Josephine Patterson (Thompson) Zell

The Descendants of John Thomson

PIONEER SCOTCH COVENANTER

———

Genealogical Notes on All Known Descendants of
John Thomson, Covenanter, of Scotland, Ireland
and Pennsylvania, with Such Biographical Sketches
as Could be Obtained from Available Published
Records or were Supplied by the Friends of Those
Individuals who were too Modest to Tell of Their
Own Accomplishments

— -

COMPILED FOR THE COUSINS BY
ADDAMS S McALLISTER
NEW YORK, N Y.
1917

———

Easton, Pennsylvania
THE CHEMICAL PUBLISHING COMPANY

DEDICATION

To Cousin Josephine Patterson (Thompson) Zell,

*without whose initiative, enthusiasm and inspiration
the present records would not have been compiled,
the compiler dedicates this volume*

PREFACE

In no way can one obtain a better idea of the character of the records it was originally hoped would be included in the present book than by reading carefully the following instructions which were sent to every descendant of Pioneer John Thomson whose address was known, on at least two occasions, namely, when the work of compilation was first started in 1912, and after the records then on hand were placed in type in 1916

The information we wish to obtain on the family tree, arranged in the order of importance, is as follows

FIRST—The *Full Name* (not merely initials) of every descendant of the Pioneer, the *Full Name* of the person married in each case, and the *Full Name* of each child born to every couple

SECOND—The *Dates* of all births, marriages and deaths

THIRD—The *Present Address* of every living descendant

FOURTH—The *Place* of birth, marriage and death of every descendant

FIFTH—A *Brief Life Sketch* of every descendant—giving only the important items, such as military service, training, education, profession and present occupation

SIXTH—The *Ancestry*—with available dates—of each person who has married into any branch of our family. That is to say, we want the *Complete* available *Ancestral Record* of every descendant

If in doubt as to exactly what is wanted, send all obtainable items of genealogical and biographical nature that would be of interest to any of the descendants of the Pioneer of our family

It is appreciated that no one person can supply all of the information desired. It is hoped, however, that each person addressed will send all information obtainable and give *Clues* as to sources of additional information. Please send whatever you have whether it is little or much

Notwithstanding the above seemingly explicit instructions, many descendants have expressed surprise that the records of certain other branches were more complete than those of their own branch—to which latter they may or may not have contributed. In can safely be stated again, as was stated in the circular letter sent to every descendant whose post office address was known in 1916, that in not one single branch are the records as they now stand too elaborate, in some branches they are quite complete, while in others they are too brief to be dignified by the title "rec d."

The compiler believes he is correct in stating that, without a single exception, every item of the above-described nature submitted by any descendant of John Thomson has been utilized in the present book—not always, however, in the exact form in which it was submitted   To all those contributing to these records, and especially to those few who have supplied material relating to branches or sub-branches other than their own, the compiler desires to express his sincere thanks and appreciation.

To the Guarantors, without whose aid the publication of the records would not have been accomplished, all members of the family are indebted for placing at the disposal of the publication committee sufficient funds to insure the prompt payment of the printer's and engraver's bills   For this purpose, a total of $900 was advanced to the committee (to be returned subsequently in the form of books or cash at their option) by the following Guarantors. Catherine Nelson Janney, J Howard Neely, Edward S Thomson, Lewis C Thompson, Henry Walters, Lucian M. Zell, and T. Burd Zell

Originally the intention was to keep the expense as low as possible and to publish the book without illustrations, but sufficient funds having been provided, it was decided to include a limited number of illustrations.

CONTENTS

Descendants of John Thomson

Pioneer Scotch Covenanter

THE PRESENT RECORDS.

To the excellent preliminary compilation made by Theodore Samuel Thompson, of Thompsontown, Juniata County, Pa., by the aid of information obtained from his mother, Mrs Charlotte Chambers (Patterson) Thompson, wife of William Thompson, Jr, son of William Thomson, Sr, and grandson of John Thomson, the Pioneer, must be attributed the completeness of the records herein presented. Without the T S Thompson notes which were added to and printed for distribution to the various branches of the family in 1887, by Heber S Thompson of Pottsville, Schuylkill County, Pa, it would not have been possible for the numerous descendants scattered throughout the United States to have kept so fully in communication with each other.

To the oldest living descendant of the Pioneer, "The Queen of the Thompson Family," Mrs. Josephine Patterson (Thompson) Zell, daughter of Mrs Charlotte Chambers (Patterson) Thompson, must be given full credit for the present compilation, for it was she who first called attention, in January, 1911, to the neglected resting place of the common ancestor, John Thomson, in the old Lock Graveyard near Thompsontown, which through her efforts has since been marked by an appropriate monument erected by the descendants. It was she who inaugurated and has kept alive the Thompson Family Assemblies, that have been held annually at Thompsontown since 1911

To the records as they now appear, all branches of the family have contributed, but the work of co-ordinating the information collected for revising the "Thompson Family" booklet was undertaken by a committee, appointed at the second Assembly in 1912, consisting of Messrs Edward S Thomson, Thompsontown, Pa ; James B Wylie, Washington, Pa, and Addams S. McAllister, New York, N Y

The financing of the undertaking, by obtaining advanced subscriptions for the publication and guarantees of the disposal of the requi

mittee consisting of Mr. T. Burd Zell, Chairman; Miss Margaret Shippen Crowther, Mrs. Catherine Janney, Mr Edward S Thomson, and Miss Juniata M Wilson. A list of the Guarantors, who practically acted as underwriters for the publication, appears in the Preface. At the 1916 assembly, at which the compilation of genealogical data was presented in proof form, appointment was made of a special committee to attend to the final details relating to the printing of the book and selection of the illustrations, consisting of Messrs. Addams S. McAllister, J. Howard Neely, Edward S. Thomson, and T Burd Zell

THOMPSON FAMILY ASSEMBLIES

From the issue in January, 1911, by Mrs. Josephine Patterson (Thompson) Zell of a call for funds from his descendants for placing a substantial head-stone over the grave of Pioneer John Thomson, must be dated the beginning of the movement which resulted in the establishment of the Thompson Family Assemblies, as well as the erection of the John Thomson monument.

On March 25, 1911, an executive board was organized consisting of Mrs. Josephine P Zell, president, Mr. Theophilus Thompson, Mr. Edward S. Thomson, Mrs Wilson Lloyd, Miss Cora E. Thompson, Miss Clara J. Thompson, Mr. Banks C. McAllister, Mrs Ella Neely, and Mrs. C N Janney, with Miss Annie G Thompson as secretary, and Mr. Theophilus M. Thompson as treasurer of the John Thomson Fund.

Chief interest naturally centers in the First Reunion of the family on August 11, 1911, when the monument to the pioneer ancestor, John Thomson, was dedicated. Mr Edward S Thomson was master of ceremonies Following a prayer by Rev Dr. J Gray McAllister, Louisville, Ky, the monument was presented to the descendants by Mrs Josephine P. (Thompson) Zell, of Passaic, N. J, and accepted for the descendants by Mr. John A. Thompson, of Cleveland, Ohio The dedicatory exercises of the morning were then brought to a close by a prayer by Mr. William Thompson Zell, of Reading, Pa In the afternoon was held the organization meeting of the Thomson Assemblies, in which the following persons took part: Misses Helen and Eunice Skaer, Augusta, Kan, General James Addams Beaver, Bellefonte, Pa.; Miss Blanche Thompson, Logansport, Ind, Miss Edith Crow-

Monument to Pioneer John Thomson

ther, Philadelphia, Pa ; Miss Mary Thompson, Philadelphia, Pa ,
Mrs. Josephine P (Thompson) Zell, and Rev. J. Gray McAllister.

In presenting the monument Mrs Zell stated that "We honor
his name not simply because he was the progenitor of a large
family, but that he was one of those who bravely stood for civil
and religious liberty, for the equal rights of humanity, and for
an open Bible, the results of which we Americans can enjoy to-
day "

The monument bears the following inscription ·

JOHN THOMSON

Pioneer and Patriot

Founder of the Thompson
Family in Juniata County

Died 1779

A Scotch Covenanter
Advocate of the Open Bible,
Civil and Religious Liberty

Wives

—— Greenlee
—— Slocum
Sarah Patterson

Erected by a Grateful
Posterity, 1911

Since 1911, the Assemblies have been held annually, the meeting place being furnished by Edward S Thomson, Thompsontown, Pa., who has acted as master of ceremonies and treasurer,
under the presidencies of Jerome N. Thompson, Wilkes-Barre,
Pa , John A. Thompson, Cleveland, Ohio, and J. Luther Thompson, Mifflintown, Pa Andrew Banks, Mifflintown, elected secretary at the first assembly, has held that office continuously since
then, with Miss Clara J Thompson, Mifflintown, as recording
secretary. Rev. J Gray McAllister, Louisville, has served as
chaplain of the assemblies

In addition to those who took part in the first assembly, the
following persons have read papers at the later assemblies · James
B Wylie, Washington, Pa ; Miss Adele Thompson, Middlefield,
Ohio, on the "Lost Uncle Isaac;" Walter M. Thompson, Topeka,

Kan , Mrs. W H Zeiders, Mifflintown, Pa , Miss Clara J Thompson, Mifflintown, J Howard Neely, Mifflintown, and William Thompson Zell, Reading, Pa

At each assembly, the descendants residing in the neighborhood of Thompsontown have provided a most bountiful dinner for those attending the meeting from far and near   Much of the preliminary work connected with the assemblies has fallen on the willing shoulders of the Committee on Invitations, of which Mrs Catherine N. Janney, Miss June Wilson, and Miss Clara J. Thompson have been active members

EARLY FAMILY HISTORY

According to the "Thompson Family" booklet of 1887, John Thomson and his brother James, originally from Scotland, emigrated from County Antrim, Ireland, about 1735 to Cross Roads, Chester County, Pa , and moved to Hanover Township (which was then in Lancaster County and is now in Dauphin County, Pa) near to Derry Church, still preserved and rebuilt in 1886 They were Scotch Covenanters and doubtless worshipped at Derry Church.

"From Hanover Township they moved to near (about 10 miles from) Harrisburg where John married his second wife, Miss Slocum; thence he moved to the farm three miles east of (what is now) Thompsontown, Pa.   He and two wives are buried in a graveyard one and one-half miles east of Thompsontown

"James Thomson settled along South Mountain (then Cumberland Valley and Cumberland County, but now Franklin County and Chambersburg) and his descendants reside there still.

"John Thomson came up the Susquehanna and Juniata Rivers and landed at the mouth of the river three miles east of what is now Thompsontown   His first wife was a Miss Greenleaf (or Greenlea), his second wife was Miss Slocum, and his third, Sarah Patterson   As his oldest daughter married a Greenleaf, the marriage of John Thomson with Miss Greenleaf may be a mistake, although marrying cousins was common."

In an old account book of Robert Thompson (born 1790, died 1860), son of William Thomson, of Thompsontown, Pa , there

Charlotte Chambers Patterson Thompson

The earliest historian of the Thompson Family. Her daughter. Josephine Patterson Thompson.

Theodore Samuel Thompson

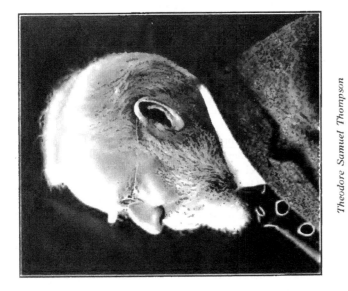

Heber Samuel Thompson

Authors of the "Thompson Family" published in 1887.

is a memorandum stating that "John Thomson, my grandfather came from Antrim, Ireland, and wore the Scotch kilt and bonnet until his death." The Thomson or Thompson family belonged to the Clan Campbell of Argyll The first of the Campbell family to take the title of Argyll was a great-grandson of Neill Campbell, King Edward's Baillie of Lands in Argyll from Lochfyne to Kilmartin, who was created Lord Campbell by James II. Argyllshire is in the southwestern portion of Scotland just across the North Channel from County Antrim, which is in the extreme northeastern part of Ireland

SCOTCH-IRISH CHARACTERISTICS.

Of John Thomson's ancestors we have no record other than the firmly believed, if not established, tradition that he was one of a number of Presbyterians who fled from Scotland to Ireland and subsequently came to America to escape persecution, oppressive taxation and political troubles Family records were not kept in Ireland and no records from Scotland were brought to America However, of the predominating characteristics of the people to whom he belonged we know much

In "Scotch-Irish Pioneers in Ulster and America,' Charles Knowles Bolton says: "New scenes must have quickened the mental processes of the transplanted Scot, and the greater community life enlarged the social instinct The Episcopalians, all-powerful in government, and the Roman Catholics, strong in numbers, pressed in upon every side, and forced the Presbyterians to an exercise of their loyalty and patience, while the spirit of proselyting which existed everywhere in Ulster sharpened their wits Under a century of these social and religious influences, the Scotch character must have changed "

"It was," said Mr Morrison, in his life of Jeremiah Smith, "the sternness of the Scotch Covenanter, softened by a century's residence abroad amid persecution and trial, wedded there to the pathos and comic humor of the Irish "

The transplanted Scot was more versatile and more fertile in resource, less clannish and less pugnacious, or in other terms, a man of wider vision. His beliefs were consistent and well defined. Against the Puritan's town meeting the Scotch-Irishman placed the legislature, for the congregation he substituted the assembly, instead of laying stress upon personality, he emphasized partnership

Whatever of military science the Scotch-Irish did not learn at the siege of Londonderry, they acquired in the French and Indian wars in the New World   Their rugged life fitted them to endure camp and march, and their inborn hostility toward England led them to forge to the front in the early weeks of the year 1775 when many good men of the old English race wavered in the face of war with Great Britain.

An excellent resumé of the causes leading to the emigration of the Scotch Covenanters, first to Ireland and then to America, was given in a paper read before the Thompson Family Assembly in 1916, by Mr J Howard Neely, who stated that "during the reigns of Charles I, Charles II and James II, bigotry and despotism marked their conduct towards the Presbyterians, and persecutions in Ulster and Scotland were employed to break down the Presbyterian faith and establish the Church of England over Scotland" The meetings of the Covenanters were denounced as seditious and to frequent them or to hold communion with those frequenting them was forbidden on pain of death   For this reason the Covenanters abandoned the land of their birth and sought an asylum among their countrymen in Ulster, in the north of Ireland   However, the British government soon began to burden the Scotch in Ireland with taxes and exactions upon their industry and trades, and the large landed proprietors demanded extravagant rents for their lands on which long time leases had expired, resulting in two great Scotch-Irish migrations to America, the first from 1717 to 1750, during which time Pioneer John Thomson came to Pennsylvania, and the second from 1771 to 1773, immediately preceding the Revolution in America against British misrule.

As Mr Neely truly said, "the industry, frugality, energy, resource and endurance fitted well the Scotch-Irish to meet the conditions in America   This race in enterprise, intelligence, education, patriotism, religious and moral character, the maintenance of civil and religious liberty, in all things that have contributed to the economic, social and religious life, has been surpassed by none other."

EARLY PROPERTY OWNERSHIP

In his "memorandum of ancestors" Robert Thompson, already referred to, showed that Pioneer John Thomson came to America in 1730, not 1735. He states that "on the 2nd day of May, 1768, grandfather John Thomson sold his estate in Hanover Township, then Lancaster County, Pa., now Dauphin County He then purchased a warrant for land granted to Samuel Sturgeon of the same place, lying in the upper end of Pfoutz Valley, which with other purchases included all the lands of Rumbaugh up to the Micheltree place (old graveyard) The deed from Sturgeon to Thomson is dated May 2, 1768. John Thomson died on the place now owned by John P' Thompson '

On page 870 of the "History of Susquehanna and Juniata Valleys in Pennsylvania," published in 1866 by Everets, Peck & Richards, Philadelphia—a book containing much information of interest to the descendants of John Thomson, and frequently referred to herein, it is stated that "John Thomson, or Thompson as later spelled, from whom most of the family of that name in Juniata County, Pa., descended, was one of several brothers who resided in Paxton Valley, and about 1768 or 1769, came up the Juniata with his family and purchased a tract of 200 acres of land (which had been previously warranted) about three miles from the present borough of Thompsontown His name is not mentioned in the tax rolls of Fermanagh Township until 1769, when he is assessed on 200 acres (now owned by Uriah Shuman) Robert, his eldest son, was also assessed on 200 acres adjoining and below Lockport.

William, the second son of John Thomson, in 1785, sold his farm adjoining his father's farm in Pfoutz's Valley and purchased the tract on which Thompsontown was located He also bought the "Happy Banks of Goshen," a farm of 400 acres three miles west of the present site of Thompsontown on the south side of the Juniata River, and also the lands (about 400 acres), mills, etc, at what is now Mexico, originally owned by Capt James Patterson

Thomas and Peter Thompson, the youngest sons of John Thomson, inherited the homestead of their father and on Feb 28, 1807, they purchased 8 acres of land of Frederick Keller,

2

which had been patented in two tracts by Isaac Yost—one named
Green Plains and the other Rivulet Grove, which two tracts they
sold in 1809 to Andrew Thompson, farmer. Thomas died a
bachelor and the old farm which then embraced 433 acres passed
to Peter.

Property tax and transfer records show that Pioneer John
Thomson owned about 500 acres of land partly on the Juniata
River and adjoining Pfoutz's Valley His sons owned all the
lands west along the Juniata to a line three-quarters of a mile
west of what is now Thompsontown, the plots containing about
1,200 acres. In an easterly direction from Thompsontown, Pa.,
there were seven adjoining farms owned by the Thompson family

HOMESTEAD OF PIONEER JOHN THOMSON

According to Mr William Albanus Logan Thompson (who
was born 1848 at the Peter Thompson homestead, about three
miles from the site of what is now Thompsontown, Juniata
County, Pa), the home of Pioneer John Thomson was about 40
rods south of the old stone house erected in 1810 by Peter Thomson, in the upper end of Pfoutz Valley, in what is now Juniata
County, near the Perry County line, which runs just east of the
farm. It was near a spring that was shaded by a big oak tree.
A stone fence built by John Thomson, the pioneer, surrounded
the meadow. The remains of this fence now form a pile of stone
by the side of the road leading south to the river

By his will, John Thomson left his farm of 412 acres to his
sons James, Thomas and Peter James died young, while Thomas
died a bachelor and Peter inherited all of the land

In 1810 Peter Thomson built the old stone house and here
most of his children were born At his death his son John
Peter bought the interests of the other heirs and kept the old
homestead until 1865 when it was sold to Judge Samuel Hepburn, of Carlisle, who sold it on Mar 4, 1869, to Uriah Shuman.

SPELLING OF THE FAMILY NAME

In the early records the name of the family was spelled
Thomson, and the wording used on the house erected by the
Pioneer's son, who located at what is now Thompsontown, Jun-

iata County, Pa , was "This House Built by W. & J. Thomson,
1798 " Even at a date earlier than this the records show a different spelling of the name   There are now in existence commissions to the son who built the above house, as second lieutenant, on May 3, 1775, in Cumberland County, Pa , Associators;
first lieutenant on May 1, 1783, in Cumberland County militia and
captain on July 11, 1792, in Mifflin County militia, in each of
which the name is spelled William Thompson   Doubtless the
records kept by the family showed how the individual spelled his
own name while the other records indicated how other people
believed the name should be spelled.

On the mill at Mexico, Juniata County, Pa , appears the following. "New Mexico Mill Built by William Thomson, 1810 "

There is now in the possession of the descendants of William
Thomson a note book owned by his son James, who had a per-
fect right to take pride in his excellent penmanship   This book
was started by him on May 23, 1799, at which time he entered
his name as James Thomson   On Jan 18, 1800, he wrote James
Thompson for the first time in this book, as his descendants now
believe, because the letter *p* added to the grace of his autograph
He is given credit for setting the fashion among the family for
spelling the name Thompson

WIVES OF JOHN THOMSON

On page 483 of Vol. III. Third Series of "Notes and Queries,"
by W H Egle, appears some items relating to the Thomson
family prepared by Mrs Charlotte Chambers (Patterson)
Thompson (born 1794; died 1863), widow of William Thompson
(descendant No 33)   In these it is stated that John Thomson,
the Pioneer, "married first a Miss Greenlee, a daughter of James
Greenlee of Hanover Township, then Lancaster County, now
Dauphin County, Pa , and connected with the Greenlees of Little
Britain Township, Lancaster County, and thus with the Bald-
ridges and Achinsons. Captain Greenlee, the Indian fighter, of
Westmoreland County, Pa , was of this family   By this mar-
riage, John Thomson had the following children Margaret,
Sarah, Elizabeth William, Robert, Susan, Jane, and Isaac
Margaret Thompson and of m   M Greenleaf. The latter was

killed by the Indians near Sunbury, Pa. The children of the family moved west."

In his will dated Mar 5, 1779, John Thomson makes no mention of a daughter Margaret, but refers to his daughter Mary According to all evidence at hand, this daughter married William Greenlee, son of James Greenlee, and he it was who was killed by the Indians in Pennsylvania His descendants went first to the Southern and Western parts of Pennsylvania and later to Ohio.

One of the sons of William and Mary (Thompson) Greenlee, Robert Greenlee, who was born in 1773 in Juniata County, Pa, and was 7 years old when his father was killed, lived for nine years with William Thomson (doubtless his mother's brother), and nine years in Stone Valley, after which in 1798, he moved to Venango County, Pa In 1892 there was in the possession of Theodore Samuel Thomson, a grandson of the above William Thomson, the original "power of attorney" given by Jean Greenlee of Washington County, Pa., under date of Oct. 27, 1795, to William Thomson, "to collect all moneys due her from the estate of William Greenlee then in the hands of James Greenlee, the administrator." This James Greenlee was doubtless the oldest son of William and Mary (Thomson) Greenlee who is known to have been born about 1754 in Pennsylvania, and died 1840 in Venango County, Pa The witnesses to the "power of attorney" were Isaac Keri and Robert Wylie Doubtless the last named was the husband of her mother's sister, Jean Thomson

Concerning the accuracy of the statement that John Thomson's first wife was a daughter of James Greenlee of Hanover Township, in what was then Lancaster County, Pa., there seems considerable doubt, although this James Greenlee did have a daughter Mary who married a Mr. Thompson The doubt expressed is based partly on the assumption that the marriage of an uncle (William Greenlee) with his niece (Mary Thomson) would not have been sanctioned, although the marriage of cousins was of common occurrence at that date. While it is highly improbable that John Thomson's first wife was a daughter of James Greenlee—in which case, his daughter, Mary Thomson, married her uncle William Greenlee yet it seems probable that

John Thomson's first wife was James Greenlee's sister—in which event, Mary Thomson's husband was her first cousin

James Greenlee, the father of Mary Thomson's husband (and probably the brother of the first wife of Pioneer John Thomson), was born in the north of Ireland about 1718, and certainly was not the grandfather of, say, William Thomson, son of John Thomson, who was born in 1752, but he probably was his uncle. He was certainly not the grandfather of Mrs Mary (Thomson) Greenlee, whose son James Greenlee was born about 1754, but was probably both her uncle and the father of her husband, William Greenlee

James Greenlee, the Pioneer, died in Hanover Township, Lancaster County, Pa., in 1778, only one year earlier than the death of Pioneer John Thomson He is said to have been a son of Alexander Greenlee The date of his emigration is not known, but his name appeared as early as 1738 on the tax list of Hanover Township, Lancaster County, Pa. He may have come to this country with John Thomson, probably then or subsequently his brother-in-law In his will dated Mar. 8, 1772, he mentioned his wife, his oldest son William, his sons James, Alexander, and Robert, and his daughter Mary Greenlee Of the descendants of his sons James, Alexander and Robert, we have no record His daughter Mary married a Mr Thompson, but concerning him and his descendants, we have no information. She was certainly not the first wife of Pioneer John Thomson, because she was evidently unmarried in 1778 when her father referred to her as Mary Greenlee. The oldest son of James Greenlee married Mary Thomson, the oldest daughter of John Thomson, and the lines of many of their descendants have been traced to the present generation

According to the notes of Mrs Charlotte Chambers (Patterson) Thompson, referred to above, John Thomson's second wife was a "Miss Slocum, by whom he had a son John, who moved from Juniata Valley to Butler County, Pa " To what family she was connected is not known At the taking of the first United States census in 1790, there were only three heads of families named Slocum in the State of Pennsylvania, all in Luzerne County, namely, Ebenezer, Ruth, and William

According to Mrs Charlotte Chambers (Patterson) Thompson, the third wife of John Thomson was Sarah Patterson, a daughter of James Patterson. She became the mother of Andrew Thomson who married Jane Stewart; of Peter Thomson who married Mary Patterson, and of Thomas Thomson   Mrs Charlotte C Thompson makes no mention of James Thomson, referred to in the will of John Thomson, and none of the "child yet unborn," when the will was written in Mar , 1779   Mary (Patterson) Thomson was the daughter of Andrew and Jane (Purdy) Patterson   Mrs. Charlotte Chambers (Patterson) Thompson, who was herself a granddaughter of Capt. James Patterson, Jr., and Mary (Stewart) Patterson, and a great-granddaughter of Capt. James Patterson, Sr , and Susan (Howard) Patterson, makes no mention of any relationship between her family and the third wife of John Thomson or the wife of his son Peter Thomson, and it is possible that none existed, although Col Samuel Evans, who probably obtained his information from Mrs Charlotte Chambers (Patterson) Thompson, is authority for the statement that Sarah (Patterson) Thompson was a daughter of Capt James Patterson, Sr   This statement has added weight by reason of the fact that Capt James and Susan (Howard) Patterson had a daughter named Sarah

WILL OF PIONEER JOHN THOMSON.

By far the most reliable source of information concerning the immediate descendants of John Thomson is his will, which was written Mar 2, 1779, in Fermanagh Township, in what was then Cumberland, but is now Juniata County, Pa , and was probated in Cumberland County, Nov. 26, 1779   The original is at Carlisle, Pa , which was then as now, the county seat of Cumberland

I, John Thomson, of Fermanagh Township and Cumberland County, being sick in body, but of sound memory, blessed be God, do this 2nd day of March, in the year of our Lord 1779, make and publish this my last Will and Testament, in manner following :

1 I do give to my son Robert one coat and jacket, likewise to John one coat and jacket, also to my sons Isaac and William five pounds each. I also give and bequeath to my daughters Mary and Sarah five pounds each, and to Jean one horse and

saddle, one cow, one bed, suitable furniture and five pounds money. I also allow my daughters Elizabeth and Susanna, if they conduct themselves prudently until they are capable of making a choice in marriage agreeable to those who shall have the oversight over them, to share equal with Jean

I do give and allow to my dear wife the use and benefit of my estate while she remains a widow, to live upon with the children and to give them schooling and learning as they come to be capable to receive it, but if otherwise that she, when a suitable opportunity is offered doth marry again, she is then to have no claim to any interest in my land, or movable estate, further than to share equally with my daughters now living with me

And I do give all my land to my sons James, Thomas and Peter, to be and remain their property with the rest of my household after every one hath got their share, but my son Andrew I allow to be put to a trade and after he hath sufficient learning and while learning his trade, he is to have necessary clothing out of my estate If any of these heirs doth decease under the age of eighteen years, their part is to remain equally divided amongst the other heirs then living on the premises.

I also allow to my son Andrew when come to twenty-one years of age to have one horse and saddle out of my estate, and James to have one horse and saddle when come to twenty-one years of age

I do also to the child unborn whether son or daughter, when come to the age of maturity, to have equal with Thomas and Peter

I do also allow my daughters Jean, Elizabeth and Susanna each one chest and a spinning wheel.

I do make and ordain my wife and son Robert to be executors of this, my last Will in trust for the intents and purposes of this my last Will contained, to take care and see the same performed according to my true intent and meaning.

In Witness Whereof. I have set my seal to this my last Will and Testament this 5th day of March in the year of our Lord 1779, in the presence of William McAllister and Thomas Palloy.

HIS
JOHN X THOMSON.
MARK

IMMEDIATE DESCENDANTS OF JOHN THOMSON

In his will John Thomson mentions his wife—not by name—and thirteen (or fourteen) children, not in the order of birth, which may have been as follows (1) Mary, (2) Jean, (3) William, (4) Elizabeth, (5) Robert, (6) Sarah, (7) Susanna, (8) Isaac, (9) John, (10) Andrew, (11) Peter, (12) Thomas, (13) James, (14) ——————?

1—Mary Thomson, wed William Greenlee Issue (1) James, (2) John, (3) Sarah, wed ——— McCullough; (4) Mary, wed George Darling; (5) Elizabeth, wed ——— Bell or Biel, (6) Susan, died young, (7) Jane, died young, (8) William, (9) Robert.

2—Jean Thomson, wed Robert Wylie Issue (1) Robert, (2) John, (3) Ann, (4) Jane Thomson, wed James Humphreys; (5) Elizabeth, wed John Moore; (6) Mary, wed Samuel Crothers, (7) Sarah, wed James Hodgens, (8) William.

3—William Thomson, wed Jane Mitchell Issue (1) John "Goshen," (2) James, (3) William, (4) Sarah, wed William McAlister; (5) Robert, (6) Isaac, (7) Jane, wed Henry Walters, (8) Elizabeth, wed William Waterhouse, (9) Samuel

4—Elizabeth Thomson, wed Robert McAlister No issue

5—Robert Thomson, wed Sarah Mitchell Issue (1) William, (2) John, (3) Robert, (4) James, (5) Andrew, (6) Jane, wed John McAlister; (7) Mitchell.

6—Sarah Thomson, wed William McAlister Issue (1) Hugh, (2) William, (3) John, (4) Isaac Thompson, (5) Mary, wed Thomas Bell; (6) Robert Harbison

7—Susanna Thomson, wed David Boal Issue (1) Sarah, wed Paul Cox; (2) John, (3) Nancy, never married, (4) Elizabeth, wed John Ulsh, (5) Thomas, (6) William, (7) Jane, wed Isaac Thompson, Jr

8—Isaac Thomson, wed twice, first Martha Larimore Issue (1) James, (2) John, died young; (3) Polly, wed Stephen Bond, (4) William He wed second time, Jane (Evans) Wells Issue (5) Robert, (6) Eliza, never married; (7) John, (8) Lydda, wed Moses Morse, (9) Robert E

9—John Thomson, wed Martha Park. Issue (1) John Park, (2) James, (3) Joseph, (4) Samuel, (5) Isabella, wed ——————, (6) Zelia, wed ——————, (7) Frances, wed James H Graham; (8) William, (9) Robert

(10)—Andrew Thomson, wed Jane Stewart Issue (1) John, (2) Elizabeth, wed James Johnson; (3) William, (4) Mary, died in infancy, (5) Stewart, (6) Julia Ann, died at the age of 21, (7) Andrew Patterson, (8) Mary Jane, wed John Barton; (9) Rebecca Stewart, wed Robert Newton; (10) Margaret Stewart, never married, (11) Gracy, died young, (12) Thomas Boston

(11)—Peter Thomson, wed Mary Patterson Issue (1) John Peter, (2) Margaret, never married, (3) Mary, wed James Curran, (4) Samuel, (5) Susannah, wed Alexander Rodgers, (6) Silas, (7) Eleanor, wed James Thompson, (8) Thomas Boal, (9) William Patterson.

(12)—Thomas Thomson, died unmarried

(13)—James Thomson, no record of descendants He was under age at the time of his father's death, and probably died unmarried

(14)—Child, possibly born after the father's death in 1779 No record

NUMERICAL DESIGNATION OF DESCENDANTS.

As will be noted, each descendant has been designated by a number for convenience in cross referencing and ease in identification For all purposes other than relationship determination, which is explained fully below, the designating numerals may well be considered as having been arbitrarily chosen in accordance with the plan practically universally employed of designating each descendant by a number when his or her name first appears in the records and subsequently referring to this descendant by the number already assigned

A little study will show that in the present records the number assigned to each descendant has been selected in accordance with the assumed order of his or her birth in his or her immediate branch of the family. For example, the numerals 3742 would be given to the second child of the fourth child of the seventh child, of the third child of Pioneer John Thomson This individual would belong to the fourth generation (four numerals) below the Pioneer. A person designated by the numerals 37156 would belong to the fifth generation below the Pioneer The parent (No 3715) is the first cousin of the one bearing the numerals 3742, because they have a common grandparent, designated by the number 37

It should be especially noted by those inclined to use the numerals not only for purposes of identification (for which all systems of numbering are equally suitable), but also for relationship determination (for which the method herein employed is particularly advantageous), that absolutely no error is introduced into the relationship determination even when the assumed order of birth in a family is not the true order, provided only that the designating numerals when once assigned to the members of a family are adhered to consistently.

For the benefit of those familiar with the arbitrarily-selected, continuously-numbered system of designation, it should be stated that in the following pages all of the records of all of the descendants of an individual are covered completely, to and including the present generation consistently throughout, before any record whatsoever is given of the descendants of his or her younger brother or sister.

If the method of numerical designation be looked upon as being purely "decimal"—with the unnecessary decimal point omitted—it will be seen that the numbers have been arranged in a perfectly logical, consecutive order throughout the book, and no difficulty whatsoever will be encountered in locating at once the record of any descendant whose designating numeral is known See "Index to Associated Family Ancestors," page 315

BRANCH NO. 1.

1—**Mary Thomson**, born probably before 1734, died after March, 1779, and before May, 1780 Married William Greenlee, son of James Greenlee, who was born about 1718, in the North of Ireland and died between March 18, 1772, and Oct, 1778, in Hanover Township, Lancaster County, Pa James Greenlee was said to have been a son of Alexander Greenlee—See the "Greenlee Genealogy," by R S and R. L. Greenlee, Chicago—The date of James Greenlee's emigration is not known but his name appears as early as 1738, on the tax list of Hanover Township, Lancaster County, Pa, where he spent the remainder of his days In his will dated March 18, 1772, he refers to his wife, but not by name, to his oldest son William Greenlee, his son Alexander Greenlee, his son James Greenlee, his daughter Mary Greenlee, to his son William's oldest son James Greenlee, and to his son Robert Greenlee, whom he appointed his sole executor The appraisal of the estate was made in Oct, 1778 William Greenlee, the oldest son, was born in Ireland Possibly it was he, whose name appears on the roll of Captain John Clark's Company, attached to Colonel Potters, Second Battalion of Northumberland County Associators, in the Revolutionary service in 1776, see "History of Susquehanna and Juniata Valleys in Pennsylvania," p 95—William Greenlee was killed by the Indians in Pennsylvania in May, 1780 According to traditions in the Thompson family, the man who married Mary Thompson "was killed by the Indians at Sunbury, Northumberland County, Pa, the children of the family went west" Mary (Thomson) Greenlee died in Pennsylvania before 1780 and William Greenlee was soon to be married a second time when he was killed He resided at Penn's Creek, near Swisher's Run in what is said to have been Juniata County, but was doubtless then Northumberland County, and is now Snyder County, Pa Issue (1) James, (2) John, (3) Sarah, (4) Mary, (5) Elizabeth, (6) Susan, (7) Jane, (8) William, (9) Robert

11—**James Greenlee**, referred to in the will of his grandfather as the eldest son of William Greenlee, was born about 1754, in Pennsylvania, died Sept, 1840, at the home of his son, James Patterson Greenlee He was a miller and farmer, in politics a Democrat, in religion a Presbyterian, raised in French Creek Township, near Franklin, Venango County, Pa He married Ann Patterson, who was born at Utica, Pa, died in 1839, near Franklin, Venango County, Pa, daughter of Peter Patterson Issue (1) William, (2) John, (3) Sarah, (4) James Patterson, (5) Margaret, (6) Elizabeth, (7) Samuel

111—**William Greenlee**, born Jan 5, 1785, or 1796, near Franklin, Pa, died July 10, 1862 or 1864, near Franklin He was a farmer, a Democrat, and 1

on Oct 15, 1818, near Franklin, Jane McClelland, who was born Feb 14, 1801 or 1795, near Franklin or Sandy Lake, Pa, and died May 30, 1876-7 near Sandy Lake, Mercer County, Pa, daughter of John and Margaret or Jane (Blackwood) McClelland Issue (1) Anna, (2) Margaret, (3) Sarah, (4) James, (5) John McClelland, (6) Elizabeth, (7) William, (8) Mary Jane, (9) Dorcas, (10) Samuel, (11) Emily, (12) Caroline, (13) Aaron, (14) Clinton De Witt

1111—**Anna Greenlee,** born Oct 27, 1819, near Raymilton, Venango County, Pa (died about 1852) Married Peter Barr, son of Samuel and Peggy Barr He was a farmer Issue (1) Mahala

11111—**Mahala Barr,** born April 13, 1849, at Raymilton, Venango County, Pa Address Farmer near Milledgeville, Pa Married on March 16, 1869, Eusebius Chatley (born near Milledgeville, Pa, or ————) son of Andrew and Ruth (Robbins) Chatley Issue (1) Bertie Milton (2) Otis Asa

111111—**Bertie Milton Chatley,** born May 19, 1870.

111112—**Otis Asa Chatley,** born Dec 22, 1877

1112—**Margaret (Peggy) Greenlee,** born Feb 1, 1821, married on————, at ————, John Patterson, son of ———— of ————. Issue (1) John Albert, (2) Peter M————

11121—**John Albert Patterson,** born on ———— at ————, lived at Raymilton, Pa in 1908

11122—**Peter M———— Patterson,** born May 14, 1844, at Raymilton, Venango County, Pa Address Raymilton, Pa Married on Feb 2, 1871, at Sandy Lake, Mercer County, Pa ; Mary A———— Cornelius (born March 10, 1850 at Leesburg, Mercer County, Pa, died Jan 2, 1894 at Raymilton) daughter of Isaac and Nancy (Cook) Cornelius Issue (1) Harry, (2) George, (3) Cora, (4) Brit, (5) Nannie, (6) Pearl

111221—**Harry Patterson,** born Nov. 29, 1872 Address————; Married on ———— at ————, Adah Snider, daughter of ———— of ————. Issue ————

111222—**George Patterson,** born May 16, 1874

111223—**Cora Patterson,** born May 21, 1877, married Walter Jewell

111224—**Brit Patterson.** born Nov 10, 1880

111225—Nannie Patterson, born April 6, 1883

111226—Pearl Patterson, born Aug. 6, 1887.

1113—Sarah Greenlee, born Oct. 10, 1822, married James Turk, died
_____

1114—James Greenlee, born May 27 1824, at Franklin, Venango County,
Pa (died March 29, 1856), farmer, Mercer County, Pa Married
about 1853, Mary Stuart (born April 1, 1820, in Ireland) daughter of
John and Martha Stuart Issue (1) James

11141—James Greenlee, born Nov. 13, 1857, at Harlandsburgh, Lawrence
County, Pa, farmer, Grove City, Pa Married May 31, 1883, at
Beaver Falls, Beaver County, Pa Mary A Crozier (born Jan 24,
1861 in Iowa) daughter of D———— and Jane (Boyd) Crozier
No issue

1115—John McClelland Greenlee, born Oct 10, 1826, at Franklin, Venango
County, Pa He was First Lieutenant in Home Guards during the
Civil War, was a farmer Lived in Gray, Iowa, in 1900 Married
on Jan 4, 1849, at Franklin, Mary Mills (born June 18, 1830, at New
Castle, Mercer County, Pa) daughter of Robert and Jane (Moak)
Mills Issue (1) Jane Mary, (2) Mills Erwin, (3) Oliver F————
(4) James Walter, (5) William Harvey, (6) John Wesley, (7)
Robert, (8) Rachel L————, (9) Charles Elmer

11151—Jane Mary Greenlee, born Nov 7, 1849, in Venango County, Pa
Married on Dec 25, 1870 at Victor, Powershick County, Iowa, Wil-
liam Allen Clarke (born Jan 20, 1842 at Jersey City, N J) son of
John and Mary (Allen) Clarke. W A Clarke served in the Civil
War from 1861 to 1864 Farmer, Audubon, Iowa Issue (1) Laura
May, (2) Wilbur Arthur, (3) Robert, (4) Charles Edwin, (5) Mary
Ella, (6) Jennie Bell, (7) John Wesley, (8) Nellie Pearl, (9) Louis,
(10) Sarah Matilda

111511—Laura May Clark, born Dec 23, 1871, married Austin Linn
Address Gray, Iowa

111512—Wilbur Arthur Clark, born Feb 28, 1872, in Poweshick County,
Iowa Address, Audubon, Iowa Married on Sept 21, 1899, at
Council Bluffs, Iowa, Clara Belle Friese (born Jan 7, 1876, at Audu-
bon, Iowa) daughter of Charles William and Phoebe Jane (Mc-
Cloughy) Friese No issue

111513—Robert Clark,

111514—Charles Erwin Clark, born November 27, 1876

111515—Mary Ella Clark, born May 5, 1882

111516—Jennie Bell Clark, born September 11, 1887

111517—John Wesley Clark, born Feb 29, 1888

111518—Nellie Pearl Clark, born December 5, 1890.

111519—Louis Clark, born September 9 1892

11151 (10)—Sarah Matilda Clark, born August 15, 1894

11152—Mills Erwin Greenlee, born April 24th, 1852 at Franklin, Venango
County, Pa Address, Templeton, Iowa Married on Dec 25, 1875,
at Avoca, Iowa, Aurildah Sinclair (born March 29, 1857 at Avoca,
Iowa) daughter of Robert and Mary (Hogan) Sinclair Issue (1)
Biol, (2) Edna, (3) Ernest, (4) Robert, (5) Viola, (6) Coquella

111521—Biol Greenlee, born April, 1877

111522—Edna Greenlee, born December 12, 1879 Married May 16, 1900,
Arthur Billick Address Templeton, Iowa

111523—Ernest Greenlee, born March 18 1889

111524—Robert Greenlee, born Feb 20. 1884 Married Feb, 1908, Jenny
Lacy Issue (1) Viola

111525—Viola Greenlee, born Oct 11, 1889

111526—Coquella Greenlee, born Oct. 5, 1897

11153—Oliver F Greenlee, born Feb 9, 1854, at Franklin, Venango County,
Pa, farmer at Shelby, Iowa, before 1908 Married on March 6, 1877,
at Avoca, Pottawatomie County, Iowa Catherine L Plummer (born
April 14, 1859 at Brooklyn, Poweshick County, Iowa) daughter of
Caleb and Rebecca (Pittinger) Plummer Issue (1) Rebecca I,
(2) Charles Elmer T

111531—Rebecca Greenlee, born July 22, 1878.

111·   ·   Jam· C Grudi· ·   11 · 11, 1889

11154—James Walter Greenlee, born Oct 27, 1856, at Juda, Green County, Wis, farmer Guthrie Center, Iowa, R F D No 6 Married on March 17, 1887 at College Springs, Page County, Iowa Luella Greenlee (born Aug 24, 1861, at Franklin, Venango County, Pa) daughter of Samuel McLean—III, (10)—and Mary Ann (Burch) Greenlee Issue (1) Leroy, (2) May, (3) Earl, (4) Bryan, (5) James Walter

111541—Leroy Greenlee, born June 28, 1888

111542—May Greenlee, born Oct 22, 1892 Married Jan 27, 1912, John F. Saltsgaver

111543—Earl Greenlee, born April 1, 1894.

111544—Bryan Greenlee, born April 4 1899

111545—James Walter Greenlee, born Sept 28, 1902

11155—William Harvey Greenlee, born December 25 1858 Married on ———— at ————; Frances Woodle, daughter of ———— of ———— Issue ————

11156—John Wesley Greenlee, born April 12, 1861, at Winterset, Madison County, Iowa Farmer, Ross, Iowa. Married on March 13, 1891, Eleanor Steere (born April 25, 1865, Iona, Iona County, Mich) daughter of Amos and Alice (King) Steer No issue.

11157—Robert Greenlee, born May 11, 1863, died Sept 21, 1864

11158—Rachel L———— Greenlee, born Nov 18, 1865, died Sept. 30, 1866

11159—Charles Elmer Greenlee, born Jan 28, 1867 Married on ———— at ————, Clara Aikman, daughter of ———— of ————. Issue ————

1116—Elizabeth Greenlee, born October 3 1829, at Franklin, Venango County, Pa Married Aug 1, 1854 at Warren, Warren County, Pa. (Born Oct 7, 1831, at Franklin, died Aug, 1895), son of ———— and ———— (Wilson) Singleton Issue (1) Orlando R————, (2) Armina, (3) Ellen Minerva, (4) Emma Jane, (5) Susie, (6) Rosa Belle

11161—Orlando R. Singleton, born April 6, 1856 Married Eva Hosack, (see 11

11162—Armina Singleton, born Sept 12, 1857   married Albi Barry

11163—Ellen Minerva Singleton, born May 26. 1859. died in infancy.

11164—Emma Jane Singleton, born Dec 9, 1860   Married Fred P———
Morris

11165—Susie Singleton, born April 6, 1864   Married Harry Osborne.

11166—Rosa Belle Singleton, born May 21, 1867.   Married Rev Thomas
P——————— Walter

1117—William Greenlee, born March 31, 1830   Resided at Tidioute, Pa ;
married Elmira Stocking   Issue (1) Aaron, (2) James, (3) Marion,
(4) Elmer   No other data on family

1118—Mary Jane Greenlee, born June 22, 1832, at Franklin, Venango
County, Pa   Married Dec 22, 1851 in Venango County, Pa   John
Sharp McChesney (born July 6, 1831, at New Castle, on Mt Jackson,
Lawrence County, Pa)   He was a farmer and resided at Tidioute,
Warren County, Pa   Issue (1) Laura Euphema, (2) Vincent, (3)
Eugene, (4) Willis, (5) Francis, (6) Eva Jane, (7) Effie Violet,
(8) Gertrude, (9) Cora, (10) Joseph

11181—Laura Euphema McChesney, born July 10, 1853   Unmarried;
died Sept 25, 1873

11182—Vincent McChesney, born March 6, 1855   Married Vista McCormick, lived at Tidioute, Pa , in 1908

11183—Eugene McChesney, born Jan 18, 1857   Married Jenny Bowles;
lived at Tidioute, Pa , in 1908

11184—Willis McChesney, born Jan 13, 1859   Married Vinnie Nickles;
lived at Grand Valley, Pa , in 1908

11185—Francis McChesney, born Feb. 14, 1869   Married Addie Wells;
lived at Ridgeway, Pa , in 1908

11186—Eva Jane McChesney, born April 16, 1864.   Married John Williams.

11187—Effie Violet McChesney, born April 21. 1866, died unmarried
July 4, 1888

11188—Gertrude McChesney, born April 10, 1868; died Dec. 17, 1880

1   1   ˀ (lˈ ʳ   ˈ   ├ ˈ ,   ˈf ˈrˈd ˈdwˈrd Campbell.

1118(10).—Joseph McChesney, born July 27, 1873 Married Edna Anderson

1119—Dorcas Greenlee, born April 17, ———, at Raymilton, Venango County, Pa (died Jan 21, 1869, at Mercer, Mercer County, Pa) Married March 30, 1854, at Raymilton, David Hosack (born June 7, 1828, in Adams County, Pa , died April 4, 1888, at Mercer) Issue (1) Wirt Quincy, (2) Lugetta, (3) Aaron Burr, (4) Eva Jane, (5) Frank Leslie, (6) Charles Fremont.

11191—Wirt Quincy Hosack, born March 1, 1855, at Mercer, Mercer County, Pa Address New York City Married Oct 23, 1882, at Sioux City, Iowa Mary Jane Glenn (born Nov 4, 1865, at Lemars, Pa) daughter of Michael Glenn Issue (1) Dorcas Bell, (2) Charles, (3) Wirt Edward

111911—Dorcas Bell Hosack, born December 21, 1883, died March 2, 1884

111912—Charles Hosack, born Nov 21, 1884, died May 5, 1886

111913—Wirt Edward Hosack, born March 31, 1887

11192—Lugetta Hosack, born Oct. 6, 1856, died Oct 7, 1858.

11193—Aaron Burr Hosack, born June 19, 1858, died Sept. 29, 1858.

11194—Eva Jane Hosack, born Nov 4, 1859 Married Olando R——— Singleton (see 11161)

11195—Frank Leslie Hosack, born Sept 13, 1861 Married Christiana Eckerson Dead

11196—Charles Fremont Hosack, born May 22, 1863. Married in 1900

111(10)—Samuel McLaine Greenlee, born June 6, 1836, at Waterloo, Venango County, Pa , lived at Webb City, Mo , in 1908 Married first on Nov 14, 1860, in Venango County Mary Ann Burck (born Jan 11, 1840, in Warren County, Pa , died Nov 4, 1872, in Warren County) daughter of William and Mary (Weaks) Burck Issue (1) Luella, (2) Rosetta Belle, (3) William Byron, (4) Aaron Burton, (5) Melda Married second time in March, 1873, at Fidionte, Warren County, Pa Clara Morrison (born Aug 30, 1853, at Fidionte) daughter of Robert D——— and Jane Morrison. Issue (6) Charles Walter, (7) Lottie Jane, (8) St...., M....

3

111(10)1—Luella Greenlee, born Aug 24, 1861, at Franklin, Venango
County, Pa Married March 17, 1887, at College Springs, Page
County, Iowa James Walter Greenlee—11154—Issue (1) Leroy,
(2) May, (3) Earl, (4) Bryan—(see 11154)

111(10) 2—Rosetta Bell Greenlee, born March 24, 1863 Married Thomas
Hurley, lived at Cartersville, Mo, in 1908.

111(10) 3—William Byron Greenlee, born Nov 14, 1865 or 1864. Unmarried in 1908; lived at Gray, Iowa

111(10) 4—Aaron Burton Greenlee, born May 3, 1867, in Warren County,
Pa Married at Goodman, McDonald County, Mo, Sarah Eliza-
beth Garoutte, daughter of James Lake and Lou Ann (Pogue)
Garoutte. Issue (1) Ethel Armenia, (2) Roy Edmund, (3)
Mable Mildred

111(10)41—Ethel Armenia Greenlee, born December 11, 1893; died Sept.
3, 1896

111(10)42—Roy Edmund Greenlee, born March 7, 1896

111(10)43—Mable Mildred Greenlee, born Nov. 5, 1897

111(10)5—Melda Greenlee, born May 18, 1869, in Pa. Married May 27,
1890, at Carterville, Eli Oliver Swoveland, son of Samuel and
Mary Ann (Chamness) Swoveland and grandson of William
Chamness Reside at Alba, Mo Issue (1) Zena Luseta, (2)
Gladys Malley, (3) Sylvia Tillie, (4) Goldie Hollen, (5) Valle
Beauford, (6) Walter Samuel, (7) Fleeta Lothefa,, (8) Treva
Myrtle Laurena, (9) Mary Glena

111(10)51—Zena Luseta Swoveland, born May 1, 1891, at Webb City, Mo

111(10)52—Gladys Malley Swoveland, born May 9, 1893, at Alba, Mo.
Married Jan 21, 1911, to Benjamin Harrison Cox Issue (1)
Arthur Hadley.

111(10)521—Austin Hadley Cox, born Aug 14, 1911, at Alba, Mo.

111(10)53—Sylvia Tillie Swoveland, born May 3, 1895, at Alba, Mo. Married Jenis Lamb, Aug 9, 1912. Issue (1) Tray Bryan

111(10)531—Tray Bryan Lamb, born Nov. 3, 1913, Alba, Mo.

11   Goldie Hollen Swoveland, born Oct 31, 1896, at Alba, Mo.

111(10)55—Valle Beauford Swoveland, born Dec. 14 1898, at Alba, Mo

111(10)56—Walter Samuel Swoveland, born Nov. 27, 1900, at Alba, Mo.

111(10)57—Fleeta Lothefa Swoveland, born June 17, 1904, at Alba, Mo

111(10)58—Treva Myrtle Laurena Swoveland, born Feb 2. 1908, at Alba, Mo

111(10)59—Mary Glena Swoveland, born April 25, 1912, at Alba, Mo , died Feb 20, 1913

111(10)6—Charles Walter Greenlee, born Feb 26, 1876 Unmarried; lived at Webb City, in 1908

111(10)7—Lottie Jane Greenlee, born Sept 18, 1879 Unmarried, lived at Webb City, in 1908

111(10)8—Stella Melissa Greenlee, born May 11, 1888, Unmarried, lived at Webb City, in 1908

111(11)—Emily Greenlee, born Aug 8. 1839, at Raymilton, Venango County, Pa Resided at Raymilton, in 1908 Married Nov. 11, 1858, at Raymilton Harvey Rose (born Aug 10, 1835, at Raymilton) son of Andrew and Mary Ann (Richmond) Rose Issue (1) Marion A———, (2) Charles A———, (3) Frederick W———, (4) Margaret J———, (5) W———, F———

111(11)1—Marion A Rose, born April 4. 1860, at Sandy Lake Mercer County, Pa Farmer, Dempseytown, Pa Married on Dec. 28, 1880, at Franklin, Venango County, Pa Nettie Wallace (born April 15, 1861, near Mercer, Mercer County, Pa), daughter of Hugh and Sarah (Dight) Wallace Issue (1) Harvey Delbert, (2) Hugh Wadsworth, (3) Olive Agnes, (4) Wallace William, (5) George DeWitt, (6) Ethel Sarah Emma, (7) Elma Jeanette

111(11)11—Harvey Delbert Rose, born July 9 1889

111(11)12—Hugh Wadsworth Rose, born Dec 3, 1883

111(11)13—Olive Agnes Rose, born April 9 1885

111(11)14—Wallace William Rose, born Sept. 6, 1886.

111(11)15—George Dewitt Rose,

111(11)16—Ethel Sarah Emma Rose, born March 18, 1893

111(11)17—Elma Jeannette Rose, born Jan 16. 1900

111(11)2—Charles A——————— Rose, born Nov 19 1863, died Feb. 21, 1874

111(11)3—Frederick W——————— Rose, born Jan 20, 1867   Married Nettie Humphrey

111(11)4—Margaret J. Rose, born Feb. 22, 1876   Married John F——————— Williams

111(11)5—W——————— F——————— Rose, born on ———————, at ———————; lived at Raymilton, Pa, in 1908

111(12)—Caroline Greenlee, born Feb 13. 1841, at Raymilton, Pa. Married Sept 14, 1863, Henry Waters (born March 15, 1840, at Ashtabula, Ohio, son of Fisher and Margaret (Wood) Waters, lived at Iona, Mich, in 1908 Issue (1) Sidney E———————, (2) Charles, (3) Jessie M———————, (4) Fred C———————, (5) John Jay

111(12)1—Sidney E——————— Waters, born Sept 2, 1865 Married in 1888, ——————— at ———————, lived at Iona, Mich, in 1908

111(12)2—Charles Waters, born in 1867, died in 1871

111(12)3—Jessie M——————— Waters, born Feb 17, 1871, at Fidionte, Warren County, Pa Married Jan 18, 1899, at Iona, Mich Charles B ——————— McCormick (born Feb 18, 1863, at Fidionte), son of John D——————— and Charlotte C——————— (Broughton) McCormick, farmer at Iona, Mich Issue ———————

111(12)4—Fred C——————— Waters, born Nov 23, 1873 Married in 1899, lived at Iona, Mich, in 1908.

111(12)5—John Jay Waters, born Jan 8, 1878 Unmarried, lived at Iona, Mich, in 1908

111(13)—Aaron Greenlee, born Sept 1, 1843, died Jan 20, 1851

111(14)—Clinton Dewitt Greenlee, born Oct 22, 1852, at Franklin, Venango County, Pa Married Oct 3, 1877, at Butler, Butler County Pa Clara May Russell (born Dec 31, 1858, at Butler) daughter of John Ebenezer and Maria (McCallen) Russell He is an oil well owner, organized the United States Oil Company of which he is Vice-President and General Manager, the wells being in Marion Wood and Wetzel Co, West Virginia Issue (1) Warren Russell,

111(14)1—Warren Russell Greenlee, born March 5, 1883

111(14)2—Paul Manwaring Greenlee, born Aug 15, 1886 Married

112—John Greenlee, born Aug 30, 1798 at Franklin, Venango County, Pa , died June 26, 1884, at Mercer, Mercer County, Pa. Married first on Aug 19, 1824, in French Creek Township, Venango County, Pa , Margaret Paterson (born May 2, 1804, at Franklin, Pa , died Jan. 28, 1849, in Jackson Township, Mercer County, Pa.) daughter of Peter Patterson and Elizabeth Donley Issue (1) Peter Patterson, (2) Anna, (3) Elizabeth, (4) James, (5) John, (6) William, (7) Samuel S——— (8) Margaret Jane, (9) Mary F ———, (10) Martha, (11) Sarah E——— Married second time on Oct. 10, 1855, in Jackson Township, Mary McKay, daughter of Enos McKay No issue

1121—Peter Patterson, Greenlee, born June 6 1825 at Mercer, Mercer County, Pa ; died Oct 23 or 24, 1864, at Toledo, Tama County, Iowa. Married Feb 19, 1856, at Washington, Washington County, Iowa, Mary Jane Guiler (born May 12, 1832 or 1831 at Irvin, Venango County, Pa) daughter of John and Margaret (Aiken) Guiler In 1863 he enlisted in the Ninth Iowa Cavalry He resided at Toledo, Iowa Issue (1) Margaret E———, (2) Mary Emily, (3) Martha Jane, (4) Anna

11211—Margaret F——————— Greenlee, born Oct. 8, 1857, died Aug 27, 1863

11212—Mary Emmeline Greenlee, born Oct 8 1858; graduated 1888 at Western College, Toledo, Ohio, died June 6, 1890

11213—Martha Jane Greenlee, born Sept. 18, 1860, at Buckingham, Tame County, Iowa, a writer of short stories Married June 30, 1884, at Toledo, Iowa, George Hale Cotton (born Oct 12, 1857, at South Bend, St Joseph County, Ind) son of Joseph and Susan (Ford) Cotton Minister in Reformed Church in America at Traer and Des Moines, Iowa, Salem, S D , New Brunswick and Dumont, N J , and New York City. Issue (1) Mary Jane, (2) George, (3) Anna Alvira

112131—Mary Jane Cotton, born June 25 1887.

112132—George Cotton, born Sept 21, 1890, died Sept. 30, 1890

112133—Anna Alvira Cotton, born Feb 28 1894.

11214—Anna Greenlee, born Sept 29, 1862, at Toledo, Tama County,
Iowa   Married Nov 19, 1885, at Toledo, Iowa   Charles Clinton
Wallace (born June 27, 1859, at Chariton, Lucas County, Iowa; died
May 10, 1898, at Des Moines, Iowa) son of Thomas D ————
and Sarah (Nichols) Wallace   At one time a worker in Presbyterian Church, Des Moines, Iowa   Issue (1) Lawrence Greenlee,
(2) Martha Lucile

112141—Lawrence Greenlee Wallace, born Aug 19, 1886

112142—Martha Lucile Wallace, born Nov 28, 1893

1122—Anna Greenlee, born Oct. 28, 1826, died March 18, 1849

1123—Elizabeth Greenlee, born Nov 5, 1828, at Pardoe, Mercer County,
Pa, died Sept 1, 1890, in Pennsylvania   Married Sept 20, 1855,
Thomas G———— Barnes (born Jan 21, 1832, at Pardoe) a farmer,
resided near Jackson Center, Pa   Issue (1) Charity Jane, (2) Margaret Florella, (3) John Quincy, (4) Anna Maria, (5) James Elmer,
(6) Edward Gibson

11231—Charity Jane Barnes, born Aug 10, 1856

11232—Margaret Florella Barnes, born June 16, 1858.

11233—John Quincy Barnes, born Feb 5, 1860, at Pardoe, Mercer County,
Pa   Married Sept 20, 1892, Anna Louvena Patterson (born March
28, 1869, at Jackson Center, Pa) daughter of Thompson and Mary
Jane (Williams) Patterson   Farmer at Grove City, Pa   Issue (1)
Mary Edna, (2) Charles Reid

112331—Mary Edna Barnes, born March 19, 1896

112332—Charles Reid Barnes, born Nov 10, 1900

11234—Anna Maria Barnes, born April 26, 1862.   Married Austin W————
Gildersleeve

11235—James Elmer Barnes, born April 15, 1866, at Pardoe, Mercer
County, Pa   Married Aug 24, 1899, at Pardoe, Pa , Mary Martha
Johnston (born June 13, 1869, at Pardoe) daughter of Gilbert and
Margaret (Paden) Johnston, florist at Grove City, Pa   Issue————

11236—Edward Gibson Barnes, born June 30, 1868.   Married Anna
Mable .

1124—James Greenlee, born Dec. 10, 1831 or 1830, at Mercer, Mercer County, Pa , died Oct 22, 1891 or 1890, at Idaho Springs, Clear Creek County, Col Married March 1, 1866, at Bald Mountain, Gilpin County, Col, Maria L——— McColgan (born in Pennsylvania, died at Central City, Gilpin County, Col, Jan 10, 1875) daughter of Thomas McColgan Issue (1) Viola, (2) Rosabel, (3) John Thomas.

11241—Viola Greenlee, born Aug 8, 1869, at Central City, Col Married Jan 15, 1896, at Nevadaville, Gilpin County, Col, Howard E——— Galton (born Jan 22, 1868, at Foochon, China) son of W——— P——— and Georgiana (Parker) Galton Farmer at Otis, Eddy County, New Mexico Issue (1) John Howard, (2) Ruth, (3) Harold Parker

112411—John Howard Galton, born Oct 29, 1896

112412—Ruth Galton, born Feb 19, 1896

112413—Howard Parker Galton, born June 18, 1871.

11242—Rosabel Greenlee, born July 18, 1871, died in infancy

11243—John Thomas Greenlee,—born Sept. 2 1873 at Central City, Col Educated at University of Colorado, Boulder Unmarried in 1901

1125—John Greenlee, born March 25, 1833 Married on Aug 11 ——— Mary Vight or Mary Dight, resided at Utica or Polk, Pa Issue (1) Louis

11251—Louis Greenlee, born ——— — at ——— He was a minister of the United Presbyterian Church, Slingo and Lumber City, Pa , before 1908

1126—William Greenlee, born Feb 27, 1835, died Oct 12, 1900 Married June 22, 1871, Jane Dodds, lived in Jackson Center, Pa

1127—Samuel S——— Greenlee, born March 15, 1837, at Mercer Mercer County, Pa In Company A 139th Regiment Pa and army of the Patomac, wounded at Gettysburg, farmer at West Middleses County, Pa Married Sept 29, 1868 at Pittsburgh, Pa, Amanda T——— Tinker (born Oct 27, 1841, at Mercer, Pa ; died June 17, 1911, at Butler, Pa , buried in Hoagland Cemetery in Mercer County, Pa, daughter of William J——— and Jane (Cook) Tinker—see 1128—Issue (1) Florence Elizabeth, (2) Vinton Lawrence, (3) Laura Mabell

11271—Florence Elizabeth Greenlee, born July 11, 1870, at Mercer, Pa. Married Oct 12, 1892, at West Middlesex, Pa, Frank William Tinker (born Feb 27, 1869, at Butler, Pa) son of Charles and Elizabeth (Morrison) Tinker, contractor at Butler, Pa Issue (1) Mildred Frances, (2) Helen Elizabeth, (3) Florence Lillian, (4) Raymond Greenlee

112711—Mildred Frances Tinker, born Aug 1, 1895 at Butler, Pa

112712—Helen Elizabeth Tinker, born Nov 19, 1899, at Butler, Pa

112713—Florence Lillian Tinker, born Jan. 12, 1907, at Butler, Pa

112714—Raymond Greenlee Tinker, born Jan 6, 1911 at Butler, Pa

11272—Vinton Lawrence Greenlee, born April 22 1874, in Jackson Township, Mercer County, Pa Unmarried Address West Middlesex, Mercer County, Pa

11273—Laura Mabell Greenlee, born Jan. 28, 1884, in Jackson Center, Pa. Married on May 29, 1904, at West Middlesex, Pa, George W——— Brown, son of Johnston and Mary (———————) Brown Address Butler Pa Issue (1) Clifford George, (2) Lucile Margery, (3) Wayne Maxwell

112731—Clifford George Brown, born Dec 14, 1907, at Butler, Pa; died Nov. 15, 1911.

112732—Lucile Margery Brown, born Sept 6, 1908, at Butler, Pa.

112733—Wayne Maxwell Brown, born Aug 21, 1911, at Butler, Pa

1128—Margaret Jane Greenlee, born June 3, 1839, near Mercer, Mercer County Married March 17, 1864, at Mercer, Ellis Wainwright Tinker (born Jan 26, 1836, at Newcastle, Lawrence County, Pa) son of William J——— and Jane (Cook) Tinker—see 1127—Address Denver, Col Issue (1) John Francis, (2) Estella Jane, (3) Adella May, (4) William Ellis, (5) Daughter

11281—John Francis Tinker, born Jan. 19, 1865 Lived in Denver, Colo., in 1908

11282—Estella Jane Tinker, born April 19, 1869 Married Fred Rowe.

11283—Adelle May Tinker, born Dec 16, 1871. Married Benjamin S——————— Smith

11284—William Ellis Tinker, born Feb 7, 1875, died July 5, 1876

11285—Daughter, born March 28, 1879, died March 30, 1879

1129—Mary E——————— Greenlee, born Aug. 1, 1841, died Nov 26, 1845

112(10)—Martha Greenlee, born Jan 18, 1884, at Mercer, Pa Married May 20, 1867, Robert Allen (born Oct. 3, 1837, at Slippery Rock, Lawrence County, Pa) son of Robert and Jane (Wilson) Allen Address 622 South Pearl Street, Denver, Col Issue (1) Margaret Jane, (2) Lizzie May, (3) Minnie Alice, (4) Robert Alvah, (5) Mary Vena, (6) Martha Pernilla, (7) Sarah Augusta, (8) Nannie Burdelia, (9) John Calvin, (10) James Greenlee

112(10)1—Margaret Jane Allen, born July 6, 1868 at Pardoe, Mercer County, Pa , died March 25, 1913 Married April 30, 1891, at Superior, Neb, John Carson (born July 19, 1857, at Ballymorey, County Antrim, Ireland; died Jan. 14, 1907) son of John and Jane (Long) Carson Address of family, University, Pash, Col Issue (1) Martha Jane, (2) Robert John, (3) James Alexander, (4) Harold William, (5) Thomas-twin, (6) son-twin, (7) Richard Cameron.

112(10)11—Martha Jane Carson, born Oct. 18, 1892

112(10)12—Robert John Carson, born April 14. 1895

112(10)13—James Alexander Carson, born Jan. 16, 1897, died Aug 16, 1898

112(10)14—Harold William Carson, born May 15. 1899

112(10)15—Thomas Carson, born Jan 30, 1901, 112(10)6 was born same time, died Feb 8, 1901

112(10)17—Richard Cameron Carson, born Jan 7, 1904, died April 20, 1910

112(10)2—Elizabeth May Allen, born Feb. 20, 1870, at Mercer, Mercer County, Pa Married on June 23, 1886, at Superior, Neb, Robert William Gilchrist (born ——————, died Sept 24. 1909) son of Andrew Symington and Eliza (———————) Gilchrist and grandson of William and Margaret (———————) Gilchrist. Mr R W Gilchrist was a farmer at Superior, Neb Issue (1) Andrew Wilson, (2) Bertha May, (3) Cora Belle, (4) Herbert C———, (5) Allen K———————, (6) Samuel J———————, (7) Robert Spence (8) Margaret Jean

112(10)21—Andrew Wilson Gilchrist, born March 19, 1887, at Mount Clare, Neb Address Superior, Neb

112(10)22—Bertha May Gilchrist, born Oct 6, 1888, at Mount Clare, Neb. Married on ————, at ———— Mr ———— Address Webber, Kan

112(10)23—Cora Belle Gilchrist, born April 2, 1891, at Mount Clare, Neb, died March 7, 1894

112(10)24—Herbert C———— Gilchrist, born Jan 1, 1895, at Los Angeles, Cal Address Superior, Neb

112(10)25—Allen K———— Gilchrist, born June 23, 1896, at Superior, Neb Address Superior, Neb

112(10)26—Samuel J———— Gilchrist, born Feb 12, 1901, at Superior, Neb Address Superior, Neb

112(10)27—Robert Spence Gilchrist, born Aug 20, 1905, at Superior, Neb Address Superior, Neb

112(10)28—Margaret Jean Gilchrist, born Feb 14, 1909, at Superior, Neb Address Superior, Neb

112(10)3—Minnie Alice Allen, born Nov 20, 1871 at Mercer, Mercer County, Pa Married on ————, at Superior, Neb, Robert Gourley Martin, son of Robert and Elizabeth (McKissick) Martin Grocer, 2134 West Jefferson St, Los Angeles, Cal Issue (1) Robert Roscoe, (2) Alice Marie, (3) Wilbert Maxwell

112(10)31—Robert Roscoe Martin, born March 15, 1891 Address Los Angeles, Cal

112(10)32—Alice Marie Martin, born July ————, 1894 Address Los Angeles, Cal

112(10)33—Wilbert Maxwell Martin, born June 14, 1898 Address Los Angeles, Cal

112(10)4—Robert Alvah Allen, born Sept 4, 1874 at ————, Pa Married on ———— at ————, Cal

112(10)5—Mary Vena Allen, born June 30, 1877, at Pleasant Hill, Lawrence County, Pa Married on ———— at ————, William A———— Bryan, son of ———— Address Lawyer, E and C Building, Denver, Col Issue (1) William A————

112(10)51—William A———— Bryan, Jr, born July 5, 1899, at Denver, Col.

112(10)52—Clyde Venroy Bryan, born July 18, 1903, at Denver, Col

112(10)6—Martha Pernilla Allen, born Jan 21, 1880, at Pleasant Hill, Lawrence County, Pa

112(10)7—Sarah Augusta Allen, born May 15, 1881, at Pleasant Hill, Lawrence County, Pa Married on Oct 9, 1907, at Denver, Col, Walter H———— Gross, son of George W———— and Rebecca (————) Gross Master mechanic, 39 Elm Ave, Rahway, N J Issue (1) Charles E————, (2) Walter H————.

112(10)71—Charles E———— Gross, born Jan 24, 1909, at Norristown, Montgomery County, Pa

112(10)72—Walter H———— Gross, Jr., born Nov. 14, 1911, at Philadelphia, Pa

112(10)8—Nannie Burdelia Allen, born May 30, 1883

112(10)9—John Calvin Allen, born Sept 4, 1886, at ———— Married on ———— at ————

112(10)(10)—James Greenlee Allen, born Aug 14, 1888, at Superior, Neb Married on April 27, 1911, at Denver, Col, Alice Benetta Burns, daughter of Patrick and Alice (————) Burns and grand-daughter of Patrick and Mary McGuinn Auto machinist, 3609 Williams St, Denver, Col Issue (1) James Alvah.

112(10)(10)1—James Alvah Allen, born May 13 1912, at Denver, Col

112(11)—Sara E———— Greenlee, born June 19, 1847; died Aug 14, 1861

113—Sarah Greenlee, born Aug ———— 1802 or 3, at Utica or North Shady, Pa, died March 4, 1879, at Franklin, Pa Married in 1827, near Utica, David Barr (born Aug 1805, at Utica or North Shady, died Feb 21, 1882, at Franklin) a farmer, brother of Samuel Barr, who married Margaret Greenlee—115 Issue (1) Silas, (2) Jane, (3) Annie, (4) Isabella, (5) Elizabeth, (6) Margaret, (7) Hettie, (8) Mary, (9) M....

1131—Silas Barr, born 1822   Maried Elizabeth Duffield, both died before 1908

1132—Jane Barr, born March 22, 1899   Married John Bole.

1133—Annie Barr, born Nov. 11, 1830, at Utica, Mercer County, Pa. Married Jan 12, 1860, near Franklin, Venango, County, Pa, David Runninger (born Feb 23, 1831, in Venango County, Pa, died May 19, 1897, at Franklin, Pa)—see 1134—He was a farmer in French Creek Township, near Franklin, Pa   Issue (1) child, (2) Katie Jane, (3) Jacob Silas, (4) James Edwin, (5) Flora, (6) Joseph, (7) Clinton, (8) Mary, (9) Susan

11331—Child, born Dec 12, 1860, died same day.

11332—Katie Jane Runninger, born Dec 26, 1861   Married Frederick McIntyre, lived at Emlenton, Pa, in 1908

11333—Jacob Silas Runninger, born Oct 24, 1864, died Jan 25 1867

11334—James Edwin Runninger, born Aug. 24, 1867   Married Mollie Ferguson, lived at St Marys, W Va, in 1908

11335—Flora Runninger, born June 1, 1869, died July 11, 1869.

11336—Joseph Runninger, born Aug. 24, 1870, died Sept. 28, 1870

11337—Clinton Runninger, born Dec 29, 1871. Married Berthene Temple

11338—Mary Runninger, born Nov 9, 1874   Married James Foster Welton

11339—Susan Runninger, born April 22, 1876. Unmarried in 1908

1134—Isabella Barr, born Jan. 9, 1833   Married Conrad Runninger—see 1133————. Issue (1) John S————.

11341—John S———— Runninger; high Sheriff of Venango County Pa; lived at Franklin, in 1901

1135—Elizabeth Barr, born 1835, died aged 18 months.

1136 Margaret Barr, ' .. 18, 5 died aged 18 months

1137—Hettie Barr, born Aug 6, 1837 or 1838, North Sandy, Mercer County, Pa Married Oct 21, 1857, at Sheakleyville, Mercer County, Pa, Elias Clayton (born Dec 2, 1827, at Huntingdon, County, Pa) Resided at North Sandy, Pa, in 1908 Issue (1) John M————

11371—John M———————— Clayton, born Aug 6, 1861 Married Maria Reagle.

1138—Mary Barr, born 1842 Married Frank Sutler

1139—Maria Barr, born 1844 Married Robert Clinton Longwell

114—James Patterson Greenlee, a farmer born Oct 13, 1805, near Raymilton, Venango County, Pa, died April 26, 1888, near Raymilton Married his first cousin in April, 1830, Elizabeth Greenlee (194) who was born in 1811, near Raymilton; died in 1847, daughter of Robert and Margaret (Porter) Greenlee, and grand-daughter of William and Mary (Thompson) Greenlee Issue (1) Margaret, (2) Robert, (3) Anna, (4) Elizabeth, (5) Samuel, (6) Jane, (7) James Married second time Margaret McGinnis (born April, 1826, at Raymilton, died April, 1889, at Raymilton, daughter of William and Mary (Dousman) McGinnis—see 196 and 197—Issue (8) Mary Ellen, (9) John William, (10) Sarah Luretta, (11) James Madison, (12) Jesse Stewart

1141—Margaret Greenlee, born Aug 20, 1831, in French Creek Township, Venango County, Pa Married April 16, 1851, near Raymilton, Pa, James Jewell (born Dec 18, 1830, near Polk Venango County, Pa) son of Jonathan and Harriet (McGinnis) Jewell, farmer at Raymilton Issue (1) Milo J————, (2) Samuel C————, (3) Frank, (4) Newell, (5) Robert, (6) Walter, (7) Chester, (8) Hettie

11411—Milo J———————— Jewell

11412—Samuel C———————— Jewell.

11413—Frank Jewell

11414—Newell Jewell

11415—Robert Jewell.

11416—Walter Jewell.

11417—Chester L———————— Jewell. Unmarried in 1908.

11418—Hettie Jewell

1142—Robert Greenlee, born —————. Married Sophia Flickner, lived at Raymilton, in 1908

1143—Anna Greenlee, born March 4, 1839, near Raymilton, Venango County, Pa Married July 7, 1864, George Walter Noel (born Oct 5, 1839, near Wallaceville, Venango County, Pa) son of Thomas Jerome and Sarah (Seely) Noel

1144—Elizabeth Greenlee. Married Seth Temple

1145—Samuel Greenlee Married Harriet Burch, lived at Raymilton, Mercer County, Pa, in 1908 Issue (1) George, (2) Elmer, (3) Fred, (4) Ida

11451—George Greenlee, born —————

11452—Elmer Greenlee, born March 7, 1870, near Raymilton, Venango County, Pa Married Nov 14, 1899, at Sandy Lake, Mercer County, Pa, Cora Frances Vogan (born Aug 17, 1878, at Sandy Lake) daughter of Simeon Vogan and Rebecca Ward, farmer at Sandy Lake Issue (1) Herman Bruce.

114521—Herman Bruce Greenlee, born Nov 14, 1900

11453—Fred Greenlee Married Jennie Richard

11454—Ida Greenlee.

1146—Jane Greenlee Unmarried in 1908, lived at Raymilton, Pa.

1147—James Greenlee; died

1148—Mary Ellen Greenlee, born Dec 3, 1850, at Raymilton, Pa Married Alvin C————— May (born March 5, 1849, at Franklin, Pa) son of John C————— and Elizabeth (Singleton) May Gas Engineer at Franklin, Pa Issue (1) Alvin Plummer, (2) Bertha L—————, (3) John F—————, (4) William C—————, (5) James LeRoy, (6) Lewis Edwin

11481—Alvin Plummer May, born May 30, 1878

11482—Bertha L————— May, born Dec 15, 1879

11483—John F————— May, born Oct 11, 1881.

11484—William C————— May, born Oct 3, 1883.

11485—James LeRoy May, born March, 14, 1886.

11486—Lewis Edwin May, born Oct. 11, 1888.

1149—John William Greenlee. Unmarried in 1908.

114(10)—Sarah Luretta Greenlee. Married Joshua Aley; lived at Raymilton.

114(11)—James Madison Greenlee, Married at Pittsburg.

114(12)—Jessie Stewart Greenlee. Unmarried in 1908; lived at Raymilton.

115—Margaret Greenlee, born on ——————— at ———————. Married on ——————— at ———————, Samuel Barr, a brother of David Barr, who married her sister Sarah, (113). Issue (1) Eliza, (2) Annie, (3) Mary, (4) Sarah, (5) Margaret, (6) Jennie, (7) Ellen, (8) Martha, (9) Peter, (10) David.

1151—Eliza Barr, born on ——————— at ———————. Married on ——————— at ——————— Dunn; died ———————; lived in Kansas.

1152—Annie Barr, born on ——————— at ———————; died ——————— Married on ——————— Austin; lived in Kansas.

1153—Mary Barr, born on ——————— at ———————; died ——————— Married on ——————— ——————— Johnson; lived in Ohio.

1154—Sarah Barr, born on ——————— at ———————. Married Pierson; lived in New Jersey.

1155—Margaret Barr. Married; Lord. Lived in Crawford County, Pa.

1156—Jennie Barr, born on ——————— at ———————; died ——————— Married on ——————— ——————— Smith; lived in Crawford County, Pa.

1157—Ellen Barr, born on ——————— at ———————; died ——————— Married on ——————— ——————— Holman; lived in Titusville, Pa., in 1908.

1158—Martha Barr, born on ——————— at ———————; died ——————— Married on ——————— ——————— Nevin.

1159—Peter Barr, born ———————; died ———————.

115(10)—David Barr, ———————.

116—Elizabeth Greenlee, born on ———————— at ————————; died
———————, Married ———————— Issue ————————

117—Samuel Greenlee, born about 1812, died unmarried aged 21 years.

12—John Greenlee, born about 1758, in Pa He probably lived with his
brother William in what was then Northumberland County, Pa, when
the first census was taken in 1790 He removed from Susquehanna
County to Woodcockboro, Pa, in 1799 He was a soldier in the War of
1812, elder in the Presbyterian Church, a Democrat; resided in Woodcock, Crawford County, Pa, until his death on May 22, 1837, aged 79
years Married Sarah Brady, who was born in 1771, in Pennsylvania,
died May 16, 1850, aged 79 years, daughter of Capt John Brady and
Mary Quigley Issue (1) William, (2) James, (3) Mary, (4) Elizabeth,
(5) John, (6) Samuel, (7) David

121—William Greenlee, born June 6, 1797, at Woodock, Crawford County,
Pa (died Jan 8, 1878, aged 78 years, 7 months and 20 days, at Wood-
cock) He was a soldier in the War of 1812 He was a saw-mill
owner and operator Married on May 4, 1827, at Waterford, Erie
County, Pa, Margaret Townley (born Sept 2, 1805, at Woodcock,
died Nov 14, 1852, at Woodcock, daughter of Robert and Mary
(Brown) Townley Issue (1) Mary, (2) John, (3) Robert, (4)
Sarah J————————, (5) Cyrus, (6) Amos, (7) William Harrison, (8)
Angeline, (9) Mary Adeline, (10) Margaret, (11) Frances Amelia

1211—Mary Greenlee, born Feb 8, 1827

1212—John Greenlee, born July 18, 1829

1213—Robert Greenlee, born May 18, 1830, at Woodcock, Crawford
County, Pa, died July 23, 1893, at Bloomington, Ill Was a building
contractor in California and Illinois Married March 27, 1858, at
Bloomington, Sarah Corman (born Jan 1, 1829, at Nicholasville,
Jessamine County, Kentucky) daughter of Abraham and Elizabeth
(Grow) Corman Issue (1) Frances Amelia, (2) Ella Louvena, (3)
Theodore Tyler, (4) John Wesley, (5) Ulysses Logan, (6) Cora
Estelle.

12131—Frances Amelia Greenlee, born Aug 28, 1859 Married A————·—
A———————— Hoffman

12132—Ella Louvena Greenlee, born Oct. 6, 1862

12133—Theodore Tyler Greenlee, born Nov 4, 1864.

1213, John Wesley Greenlee, born April 6, 1866

12135—Ulysses Logan Greenlee, born Sept 8, 1867 Married Sept 16, 1897, Nellie Irene Sanders

12136—Cora Estelle Greenlee, born Dec 14, 1872

1214—Sara Jane Greenlee, born April 18, 1832, at Woodcock, Crawford County, Pa Married in 1857, at Cambridge Springs, Pa, John Smith (born about 1825, in Scotland; died Oct 8, 1889, aged 64 years, at Akron, Ohio Issue (1) Anna E————

12141—Anna E———— Smith, born Nov 22, 1860, at Woodcock, Crawford County, Pa Married June 15, 1881, at Akron, Ohio, to Park B Field, owner of the "Repository" at Canton, Ohio, son of Asa Field and Mary Ann Catherine (Cady) Field He was Secretary to President McKinley in 1896 Her address 1914 is 117 E William St, Canton, Ohio Issue (1) John Asa Field

121411—John Asa Field, born Akron, Ohio, March 23, 1882 Married Maude Anna Covell, of Clyde, Ohio, is now (1914) designing engineer. Address Akron, Ohio

1215—Cyrus Greenlee, born Sept 2, 1834 at Woodcock, Crawford County, Pa, moved to Springfield, Mo, in 1859 Was Sergeant Major of the 8th Missouri Volunteer Cavalry A contractor and builder, died Oct 21, 1900, at Springfield, Mo Married twice, first ———— Randolph; second in March, 1874, at Springfield, Mo, Mrs Harriet E———— (McFarland) Davis (born Oct, 1833 or Feb 20, 1835, at Sedalia, Pettis County, Mo) daughter of William H———— McFarland Issue (1) Charles

12151—Charles Greenlee, born Aug 17, 1875, at Springfield, Mo. Unmarried in 1908

1216—Amos Greenlee, born Jan 10, 1837, at Woodcock, Crawford County, Pa, died Jan 25, 1887, at Woodcock Was a farmer in Richmond Township, seven miles from Cambridge Springs Married on Jan 1, 1866, at Cambridge Springs, Crawford County, Pa, Adelaide H Chamberlain (born Dec 24, 1848, at Cambridge Springs) daughter of Emerson and Elvin (Aiken) Chamberlain Issue (1) Myrtle, (2) Mortimer R————, (3) Albert A————

12161—Myrtle Greenlee, born May 31, 1868, at Cambridge Springs Unmarried in 1899, lived at Buffalo, N Y

12162—Mortimer R Greenlee, born March 17, 1870, at Cambridge Springs Unm...

4

12163—Albert A. Greenlee, born Oct 27, 1876 Unmarried in 1899

1217—William Harrison Greenlee, born Feb 3, 1839, at Woodcock, Crawford County, Pa , died April 9, 1892, at Woodcock Married June
17, 1869, Mary Elizabeth Quay (born Feb 8, 1827, at Cambridge,
Crawford County Pa , died June 4, 1889, at Woodcock) daughter
of Archie and Jane (Clark) Quay Issue (1) Adriel Laduff, (2)
William Albert

12171—Adriel Laduff Greenlee, born June 12 1872, at Woodcock, lived
at Woodcock, in 1908

12172—William Albert Greenlee, born Aug. 10, 1874

1218—Angeline Greenlee, born Aug 12, 1842, died unmarried July 15,
1874

1219—Mary Greenlee, born Aug 22 1844, at Woodcock, Crawford County,
Pa ; died May 23, 1870 (or 1869) at Woodcock Married Dec 25,
1864, at Woodcock, Dr Albert Logan (born June 4, 1831, at Hartstown, Crawford County, Pa , died July 17, 1885, at Woodcock) son of
David Logan, Jr , Physician at Woodcock Issue (1) James Albert,
(2) Mary Adelaide

12191—James Albert Logan, born Dec 25, 1866; lived at Cambridge
Springs, Pa , in 1908 Married Ida May Swift

12192—Mary Adelaide Logan, born March 24 1869, at Woodcock, Pa
Married on April 10, 1892, William Clendenin (born March 12, 1868,
at Cincinnati, Ohio) son of Dr William and Sabra (Birchard) Clendenin A physician at Madisonville, Ohio, in 1908 Issue (1) Mary
Elizabeth

121921—Mary Elizabeth Clendenin, born March 10, 1894

121(10)—Margaret Greenlee, born June 26, 1846 Unmarried in 1908, lived
at Springfield, Mo

121(11)—Frances Amelia Greenlee, born March 15, 1848, at Woodcock,
Pa ; died April 1, 1895, at Springfield, Mo Married Nov 1, 1878,
at Springfield, Mo, John (or Joseph) M Jarrett (born Nov 3,
1824 or 1844, in McMinn County, Tenn , died Sept 28, 1890, at
Springfield, Mo) son of Aaron and Mary (Moore) Jarrett Issue
(1) Lyman Hampton, (2) Effie Glenn, (3) Elfred Logan

121(11)1—Lyman Hampton Jarrett, born Aug 11, 1880 Lived at Spring-

121(11)2—Effie Glenn Jarrett, born Aug 11, 1880, died before 1908.

121(11)3—Alfred Logan Jarrett, born Feb 24 1883, died before 1908

122—James Greenlee, born in 1799, at Woodcock, Crawford County, Pa died Sept 15, 1868, aged 70 Married on ————, Hannah Bracken, of Columbus, Pa (born Aug 23, 1808, at Woodcock), died Dec 30, 1898 Issue (1) George Bracken, (2) Sarah, (3) Irene E————.

1221—George Bracken Greenlee, born ————, died in 1866 Married Sarah Rabel, of Woodcockboro, Pa, who later married A C. Gibson. Children of G B and S Greenlee (1) Clayton, (2) George

12211—Clayton Greenlee, born ————, lived in Brooklyn, in 1908

12212—George Greenlee, born ————, lived with his mother near Woodcockboro, Pa, in 1908

1222—Sarah Greenlee, born ———— at ————.

1223—Irene E Greenlee, born 1845, died April 15, 1852, aged 7 years.

123—Mary Greenlee, born May 2 1802, at Woodcock, Crawford County Pa, died July 21, 1873, at Erie, Pa Married on Feb 24, 1820, at Woodcock, John Meredith Taylor Dunn (born May 4 1796 at Londonderry, Ireland; died May 2, 1860, at Erie or McKean, Erie County, Pa) son of Oliver and Rachel (Taylor) Dunn ————. A farmer of McKean, Pa. Issue (1) Sarah Ann, (2) Rachel (3) Oliver Brady, (4) Mary Esther (5) Elizabeth, (6) Emily, (7) Martha Jane, (8) Lafayette, (9) John Greenlee.

1231—Sarah Ann Dunn, born Dec 25 1820, died Oct. 20, 1854. Unmarried

1232—Rachel Dunn, born Feb 11 1822. Married at Erie, Pa., Joseph A. French, died March, 1894 Issue (1) Clara, (2) George Dunn, (3) Joseph S

12321—Clara French, born ———— died in her 'teens

12322—George Dunn French, born at Cincinnati, Ohio Married, Attorney at Law, Cincinnati, Ohio

12323—Joseph S. French, born ————, lived at Pittsburgh, Pa. in 190~

1233—Oliver Brady Dunn, born June 10, 1824; died 1904-5, Monmouth, Ill Married in Erie County, Pa, Harriet Dunn Issue (1) Nannie V, (2) Emmet Thomas, (3) Robert Monroe, (4) Lenoir G, (5) Clyde Gilson

12331—Nannie V. Dunn, born Dec 4, 1852, at Erie, Pa Address 1913, 942 N 4th St, Pomona, Calif

12332—Emmet Thomas Dunn, born ————, lived at Seattle, Wash, in 1908

12333—Robert Monroe Dunn, born ————, at ————

12334—Lenoir G Dunn, born ———— Lived at Seattle, Wash, in 1908

12335—Clyde Gilson Dunn, born ————. Lived at Kent, Wash, in 1908

1234—Mary Esther Dunn born July 18, 1826, died April 14, 1857. Unmarried

1235—Elizabeth Dunn, born April 12, 1829, at Woodcock, Pa, died March 27, 1901 Married Feb 24, 1870, at Erie, Pa, John Robison Dumars, (born Dec 1, 1807, at Erie, Pa, died April 10, 1895, at Erie, Pa) son of James and Margaret (Robison) Dumars No children.

1236—Emily Dunn, born Sept 15, 1832, died March 2, 1855 Unmarried

1237—Martha Jane Dunn, born June 2, 1834, at McKean, Erie, Pa Married Oct 18, 1854, at McKean, Samuel LeRoy Glover (born July 4, 1832, at Morris, Ostego County, N Y) son of Ezra Jarvis and Hannah (Mudge) Glover, lived at Comstock, Neb (R F D No 1), in 1913 Issue (1) Deett, (2) Mary Emily, (3) Grace, (4) Henry Bion, (5) Percy Dunn, (6) Sidney Lynn

12371—Deett Glover, born April 22, 1856, in Erie County, Pa Married on April 9, 1893, in Custer County, Neb, Joseph Warren McRae, son of Daniel Brown and Nancy (Wright) McRae His grandparents were C. C and Mary McRae He is a farmer Address Republican City, Neb, R F D No 2 Issue (1) Orlo, (2) Mott

123711—Orlo McRae, born April 11, 1894, at Weisen, Neb

12712 Mott McRae, born Jan 3, 1876, at Weisen, Neb

12372—Mary Emily Glover, born Aug 4, 1858, at La Salle County, Ill. (Address, Comstock, Neb, R F D No 1) Married on April 22, 1886, at Campus, Ill, Elvie Thurston Potter (born ————; died May 21, 1902, at Campus, Ill) son of Stephen and Mary Ann Potter No children

12373—Grace Glover, born Dec. 12 1859, at La Salle County, Ill Married on April 4, 1889, in Dundy County, Rev Eugene Victor Sparks, son of Thomas Cook and Esther Ann (Dunn) Sparks and grandson of Ephriam and Sarah (Cook) Sparks and of James and Asenath (Grable) Dunn Farmer, Jaqua, Kan. No children.

12374—Henry Bion Glover, born Sept 24 1861, at ————. Married on April 5, 1907, at Lincoln Neb, Cordelia A——— Johnson. Farmer Address Comstock, Neb, R. F D No 1

12375—Percy Dunn Glover, born April 27, 1863. at ————. Farmer Address, Comstock, Neb, R F D No 1 Married on Jan 24, 1887, at Campus, Ill, Augusta Susan Lower Issue (1) Earl, (2) Fay, (3) Guy, (4) Ruth, (5) Loyd, (6) Glen, (7) Rex, (8) daughter, (9) Frank, (10) Ray, (11) Seth, (12) Ted, (13 Max, (14) Grace, (15) Ralph, (16) Clyde.

123751—Earl Glover,—born May 19, 1888

123752—Fay Glover, born Nov 19, 1889

123753—Guy Glover, born March 1, 1891.

123754—Ruth Glover, born May 12, 1892.

123755—Loyd Glover, born Dec 28, 1893

123756—Glen Glover, born May 14, 1895

123757—Rex Glover, born Oct 16, 1896

123758—Daughter, born Feb 23, 1899, died Sept. 20, 1899

123759—Frank Glover, born Feb 5, 1901.

12375(10)—Ray Glover, born March 18, 1902.

12375(11)—Seth Glover, born July 11 1903

12375(12)—Ted Glover,

12375(13)—Max Glover, born Dec 29, 1905

12375(14)—Grace Glover, born Feb 23, 1907.

12375(15)—Ralph Glover, born July 18, 1908

12375(16)—Clyde Glover, born July 15, 1909

12376—Sidney Lynn Glover, born Dec 29, 1864 Address Comstock, Neb Married on ————, at York, Neb , Lena Peterson Issue (1) Mary, (2) Lillie, (3) Beulah

123761—Mary Glover, born Aug 15, 1905

123762—Lillie Glover, born Feb 21, 1907

123763—Beulah Glover, born Nov ————, 1908

1238—Lafayette Dunn, born Sept 4, 1836; died Oct 10, 1863, in the Civil War, was master mate on the U S Steamer "Tawak"

1239—John Greenlee Dunn, born April 27, 1838, died ———— 1906. Married Caroline Matilda Luce No children Address Ashtabula, Ohio

124—Elizabeth B———— Greenlee, born April 27, 1805. at Gravel Run, Crawford County, Pa , died May 29, 1884. Married on ————, at ————, John M———— Humes (born April 13, 1790, at Lockhaven, Pa , died Dec 2, ————) son of Archibald and Mary Humes John M———— Humes was a soldier in the War of 1812 Issue (1) Jasper Newton, (2) Porter C————, (3) Dickson, (4) ————, (5) ————

1241—Jasper Newton Humes, born June 7, 1846 Married Amanda Bole

1242—Porter C———— Humes, born Feb 20, 1849, at Woodcock, Pa , was a Justice of the Peace at Woodcock for five years Married three times, first on Oct 20, 1869, at Woodcock, Julia Dedrich (born Nov 15, 1848, at Friendship, N. Y , died May 10, 1880, at Woodcock) daughter of Peter and Mary Dedrich No issue Married second time on Jan 8, 1885, at Cambridge Springs, Pa, Kate Fisher (born March 5, 1865, in Woodcock Township, Crawford County, Pa , died April 21, 1898, in Woodcock) daughter of Frederick and Lena Fisher Issue (1) Ransom P Married third time on March 17, 1897, at Cambridge Springs, Pa , Jeanette C Mann (born Oct 30, ————, in W———— T———————— Crawford County Pa. died June 26, 1898, at ———————— Joseph and Sarah Mann

12421—**Ransom P Humes**, born Feb 10, 1888

1243—**Dickson Humes**, born Aug 10, 1851

1244———————— Humes, born ———————, died in infancy

2245——————— Humes, born ———————; died in infancy

125—**John Greenlee**, born ———————, 1808 Unmarried Killed by a train in Meadville, Pa, Sept 15, 1865

126—**Samuel Greenlee**, born ———————, 1810, died April 16 1826

127—**David Greenlee**, born 1816. Unmarried, died May 14, 1841

13—**Sarah Greenlee**, born ——————— at ———————. Married on ——————— at ——————— ——————— McCullough Issue ———————

14—**Mary Greenlee**, born ——————— at - Married on ——— —, George Darling ——————— Issue ———————

15—**Elizabeth Greenlee**, born on ——————— at ———————. Married on ———————, ——————— Bell or Biel Issue ———————

16—**Susan Greenlee**, born ———————, died young from fall in a barn

17—**Jane Greenlee**, born ———————; died when quite young of smallpox at Washington, Pa, at the home of her aunt Jean (Thomson) Wylie (No 2), with whom she lived after the murder of her father by the Indians Under date of Oct 21, 1795, Jean Greenlee, of Washington County, Pa, sent power of attorney (original in the hands of Theodore Samuel Thompson, No 338, on May 10, 1802) to William Thomson (No 3) to collect all moneys due her from the estate of William Greenlee (her father, No 1) in the hands of James Greenlee (her brother, No 11), the administrator Witnesses Isaac Kerr and Robert Wylie (the husband of her aunt Jean Thomson, No 2)

18—**William Greenlee**, born Nov 15, 1771, at Pottsville Schuylkill County, Pa, died in 1854, aged 82 years, 3½ months, at McZena, Ashland, County, Ohio He probably lived with his brother John in what was then Northumberland County, Pa, in 1790 He moved from Susquehanna County, Pa, to Ohio, about 1810, and located on a farm of 160 acres on the south side of the Big Mohican River, in Wayne (now Ashland County) He married on March 13, 1798, in Pennsylvania, Rebecca Hughes Issue (1) Nancy, (2) Mary, (3) John, (4) Ellen, (5) Elizabeth, (6) Elizabeth, (7) Jane, (8) Sarah (9) William, (10) James, (11) Wesley, (12) L Matilda, (13) George Washington Married second time to ——————— Smith, who died at McZena, Ohio, daughter . ⁔

181—Nancy Greenlee, born Dec 15, 1799

182—Mary (Polly) Greenlee, born April 4, 1802 Married on ————————
at ———————— ———————— Musgrove Issue ————————————

183—John Greenlee, born Feb 17, 1804, in Pa , died June 13, 1877, at
McZena, Ashland County, Ohio Married on May 18, 1837, at Lake-
ville, Wayne County, Ohio, Susan Mary Warner, of Lake Township
(born Sept 18, 1815, at McZena, Ohio, died Aug 31, 1835, at McZena)
daughter of Henry and Mary (Muchler) Warner (or Elizabeth (Bals-
ley) Warner Issue (1) Sophronia, (2) Nancy Ann, (3) Luserbia
Livonia, (4) John Slone, (5) William, (6) Daniel Warner, (7) James
Lewis, (8) Mary Elizabeth, (9) Curtis, (10) Bell, (11) Xenis, (12)
Edward Stewart, (13) Susan Otello, (14) Eliza Rolland, (15) Martha
Jane

1831—Sophronia Greenlee, born March 3, 1838; died Feb 16, 1879
Married June 15, 1865, Isaac N Bonnett. Issue (1) Harry, (2) Ida
Nettie, (3) Isaac Dean, (4) ————————, (5) ————————.

18311—Harry Bonnett, born ————————. He was a druggist; died at
Perrysville, Ohio

18312—Ida Nettie Bonnett, born ————————. Married Pearl Showalt-
ter, of Kentucky, Superintendent of the Prudential Insurance Company, lived at Denver, Col, in 1908

18313—Isaac Dean Bonnett, born ————————. Graduated at Lafayette,
Ind

18314———————— Bonnett, born ————————, died in infancy.

18315———————— Bonnett, born ————————, died in infancy.

1832—Nancy Ann Greenlee, born Sept 1, 1839. Unmarried in 1908

1833—Luserbia Livonia Greenlee, born Aug 30, 1841, died Aug. 27, 1842

1834—John Slone Greenlee, born March 2, 1843; died March 26, 1866.
He was a soldier in the Civil War, Company H. 82nd Regiment,
Ohio Volunteers Infantry Married April 21, 1864, Sarah Wachtel,
Issue (1) Hettie

18341—Hettie Greenlee, born in 1865, died in 1875

183, William Greenlee, on Nov 4, 1844, died March 8, 1846

1836—Daniel Warner Greenlee, born April 11, 1846; died Aug 13, 1897, at Davis, Indian Territory Married March 2, 1867, Melissa Ann Plank Issue (1) daughter, (2) Zella

18361—(Daughter) Greenlee, born ——————, died in infancy

18362—Zella Greenlee, born ——————. Married ——————, lived at Cleveland, Ohio, in 1908

1837—James Lewis Greenlee, born Feb 22 1848; died Dec 7, 1875

1838—Mary Elizabeth Greenlee, born Jan 5, 1850, at McZena, Ashland County, Ohio Married Dec 27, 1870, at McZena, John Wesley Esterday (born Feb 27, 1849, at Sparta, Marrow County, Ohio) son of Conrad and Hannah (Green) Esterday, a farmer at Overton, Wayne County, Ohio Issue (1) John Conrad, (2) Elva Gertie, (3) Susan Hannah, (4) Bernice Luella

18381—John Conrad Esterday, born Sept. 22, 1871. Married Callie Hempertz, lived at Mansfield, Ohio, in 1908

18382—Elva Gertie Esterday, born April 3, 1874, at Big Prairie, Wayne County, Ohio Married Jan 30, 1890, at Wooster, Wayne County, Ohio William Eugene Hawk (born Nov. 22, 1870, at Wooster, Ohio) lived at Wooster, Ohio, in 1908 Issue (1) Frankie Luella, (2) Mary Arminta, (3) Charles Glen.

183821—Frankie Luella Hawk, born March 24, 1891

183822—Mary Arminta Hawk, born May 3. 1893

183823—Charles Glen Hawk, born July 8. 1895

18383—Susan Hannah Esterday, born Jan 22, 1879.

18384—Bernice Luella Esterday, born Sept 29, 1882

1839—Curtis Greenlee, born March 1, 1851 at McZena, Ashland County, Ohio Married Dec. 4, 1872, at Haysville, Ashland County, Pa, Mina Marks (born Oct 6, 1857, at McZena) daughter of Robert and Mary Ann (Pierce) Marks, lived at Columbus, Ohio, in 1908 Issue (1) Alice May, (2) Curtis Earl, (3) Harmon Victor, (4) Cloyd Steward

18391—Alice May Greenlee, born May 23, 1875

18392—Curtis Earl Greenlee, born April 6. 1877. A soldier in the Spanish Am   n W .

18393—Harmon Victor Greenlee, born June 16, 1878

18394—Cloyd Steward Greenlee, born Aug 25, 1879, at McZena, Ohio.

183(10)—Bell Greenlee, born Feb 13, 1852, died Feb 10, 1857

183(11)—Xenis Greenlee, born June 2, 1854; died Sept 10, 1854.

183(12)—Edward Stewart Greenlee, born June 2, 1855, at McZena, Ashland
County, Ohio   Served for five years as secretary of Holmes
County, Mutual Insurance Company   Address, Mansfield, Ohio
Married on Dec 31, 1885, at Mohican, Ashland County, Ohio,
Filora Bell Emerich (born April 14, 1866, at McZena, Ohio) daugh-
ter of George Washington and Caroline (Crumlick) Emerich
Issue (1) Arden Deane, (2) Zodie Vern, (3) Vulah Constance,
(4) Eolis Erma, (5) Zelda Zula

183(12)—Arden Deane Greenlee, born Oct. 29, 1886.

183(12)2—Zodie Vern Greenlee, born Jan 6, 1889.

183(12)3—Vulah Constance Greenlee, born Oct 11, 1891.

183(12)4—Eolis Erma Greenlee, born March 24, 1893.

183(12)5—Zelda Zula Greenlee, born Jan 22, 1896

183(13)—Susan Otello Greenlee, born Sept 30, 1857, died May 14, 1881.

183(14)—Eliza Rolland Greenlee, born March 4, 1860, at McZena, Ohio.
Address, McZena, Ohio   Married on Jan 14, 1886, at Mohican,
Ohio, Mary Long (born Dec 30, 1860, at Mohican, died Nov 3,
1896, at McZena, Ohio) daughter of Peter B——— and Saloma
(Kantzer) Long   Issue (1) Herbert Clarence, (2) George Glell,
(3) Grace Bell

183(14)1—Herbert Clarence Greenlee, born Nov 11, 1886.

183(14)2—George Glell Greenlee, born June 3, 1890.

183(14)3—Grace Bell Greenlee, born Aug. 15, 1893.

183(15)—Martha Jane Greenlee, born Aug 10, 1861, died same day

184—Ellen Greenlee, (twin), born Jan 11, 1806

185 Elizabeth Greenlee, (twin) born Jan 11 1806, died young

186—Elizabeth Greenlee, born March 11, 1808

187—Jane Greenlee, born Feb 20, 1810. Married on ——————— at
——————, William Bell, son of ————— Issue ———————

188—Sarah Greenlee, born Dec 7, 1812, at Londonville, Ashland County,
Ohio, died Nov 1, 1899, at Londonville. Married on Jan 2, 1837,
Ephraim Chidister Marks (born Oct 7, 1813, at Mohican, Ashland
County, Ohio, died May 26, 1864, at Londonville) a merchant and a
lawyer at Londonville Issue (1) Jane Bell, (2) Lusasba, (3) George
Washington, (4) William Miner, (5) Budd Frank.

1881—Jane Bell Marks, born Oct 1, 1838 Unmarried, died Dec 1, 1896.

1882—Lusasba Marks, born Sept 26, 1839

1883—George Washington Marks, born July 1, 1841 Married on ———————
————————, 1861, at ——————— No issue

1884—William Miner Marks, born June 5, 1850, in Ashland County, Ohio.
Address, Londonville, Ohio Married on ———————, 1880, in Ashland, Ohio, Effie May Wallace (born April 3, 1859, in Londonville,
Ohio) daughter of Robert P——————— and Electa Jane (McGuier)
Wallace Issue (1) Robert Wallace, (2) C——————— V———————,
(3) Beulah, (4) Mabel Irene, (5) Irma Fay, (6) Florence Alline,
(7) Ralph Gordon

18841—Robert Wallace Marks, born Jan 2, 1881.

18842—C——————— V ——————— Marks, born Aug. 27, 1882

18843—Beulah Marks, born ——————— 1887

18844—Mabel Irene Marks, born Dec 31, 1888

18845—Irma Fay Marks, born Jan 16, 1891

18846—Florence Alline Marks, born Nov 29, 1893

18847—Ralph Gordon Marks, born June 2, 1896

189—William Greenlee, born Oct. 7, 1818. Lived at Sumner, Ill in 1901

18(10)—James Greenlee, born Sept. 17, 1820

18(11)—Wesley Greenlee,   —— —— — ,   — — —

18(12)—L———— Matilda (Martha) **Greenlee,** born June 7, 1825 (died about ———— 1871) Married on ———— at ———— John Burwell, son of ———— of ———— Issue (1) Herbert

18(12)1—Herbert **Burwell,** born on ———— at ————.

18(13)—George Washington **Greenlee,** born Oct 23, 1827.

19—Robert **Greenlee,** born May 30, 1773, at Penns Creek, near Swishers Run, Snyder County, Pa , died March, 1856, near Franklin, French Creek Township, Venango County, Pa He was seven years old when his father was killed by the Indians He lived with William Thompson (probably No. 4) nine years, then went to Stone Valley and lived nine years He settled in Franklin, April 17, 1798 His farm joined that of his brother, James, near Raymilton He served in the War of 1812 He married April, 1804, near Franklin, Margaret Porter, who was born in 1786-7, in Venango County, Pa , died March 30, 1840, at Franklin, daughter of Robert and Rebecca (Stewart) Porter Issue (1) William, (2) Rebecca, (3) Mary, (4) Elizabeth, (5) Robert Porter, (6) Jane, (7) Stewart, (8) Joseph

191—William **Greenlee,** born on Aug 12, 1805, at Franklin, Venango County, Pa , died in 1866, at Franklin. Married in 1827, at Franklin, Mary Jane Vogan (born 1807, at Sandy Lake, Mercer County, Pa ; died in 1879, at Clay Center, Clay County, Kan), daughter of William and Jane (Hassan) Vogan Issue (1) Robert Thompson, (2) Jane H————, (3) Margaret P————, (4) William W————, (5) Hugh Hassan, (6) Joseph, (7) Mathew B————, (8) James V————, (9) Samuel S————

1911—Robert Thompson **Greenlee,** born June 15, 1828, at Franklin, Venango County, Pa. He served in the Civil War, Company G, 100th Illinois Volunteers Farmer   Address Idana, Clay County, Kan Married twice First on Jan 11, 1855, at Sandy Lake, Mercer County, Pa , Rachel Beggs (born ————, 1830, in County Tyrone, Ireland, died Jan 13, 1861, at Channahon, Will County, Ill, daughter of William and Martha (Wilson) Beggs Issue (1) Mary J————, (2) Martha E———— Married second time on Nov 20, 1866, in Mercer County, Pa , Amanda J———— Porter (born ———— 1840, near Sandy Lake, Pa) daughter of David and Anna (White) Porter. Issue (3) David Howard, (4) Anne E————, (5) Matthew Wilken, (6) Robert Allen, (7) Jesse Forrest, (8) Nannie B————, (9) John K————

1911r—Mary J———— Greenlee, born Dec 28 1857 Married James

19112—Martha E——————— Greenlee, born March 10, 1859 Married Robert J——————— Rea

19113—David Howard Greenlee, born Oct 12, 1867, died Oct 17, 1872

19114—Anne E——————— Greenlee, born Aug 17, 1869 Married J——————— E——————— Hamilton.

19115—Matthew Wilkin Greenlee, born Dec 10, 1870

19116—Robert Allen Greenlee, born Jan 7, 1873, died Aug 7, 1878

19117—Jesse Forrest Greenlee, born Sept 7, 1874, died July 30, 1878

19118—Nannie B——————— Greenlee, born Dec 18, 1877

19119—John K——————— Greenlee, born June 8, 1880

1912—Jane H——————— Greenlee, born ——————— 1830 Married David Glenn

1913—Maragret P——————— Greenlee, born ——————— 1832 Married John Lynch

1914—William W——————— Greenlee, born 1835 Married Margaret Johnson

1915—Hugh Hassan Greenlee, born Nov 5, 1837, at Polk, Venango County, Pa , died Jan 2, 1900, at Derrick City, McKean County, Pa Married twice First on Dec 15, 1859, at Polk, Amanda M——————— Hedglin (born June 10, 1845, at Polk, died May 7, 1886, at Derrick City) daughter of Stephen Decatur and Hannah W (Lane) Hedglin Issue (1) Aramanda Araminta, (2) George W, (3) Ira R——————— Married second time on July 4, 1887, Ellen Lee (born May 3, 1861) Issue (4) Thomas S———————, (5) Charles H———————, (6) Clyde, (7) Lucy M———————, (8) Harold

1915:—Aramanda Araminta Greenlee, born Jan 22 1861, near Polk, Mineral Township, Venango County, Pa Married on July 10, 1879, at Parkers City, Armstrong County, Pa, Walter E——————— Brown (born May 5, 1859, at Scrubgrass, Venango County, Pa) son of Marcus Lucian and Annie Eliza (Phipps) Brown Oil producer Address, Four Mile Cittarangus County, N Y Issue (1) George W———————, (2) Willard L———————, (3) Myrtle M———————, (4) Hazel A———————, (5) Ivy B———————, (6) Laurel E———————

191511—George W——————— Brown, born April 21, 1880, died May 7, 188.

191512—Willard L——————— Brown, born June 18, 1882.

191513—Myrtle M——————— Brown, born May 30, 1885.

191514—Hazel A——————— Brown, born June 11, 1888

191515—Ivy B ——————— Brown, born Oct 25, 1890

191516—Laurel E——————— Brown, born May 12, 1894.

19152—George W——————— Greenlee, born Jan 20, 1863

19153—Ira R——————— Greenlee, born April 9, 1885 died Mar 14 1899.

19154—Thomas S——————— Greenlee, born Nov 5, 1889

19155—Charles H——————— Greenlee, born Nov. 5, 1889

19156—Clyde Greenlee, born Jan 22, 1892

19157—Lucy M——————— Greenlee, born Jan 26, 1897.

19158—Harold Greenlee, born Aug 12, 1897

1916—Joseph Greenlee, born ——————, 1841.

1917—Matthew B——————— Greenlee, born ——————— 1843 Married Sarah Furst

1918—James V——————— Greenlee, born ——————— 1847

1919—Samuel S——————— Greenlee, born ——————— 1853

192—Rebecca Greenlee, born May 30, 1807, died 1813

193—Mary Greenlee, born 1809 or 1813, at Waterloo, Venango County, Pa , died May 7, 1855, 1856, at Waterloo Married David Irwin Nicholson, who was born at Waterloo and died at Newton, June 11, 1863 He was a farmer, resided at Waterloo Issue (1) Mary, (2) Margaret, (3) James, (4) Robert Greenlee, (5) Nancy, (6) William, (7) Jennie, (8) Andrew.

1931—Mary Nicholson, born Jan 4, 1836 Married Josiah Stanford No issue Address Dunlap, Kan

1932—Margaret Nicholson, born Oct. 12, 1840 Married twice. First Abraham Douht, second C—— G——————— McCracken Ad-

1933—James Nicholson, born June 10, 1842 Married Molly Thompson

1934—Robert Greenlee Nicholson, born March 4 1844 in Venango County, Pa He served in Company G 100th Pennsylvania Volunteers and Company I, 10th Pennsylvania Volunteers in the Civil War. Married twice First on Feb 14, 1866, Mary Ann Thompson Issue (1) Alice Violett, (2) Mary M————, (3) William Walker, (4) Sara Evaline Married second time ———————— No issue

19341—Alice Violette Nicholson, born ———————, died ————

19342—Mary M———————— Nicholson, born ————————, died ————.

19343—William Walker Nicholson, born ————————, died ————————.

19344—Sarah Evaline Nicholson, born ———————— Married Charles A ———— McDugal Address, Grove City, Pa

1935—Nancy Nicholson, born ———————— Married John Huddleston (born ————, died ———————— Issue one son ————————

1936—William Nicholson, born Sept 12 1847, at Raymilton, Venango County, Pa Address, Sheakleyville, Pa Married July, 1867, at Utica, Pa, Anna Pierce (born Nov 3, 1846, at Cochranton, Crawford County, Pa) daughter of William and Cinderella (————————) Pierce Issue (1) Clinton, (2) Cora, (3) Maude, (4) Nellie, (5) Minnie, (6 James, (7) Claude, (8) Charles, (9) Pearl, (10) Walter, (11) Mary

19361—Clinton Nicholson, born Oct. 14, 1867

19362—Cora Nicholson, born March 26, 1868

19363—Maude Nicholson, born Feb 13, 1870

19364—Nellie Nicholson, born Nov. 26, 1872 Married Lewis Heasley

19365—Minnie Nicholson, born June 13 1874.

19366—James Nicholson, born Sept 14, 1876

19367—Claude Nicholson, born Dec 2 1878

19368—Charles Nicholson, born Sept. 4 1880

19369—Pearl N

1936(10)—Walter Nicholson, born Oct. 24, 1886

1936(11)—Mary Ncholson, born Aug 26, 1890

1937—Jennie Nicholson, born April 15, 1849, at Franklin, Venango County,
Pa Married on March 1, 1870, Michael Hayes (born Nov 20, 1844,
at Innis County Clare, Ireland, died June, 1896) son of Thomas
Hayes, lived at Bradford, Pa Issue (1) John G————, (2) Ed-
mond I——— , (3) Dot ————, (4) William M————, (5)
Joe, (6) Jennie A————

19371—John G———— Hayes, born Jan 21, 1871 Married Ada Myer.
Issue two sons and one daughter

19372—Edmond I———— Hayes, born Feb 5, 1873 Married Mary
Keating, died March 19, 1900 Issue one daughter

19373—Dot Hayes, born April 25, 1875

19374—William M———— Hayes, born June 2, 1877.

19375—Joe Hayes, born Nov 20, 1879

19376—Jennie A———— Hayes, born March 1, 1881

1938—Andrew Nicholson, born June 12, 1852

194—Elizabeth Greenlee, born 1811, near Raymilton, died 1847 Married
in April, 1830, James Patterson Greenlee, (see 114) son of James and
Ann (Patterson) Greenlee Issue (1) Margaret, (2) Robert, (3)
Anna, (4) Elizabeth, (5) Samuel, (6) Jane, (7) James ————,
(see 114)

195—Robert Porter Greenlee, born April 12, 1815, in Venango County,
Pa , died April 2, 1884, at New Lebanon, Mercer County, Pa Married
on Aug 20, 1844, at Jackson Center, Pa , Elizabeth Bainbridge Johnston (born June 20, 1820, at Evansburgh, Crawford County, Pa , died
May 12, 1889, at New Lebanon, Pa) daughter of Ephraim and Maria
Ann (Peart) Johnston He was a farmer at New Lebanon, Pa. Issue
(1) Abner Bainbridge, (2) Robert William, (3) son

1951—Abner Bainbridge Greenlee, born April 23, 1846, in French Creek
Township, Venango County, Pa Farmer, resided at Carlton, New
Lebanon, Pa Married on Nov 27, 1870, at Carlton, Mercer County,
Pa, Mary Smith Stevens (born June 3, 1848, in French Creek Town-
ship) daughter of Peter Case and Margaret (Robb) Stevens. Issue
(1) Laura Bell, (2) William Charles, (3) Susan Peart, (4) Carrie
Olive, (5) Peter Case, (6) Robert Porter, (7) Hattie Ellen, (8)
     and (10) Joseph Presley

19511—**Laura Bell Greenlee**, born March 15, 1872 or 1873 Married John Frank Wiser

19512—**William Charles Greenlee**, born Nov. 11, 1874 Married Emma Cullow

19513—**Susan Peart Greenlee**, born July 18, 1876. Married Nov. 15, 1896, David Henry McWilliams

19514—**Carrie Olive Greenlee**, born Oct 31, 1878 Married Oct 1, 1896, Oscar Ived Firster

19515—**Peter Case Greenlee**, born June 30, 1880

19516—**Robert Porter Greenlee**, born Jan 20, 1882.

19517—**Hattie Ellen Greenlee**, born Oct 12, 1883.

19518—**Henry Pratt Greenlee**, born March 30, 1886

19519—**Mary Ann Greenlee**, born Sept 25, 1888

1951(10)—**Joseph Presley Greenlee**. born Oct 25, 1888.

1952—**Robert William Greenlee**, born June 6, 1848, at Polk, Venango County, Pa Married on April 10, 1873, at Sandy Lake, Mercer County, Pa, Clara Josephine Firster (born July 22, 1853, at New Lebanon, Pa) daughter of John and Barbara (Grove) Firster, lived at New Lebanon, Pa Issue (1) Addison, (2) Lilly, (3) David Porter, (4) Olive Cromwell, (5) James Adams, (6) Josephine, (7) John Coulter.

19521—**Addison Greenlee**, born Dec 9, 1874.

19522—**Lilly Greenlee**, born April 13, 1876 Married Dec, 1896, James Vick Hollibaugh

19523—**David Porter Greenlee**, born Dec. 10, 1877

19524—**Olive Cromwell Greenlee**, born May 10, 1881, died March 18, 1884.

19525—**James Adams Greenlee**, born June 17, 1885

19526—**Josephine Greenlee**, born Nov 30, 1887.

19527—**John Coulter Greenlee**

1953—Son ——————— Greenlee, born April 8, 1852, died April 11, 1852

196—Jane Greenlee, born March 7, 1819, near Raymilton, Venango County, Pa. Married in the fall of 1847, at Polk, Venango County, Pa., Andrew McGinnis (born Feb., 1821, near Raymilton, Pa., died April 3, 1878, near Raymilton) son of William and Margaret (Douceman) McGinnis—see 114 and 197—He was a farmer. She lived at Parkers Landing, Pa., in 1899. Issue (1) William C———, (2) Robert, (3) Isaac Newton, (4) Margaret Beulina, (5) Peter Jasper, (6) Sarah Elizabeth, (7) Francis Stewart

1961—William C——— McGinnis, born 1848, in Venango County, Pa. Married Josephine White. Address Butler, Pa.

1962—Robert McGinnis, born March 7, 1850, in Venango County, Pa., died May 31, 1898, at Kidwell, W. Va. Married on June 25, 1886, at Parkers Landing, Pa., Minnie Downing (born Oct. 17, 1869, in Venango County, Pa.) daughter of Jacob G——— and Harriet (Truby) Downing. Issue (1) Jennie, (2) Newton, (3) Mabel Elizabeth, (4) Grant

19621—Jennie McGinnis, born March 10, 1887, died ————————

19622—Newton McGinnis, born March 29, 1889, died ————————

19623—Mabel Elizabeth McGinnis, born March 14, 1897

19624—Grant McGinnis, born ————————.

1963—Isaac Newton McGinnis, born Dec. 14, 1852, at Waterloo, Pa. Unmarried in 1908, lived at Sturgeon, Pa.

1964—Margaret Beulina McGinnis, born May 6, 1856 at Polk, Pa., died, 1906. Married on Sept. 19, 1887, at Parkers Landing, Armstrong County, Pa., to Robert Snow (born May 6, 1840), son of Nicholas and Elizabeth (Croyar) Snow. Address Butler, Pa. Issue (1) Josie E———, (2) Rose N———, (3) Florence, (4) Joe Wesley

19641—Josie E——— Snow, born Jan. 26, 1890.

19642—Rose N——— Snow, born July 10, 1891.

19643—Florence Snow, born March 19, 1893

1   Joe Wesley Snow, born Jan. 1897

1965—Peter Jasper McGinnis, born ———— 1857, in Venango County,
Pa Married Sarah Cousins

1966—Sarah Elizabeth McGinnis, born July 17, 1859, at Raymilton, Venango County, Pa Married on Ian 11, 1878, at Petersburg, Clarion
County, Pa, Joseph Carey (born Sept 25, 1852 or 1856, in Wisconsin)
son of Nathaniel and Eliza (Wagner) Carey, school teacher, Thorn-
hill, Allegheny County, Pa Issue (1) Earl F————, (2) Clarence
B————, (3) William F ————, (4) Herbert C————,
(5) Newton O————, (6) Maggie B————, (7) Joseph B————,
(8) Andrew Jay, (9) Helen Irene

19661—Earl F———— Carey, born July 11, 1879

19662—Clarence B———— Carey, born April 24, 1881, died Dec 2,
1894

19663—William F———— Carey, born April 6 1883

19664—Herbert C———— Carey, born July 10, 1885; died Aug 25,
1887

19665—Newton O———— Carey, born Dec 11, 1887

19666—Maggie B———— Carey, born Aug. 22, 1893, died March 17,
1899

19667—Joseph B———— Carey, born Feb 17, 1895

19668—Andrew Jay Carey, born April 25, 1897.

19669—Helen Irene Carey, born Jan 13, 1901

1967—Francis Stewart McGinnis, born 1863 Married Nannie Cousins
Address Sturgeon, Pa

197—Stewart Greenlee, born April 30, 1821, at Polk, Pa, died May 30,
1899, in his 79th year, at Stony Point, Crawford County, Pa He was
a farmer and a Justice of the Peace for ten years at Hartstown He
resided in Mercer and Venango Counties until 1865, when he moved
to Crawford County, Pa Married first time on May 27, 1841, at
Sandy Lake or Waterloo, Sara Ann McGinnis (born Dec 24, 1817, at
Sandy Lake, died June 12, 1896, at Hartstown, Pa) daughter of
William and Margaret (Douceman) McGinnis—see 114 and 196—Issue
(1) Jeremiah Porter, (2) Andrew McGinnis, (3) Mary Jane, (4)
Robert Stewart, (5) William Harrison, (6) Isaac Newton, (7) Grace
M————, (8) Sarah Elizabeth, (9) Harriet Ann He married
second time on April 30, 1898, Mrs Susan E———— (Wood) Williams, of Greenwood Township, widow of George W———— Williams, born March 27, 1834, daughter of John M———— and Catherine (Harkins) Wood

1971—Jeremiah Porter Greenlee, born March 26, 1842 Killed in battle
at Bermuda Hundred, May, 1864

1972—Andrew McGinnis Greenlee, born July 13, 1844   Drowned May 25,
1861

1973—Mary Jane Greenlee, (twin), born April 24, 1847   Married on July
31, 1867, John Lyons   Address, Pithole, Venango County, Pa.

1974—Robert Stewart Greenlee, (twin), born April 24, 1847, at Waterloo,
Venango County, Pa ; died before 1913   Married on Sept 6, 1872,
at New Lebanon, Pa , Amelia Jane Dufford (born Sept 24, 1855, in
Pennsylvania) daughter of George M——— and Martha (Sagizer)
Dufford   Oil well contractor at Findlay, Ohio   Issue (1) Donella
J———, (2) William S———, (3) Albert, (4) Roy, (5)
Georgia, (6) Margaret, (7) John C———, (8) Kittie, (9) Dollie

19741—Donella J——— Greenlee, born Sept 13, 1873 Married
June 30, 1895, Clarence Graves; died July 12 1896

19742—William S——— Greenlee, born Nov. 11, 1847, at Hartstown, Crawford County, Pa. Married twice, first on Jan. 2, 1895,
at Findlay, Ohio, Grace E——— Packard (born June 28, 1878, at
Dunkirk, Ohio) daughter of Milton and Sarah (———) Packard, lived for a time at Findlay, Ohio   Married second time to
Mary Vinton Issue (1) Ray R———.

197421—Ray R——— Greenlee, born Jan 12, 1896.

19743—Albert Greenlee, born Sept. 3, 1876.

19744—Roy Greenlee, born Nov. 29, 1878, lived at Findlay, Ohio, before
1908 Married Bertha Moyer   Issue (1) Ruth.

19745—Georgia Greenlee, born Dec 23, 1884

19746—Margaret Greenlee, born ———

19747—John C——— Greenlee, born ———

19748—Kittie Greenlee, born Jan 15, 1889.

19749 Dollie Greenlee, born Feb 16, 1897

1975—William Harrison Greenlee, born June 28, 1849, at Waterloo, Ven-
ango County, Pa Farmer near Pottstown, Pa , died Nov 18, 1912, at
Hartstown, Pa Married Feb 1, 1877, at Linesville, Crawford County,
Pa, Mary Ann Shellito (born June 5, 1858, at Hartstown, Crawford
County, Pa) daughter of William and Harriet (McDowell) Shellito,
and grand-daughter of David and Bell (Kendall) Shellito and of
Samuel and Mary Ann (Frame) McDowell Issue (1) Frederick
Harrison, (2) Robert Clyde, (3) Mabel Harriet.

19751—Frederick Harrison Greenlee, born March 28, 1878, at Hartstown,
Pa. Married in Aug, 1903, at Meadville, Pa, Jennie Ewing, daugh-
ter of —————— and Ina (Peterman) Ewing. Address 407 Gould
Building, Atlanta, Ga Piedmont Fertilizer

19752—Robert Clyde Greenlee, born Nov. 20, 1883, at Hartstown, Pa
Unmarried, died Dec 2, 1907, at Hartstown, Pa

19753—Mabel Harriet Greenlee, born Sept. 10, 1891, at Hartstown, Pa
Teacher at Hartstown, Pa Unmarried

1976—Isaac Newton Greenlee, born July 23, 1851, died Dec. 8, 1861

1977—Grace M————Greenlee, born Oct 26, 1853 Married Dec
1879, at Hartstown, Pa, George Washington Mason Address, Greenville, Pa Issue (1) Eddy, (2) Charles, (3) Sadie.

19771—Eddy Mason, born 1881.

19772—Charles Mason, born 1884

19773—Sadie Mason, born 1894.

1978—Sarah Elizabeth Greenlee, born Jan 24 1856, at Milledgeville, Pa.
Married May 5, 1879, at Hartstown, Pa, Edward N———— Hall
(born Aug 12, 1854, at Geneva, Crawford County, Pa) son of John
and Clynda (Newton) Hall Farmer at Geneva, Pa Issue (1) Ira
Stewart, (2) Ida, (3) Thomas, (4) Robert Harrison

1978—Ira Stewart Hall, born Feb. 17, 1882.

19782—Ida Hall, born Feb 18, 1884

19783—Thomas Hall, born May 19, 1891.

19784—Robert Harrison Hall,   — - -

1979—Harriet Ann Greenlee, born July 1, 1858, at Milledgeville, Pa. Married Oct 14, 1880, at Conneaut Lake, Pa, Joseph Elbert Ellis (born Feb, 1857, at Hartstown) son of Benjamin Ford Ellis and Mary S. (Kinney) Ellis, grandson of Rosanna (Bartlett) Kinney Address Chagrin Falls, Ohio, to Kit C Dull Address, Kent, Ohio, in R R business Issue (1) Harrison Eugene, (2) Rosa Elbertine, (3) Grace Emma

19791—Harrison Eugene Ellis, born Sept. 18, 1881, at Hartstown, Pa. Married Sept 17, 1910, at Ashland, Ohio, Kit C. Dull. Address, Kent, Ohio

19792—Rosa Elbertine Ellis, born Nov. 23, 1884, at Atlantic, Pa. She is a teacher at Crestline, Ohio

19793—Grace Emma Ellis, born May 13, 1887, at Sandy Lake, Pa Married Nov 23, 1904, at Crestline, Ohio, to Henry Edward Klinkle (son of Gearhart and Eva Rosella Klinkle) engineer on Penn R R, residing at Crestline, Ohio Issue (1) Harriett Naomi, (2) Eva Rosella

197931—Harriet Naomi Klinkle, born Feb 3, 1907, Crestline, Ohio

197932—Eva Rosella Klinkle, born Dec 24, 1909, Crestline, Ohio

198—Joseph Greenlee, born July 14, 1823, at Sandy Lake or Waterloo, Pa, died before 1899 Married in March, 1843, in Venango County, Pa, Harriett McNeal (born May 3, 1820, in Lancaster County, Pa, died Feb 29, 1892, in Columbia County, Ohio) daughter of Jonathan McNeal He was a farmer, and lived five miles from Lisbon, Columbiana County, Ohio Issue (1) Curtis or Licurdis, (2) Susan Rebecca, (3) Margaret Jane, (4) Jemima, (5) Alexander, (6) Joseph P———, (7) Lydia A———, (8) child ———, (9) Amos

1981—Curtis or Licurdis Greenlee, born March 20, 1845, at Waterloo, Venango County, Pa Married on Nov 9, 1865, Maria McGinnis (born Feb 12, 1850, at Waterloo) Farmer Address Bertrand, Neb No issue

1982—Susan Rebecca Greenlee, born April 11, 1846, near Waterloo, Pa Married on May 6, 1872, in Pennsylvania, George Washington Myers (born Feb 23, 1836, at New Middleton, Ohio) son of George W and Saloma (Raub) Myers Address, New Middleton, Ohio Issue (1) Maggie Luella, (2) Clara Belle, (3) Viola, (4) Harry Dole, (5)

19821—Maggie Luella Myers, born March 15, 1872. Married Ollie G Kruner.

19822—Clara Belle Myers, born July 26, 1874

19823—Viola Myers, born April 16, 1876 Married John P Hardesty

19824—Harry Dole Myers, born ————————, died ————————

19825—Homer O———————— Myers, born Oct 2, 1880

19826—Harvey E Myers, born Nov 8, 1882

1983—Margaret Jane Greenlee, born Dec 30, 1847, at Sandy Lake, Venango County, Pa Married June 9, 1870, at Leetonia, Columbiana County, Ohio, Jabez Whitton (born July 31, 1841, at Staffiger, England) son of John and Mary (White) Whitton Issue (1) George, (2) Wilbert, (3) Nellie, (4) Etta, (5) Eva

19831—George Whitton, born Aug 14, 1874 Married Minnie Patric. Address Salem, Ohio

19832—Wilbert Whitton, born April 9 1879

19833—Nellie Whitton, born Oct 3, 1882, died Dec. 22, 1882

19834—Etta Whitton, born June 23, 1885.

19835—Eva Whitton, born March 13, 1887.

1984—Jemima Greenlee, born July 4, 1840 Married Thomas Aley, died about 1886

1985—Alexander Greenlee, born Aug 15, 1852. Married Emma Vanskiver Address Columbiana County, Ohio

1986—Joseph P Greenlee, born Feb 7, 1854 died Aug 17 1866

1987—Lydia A. Greenlee, born Sept 15, 1856, at New Lebanon, Mercer County, Pa Married June 1, 1881, at Washingtonville, Columbiana County, Ohio, George W Webber (born June 15, 1848, at Lisbon, Columbiana County, Ohio Farmer at Lisbon, Ohio Issue (1) Hattie M————————, (2) Bertha L————————, (3) Harry L————————, (4) Albert R————————, (5) Frank Leroy

19871—Hattie M Webber

19872—Bertha L———————— Webber, born March 22, 1885

19873—Albert R Webber, born Nov 5, 1889

19874—Frank Leroy Webber, born Oct 6, 1892

1988——————Greenlee, born ——————, died in infancy, Dec ———,
18—————

1989—Amos Greenlee, born Aug. 24 1863 or 1862 Married Sarah
Malenlé (or Morlanee) Address, Leetonia, Ohio

BRANCH NO. 2

2—Jean Thompson, born ———— 1758 Married in 1774, at Thompsontown, Pa, Robert Wylie (born 1743, in County Antrim, Ireland, died at Washington, Pa). He was a soldier in the American Revolution The home of Robert and Jean (Thomson) Wylie, a substantial building which is still standing, was erected on land patented under the name of "Silver Springs" adjoining the borough of Washington, Pa Robert Wylie's ancestors were Covenanters Issue (1) Robert, (2) John, (3) Ann (4) Jane Thompson, (5) Elizabeth, (6) Mary, (7) Sarah, (8) William

21—Robert Wylie, born ————; died at Baltimore, Md Unmarried

22—John Wylie, born ————. Married ———— Issue "three sons and one daughter in the South" (Note There are many Wylies in Virginia, especially Augusta County, whose ancestors doubtless came from Pennsylvania)

23—Ann Wylie, born Aug 9, 1794, in Canton Township, Washington County, Pa, died Nov 6, 1878, aged about 84 Married on Nov 2, 1820, in Canton Township, Washington County, Pa, Samuel Brownlee (born ————; died June 25, 1858), son of James and Jane (Leman) Brownlee, and grandson of Archibald and Margaret (Hamilton) Brownlee. Issue (1) Jane Thompson, (2) Elizabeth Leman, (3) William Carlisle, (4) Mary Crothers, (5) Ann Maria, (6) Robert Wylie, (7) Agnes Virginia, (9) Sarah Margaret

231—Jane Thompson Brownlee, born on Dec. 1, 1821, in Canton Township, Washington County, Pa, died Sept 30, 1889 Married on Dec 17, 1845, at Washington, Pa, Rev Jacob Piper Fisher (born ————; died Sept 3, 1857), son of George and ———— (Piper) Fisher J. P. Fisher was a minister of the Associated Presbyterian Church at Cherryfork, Adams County, Ohio Issue (1) Samuel Brownlee, (2) George McVey

2311—Samuel Brownlee Fisher, born Oct 24 1846, at Cherryfork, Adams County, Ohio. Graduated Washington and Jefferson College, B S 1868, M S 1871, Dr Sc 1909 Civil engineer. He was chief engineer of the Milwaukee and Northern Railroad, 1873-85; Minneapolis, St Paul and Sault Ste Marie Railway, 1890-2, Everett and Monte Cristo Railway, Everett, Wash, 1893-4, M. K & T since 1895 Member of the American Society of Civil Engineers and Western Society of Engineers See Biographies in Who's Who in America," "International Who's Who" Address, 4606 Maryland Ave, St Louis, Mo Married on Feb 7, 1882, at Pittsburgh, Pa, Agnes Crooks (born —————, died Dec 1, 1906), daughter of James and Anna (Palmer) Crooks and a descendant of John Palmer, one of the lieutenants of William, the Conqueror Issue (1) Samuel Brownlee, (2) Anna Palmer

23111—**Samuel Brownlee Fisher,** born Dec. 24, 1882, at Allegheny City, Pa Unmarried

23112—**Anna Palmer Fisher,** born Feb 2, 1886, at Allegheny City, Pa. Unmarried

2312—**George McVey Fisher,** born Oct 31, 1847, at Cherryfork Adams County, Ohio He graduated from Washington and Jefferson College in 1875 and from the Union Theological Seminary, New York City, in 1882 He organized two Presbyteries under the instruction of the General Assembly of the Presbyterian Church, U S A and also helped to organize seven Presbyterian Churches in Montana Address, Kalispell, Mont He married on Jan 14, 1886, at Missoula, Mont, Mary Elizabeth Swaney, daughter of Hugh and Criscilla (Fullerton) Swaney and grand-daughter of Thomas and Elizabeth (Linn) Swaney, of Scotland, and of James and Mary (Wilson) Fullerton, of Antrim, Ireland Issue (1) Crystal Jane, (2) Miriam Elizabeth, (3) Ruth, (4) Mary, (5) George McVey, (6) Hugh Gordon

23121—**Crystal Jane Fisher,** born Jan 10, 1887, at Missoula, Mont Address, Kalispell, Mont

23122—**Miriam Elizabeth Fisher,** born Oct 16, 1888, at Massonla, Mont Married on July 1, 1907, at Minneapolis, Minn, Carl Henry Scherf (born Oct 27, 1880, in New York City), son of Peter Francis and Margaret Louise (Schwartz) Scherf and grandson of Christian and Katharine (Hammer) Schwartz and of Francis Casper Scherf, of Germany C H Scherf is a school teacher Address, Elizabeth, N J Issue (1) Margaret Louise, (2) Mary Elizabeth

231221—**Margaret Louise Scherf,** born April 1, 1908, Fairmont, West Va

231222—**Mary Elizabeth Scherf,** born Oct. 28, 1910, Elizabeth, N J.

231223—**Ruth Fisher,** born Sept 9, 1892, at Kalispell, Mont Married 1913, at Kalispell, Mont, Sydney Godfrey Rubinow, son of George Rubinow S C Rubinow is a teacher in the A & M College of Texas, College Station, Texas Issue (1) Sydney Godfrey.

231 Sidney Godfrey Rubinow, Jr, born — — 1914, at Eliza-

23124—Mary Fisher, born April 12, 1896   Address, Kalispell. Mont

23125—George McVey Fisher, Jr., born Sept 12, 1899   Address Kalispell, Mont

23126—Hugh Gordon Fisher, born Nov 21. 1903   Address. Kalispell, Mont

232—Elizabeth Leman Brownlee, born Oct 11, 1832, in Canton Township, Washington County. Pa , died Aug 21, 1886   Married on Jan 23, 1850, in Canton Township, Washington County. Pa , William Sutton Moore (born —————— , died Dec 30, 1877), son of Joseph and Ann (Sutton) Moore and grandson of William and Margaret (Paul) Sutton   Joseph Moore, who came from Ireland, was a cousin of Joseph Moore, father of Samuel Ross Moore—see 238—William S—————— Moore was editor of the *Washington Reporter* and member of Congress from the twenty-fourth district of Pennsylvania for two terms   Issue (1) Annie Brownlee, (2) Alice Virginia (3) Joseph Henderson

2321—Annie Brownlee Moore, born —————————, 1850, at Washington. Pa   Married on Feb 26, 1885, at Washington, Pa , Alexander McCarrell Patch   Mr Patch graduated from the West Point Military Academy and was stationed in the South West for several years with the rank of lieutenant   He resigned and now owns and conducts a store at Lebanon, Pa   Issue (1) Joseph Dorst, (2) Elizabeth Moore. (3) William Moore, (4) Lida Wint, (5) Alexander McCarrell

23211—Joseph Dorst Patch, (twin), born cDe. 8, 1885

23212—Elizabeth Moore Patch, born Dec 8, 1885, died July 27. 1887.

23213—William Moore Patch born July 30, 1887

23214—Lida Wint Patch born Oct 8 1888   Married on July 19, 1913, at Lebanon, Pa , Philip Gordon   Philip Gordon is a lieutenant in the Second U S Cavalry

23215—Alexander McCarrell Patch, born Nov 23, 1889

2322—Alice Virginia Moore, born Aug 25. 1856, died Aug 10, 1860

2323—Joseph Henderson Moore, born March 17 1859, at Washington. Pa   Married June 20, 1888, at Washington, Pa , Martha Ramsey McKennan, son of William Bowman and Adaline Dodridge (Ramsey) McKennan, and grandson of John Thompson McKennan   J H Moore is a member of the brokerage firm of Moore, Leonard & Lewis N Y N C   B   D   of the M N

23231—William McKennan Moore, born Sept 7, 1891   He graduated from St Lukes, at Wayne, Pa, in 1911

233—William Carlisle Brownlee, born Feb. 28, 1826, in Canton Township, Washington County, Pa   He is a farmer   Address (1913), Washington, Pa. He married on Oct 12, 1848, Nancy Maria Logan (born ————, died Feb 13, 1898), daughter of James and Mary (Bryson) Logan and grand-daughter of John and Elizabeth (Bouner) Logan and of Patric and Elizabeth (McCracken) Bryson   Issue (1) Ellen Maria, (2) Alton Warren, (3) Emma Jane, (4) Thomas Logan

2331—Ellen Maria Brownlee, born Sept 15, 1849, in Franklin Township, Washington County, Pa   Married Sept 18, 1865, at Washington, Pa, James Liberty McKee, son of James and Mary (Moore) McKee and grandson of Joseph and Mary Jane (Milligan) McKee   J L McKee is a farmer   Address, Deerlick, Greene County, Pa, R F D No 1   Issue (1) William Thomas, (2) Thomas Bryson (3) Martha Jane, (4) Edward Harrison, (5) Charles Leslie, (6) Jurdie Evalena

23311—William Thomas Bryson McKee, born Feb 8, 1867, in Franklin Township, Washington County, Pa   Married on ————, at Waynesburg, Greene County, Pa, Laura M———— Miller   Address, Mount Morris, Greene County, Pa   Issue (1) Horace James (2) Willis

233111—Horace James McKee, born June 2, 1894

233112—Willis McKee, born Feb. 20, 1898

23312—Thomas Bryson McKee, born April 13, 1869, Franklin Township, Washington County, Pa   Married at Waynesburg, Greene County, Pa, Florence Everly   Address, Rice's Landing, Greene County, Pa   Issue (1) Donald, (2) ————, (3) Thomas Brownlee, (4) Nellie Madeline, (5) Harriet Gladys, (6) Martha Elizabeth, (7) James Albert, (8) Russel Blair

233121—Donald .McKee, born July 24, 1894.

233122—————— McKee, born 1896, died in infancy

233123—Thomas Brownlee McKee, born Sept 9, 1898

233124—Nellie Madeline McKee, born Sept. 12, 1900.

2?   ' ' '' Glady McKee, born May 15, 1903

233126—Martha Elizabeth McKee, born Feb 21, 1905.

233127—James Albert McKee, born —————, 1907.

233128—Russel Blair McKee, born —————

23313—Martha Jane McKee, born May 31, 1872, in Franklin Township, Washington County, Pa Married on Oct 12, 1899, in Morris Township, Greene County, Pa, John Scott Elliott, son of John Morgan and Elizabeth Ellen (Danley) Elliott, and grandson of William and Jemima (Winget) Elliott and of Samuel and Ruth (Enlow) Danley J S Elliott is a farmer Address, Clayville, Washington County, Pa, R. F D No 3 Issue (1) Jurdie Evalena, (2) Cora Bell

233131—Jurdie Evalena Elliot, born May 14, 1900

233132—Cora Bell Elliott, born Oct 14, 1901.

23314—Edward Harrison McKee, born Nov 13, 1875 Unmarried.

23315—Charles Leslie McKee, born Jan 29, 1877, in Morris Township Greene County, Pa Married June 8, 1902, at Newmartinsville, W Va, Sadie E————— Polton, daughter of John and Mary (Rose) Polton Address, Bristoria, Greene County, Pa Issue (1) Beula Rose, (2) Beatrice Evalena, (3) James Earle

233151—Beula Rose McKee, born Oct 26, 1903.

233152—Beatrice Evalena McKee, born Oct 18, 1905.

233153—James Earle McKee, born Oct. 27, 1907

23316—Jurdie Evalena McKee, born Feb. 6, 1879 Unmarried.

2332—Alton Warren Brownlee, born Jan. 3, 1851, in Franklin Township, Washington County, Pa, died March 13, 1900 Married twice, first on May 7, 1873, in Canton Township, Washington County, Pa, Matilda Mountz (born —————, died —————), daughter of James K————— and Caroline (Rodgers) Mountz and granddaughter of Richard Mountz No children He married secondly on Oct 3, 1888, at Maitland, Holt County, Mo, Mary A McNeal, daughter of James Gibson and Margaret (Shore) McNeal and granddaughter of James and Margaret (Gibson) McNeal A W. Brownlee was a farmer Issue (1) Laura V.

23321—Laura Mae Brownlee, born June 19, 1899, at Maitland, Mo   Married July 2, 1911, at Maitland, Ernest Hodgin, son of William N———— and Margaret (Haskett) Hodgin and grandson of John and Mary Ann (Hill) Hodgin   E. Hodgin is a storekeeper at Maitland, Mo   No children

2333—Emma Jane Brownlee, born Dec 12, 1854.   Unmarried

2334—Thomas Logan Brownlee, born June 16, 1867   Unmarried   Historian of the Brownlee Family   Address Washington, Pa

234—Mary Crowthers Brownlee, born April 19, 1828, in Canton Township, Washington County, Pa , died June 22, 1912   Married on April 29, 1847, in Canton Township, Joseph Dennis Wolfe (born ————, died May 25, 1897), son of William and Catherine (Dennis) Wolfe.   J D Wolfe was a graduate of Washington and Jefferson College and of the Associate Theological Seminary, Canonsburg, Pa.   He was licensed to preach in 1846, and served as a pastor for some time of a church in New York City   Afterward he studied law and was admitted to practice at Monmouth, Ill   He entered and left the Union Army in the Civil War with the rank of Captain   He moved to Pensacola in 1866 and practiced law and finally became editor of the *Pensacola Commercial*   He was well known as a writer on economics Issue (1) Lilas Anne, (2) Jane Clark, (3) William Wylie, (4) Agnes Brownlee, (5) Mary Eva, (6) Joseph Emmett, (7) Elmer Ellsworth

2341—Lilas Anne Wolfe, born Feb 15, 1848   She graduated from the Monmouth College, Ill   Married Nov 3, 1876, William Hamilton Eakin   Address, 253 North Conception Street, Mobile, Ala   Issue (1) Robert Elmer, (2) William Sterling, (3) Minnie Eva, (4) Lillie Bell, (5) Alice Hamill, (6) Edwin Earl

23411—Robert Elmer Eakin, born Aug 1, 1877, died May 3, 1878

23412—William Sterling Eakin, born Feb 23, 1879.   Married Jan. 18, 1905, Dora Roberts   Issue (1) Elizabeth Lilas.

234121—Elizabeth Lilas Eakin, born Jan 1, 1906

23413—Minnie Eva Eakin, born May 18, 1881.   Unmarried

23414—Lillie Bell Eakin, born Oct. 15, 1883, died Aug. 24, 1887.

23415—Alice Hamill Eakin born May 13, 1886   Married Aug. 20, 1913, Henry Abbott Heblon

23   Edwin Earl Eakin, born Nov 10, 1888   died June 2, 1889.

2342—Jane Clark Wolfe, born May 30, 1850. Married May 24, 1892, at Vinita, Okla, Robert Selden Liggett, son of William and Jane Mc Coombs (Henderson) Liggett and grandson of John and Annie (Jack) Liggett   R S Liggett is an electrician   Address, 1613 Ohio St, Joplin, Mo   Issue (1) Nellie Vinita

23421—Nellie Vinita Liggett, born Dec 28, 1893

2343—William Wylie Wolfe, born April 9, 1853   Married May 1, 1877, Addie Gisque Austin   Address, East Strong St, Pensacola, Fla Issue (1) Joseph Dennis, (2) Arthur Emmett, (3) Brownlee Fisher, (4) William Wylie, (5) James Herron, (6) Joseph Dennis—No 2, (7) Mary Brownlee, (8) Agnes Mabel, (9) Susie May

23431—Joseph Dennis Wolfe, born March 20, 1879, died —————, 1880

23432—Arthur Emmett Wolfe, born June 23, 1880, died Aug 3, 1897

23433—Brownlee Fisher Wolfe, born Sept 24 1883

23434—William Wylie Wolfe, born March 4, 1885; died Oct —————, 1911

23435—James Herron Wolfe, born June 16, 1886

23436—Joseph Dennis Wolfe, (No 2), born April 14 1888, died Oct 1889.

23437—Mary Brownlee Wolfe, born June 11, 1893.

23438—Agnes Mabel Wolfe, born June 8 1897.

23439—Susie May Wolfe, born Feb 17, 1901

2344—Agnes Brownlee Wolfe, born Feb 23 1855   Married —————, 1885, Orlando Erwin McReynolds, school teacher   Address, 924 Polafox St, Pensacola, Fla   No children

2345—Mary Eva Wolfe, born May 3, 1857   Married on ————— David Blair Rutherford, son of Dr Walter and Rosina (Blair) Rutherford   D B Rutherford died April 8, 1913   Mrs Mary E (Wolfe) Rutherford is a music teacher   Address, 924 Polafox St, Pens...

2346—Joseph Emmett Wolfe, born Nov. 22, 1859   Married Aug 15, 1906, Mattie V——— Vinson   He graduated from the Peabody Institute, Nashville   He served as a member of the State Assembly of Florida   He is now Judge of the Circuit Court   Address, 902 North Polafox St, Pensacola, Fla   Issue (1) Joseph Emmett, (2) Earl Vinson

23461—Joseph Emmett Wolfe, Jr, born May 30, 1907

23462—Earl Vinson Wolfe, born June, 1910

2347—Elmer Ellsworth Wolfe, born Oct 25, 1861. Married ———, 1887, Mary Gabel   Carpenter   Address, 709 E Cervantes St, Pensacola, Fla   Issue (1) Emmett Leslie, (2) Albert Cecil, (3) Austin Seabrook, (4) Elmer Ellsworth, (5) Emma Day, (6) William Hannah, (7) Stanley Reed, (8) Edna Amanda, (9) Loyd Oliver, (10) Margaret Crothers

23471—Emmett Leslie Wolfe, born Jan 4, 1889, died Feb. ———, 1890

23472—Albert Cecil Wolfe, born Sept 21, 1890, at Pensacola, Fla   Married Sept 2, 1902, Desdemona Williams   Issue (1) Cecil

234721—Cecil Wolfe, born July 22, 1913

23473—Austin Seabrook Wolfe, born Sept 22, 1892

23474—Elmer Ellsworth Wolfe, born July 5, 1896

23475—Emma Day Wolfe, born March 11, 1899

23476—William Hannah Wolfe, born Aug 8, 1901

23477—Stanley Reed Wolfe, born Sept 6 1903

23478—Edna Amanda Wolfe, born Dec 4, 1905

23479—Loyd Oliver Wolfe, born Aug ———, 1907.

2347(10)—Margaret Crothers Wolfe, born May 27, 1911

235—Ann Maria Brownlee, born May 15, 1830, in Canton Township, Washington County, Pa ; died Nov 21, 1911   Married May 11, 1859, in Canton Township, Samuel Stewart Hamill (born ———, died ———), son of John Lawry and Martha L——— (Stewart) Hamill   S S Hamill was a well-known teacher of elocution in the West   Issue (1) Alice. (2) Harry (3) Edwin, (4) John

2351—**Alice Hamill**, born Sept 18, 1860 She taught elocution with her father prior to her marriage on Sept 10, 1892, in Chicago, Ill, to Cecil Statford Handcock, son of John Statford and Elizabeth Penelope Blair Carlisle (Kent) Handcock Issue (1) Cecil Kent Statford, (2) Evelyn Ann

2352—**Harry Hamill**, born Dec. 6, 1861 Graduated from the Union College of Law, Chicago, Ill, with the degree of B L, 1888, and is practicing law with offices at 9 S LaSalle St, Chicago Married twice, first on ————, 1887, at Henosha, Wis, Carrie Elizabeth Calkins, daughter of William T———— and Arabella (Reeves) Calkins No children He married secondly on Sept 12, 1899, at Oak Park, Ill, Katherine Montague Tooky, daughter of John B———— and Sarah A———— (Chandler) Tooky No children

2353—**Edwin Hamill**, born June 24, 1863. He graduated from the Rush Medical College, 1888, and is now a practicing physician, Chicago, Ill Unmarried

2354—**John Calvin Hamill**, born Jan 17, 1867 He is a dentist at Sandwich, Ill. Married on June 19, 1901, Anna Laura Achison, daughter of Nathaniel and Elizabeth (Danley) Achison Issue (1) John, (2) Alice Elizabeth, (3) Virginia

23541—**John Hamill**, born June 17, 1902.

23542—**Alice Elizabeth Hamill**, born Aug 19, 1903

23543—**Virginia Hamill**, born Dec. 7, 1907

236—**Robert Wylie Brownlee**, born March 7, 1832; died Sept. 23, 1902. He was a soldier in the Union Army during the Civil War He enlisted with the 15th Pennsylvania Cavalry, served through the war and was discharged at the close of the war with the rank of First Sargeant He married on June 30, 1868, in Canton Township, Washington County, Pa, Matilda Patton (born ————, died ————), daughter of Thomas Jefferson and Elizabeth (Ury) Patton Issue (1) Edwin Patton, (2) Charles Ury

2361—**Edwin Patton Brownlee**, born Oct 12, 1870, in Franklin Township, Washington County, Pa Married on Oct 12, 1899, Lillian Bell Butler, daughter of Walter and Mary Ann (Varco) Butler Address, Hellam Ave, Washington, Pa. Issue (1) Eva Grace, (2) Robert Walter, (3) Mary Matilda, (4) Elizabeth Moore

23611—**Eva Grace Brownlee**, ...

6

23612—Robert Walter Brownlee, born March 9, 1906

23613—Mary Matilda Brownlee, born Nov 2, 1907.

23614—Elizabeth Moore Brownlee, born Feb 27, 1910.

2362—Charles Ury Brownlee, born March 6, 1872, in Franklin Township, Washington County, Pa He enlisted with Company H, 10th Pennsylvania Volunteers and served through the Spanish-American War He was in the Philippines during the war and was discharged at the close He is a building contractor, Washington, Pa Married Oct 7, 1896, at Washington, Pa , Georgia Maggie Stewart, daughter of John James and Elizabeth Margaret (Hannah) Stewart Issue (1) Edwin Stewart

23621—Edwin Stewart Brownlee, born ——————.

237—Agnes Virginia Brownlee, (twin) born Dec 19, 1836, died Jan 3, 1911 Married twice, first on March 3, 1859, in Canton Township, Washington County, Pa , David P———— Stewart No children. Married secondly on May 30, 1867, in ——————, Iowa, Peter Leslie (born ——————, died ——————). Peter Leslie served in the Ohio Infantry until the close of the Civil War Issue (1) Mabel, (2) Sadie Virginia, (3) Robert Brownlee, (4) Williard Wylie

2371—Mabel Leslie, born Feb 29, 1868 Unmarried

2372—Sadie Virginia Leslie, born Jan 22, 1871. Unmarried.

2373—Robert Brownlee Leslie, born Jan 6, 1872, at Mt Ayr, Iowa Married on Sept 2, 1897, at Washington, Pa , Fannie Luella Pollock, daughter of James and Mary (McNary) Pollock No children

2374—Williard Wylie Leslie, born March 29, 1874, at Mount Ayr, Iowa He is a building contractor, Washington, Pa Married March 17, 1903, at Washington, Pa , Susan Grimes, daughter of John Thomas and Ann Eliza (Carter) Grimes and grandson of William and —————— —————— (McRoberts) Grimes Issue (1) Virginia Ann

23741—Virginia Ann Leslie, born Nov. 3, 1912

238—Sarah Margaret Brownlee, (twin), born Dec 19, 1836, in Canton Township, Washington County, Pa , died Sept. 23, 1911 Married on Jan 8, 1880, in Franklin Township, Washington County, Pa , Samuel P   Joore, son of Joseph and Sarah (Ross) Moore Joseph Moore   son of William Sutton Moore 232 No children

24—Jane Thompson Wylie, born in Canton Township, Washington County, Pa Married in Canton Township, James Humphreys Issue (1) James Wylie.

241—James Wylie Humphreys, born in 1828, died in 1911, in Nevada, Married Issue five children, names and addresses unknown

25—Elizabeth Wylie, born ————. Married John or William Moore Not related to William Sutton Moore (232) or Samuel Ross Moore (238) Lived at Burgettstown, Pa, and later at Holmes Mills, Jefferson County, Ohio. Issue (1) Jane Thompson

251—Jane Thompson Moore, born ————. Married George Day Jefferson County, Ohio George Day studied at the Cincinnati Medical College and practiced medicine in Evansburgh, Ohio Issue (1) Elizabeth Wylie, (2) Sarah Rogers

2511—Elizabeth Wylie Day, born in Evansburgh, Ohio in 1837 Married Samuel Luccock Issue (1) George N————

25111—George N———— Luccock, born ———— He is a minister Address, 523 N Kenilworth Ave, Oak Park, Ill

2512—Sarah Rodgers Day, born June 28, 1841, at Evansburgh, Ohio Married on April 14, 1864, at Evansburgh, Ohio, John Pearson Peck (born April 2, 1834, at Cambridge Ohio; died Oct 7, 1897, at Coshocton, Ohio), son of Richard Anson and Hester (Chambers) and grandson of Richard and Parmella (Ray) Peck and of Robert and Elizabeth (Sprangle) Chambers Richard Peck was a descendant of William Peck, who came from London, England, to New Haven, Conn, in 1637 and signed the New Haven Constitution in 1639 Three generations of his descendants served in the Revolution—See "The Peck Family" by Judge Delins Peck Richard Chambers was a descendant of Benjamin Chambers, the pioneer of Chambersburg J P Peck was president of the Farmers Bank at Coshocton, Ohio Issue (1) Jean Wylie, (2) Hester Howard.

25121—Jean Wylie Peck, born June 8, 1865, at Evansburgh, Ohio Married twice, first on Aug 4, 1885, at Coshocton, Ohio, Stacy Bancroft Bube (born ————; died Aug, 1889 Married second time on Dec 27, 1892, in Coshocton, Ohio, William Don Washburn, son of Joseph and Elizabeth (Cline) Washburn and grandson of Gabriel Washburn, lawyer, 1201 Title and Trust Building, Chicago, Ill Issue (1) Sarah F, (2) Hester Spangler, (3) William Day, (4) John Peck

251211—Sarah Elizabeth Washburn, born Oct. 17, 1893, Chicago, Ill
Student at Wellesley

251212—Hester Spangler Washburn, born Feb 22, 1895, Chicago, Ill.

251213—William Day Washburn, born Nov 5, 1896, Chicago, Ill.

251214—John Peck Washburn, born Sept 29, 1898, Chicago, Ill   Address
461 Maple Ave, Wonnetha, Ill

25122—Hester Howard Peck, born Oct 28, 1870, at Evansburgh, Ohio.
Address Coronado, Cal   Married June, 1889, Charles Etherington
Spangler (born ————, died in 1901)   Issue (1) Etherington
Thomas

251221—Etherington Thomas Spangler, born April 12, 1892   Architect-
tural student, Coronado, Cal

26—Mary Wylie, born ————, 1788 Married ————, Samuel
Crothers, son of Robert and Mary (Johnson) Crothers His father
laid out in Oct, 1803, the town of Mount Pleasant, Ohio—See 2613
Issue (1) Samuel Johnson, (2) Mary, (3) Hugh Wylie.

261—Samuel Johnson Crothers, born June 25, 1812, at Mount Pleasant,
Ohio, died July 20, 1889 Married on March 4, 1835, near Washing-
ton, Pa, Jane Brownlee—see 23—daughter of William and Hannah
(McCracken) Brownlee Issue (1) William Brownlee, (2) Robert
Wylie, (3) Hannah Jane, (4) Leamon McCarroll, (5) Mary Almira,
(6) Elizabeth McCabe, (7) Ella Hodgens

2611—William Brownlee Crothers, born June 14, 1836, at Taylorstown, Pa ;
died Jan. ——, 1907 Married on Feb 28, 1861, at Buffalo, Pa , Emmaline Maxwell (born June 29, 1837, died Aug. 9, 1911)   Issue
(1) Anna Bell, (2) Wylie Frank, (3) Margaret Jane, (4) Harry
Milton, (5) Samuel Albert, (6) James Maxwell, (7) William Dinsmore, (8) Arthur Brownlee, (9) John McDowell

26111—Anna Bell Crothers, born June 19, 1862, at Taylorstown, Pa. Married Samuel Cleland   Address, Washington, Pa Issue (1) James

261111—James Cleland, born ————.

26112—Wylie Frank Crothers, born June 19, 1864, at Taylorstown, Pa.
C   ", Pa Married Annette Noble Issue (1) Beulah,

26113—Margaret Jane Crothers, born April 2, 1866, at Taylorstown, Pa. Married Walter Coulson Address, 247 North Ave, Washington, Pa Issue (1) William, (2) Harry, (3) Emmaline

26114—Harry Milton Crothers, born Sept. 2, 1868, at Taylorstown, Pa. Address Crothers, Pa Married Anna Knapp Issue (1) Felix, (2) Ruth—died, (3) William, (4) Gaylord, (5) Wylie

26115—Samuel Albert Crothers, born Oct 12, 1870, at Taylorstown, Pa.

26116—James Maxwell Crothers, born Jan 23, 1873, at Taylorstown, Pa Address, Washington, Pa Married Mary Leonard Issue (1) Ethel, (2) Donald

26117—William Dinsmore Crothers, born April 19, 1875, at Taylorstown, Pa , died Jan 26, 1876

26118—Arthur Brownlee Crothers, born Jan 12, 1877, at Taylorstown, Pa. Address, Elgin, Ill. Married Miss Moore

26119—John McDowell Crothers, born Nov 12, 1879, at Taylorstown, Pa Address, Erie, Pa Married Blanch Hollister Issue (1) Albert

2612—Robert Wylie Crothers, born Dec 16, 1837, at Taylorstown, Pa Married on Sept 11, 1872, at West Middletown, Pa , Charlotte Moore Murdock, daughter of Milton and Nancy (White) Murdock, and granddaughter of James and Jane (Templeton) Murdock and of Jacob and Elizabeth (Mitchell) White. Issue (1) Minnie Caldwell, (2) Laura Brownlee, (3) Charles Edgar, (4) Chester Murdock, (5) Irene, (6) Pauline Almira

26121—Minnie Caldwell Crothers, born July 22, 1873, at Taylorstown, Pa.

26122—Laura Brownlee Crothers, born July 28, 1875, at Taylorstown, Pa.

26123—Charles Edgar Crothers, born March 19, 1878, at Taylorstown, Pa. Married on Nov 20, 1907, at Wellsburg, W Va, Mary Josephine Waugh, daughter of David and Mary (Bechtell) Waugh and granddaughter of Richard and Eliza (Moon) Waugh and of William and Jane (White) Bechtell Issue (1) Robert Waugh, (2) Mary Virginia, (3) Jane Margaret

261231—Robert Waugh Crothers, (twin), born Aug 25, 1908, at Taylorstown, Pa

261232—Mary Virginia Crothers ⸱⸱ ⸱ ⸱ Aug 25 ⸱ ⸱ - Taylorstown, Pa.

261233—Jane Margaret Crothers, born Jan 12, 1911, at Taylorstown, Pa.

26124—Chester Murdock Crothers, born Aug 9, 1880, at Taylorstown Pa ; died Jan 10, 1911

26125—Irene Crothers, born July 24, 1885, at Taylorstown, Pa. Married on June 24, 1909, at Taylorstown, Pa, Rufus Emery (born Jan 25, 1881), son of John Anson and Mary Tassy (Morrison) Emery, and grandson of John and Almira (Harding) Emery and of John and Hannah Ann (David) Morrison Address, 3733 Hiawatha St , North Side, Pittsburgh, Pa

26126—Pauline Almira Crothers, born April 25, 1889, at Taylorstown, Pa

2613—Hannah Jane Crothers, born Oct 19, 1839, at Taylorstown, Pa ; died Aug 31, 1897 Married on June 5, 1867, at Crothers Station, Pa, Joseph Bradford Johnson (born Sept. 27, 1842, near Cannonsburg, Pa , died Dec 11, 1912), son of John and Rebecca (Van Erman) Johnson, and grandson of Richard and Jane (Bradford) Johnson, and John Johnson—See 26 Issue (1) Ella Maude, (2) John Tracy, (3) Charles Crothers

26131—Ella Maude Johnson, born Dec 27, 1868, at Cannonsburg, Pa Married on June 14, 1893, at Mill Seat, near Cannonsburg, Rev Charles Gaston Williams (born March 9, 1867), son of Ralston and Sarah H (Gaston) Williams and great-grandson of Aaron Williams, who hewed the logs for the first fort on the site of Wheeling, W Va Address, 2951 E 11th Ave, Denver, Colo. Issue (1) Bradford Ralston, (2) Jay Tracy

261311—Bradford Ralston Williams, born April 2, 1894, at Cross Creek, Pa

261312—Jay Tracy Williams, born March 5, 1897, at Cross Creek, Pa

26132—John Tracy Johnson, born May 17, 1871, at Cannonsburg, Pa Unmarried Address, Cannonsburg, Pa

26133—Charles Crothers Johnson, born Dec 17, 1872, at Cannonsburg, Pa He graduated from Washington and Jefferson College in 1893 and is now President of the Citizens Trust Company, Cannonsburg, Pa Married on June 20, 1903, at Cleveland, Ohio, Grace Moreland Henderson, daughter of John Moreland and Anna Ramsey (Cary) Henderson, and granddaughter of James Patterson and Anne Gillilland ' l (l s   n, and of Freeman Grant and Malvina , (,   Iuldren Anne Patterson was the son of

Rev. Mathew Henderson, Jr, and the grandson of Rev Mathew Henderson, both United Presbyterian ministers—see (28) Freeman Grant Cary was a grandson of Roswell Fenton, soldier of the Revolution and a descendant of John Cary, who came from England to America, in 1632.

2614—**Leamon McCarroll Crothers,** born Sept 9, 1841, at Taylorstown, Pa ; died July 11, 1902 Married on July 25, 1878, at Cannonsburg, Pa, Mary Price Ritchie, daughter of Craig and Mary Ann (Chickering) Ritchie Issue (1) Mary Charlotte Ritchie

26141—**Mary Charlotte Ritchie Crothers,** born June 27, 1879, at Taylorstown, Pa Married on Nov 6, 1901, at Washington, Pa, George Lawrence Claypool, (born at Marysville, Ky, Aug 27, 1871), son of John and Eliza Coons (Blaine) Claypool Address, 913 Aiken Ave, Pittsburgh, Pa Issue ——————————————

2615—**Mary Almira Crothers,** born May 29 1843, at Taylorstown, Pa, died Jan 1, 1890 Married William W McClay No children

2616—**Elizabeth McCabe Crothers,** born Jan 21, 1845, at Taylorstown, Pa ; died July 11, 1896 Unmarried

2617—**Ella Hodgens Crothers,** born Jan 29, 1859, at Taylorstown, Pa Married on May 17, 1882, at Taylorstown, Pa, Robert Miller Dorrance Address, 13372 Euclid Ave, Cleveland, Ohio Issue (1) Elizabeth Crothers, (2) Helen Roberta

26171—**Elizabeth Crothers Dorrance,** born April 29, 1883. Married April 24, 1906, Cleveland, Ohio, James Edward Graham Address, Cleveland, Ohio Issue (1) Elizabeth Crothers

261711—**Elizabeth Crothers Graham,** born Oct. 30, 1909

26172—**Helen Roberta Dorrance,** born April 30, 1893. Address Cleveland, Ohio.

262—**Mary Crothers,** born ——————.

263—**Hugh Wylie Crothers,** born Dec 18, 1820 at Mount Pleasant, Ohio ; died Dec 5, 1880 He was a merchant In the Civil War he served as aid to Pierpont, subsequently Governor of Virginia with the rank of colonel He was a member of the first Legislature of West Virginia Married in 1847, Ann Hoopes Du Val, a descendant of Warren Du Va̶̶ ̶ ̶ ̶ ̶ ̶ ̶ 'd, in 165̶ ̶ ̶ ̶ ̶ ̶

2631—Sallie Harding Crothers, born Aug 20, 1848; died Dec. 1872. Married William Merwin Woolcott No children

2632—Anna Julia Crothers, born Aug. 28, 1861 Married on —————, Clayton Alexander Crisman, a clergyman of the Episcopal Church Address, Croom, Prince George County, Md No children

27—Sarah Wylie, born 179—, died —————. Married James Hodgens Issue (1) John, (2) James, (3) Robert Wylie, (4) Thomas, (5) Sarah, (6) Mary, (7) Helen—no record

28—William Wylie, born Sept, 1800, in Canton Township, Washington County, Pa ; died March 3, 1877 in Canton Township He attended Washington College In 1835 he established the wool commission business now conducted by James B Wylie—2812 Married in 1828, in Hopewell Township, Washington County, Pa, Mary Clark, daughter of David and Jane (Henderson) Clark and granddaughter of James Clark, a soldier of the Revolution and of Rev Mathew Henderson (See 26133) Rev Mathew Henderson was the first seceder minister to cross the Allegheny Mountains westward He came to this country from the University at Edenburg, Scotland, in 1758, and founded several congregations in eastern and central Pennsylvania In 1779 he settled in Washington County, Pa, where he established two strong congregations He was a member of the first board of trustees of Jefferson College, Cannonsburg, Pa, ,and president of the first board of trustees of the Washington College, at Washington, Pa, and was one of the founders of the institution which has since become the University of Pittsburgh He was a descendant of Alexander Henderson, of Edinburg, Scotland, (1583-1646) Episcopal Bishop, who later became a leader in the Scotch Presbyterian Church and was author of "The League of the Covenant" Issue (1) Robert, (2) Jane Clark, (3) Annie E, (4) James Clark.

281—Robert Wylie, born Aug 25, 1830, in Canton Township, Washington County, Pa ; died March 27, 1912 He was a farmer and wool commission merchant He attended the Washington College in 1848-50 Married on Feb 2, 1857, at Independence Township, Washington County, Pa, Elizabeth Beall, daughter of James and Mary (Stricker) Beall—See 282 The Pioneer American of the Beall family was Ninian Beall, who came from St Ninian Parish, Ireland, to Maryland, in 1652, and became the military leader of the Province He was instrumental in founding the first Presbyterian Church in the Colony. His great-grandson, Ninian Beall (3rd), married Mary Stricker, daughter of Col George Stricker, of the Revolutionary Army and sister to Gen John Stricker of the Army of 1812 Ninian Beall (4th), was a
‘   ‘ ‘   ‘ ‘ ‘ ‘   ‘ -th (1) William, (2) James Beall, (3)

2812 James Beal Wylie

281 Robert Wylie

28 William Wylie

281211 – James B. Wylie Murphy

28122—Garvin R. Wylie

283—Annie (Wylie) Thompson

2811—William Wylie, born Nov 10, 1859, in Canton Township, Washington County, Pa Civil engineer Address, Washington, Pa Married on June 16, 1885, at Wellsburg, W Va, Mary W Gist—see 2813—daughter of Joseph Christopher and Elizabeth (Culver) Gist and granddaughter of Cornelius and Eliza (Reinicker) Gist Issue (1) Elizabeth Beall, (2) Clara Virginia, (3) William Clark Gist

28111—Elizabeth Beall Wylie, born Oct 6, 1887, in Canton Township, Washington County, Pa Graduated from Washington Seminary, 1908 Address, Washington, Pa

28112—Clara Virginia Wylie, born Nov. 21, 1891, in Canton Township, Washington County, Pa Graduated from Washington Seminary, 1910 Address, Washington, Pa

28113—William Clark Gist Wylie, born Jan 28, 1898, in Washington County, Pa Address, Washington, Pa

2812—James Beall Wylie, born Sept 24 1862, in Cumberland Township, Greene County, Pa He graduated from the Washington and Jefferson College in 1882 Elder, First United Presbyterian Church, Washington, Pa Director, Union Trust Company and People's National Bank, Washington, Pa Member, Board of Trustees, Washington Seminary, established 1835 J B Wylie is a well-known breeder of registered stock, and belongs to a number of record and live stock breeders associations and to the Luther Burbank Society He married on June 24, 1890, at Senatobia, Miss, Helen Cornelia Roseborough, daughter of William and Elizabeth (Williamson) Roseborough of Scotch and Huguenot ancestry Her great-grandfather Alexander Roseborough married into the Gaston family which traces ancestry to Henry V of Navarre and France, through the Duke of Orleans who was banished from France in 1642, because he would not swear allegiance to the Catholic church Address, Washington, Pa Issue (1) Marion Margaret, (2) Garvin Roseborough, (3) Laura Jean Gaston

28121—Marion Margaret Wylie, born May 14, 1891, in Canton Township, Washington County, Pa Graduated 1908, Washington Seminary, Student Wheaton Seminary (Mass) 1908-9 Married on Dec 1, 1910, at Washington, Pa, Robert Martin Murphy, son of Hugh McIsaac and Margaret Eleanor Murphy Address, Washington, Pa. Issue (1) James Beall Wylie

281211—James Beall Wylie Murphy, born Nov 17 1911.

28122—Garvin Roseborough Wylie, born May 24, 1893, in Canton Township, Washington, Pa   He graduated from Washington and Jefferson, 1913   Attended Pennsylvania State College, 1913-4   Address, Washington, Pa

28123—Laura Jean Gaston Wylie, born Oct. 1, 1898 in Canton Township, Washington County, Pa   Graduated from Washington Seminary, 1914   Address, Washington, Pa

2813—Laura Virginia Wylie, born Oct 1, 1898, in Canton Township, Washington County, Pa   Married on Oct 7, 1890, in Canton Township, Washington County, Pa, Joseph Christopher Gist—see 2811—son of Joseph Christopher and Elizabeth (Culver) Gist, and grandson of Cornelius and Eliza (Reiniker) Gist   Address, Wellsburg, Brooke County, W Va   Issue (1) Robert Wylie, (2) Wilbur Boyle, (3) James Beall, (4) Joseph Christopher

28131—Robert Wylie Gist, born June 11, 1892, at Wellsburg, W Va ; died March, 1902

28132—Wilbur Boyle Gist, born Nov 29, 1894, at Wellsburg, W. Va   Address, Wellsburg, W Va

28133—James Beall Gist, born Sept. 3, 1896, at Wellsburg, W. Va.   Address, Wellsburg, W Va

28134—Joseph Christopher Gist, born Oct 15, 1898, at Wellsburg, W. Va   Address, Wellsburg, W Va

282—Jane Clark Wylie, born Oct 20 1833 in Canton Township, Washington County, Pa , died March 27, 1903, at Wellsburg, W Va   Married May ——, 1852, at Washington, Pa, John Stricker Beall, son of James and Mary (McCormick) Beall, and grandson of Ninian and Mary (Stricker) Beall—See 281   Issue (1) Annie Clark, (2) Wilson, (3) William Wylie

2821—Annie Clark Beall, born Aug 1853, at Wellsburg, W Va   Married on April 22, 1885, at Wellsburg, W Va, Edwin Hammond, son of Henry Hammond   Issue (1) John Beall, (2) Grace Raymond, (3) Mary Wylie

2822—Wilson Beall, born in 1856, at Wellsburg W Va , died 1864

2823—William Wylie Beall, born March 21, 1871, at Wellsburg, W Va.
                    [·   (.ll R· · ·   Issue (1)

28231—Eleanor Beall, born Oct. 31, 1894

28232—W———————— Wilson Beall, born Jan 29, 1900.

283—Annie E———————— Wylie, born Jan 18, 1837, at Washington, Pa
Address, Cannonsburg, Pa   Married on Dec 2, 1858, at Washington,
Pa, Rev Joseph Russell Thompson (born ————————, died Dec 16,
1861, at Mount Pleasant, Pa)   Graduated from Jefferson College and
the Associate Presbyterian Theological Seminary, of Western Pennsylvania   See sketch of Rev Alexander and Joseph Thompson by (their
brother), Rev James Thompson, 1862   Issue (1) William Wylie

2831—William Wylie Thompson, born April 16, 1860, at Hickory, Pa,
died Nov 16, 1864

284—James Clarke Wylie, born Aug 7, 1841, in Canton Township, Washington, County, Pa, died Jan, 1862   Unmarried

BRANCH NO. 3

3—**William Thomson** was born in Chester County, Pa., "in the year of our Lord 1752, January 2nd"—taken from his own personal Bible, now in the possession of Mrs Catherine Nelson (Wilson) Janney (3814) He died at Thompsontown, Juniata County, Pa., Jan 3, 1813, "in the 58th year of his age"—taken from his ledger gravestone in the family graveyard, 1½ miles from Thompsontown. This village was laid out by him in 1790 upon land purchased in 1785 from Michael Quiggle Upon taking possession of the property he built thereon a store, a grist-mill, and a saw-mill Near the grist-mill he erected later a stone dwelling house, still in the possession of his descendants, the corner stone of which bears the inscription "This House Built by W and J Thomson, 1798" William Thomson owned a farm near what is now Mexico in Walker Township, Juniata County, Pa He built at Mexico, a stone flour-mill on which there are two tablets containing the following inscriptions, "New Mexico Mill, Built by William Thomson, 1810" and "Virtue, Liberty and Independence Be Thine Success to Farmers and Mechanics" The farm near Mexico was inherited by his son Samuel His son John inherited a tract of land opposite Van Dyke Station, patented as the "Happy Banks of Goshen" on account of its fertility, which was purchased from the heirs of Joseph Poultrey in 1804 William Thomson's son, Isaac, was given by him a farm in Lost Creek Valley, "adjoining the Hugh McAlister property called Hugh's Fancy" Some interesting facts concerning the enterprises in which William Thomson (or Thompson, as later spelled) was engaged and the disposal made of his taxable industries, are given in the tax records of Fermanagh Township, Juniata County, Pa From 1785 to 1813, he was taxed on a grist-mill at Thompsontown and from 1809 to 1813 on one at Mexico, he was taxed on a fulling-mill from 1809 to 1813, a distillery from 1809 to 1813, a saw-mill from 1790 to 1813 and on a store from 1801 to 1813 and a second store in 1812 After his death in 1813, these properties passed to his sons, who were taxed as follows James and Samuel, grist-mill, 1814-31, William and Robert, grist-mill, 1814-31 and 1823-31; James and Samuel, fulling-mill, 1814-31, William and Robert, distillery, 1814, and 1823-31; William and Robert, saw-mill, 1814-22 and 1823-31, John, saw-mill, 1817-24; James and Samuel, saw-mill, 1817-31, William and Robert, store, 1814-27, James and Samuel, store, 1814-23 Some idea of the difficulty encountered in establishing the military record of early ancestors can be gained from the fact that in the Index to the Fifth Series of the Pennsylvania Archives (which Index in Part 1 and Part 2 is Vol XV of the Sixth Series of Pennsylvania Archives) there are exactly 100 references under the name of William Thompson, showing conclusively that tl   , of that name in the Revolutionary Service According to   of the Pennsylvania Archives, our Wil-

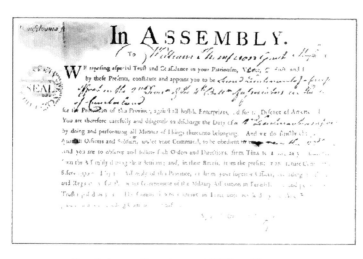

Revolutionary Commission of William Thomson

*Home of William and Jean Mitchell Thomson, Thompsontown, Pa.
Built by them in 1798.*

Tablets on Thomson Mill, Mexico, Pa.

Tablet on Thomson Homestead, Thompsontown, Pa.

liam Thompson was chosen on July 12, 1774 a member of the committee
on Observation, Cumberland County—see Penn Archives, Second Series,
Vol XIV, p 371—he was appointed second lieutenant of a company of
foot, second division, Fourth Battalion of Associators of Cumberland
County, on May 3, 1775, and was made captain of a company in the
Fifth Battalion of Cumberland County Associators in July, 1776, in
service in the New Jersey Campaign of that year—See Penn Archives,
Second Series, Vol XIV, p 372   There is now in the possession of his
great-granddaughter, Josephine P Thompson (3312), the original of
William Thompson's commission as second lieutenant and photographic
copies of it have been obtained by other descendants   On account of his
service in the Revolution, his descendants are eligible to membership in
the "Sons of the Revolution" or the "Daughters of the Revolution"—see
the sketch of his great-great-granddaughter, Henrietta Baldwin (34524).
That he continued to hold the confidence of his fellow citizens
is shown by the facts that at about the close of the Revolutionary
War, on May 1, 1783, the Supreme Executive Council of the Commonwealth of Pennsylvania gave him a commission as lieutenant of a company of foot in the Seventh Battalion of Militia of County of Cumberland, and, on July 11, 1792, Thomas Mifflin, Governor of Pennsylvania,
gave him a commission as captain of the Fifth Company, of Foot in the
Lost Creek Battalion of Militia, County of Mifflin   These two original
commissions, dated 1783 and 1792—in times of peace—are now in the
possession of Edward Shippen Thomson (3383)   Among the papers now
in the possession of the family of Edward Patterson Thompson (331) is
one showing the activity of William Thompson in the public welfare up
to the year of his death, as follows. "Headquarters, Meadville, Oct
20th, 1812   I do certify that Captain William Thompson has served
six days as a member of a General Court Martial, ordered by Brigadier
General Tannyhill—signed by—(Gen) James Irwin, President   William
Thompson was married on March 30, 1780, by Rev Alexander Dobbin
of Gettysburg, Pa, to "Jane Mitchell of Letterkenny"   (See p 26, History of Adams County, Pa, published 1886 by Warner Beers & Co,
Chicago) According to Hugh Nelson McAllister (343) son of Sarah
(Thompson) McAllister and grandson of Jane (Mitchell) Thompson
Jane Mitchell "was born within one mile of Strasburg, now Franklin
(then Cumberland) County   Her father was killed by the Indians in a
harvest field during the French and Indian War (1754-60) near what is
now called St Thomas, seven miles west of Chambersburg"   Letterkenny is a township of Franklin County, Pa, of which Strasburg is
the chief post office   The township extends from say 2 to 15 miles
north of Chambersburg and from say 5 to 25 miles west of Shippensburg   Among the earliest of land titles in this township was that of
James Mitchell, dated July 10, 1752   On May 9, 1754, Joseph Mitchell
and William Mitchell were referred to as "neighbors" of John Maughan
in that township   On p 169 of the "History of Franklin County, Pa"
 . . . it is . .   !   \   . . ir C . .   aque

was shot and killed by a band of Indians while at work in the
harvest field" On p 59 of the "History of Cumberland County, Pa"
(published in 1886 by Warner Beers & Co, Chicago) appears an account
of an Indian raid during which four people were captured and ten people
killed in a harvest field near Shippensburg on July 19, 1757 Among
the killed were Joseph, James, and William Mitchell According to
Robert Thompson (35) son of Jane (Mitchell) Thompson, his father
William Thompson "married Jane Mitchell, a daughter of James Mitchell
in Cumberland Valley near Chambersburg" A sister of Jane Mitchell,
Sarah Mitchell, married Robert Thompson (5) brother of William
Thompson It is probable that it was another sister, Agnes Black, who in
1812 wrote from Blount County, Tenn, to her "brother" William Thomp-
son, at Thompsontown, Pa This Agnes was not a daughter of Pioneer
John Thompson—as stated on p. 871 of the "History of Juniata and
Susquehanna Valleys in Penn," and was not a sister but a sister-in-
law of William Thompson She may have married one of the sons of
John and Abigail Black who went from Perry County, Pa, to Tennessee
(See p 1108 of the history just mentioned) Jane (Mitchell) Thompson
died Feb 9, 1813, "in the 57th year of her age" one month and six days
after the death of her husband from camp fever (typhoid-pneumonia)
which they both contracted from their soldier sons, William and Isaac,
who recovered They are buried in the Thompson family graveyard
one and one-half miles east of Thompsontown Children of William
and Jane (Mitchell) Thompson (1) John "Goshen," (2) James, (3)
William, (4) Sarah, (5) Robert, (6) Isaac, (7) Jane, (8) Elizabeth,
(9) Samuel

31—**John Thompson,** "Goshen John," was born Dec 28, 1780, died Oct
2, 1855 In 1809 he settled on the old Poultney tract on which was
subsequently located the Van Dyke Station This tract was known as
the "Happy Banks of Goshen," and he was known as "Goshen John"
or "John Goshen" to distinguish him from "Bridge John" Thompson,
who lived below Thompsontown John Goshen Thompson married
Abigail North (born July 15, 1783, died Dec 24, 1852) Issue (1)
Jane, (2) Rachel, (3) Martha, (4) Wilhelmina, (5) William, (6) John

311—**Jane Thompson,** married twice first, William (or Joseph) Montgomery, second John Lukens of Port Royal—no data—see 533, 542 and
572—see also "History of Juniata and Susquehanna Valleys in Pennsylvania," p 854—A certain John Lukens who died in Port Royal, Sept,
1885 was a son of Gabriel, grandson of Abraham and great-grandson
of John Lukens of Juniata County, Pa

312—**Rachel Thompson,** born Aug 4, 1801, died March 22, 1842, in Mil--
ford Township, Juniata County, Pa Married Jan 8, 1835, William
Strock of Lancaster County, Pa. (born Jan 25, 1801, died Jan 25,

1889) son of James and Mary (McClure) Sterrett and grandson of James Sterrett, Sr James Sterrett, Sr, lived near Mount Joy, Lancaster County, Pa He had sons James, Jr, Robert, Charles, and William—see "History of Juniata and Susquehanna Valleys in Pennsylvania," p 746 Robert removed to Mifflin County and had sons, David and John Charles removed to New York William remained in Lancaster County The children of James Sterrett, Jr, who married Annie Kennedy were James, Samuel (who died near Academia in 1849) Polly (wife of Alexander Patterson) Robert (married to Margaret Patterson, daughter of John (died in 1862) Sarah, and William (married a daughter of John Goshen Thompson) The sons of Robert are Judge James P Sterrett of the Supreme Court and Dr John P Sterrett, of Pittsburg The statement that James Sterrett, Jr, "married Annie Kennedy" is probably a mistake because it was Dr John P Sterrett whose "wife was Annie Kennedy of Chester County, Pa" See "History of Juniata and Susquehanna Valleys," p 696 James Sterrett, father of Robert and William Sterrett, purchased a tract of land in Milford Township, Juniata County, Pa, taken up in part by John Lyon, Sr, in 1767 and John Lyon, Jr, in 1793 Robert Sterrett married one of the daughters of John Patterson (the merchant) by his wife Isabella (Lyon) Patterson, daughter of James Lyon, son of John Lyon, Sr—see "History of Juniata and Susquehanna Valleys," p 760, 551 and 571 In 1773 James Sterrett was assessed on 600 acres in Armagh Township, Mifflin County, Pa The first mill in the east end of Kishacoquillas Valley, Mifflin County, Pa, was erected in 1816 by John Sterrett, who died Nov 7 ot that year, this was sold by his widow Rebecca (Woods) Sterrett to his nephew John Sterrett, son of Robert Sterrett Children of William and Rachel (Thompson) Sterrett, (1) John Thompson, (2) James A McClure, (3) William North, (4) Robert

3121—**John Thompson Sterrett**, born on July 16, 1836, at Milford Township, Juniata County, Pa (died on Thursday, Dec 14, 1911, at the home of Mrs John Brown Mitchell, Lewistown, Pa, aged 75 years, 4 months and 28 days) He attended the Port Royal Academy Served as Sergeant in Company A, First Pennsylvania Volunteer Cavalry. He married twice, first on Jan 16, 1866 at Locks Mills, Pa, Margaret Isabella Sterrett (born in Mifflin County, Pa, died Dec 18, 1875 in Kansas) daughter of Nathaniel Woods and Rebecca (Sterrett) Sterrett, granddaughter of John and Rebecca (Woods) Sterrett and of Robert and Rosanna (Green) Sterrett and great-granddaughter of James Sterrett (father of John) of Scotch-Irish ancestry, who lived in Lancaster County, Pa See "Biographical Encyclopedia of Juniata Valley," pp 668 and 703 Issue (1) Nathaniel Woods, (2) Rachel T . . . . argaret I . . . . Pa,

Hephzibah S———— Wright (born Jan. 30, 1825, died March 12, 1903, aged 78 years, 1 month and 13 days) daughter of John Wright of Walker Township No issue

31211—**Nathaniel Woods Sterrett**, born Oct. 28, 1866, died Jan 14, 1868, in Milford Township, Juniata County, Pa

31212—**Rachel Thompson Sterrett**, born on June 19, 1868, in Milford Township, Juniata County, Pa Married on Jan 17, 1897, at Mifflin, Pa, John Brown Mitchell Address Lewistown, Pa

31213—**Sallie Sterrett Sterrett**, born Jan 17, 1872, in Kansas Married on Dec. 20, 1893, in Mifflin, Juniata County, Pa, Harry Hertzler Heikes (born Sept 16, 1869), son of Edward and Elizabeth (Hertzler) Heikes of near Denholm, Pa, and grandson of George and Christiania (Kepner) Heikes H H Heikes is wreck master Penn R R, Mifflin Issue (1) Arthur Chester, (2) John Thompson, (3) Margaret Christenia

312131—**Arthur Chester Heikes**, born Sept. 25, 1894 Address, Mifflin, Pa.

312132—**John Thompson Heikes**, born Sept. 13, 1900 Address, Mifflin, Pa.

312133—**Margaret Christenia Heikes**, born Oct 1, 1902 Address, Mifflin, Pa

31214—**James Charles Sterrett**, born on Feb 8, 1873, in Kansas Married May 7, 1903, at Mifflin, Pa, Bessie May Leach (born Sept 26, 1878). He is a farmer Address Mifflin, Juniata County, Pa

31215—**Margaret Isabella Sterrett**, born Oct 28, 1875, in Kansas Married April 18, 1894, at Camden, N J, William Edward Kurtz, son of John and Ida Kurtz Address Naginey, Pa Issue (1) Estella Isabella, (2) Ruth Irene

412151—**Estella Isabella Kurtz**, born May 13, 1895, at ———— Address, Naginey, Pa

312152—**Ruth Irene Kurtz**, born Aug 7, 1896, at ————. Address, Naginey, Pa

3122—**James A ———— McClure Sterrett**, born June 10, 1838, in Mil-
      ··· ··· ··· County Pa; died Jan 10, 1839 in Milford
      ·· ·· ··

3123—William North Sterrett, born Mar 21, 1840, in Milford Township, Juniata County, Pa , died Jan 22, 1912 at Mifflintown, Pa For eight years he was engaged in the mercantile business at Patterson, Pa , but resided on a farm He served as county commissioner and associate judge of Juniata County Married April 27, 1871, at New Bloomfield, Pa , Jane Elizabeth Black (born Feb 16, 1845, at New Bloomfield, Pa) daughter of Thomas and Margaret Ann (Zimmerman) Black and great-granddaughter of George and Jane (McMillen) Black and of John Zimmerman, and great-great-granddaughter of George and Susanna (Crane) McMillen of Scotch-Irish ancestry who came from Lancaster to Perry County in 1785, and great-great-great-granddaughter of John and Abigail Black, who came to Perry County, Pa , from Ireland, prior to 1750, see "History of Juniata and Susquehanna Valleys in Pennsylvania," pp 1001, 1018 and 1108 Children of William North and Jane Elizabeth (Black) Sterrett (1) William Edward, (2) Samuel Thomas, (3) James Thompson, (4) Edgar Black

31231—William Edward Sterrett, born Feb 2, 1872 Attended Pittsburgh Business College Clerk of Pennsylvania Railroad at Denholm, Pa Married Oct 25, 1899, Bertha Elizabeth Shirk (born Sept 5, 1873; died May 2, 1907, in Mifflintown, Pa), daughter of Solomon S Shirk (born July 3, 1843, died Nov 27, 1904, in Mifflin, Juniata County, Pa) and Mary T (Beale) Shirk (born Dec 6, 1850; died Mar 23, 1901, in Milford Township, Juniata County, Pa)

31232—Samuel Thomas Sterrett, born Aug 16, 1875 A farmer at the old homestead Married April 17, 1900, Norma Ernest Issue (1) Harold Earl, (2) Samuel Glen, (3) James Fay, (4) Ann Elizabeth, (5) Edgar Ernest, (6) Emma Jane

312321—Harold Earl Sterrett, born Dec 12, 1901 Address, Mifflin, Pa

312322—Samuel Glen Sterrett, born Dec 15, 1903 Address, Mifflin, Pa.

312323—James Fay Sterrett, born June 22, 1907 Address, Mifflin, Pa.

312324—Ann Elizabeth Sterrett (twin), born July 15, 1911

312325—Edgar Ernest Sterrett (twin), born July 15, 1911

312326—Emma Jane Sterrett, born Aug 26, 1913.

31233—James Thompson Sterrett, born Sept 17, 1881 Attended Pierce's Business College clerk of Penn R R at Denholm He is assistant cashier of the first N   R   Co   Pa Married   1   t   u Ni   R son,

7

daughter of James Kenney and Katherine (Goshen) Robison and granddaughter of Col John Kenney and Isabella (McKennan Robison, great-granddaughter of John and Jane (Kincaid) Robison and of Patrick McKennan of Juniata County, Pa John Robison, Sr, was born near Mifflintown about 1792 He was an elder in the Presbyterian Church at Mifflintown In 1858, his son John Kennedy Robison was elected first lieutenant of the Juniata County troops which became Company A of the First Pennsylvania Cavalry of which he was put in command as captain Subsequently he was placed in command of the Sixteenth Cavalry, and at the close of the war was made brevet colonel and brigadier general having participated in all of the battles fought by the Army of the Potomac In 1867 he was elected State Senator He was appointed aid-de-camp on the staff of Governor James Addams Beaver—see 3431 Governor Hastings appointed him one of the factory inspectors of the State of Pennsylvania—see Biographical Encyclopedia of Juniata Valley of Pennsylvania, p 802 Children of James Thompson and Alma Virginia (Robison) Sterrett No data

31234—**Edgar Black Sterrett,** born June 26, 1888. Attended Banks' Business College of Philadelphia Bookkeeper in Philadelphia Married Oct 14, 1914, Elizabeth R Frailey (born Dec 10, 1891, at Philadelphia), daughter of William Moore and Jessie May (Harrar) Frailey

3124—**Robert Sterrett,** born Feb 14, 1842, in Milford Township, Juniata County, Pa , died in infancy

313—**Martha Thompson,** born on ————, at ———— Married on Dec 18, 1832, in Juniata County, Pa, Robert Jordan, son of ———— of ————, Newport, Perry County, Pa Line said to be extinct

314—**Wilhelmina Thompson,** born on Jan 16, 1818, at ————, died ————, 1889, at ———— Married on March 20, 1845, at "The Lock" below Thompsontown, Pa, (525) James Thompson, (born ————, 1819, died June 18, 1854) son of John and Jane (Gilfillen) Thompson and grandson of Robert and Sarah (Mitchell) Thompson and of James Gilfillen, see 315, 3212, 3213, and 72 Issue (1) Mary Evaline, (2) Heber, (3) James Addison—see 525

315—**William Thompson,** born Dec 4, 1820, at Goshen, Pa , died Oct 30, 1887, at McAlisterville, Pa Married on Jan 14, 1845, at John Patterson Thompson's homestead, Margaret Gilfillen (born Jan 19, 1825, died Aug 14, 1911), daughter of James Gilfillen (1781-1852) and Sarah (Jones) Gilfillen (1784-1854), granddaughter of James Gilfillen (1751-1801) and Nancy (Watts) Gilfillen and of Lewis and Phœbe (Landin) Jones, great granddaughter of Robert and Jean

(McConnell) Gilfillen and great-great-granddaughter of James and Margaret (Briton) McConnell—see 72   James Gilfillen, Sr and Lewis Jones served in the Revolution   Lewis Jones was a grandson of David Jones (married Sarah Bertram, daughter of Rev William Bertram) who came to America in 1701 and obtained from William Penn, title to land now called Overbrook, Pa , where some of his descendants now live   Children of William and Margaret (Gilfillen) Thompson (1) Theophilus Mitchel, (2) Elmira

3151—Theophilus Mitchel Thompson, born July 6, 1847, at Oakland Mills, Pa ; died April 25, 1912   Married Jan 15, 1884 at McAlisterville, Pa , Maggie Jacobs, daughter of Allen and Mary (Louch) Jacobs Issue (1) Anne Gilfillen, (2) Mary Gilfillen, (3) James Sharon Gilfillen

31511—Annie Gilfillen Thompson, born Feb. 24, 1885, at McAlisterville, Pa   Married June 30, 1915, Samuel Curran Watts, son of Samuel and Anna B (Curran) Watts, grandson of Samuel and ———— (Kauffman) Watts, great-grandson of Samuel and ———— (Cramer) Watts, and great-great-grandson of Samuel Watts, the founder of the family in America, who fought in the Revolution and was killed in the Battle of Monmouth   Issue (1) Hugh Curran

315111—Hugh Curran Watts, born Feb ——, 1917, at McAlisterville, Pa

31512—Mary Gilfillen Thompson, born Apr. 17, 1889, at McAlisterville, Pa   Address, McAlisterville, Pa

31513—James Sharon Gilfillen Thompson, born Dec 27, 1892 at McAlisterville, Pa   Unmarried   Farmer, McAlisterville, Pa

3152—Elmira Thompson, born Oct 10, 1849, at Oakland Mills, Pa.   Married on Dec 27, 1883, at McAlisterville, Pa , James Miller McDonald, son of James Smith and Mary Ann (Enslow) McDonald, of McCoystown, Pa   Issue (1) William Thompson, (2) James Lamont, (3) Margaret Gilfillen

31521—William Thompson McDonald, born June 15, 1885, at Mifflintown, Pa

31522—James Lamont McDonald, born Jan 26, 1887, at Mifflintown, Pa. Address, Mifflintown, Pa   Married June 24, 1908, at Mifflin, Pa , Nora B Cramer   Issue (1) Alice E, (2) Mary E

315221—Alice E———————— McDonald, born June 21 1909

315222—Mary E   —   McDonald.   - -   24 191

31523—**Margaret Gilfillen McDonald,** born Oct 19, 1890, at Mifflintown, Pa Married June 24, 1908 at Mifflin, Pa, Grover C Cramer

316—**John Thompson,** born —————, at Goshen Farm. Married April 7, 1846 in Juniata County, Pa, Margaret Wright —No data

32—**James Thompson,** born Feb 2, 1782, near Thompsontown, Pa, died Dec. 14, 1847 at Mexico, Pa He spelled his name Thomson up to 1800 He was appointed postmaster at Mexico, Pa, Oct 11, 1815 He was a merchant and a miller at Mexico He was married on April 2, 1810 by Rev Thomas Smith to Martha Porter Allen (born Sept 19, 1788, died Nov 22, 1855, in Mexico, Pa) daughter of David and Mary (Nelson) Allen David Allen was a soldier of the Revolution who came to Juniata County in 1783, married Mary, daughter of Robert Nelson, and became the father of two daughters, both of whom married Thompsons, Martha becoming the wife of James Thompson of Mexico, and Jane, the wife of Mitchell Thompson (57) who resided about two miles below Thompsontown—see "History of Juniata and Susquehanna Valleys in Pennsylvania," p 858—Robert Nelson (born 1725, died 1805 at Bowling Green, Ky, aged 83) was said to have been a nephew of Thomas Nelson and his second wife, Mrs Fannie (Houston) Tucker Nelson and a grandson of Hugh and Sarah Nelson of Penrith, County of Cumberland, England—see the *Baltimore Sun,* May 13, 1906 His wife was Martha (Patterson) Nelson (born 1731, died 1794 at Cedar Springs, Pa), daughter of Walker and Margaret (Scott) Patterson of the Parish Harwick—see No 381 Children of James and Martha (Allen) Thompson (1) Charles Allen, (2) Lucinda Mitchell, (3) Allen Mitchell, (4) Lewis Nelson, (5) Jerome Nelson, (6) Horace Nelson

321—**Charles Allen Thompson,** born Jan 11, 1811, at Mexico, Pa., died Oct 19, 1854, at Mexico, Pa He was a merchant, miller and coal dealer Married by Rev John Hutchinson of Mifflintown on March 11, 1834, at Millerstown, Pa, Mary Ann Cochran (born June 14, 1815, at Millerstown, Pa., died June 14, 1887, at Mexico, Pa, daughter of Thomas and Sophia Maria (Porter) Cochran—see 32134 and 571. Thomas Cochran was born 1776 in Redcastle, near Londonderry, Ireland and died Feb 10, 1846 at Millerstown, Pa His wife was born Oct 16, 1776, near Redcastle, Ireland and died March 29, 1852 in Pennsylvania She was the daughter of Robert Porter who served as Colonel in the Revolution and participated in the battle of Brandywine—see Biographical Encyclopedia of Juniata Valley, Pa, p 1272 Thomas Cochran and his brothers Samuel, Robert and William, bought land in Chester County, Pa, upon which they laid out a town called Cochranville In 1801 he moved to Millerstown, Pa, where he kept the first tavern in the town and lived as postmaster From 1813 to 1835 he was a merchant in Millerstown Children of C A and Mary Ann (Cochran)

*Home of James Thompson 32 and Martha Allen Thompson,
Mexico, Juniata Co., Pa.*

Residence of the Late William Porter Thompson, Mexico, Juniata Co., Pa.

Locati........which has been held by only two families since being patented, namely,
those .... No. 32
and h......W.. Captain
James ....

Home of Charles Allen Thompson (321) and Mary Ann (Cochran) Thompson, Mexico, Juniata Co., Pa., now the home of Mrs. Charles Allen Thompson, Jr. (3218).

Thompson (1) Martha Jane Allen, (2) James Horace, (3) William Porter, (4) Emma Sophia, (5) Eliza Ellen, (6) Ada Marion, (7) Anna Mary, (8) Charles Allen

3211—Martha Jane Allen Thompson, born Apr 22, 1835, at Mexico, Pa., died March 1, 1901 at Hawleyville, Iowa Married on April 12, 1864 at Mexico, Pa, George Ruffer Rumbaugh (born April 19, 1829 at Millerstown, Pa, died June 25, 1882 at Hawleyville, Iowa) son of ———— John and Elizabeth (————————) Rumbaugh G A Rumbaugh was a physician at Hawleyville, Iowa Issue (1) Gus Thompson, (2) Nettie May

32111—Gus Thompson Rumbaugh, born Jan 7, 1867, at Hawleyville, Iowa Address, G T Rumbaugh, M D, Villisca, Iowa Married March 8, 1893, at Villisca, Iowa, Nettie Hutton (born May 1, 1866, at Williamsburg, Ohio) daughter of Pleasant Miles and Mary Ann (McDonough) Hutton and granddaughter of George and Eva (————————) McDonough No issue

32112—Nettie May Rumbaugh, born Jan. 27, 1869 at Hawleyville, Iowa Married Dec 15, 1887, at Hawleyville, Iowa, Forney W. Ammons Farmer, Clarinda, Iowa Issue (1) Eugene Rumbaugh, (2) Adda Marion

321121—Eugene Rumbaugh Ammons, born Mar 1, 1892, at Hawleyville, Iowa Address, Seattle, Wash

321122—Adda Marion Ammons, born Oct 26, 1896, at Hawleyville, Iowa Address, Clarinda, Iowa

3212—James Horace Thompson, born Mar. 26, 1837, at Mexico Pa ; died July 22, 1894, at Tyrone, Pa Married twice, first Jan 18, 1872, at Millerstown, Pa, Annie Eliza Gilfillen (born at Millerstown; died June 3, 1882 in Mexico, Pa) daughter of James and Margaretta Hollingsworth (Alexander) Gilfillen, and granddaughter of James and Sarah (Jones) Gilfillen, and of Benjamin and Rebecca (Woodland) Alexander—see 315, 3213, 626 and 72 He married secondly on April ————, 1886 at Philadelphia, Mary C Cadwalader of Tyrone, Pa Address, Mrs. Mary Cadwalader Thompson, Los Angeles, Cal

3213—William Porter Thompson, born Apr 26, 1839, at Mexico, Pa, died July 31, 1915 at Mexico, Pa Married Dec 16, 1858 near Millerstown, Pa, Sarah Jane Gilfillen (born Sept 15, 1839, died Oct 6, 1916 at Mexico, Pa, buried at Mexico) daughter of James Gilfillen and M——d-

daughter of James and Sarah (Jones) Gilfillen of Mt Pleasant and
of Benjamin and Rebecca (Woodland) Alexander—see 315, 3212, 626
and 72   Issue (1) Cora Emily, (2) Clara Gilfillen, (3) Nettie Leo-
nore, (4) Jerome Nelson, (5) James Gilfillen

32131—**Cora Emily Thompson** (twin), born Sept. 6, 1859   Unmarried
Address, Mexico, Pa.

32132—**Clara Gilfillen Thompson** (twin), born Sept 6, 1859, died Jan 2,
1889

32133—**Nettie Lenore Thompson**, born Apr 6, 1862, at Mexico, Pa , died
Sept 30, 1866

32134—**Jerome Nelson Thompson**, born Apr 14, 1865, at Mexico, Pa , died
Jan 16, 1915 at Wilkesbarre, Pa , buried at Lewistown, Pa   He was
educated at the Airy View Academy, Port Royal, Pa   At the age of
23 years he started the First National Bank at Middleburg, Snyder
County, Pa   He became later director of the Belleville Bank, Belleville, Pa ; director of the Plymouth Bank, Plymouth, Pa , director
of the Russell National Bank, Lewistown, Pa , and Treasurer of the
Wyoming Valley Trust Co , Wilkes Barre, Pa   He was also a
director in the Connecticut River Power Plant, and of the Wyoming
Valley Gas & Electric Light Co   He served for two years as the
president of the Thompson family assemblies held annually at
Thompsontown, Pa , since 1911, although his health would not per-
mit his attendance at the exercises   He married on Jan 20, 1905
at Lewistown, Pa , Gertrude Mann (born April 3, 1875, at Manns
Mifflin Co , Pa , daughter of William (3rd) and Mary Jane (Cochran)
Mann and granddaughter of William (2nd) and Ann (Hutcheson)
Mann and of Thomas Preston Cochran, granddaughter of Thomas
and Sophia Maria (Porter) Cochran and great-granddaughter of
Colonel Robert Porter—see 321 and 571   The pioneer of the Mann
family was Thomas Mann, who was born in County Derry, Ireland,
and died 1820 in Wales, Erie County, N Y   His son William Mann,
Sr , who married Rachel Gillette, daughter of Stephen Gillette of
Hartford, Conn , was born Aug 18, 1779, in Braintree, Mass , and
died at Boiling Spring, Center County, Pa Feb , 1860   William
Mann, Jr , who married Ann Hutcheson, was born Oct 18, 1802 in
Johnstown, N Y , and died June 11, 1855 in Mifflin County, Pa
William Mann (3rd) was born Jan 7, 1837 at Manns, Mifflin County,
Pa , and died May 17, 1876, on the Ohio River near Shancetown,
Ohio   Child of J N and Gertrude (Mann) Thompson (1) Mary
Cochran

32   ... Cochran Thompson, ... Address Wilkes-

32135—James Gilfillen Thompson, born Dec. 26, 1868, at Mexico, Pa. Cashier First National Bank, Middleburg, Snyder County, Pa Married Edna Rebecca Leisenring (born June 27, 1884) daughter of Edwin Hutter and Ida Elizabeth (Atkinson) Leisenring, and granddaughter of Gideon and Louise (Shindle) Leisenring and of William Frederick and Anna Rebecca (Altwater) Atkinson Issue (1) James Gilfillen

321351—James Gilfillen Thompson, Jr., born Mar 13, 1910, at Middleburg, Snyder County, Pa

3214—Emma Sophia Thompson, born June 12, 1841, at Mexico, Pa , died April 30, 1906 at Clearfield, Pa Married by Rev Wm Porter Cochran on Jan 2, 1868, at Mexico, Pa, to John W Wright, who was born at Clearfield, Pa , April 30, 1839 and died at Lockhaven, Pa , April 29, 1874 Issue (1) Abram Keggy

32141—Abram Keggy Wright, born Oct 2, 1868, at Clearfield, Pa Unmarried Address, Clearfield, Pa.

3215—Eliza Ellen Thompson, born Nov 7, 1843, in Mexico, Juniata Co, Pa Married March 6, 1873, Dr James Thompson Mahon (born Dec 8, 1841 near Chambersburg, Franklin County, Pa , died Feb 1, 1895 at Lewistown, Mifflin County, Pa) son of Dr David D———— and Martha S———— (Cochran) Mahon of Newton Hamilton, Mifflin County, Pa James T Mahon graduated with honors from the Baltimore Medical College (Um of Md) in 1864 and located first in Newton Hamilton, where his father was a practicing physician In 1885 he moved to Lewistown, Mifflin County, Pa He served as assistant surgeon of the 187th Pennsylvania Volunteers during the Civil War and was surgeon for Colonel Huling Post of Lewistown, for several years For 27 years he was physician for the Penn R R and was a member of the U S Pension Board of Examining Surgeons in Mifflin County, Pa No children

3216—Ada Marion Thompson, born Nov. 10, 1845, at Mexico, Pa , died Jan 19, 1900, Mifflintown, Pa Married Jan 5, 1870, at Mexico, Pa Hon Jeremiah Lyons (born Sept 16, 1839 in Saville Township, Perry County, Pa , died Nov 14, 1900) son of Nicholas and Sarah (Yohn) Lyons Jeremiah Lyons was one of the organizers and first president of the First National Bank of Mifflintown, Pa In 1891 he was elected Judge of the Forty-first Judicial District of Pennsylvania He was truste. of the First . . .   — . H st. . . mi. Valley in Penn . - c

3217—Anna Mary Thompson, born Mai 7, 1848, at Mexico, Pa , died Nov. 21, 1916, at Lewistown, Pa   Married Dec 21, 1871, at Mexico, Pa, Jacob Rickenbaugh (born Nov 11, 1844, in Walker Township, Mifflin County, Pa) son of Jacob and Mary (Seiber) Rickenbaugh, grandson of Jacob and Barbara (Hartzler) Rickenbaugh, great-grandson of John and Reionicica (Rickenbaugh) Hertzler and great-great-grandson of Julius Rickenbaugh of Switzerland, who came to Philadelphia from Holland (Rotterdam) in the ship Rick Mary in 1733   Jacob Rickenbaugh, the husband of Anna Mary Thompson, served in the 194th Pennsylvania Volunteers under Col William B Elder in 1864   Issue (1) Mary Thompson, (2) Gertrude May, (3) Charles Allen, (4) Margery Edith, (5) Guy Blain

32171—Mary Thompson Rickenbaugh, born Feb. 13, 1873, at Mexico, Pa. Address, Lewistown, Pa   Unmarried

32172—Gertrude May Rickenbaugh, born Apr 4, 1875, at Mexico, Pa. Address, Lewistown, Pa   Unmarried

32173—Charles Allen Rickenbaugh, born Jan 30, 1877, at Mexico, Pa   Coal operator, general manager of Moshanon Coal Co, Osceola Mills, Pa   Married Eva Magdalene Miller. No children

32174—Margery Edith Rickenbaugh, born May 22, 1880, at Mexico, Pa   Married on June 7, at Meiia, to John Walter Leonard, Superintendent of United States Leather Co, Titusville, Pa   No children

32175—Guy Blain Rickenbaugh, born June 12, 1883, at Mexico, Pa   Assistant cashier, First National Bank, Tyrone, Pa, to Feb 1, 1915, then became treasurer, Tarentum (Pa) Savings & Trust Co , then cashier, Bank of Waynesboro, Pa, and on Aug 1, 1916, became assistant cashier of the Irving National Bank, New York City.

3218—Charles Allen Thompson, born Jan. 22, 1851, at Mexico, Pa , died Oct. 12, 1897, at Mexico, Pa   Married Feb 10, 1881, at Mexico, Jennie Hetrick (born Dec 19, 1861), daughter of William and Sarah (Seiber) Hetrick   Address, Mrs Jennie (Hetrick) Thompson, Mexico, Pa   Issue (1) Charles Allen, (2) Martha Jane

32181—Charles Allen Thompson, Jr, born Jan 20, 1884, died Feb. 10, 1884, at Mexico, Pa

32182—Martha Jane Thompson, born July 3, 1897

322 Lucinda Mitchell Thompson, born Dec, 30, 1842, at Mexico, Pa ,
     . . . , at Issue Pa

Home of Jerome Nelson Thompson (325) and Jane Wright Thompson, on the Juniata, near Mexico, Juniata Co., Pa., now owned by their grand-niece, Martha Jane Thompson (32182).

331   *Edward Patterson Thompson*

33241   *Edward Walter Thompson*

323—**Allen Mitchell Thompson,** born Feb 3, 1814, at Mexico, Pa , died April 13, 1844, at Mexico, Pa Married on May 16, 1843, at ————, ————, Sophia Porter McDowell No issue

324—**Lewis Nelson Thompson,** born Oct 19, 1815, at Mexico, Pa.; died June 25, 1816, at Mexico, Pa

325—**Jerome Nelson Thompson,** born Sept. 27, 1817, at Mexico, Pa , died April 26, 1895, at Mexico, Pa Married on Oct 1, 1840, at ————, Jane Wright (born July 11, 1816, died ————) daughter of John and Elizabeth (McCrum) Wright Issue three children who died in infancy

326—**Horace Nelson Thompson,** born Nov 3, 1825, at Mexico, Pa , died March 11, 1827, at Mexico, Pa

33—**William Thompson, Jr,** born Dec 15, 1785, in Pfoutz's Valley Pa , died March 18, 1834 at Thompsontown, Pa He and his brother Isaac (36) served in the war of 1812 at Black Rock encampment William Thompson was captain of the company from his county, which rendered service during that war On Aug 8, 1833 he set sail for England and France in search of health but evidently was not benefited by the trip for his death occurred at Thompsontown during the following March He was married on June 14, 1816 at Chestnut Hill, Pa , by the Rev Mr. Brown, of the Presbyterian Church, to Charlotte Chambers Patterson (born at Mexico, Pa , March 9, 1794, died at Marietta, Pa , March 20, 1863) daughter of George and Jean (Burd) Patterson, granddaughter of Capt James Patterson, Jr and Mary (Stuart) Patterson and of Colonel James and Sarah (Shippen) Burd; great-granddaughter of Capt James Patterson, Sr , and Susan (Howard) Patterson of George and Jean (————) Stuart of Edward and Jean (Haliburton) Burd and of Judge Edward and Sara (Plumley) Shippen Edward Shippen was the son of Joseph and Abigail (Grosse) Shippen, the grandson of Edward Shippen, the first mayor of Philadelphia, and his wife Elizabeth (Lybrand) Shippen, and great-grandson of William Shippen, member of Parliament, and his wife Mary (Nunnes) Shippen, daughter of John and Effan (Crossfield) Nunnes Sarah (Plumley) Shippen was a daughter of Charles and Rose (Budd) Plumley and granddaughter of Charles and Margaret (Page) Plumley and of Thomas and Sarah (————) Budd Abagail (Grosse) Shippen was a daughter of Thomas and Elizabeth (Atherton) Grosse, a granddaughter of Clement Grosse and a great-granddaughter of Isaac Grosse The Shippen family occupied positions of importance and were kn . . . . al Councille . . . . as born on his ancestoral estate, Hillham, England, moved to Philadelphia to better his fortune and was named the first Mayor of Philadelphia, Oct 25, 1701, by William Penn His country house stood near the present S W corner of South and Broad Streets, and his property stretched along the south side of the old city—from Front to 16th His grandson Edward Shippen of Lancaster, as he was commonly known was Judge of the Philadelphia Court of Common Pleas His advanced age only, prevented his taking active service during the Revolution—but he was untiring in his efforts to help to the best of his ability He was a Committeeman of Lancaster County He did not live to hear of the surrender of Cornwallis—but his faith in the success of the righteous cause, seems never once to have wavered—see Provincial Councillors of Pennsylvania, pp. 46-52 Col James Burd was captain, major and colonel in the Provincial Service of Pennsylvania 1755-64 He was colonel of Second Battalion of the Pennsylvania Regiment, Provincial Service—Jan 2, 1758-64 He was a chairman of a Town Meeting in favor of Action of Colonies, in Middletown, Pa, June 8, 1774, and was Committeeman in Lancaster County, Pa, for Paxtang Township 1774-75 He was elected colonel of the Fourth Battalion of the Associated Battalion of Lancaster County, Sept 18, 1775 He resigned Dec, 1776, owing to dissentions and reluctance of the men to serve in any place except in their own immediate neighborhood His journal dating from 1756-57, giving interesting accounts of the operations of the Colonial forces—the building of Fort Agusta at Sunbury—and part of Washington's early career, was published by the State of Pennsylvania Edward Burd, the son of Col Burd, went to Boston in 1775, with Thompson's Battalion of Riflemen He was major of Flying Camp, and taken prisoner at Long Island For his active service, see Vol XIII, Second Series, Pennsylvania Archives, p 307 Captain James Patterson, son of James Patterson, Sr, who came from Salisbury, England, and settled in 1717 on the northern line of Conestoga Manor, Lancaster County, Pa, was "the most illustrious pioneer settler in Juniata County, Pa"—see History of Juniata and Susquehanna Valleys in Pennsylvania, p 851 He obtained the first warrant for land in Juniata County on Feb 4, 1755, for 400 acres at what is now Mexico, Pa In 1767 he built the first gristmill and saw-mill east of the river, then known as Patterson's Mills, but now Mexico George, the youngest son of Capt James and Mary (Stuart) Patterson, "married Jean, daughter of Colonel James Burd, the most noted military man in this province during the French and Indian War" Children of William and Charlotte Chambers (Patterson) Thompson (1) Edward Patterson, (2) William Shippen, (3) Maria Louisa, (4) George, (5) Lucian Mitchell, (6) Theophilus, (7) Mary Patterson, (8) Theodore Samuel, (9) Robert Mitchell, (10) Josephine Patterson On ————, 1840, at ————, the widow o Thompson Charlotte Chambers (Patterson) Thompson, b and of Andrew Thompson No children

331—Edward Patterson Thompson, born May 24, 1817, at Thompsontown, Pa ; died April 12, 1904 on his farm near Wichita, Kans   Married on March 4, 1839, at Mexico, Pa, Matilda Snyder (born ——————; died March 29, 1911 at Wichita, Kans)   Issue (1) Cora Burd, (2) Josephine Patterson, (3) Charlotte Chambers—dead, (4) Matilda Shippen   Address, 1320 North Topeka Ave, Wichita, Kan

332—William Shippen Thompson, born Oct. 31, 1818, at Thompsontown, Pa , died Dec 31, 1891, at Topeka, Kan   He was married on April 6, 1848 at Milton, Pa , by the Rev David Longmore, to Isabella Hunter Marr (born July 4, 1823, died July 23, 1878, at Topeka), daughter of Allen Marr (born June 18, 1787; died March 29, 1843 and Margaret (Hunter) Marr, and granddaughter of Joseph Marr (born June 5, 1750, died Sept 3, 1796) and Susanna (Price) Marr, and of David and Isabella (Patterson) Hunter, and great-granddaughter of William and Esther (Finley) Patterson   Issue (1) Theodore, (2) Robert Shippen, (3) William, (4) Walter Marr, (5) Ella, (6) Isabella Marr

3321—Theodore Thompson, born Jan 12, 1849, died Aug 12, 1849, at Thompsontown, Pa

3322—Robert Shippen Thompson, born May 12, 1852, at Thompsontown, Pa   Furniture dealer   Address, 808 Kansas Ave, Topeka, Kan   Unmarried

3323—William Thompson, born Sept 22, 1854, at Thompsontown, Pa ; died Jan 12, 1859, at Thompsontown, Pa

3324—Walter Marr Thompson, born May 24, 1857, at Thompsontown, Pa   Furniture dealer   Address 1100 West 6th St, Topeka, Kan   Married on Jan 23, 1896, at Johnstown, Pa. Anna Elizabeth Keim, daughter of Mahlon Walter and Elizabeth (Dibert) Keim and granddaughter of John and Sarah (——————) Keim and of John and Rachel (——————) Dibert   Issue (1) Edward Walter, (2) William Keim, (3) Charles Frederick, (4) Elizabeth, (5) Isabella Mildred

33241—Edward Walter Thompson, born Nov 5, 1896, at Topeka, Kans

33242—William Keim Thompson, born July 21, 1898, at Topeka, Kans

33243—Charles Frederick Thompson, born Jan. 1900, at Topeka, Kans

33244—Elizabeth Thompson, born Sept 14, 1901, at Topeka, Kans

33245—Isabella Mildred Thomps.   —   —   s.,
       died 1 in. _ 1 2   \

3325—Ella Thompson, born Dec 7, 1859, at Thompsontown, Pa , died
   Feb 7, 1912, at Topeka, Kans

3326—Isabella Marr Thompson, born Aug. 19, 1864, at Thompsontown,
   Pa , died June 12, 1909, at Topeka, Kans

333—Maria Louisa Thompson, born Aug 6, 1820, at Thompsontown, Pa ;
   died Jan 27, 1821, at Thompsontown, Pa

334—George Thompson, born Nov 1, 1821, at Thompsontown, Pa , died
   Sept 1, 1826, at Thompsontown, Pa

335—Lucien Mitchell Thompson, born Mar. 26, 1823, at Thompsontown,
   Pa , died Aug 30, 1894, or June 12, 1909, at Mahanoy City, Pa   Phy-
   sician, Mahanoy City, Pa   Married on Nov 28, 1848, at Philadelphia,
   Pa , Kate Trautman, daughter of George Christian and Sarah (———)
   Trautman   No issue.

336—Theophilus Thompson, born Feb. 27, 1825, at Thompsontown, Pa.;
   died Mar 12, 1912, at Leeds, Mo Married on ————————, at
   ————————, Elizabeth Harington, daughter of Thomas and Hettia
   (Pitcher) Harington Issue (1) William.

3361—William Thompson, born June 4, 1861, in Clay County, Mo   Married on July 28, 1888, at Kansas City, Mo, Sarah Jane Remy,
   daughter of Jasper Remy and granddaughter of Burgis W————
   Ray Address, Leeds, Jackson County, Mo Issue (1) William, (2)
   Mary Ellen, (3) Edward Francis, (4) Thomas Alva, (5) Sarah Jane.

33611—William Thompson, born Oct. 27, 1889, at Kansas City, Mo   Address Leeds, Mo

33612—Mary Ellen Thompson, born Sept 24, 1891, at Kansas City, Mo
   Married June 9, 1908, at Leeds, Mo , Martin Cornelius Mitt. Issue
   (1) William Martin, (2) Mary Ellen

336121—William Martin Mitt, born July 1, 1909, in Jackson County, Mo.

336122—Mary Ellen Mitt, born May 26, 1915

33613—Edward Francis Thompson, born June 2, 1894 Address, Leeds, Mo.

33614- Thomas Alva Thompson, born Aug. 13, 1901   Address, Leeds, Mo.

33615 Sarah Jane Thompson, born Dec 24, 1904   Address, Leeds, Mo

337—Mary Patterson Thompson, born June 14, 1828, at Thompsontown, Pa , died Feb 26, 1829, at Thompsontown, Pa

338—Theodore Samuel Thompson, born Feb. 2, 1829, at Thompsontown, Pa , died April 22, 1904, at Thompsontown, Pa It was he who co-operated with his first cousin Heber Samuel Thompson—304—in the preparation of the "Thompson Family" booklet upon which the present family records have been based He married on Jan 8, 1861, at Marietta, Lancaster County, Pa , Annie Elizabeth Cassel (born July 9, 1833, at Marietta, Pa , died Oct 29, 1914, at Thompsontown, Pa), daughter of Abraham and Amelia Caroline (Quest) Cassel and grand-daughter of David and Catherine (Hernly) Cassel and of John and Margaretta (Cossart) Quest David Cassel was a son of Abraham and Esther (Weiss) Cassel, grandson of Abraham and Catherine (——————) Cassel, great-grandson of Johannes Cassel and great-great-great-grandson of Yelles Cassel Children of Theodore Samuel and Annie Elizabeth (Cassel) Thompson, (1) Emma Cassell, (2) Herbert Moodie, (3) Edward Shippen

338i—Emily Cassel Thompson, born at Ashland, Pa. Educated at St. Mary's Hall, Burlington, N J Resides in the William Thompson, Sr , homestead, Thompsontown, Pa Married May 30, 1882, Thomas Wood Haldeman of Columbia, Lancaster County, Pa , son of George Washington and Jennie Maria (Wood) Haldeman of Columbia, Pa , grandson of Peter and Sarah Atlee (Barber) Haldeman and of Thomas and Maria (Fleetwood) Wood, great-grandson of John and Maria (Brenneman) Haldeman and Nathaniel (2nd) and Rachel Jane (Atlee) Barber, great-great-grandson of Jacob and Maria (Miller) Haldeman and Nathaniel (1st) and Mary (Connor) Barber and Colonel Samuel John and Sarah (Richardson) Atlee Jacob Haldeman was a grandson of the Honotte Gaspard Haldimand of Thun, Canton Berne, Switzerland, who with four sons removed to Yverdon, Canton Vaud, April 1, 1651 (Miscellana Geologica et Heraldica, Vol IV, p 369) Member Committee of Observation (Penna Archives, 2nd Series, Vol XXIII, p 294) Corporal in the Lancaster County Bat-talion of the "Flying Camp" and participated in the Battle of Long Island, etc (Penna Archives, 2nd Series, Vol XIII, pp 295 and 397, 3rd Series, Vol XXIII, p 463) The eldest brother of Jacob Halde-man was the noted British general, Sir Frederick Haldimand, K B , Commander-in-Chief of His Majesty's forces in America, succeeding Guy Carleton, Lord Dorchester (Penn Monthly, Aug , 1881). John Haldeman was a private in Lancaster County Battalion (3rd and 7th) (Penna Archives, 5th Series, Vol VII, pp 198, 204, 452, 725, 785) and served in Pennsylvania Legislature in 1795 Colonel Samuel John Atlee a .... -1 En_ . . . -70- 1710 . . . . yor afterw. d Colon. . . . . In.. . ars

Served as Colonel of the First Regiment of Pennsylvania Musketry and was captured at the Battle of Long Island Upon his exchange he was elected member of the Continental Congress 1778, served as Lieutenant of Lancaster County 1780, member of Supreme Executive Council 1783, member of Assembly 1782-5-6 (*Penna Magazine*, Vol II, p 74). Children of Thomas Wood and Emily Cassel (Thompson) Haldeman, (1) George Thompson, (2) Theodore Thompson, (3) Jennie Wood Thompson, (4) Thomas Wood

33811—George Thompson Haldeman, born March 1, 1883, at Columbia, Pa Attended the Pennsylvania State College and received the degree of Mining Engineer from the University of Pittsburgh Member of American Institute of Mining Engineers, Engineers Society of Western Pennsylvania, Societe Geologique de France, Societè Geologique de Belgique Address, Thompsontown, Pa Married June 8, 1910, in New York City, Agnes Wallace Campbell MacIndoe (born in New York City, Oct 23, 1885), daughter of Walter James and Annie Lee (Millar) MacIndoe and granddaughter of William and Agnes Wallace (Campbell) MacIndoe and William Guernsey and Susan Leroy Millar. Agnes Wallace Campbell (MacIndoe) Haldeman is a descendant of Sir William Wallace and of Robert the Bruce, King of Scotland Attended Miss Graham's School, New York City, graduated from the Horace Mann School of Columbia University Issue (1) Janet Emily

338111—Janet Emily Haldeman, born May 20, 1911, at Wilkes-Barre, Pa

33812—Theodore Thompson Haldeman, born Aug 4. 1884, at Columbia, Pa. Married May 13, 1913, May Nixon of Washington, Pa Issue (1) Frederick

338121—Frederick Haldeman, born Feb 20 1914, at Dover, Del

33813—Jennie Wood Thompson Haldeman, born March 8, 1886, at Columbia, Pa Graduated Hannah Moore Academy, Reisterstown, Md Married Feb 19, 1909, Joseph Bird Cummins Address, New York City No issue

33814—Thomas Wood Haldeman, Jr, born July 9, 1899, at Shamokin, Pa ; died Dec 14, 1902.

3382—Herbert Moodie Thompson, born Oct. 8, 1865, at Marietta, Pa ; died Dec. 19, 1906, at Thompsontown, Pa Unmarried

33—Edward Shippen Thomson, born at Marietta. Pa, on May 23, 1869 at Thompsontown, Pa He has served as treasurer of the [...] Association since its formation in 1911 To him

must be given most credit for the success which has attended the
Thompson Family Assemblies held annually under his personal direction at Thompsontown   He married on June 3, 1912, at Oak Lane,
Philadelphia, Pa , Charlotte Patterson Crowther—33(10)36—daughter
of Henry and Josephine Patterson (Zell) Crowther, granddaughter
of Henry and Amelia (Homan) Crowther, and of Thomas and
Josephine Patterson (Thompson) Zell   Issue (1) William Haliburton, (2) Charlotte Patterson, (3) Edward Shippen

33831—William Haliburton Thomson, born Apr. 26, 1913, at the William
Thomson, Sr , homestead, Thompsontown, Pa

33832—Charlotte Patterson Thomson, born July 28, 1914. at the William
Thomson, Sr , homestead

33833—Edward Shippen Thomson, Jr , born Feb. 19. 1916, at the William
Thomson, Sr , homestead

339—Robert Mitchell Thompson, born Dec 22, 1831, at Thompsontown,
Pa , died Nov 7, 1832, at Thompsontown, Pa.

33(10)—Josephine Patterson Thompson, born Dec. 6, 1833, at Thompsontown, Pa   It was she who first called the attention of the family
to the resting place of Pioneer John Thomson, and to her must be
credited the enthusiasm that has kept alive the Thompson Family
Assemblies   The "Queen of the Thompsons"—see the Introduction
She married on Dec 23, 1851, at Green Dale Farm, Pa , Thomas
Zell (born Mar 18, 1821, at Marietta, Pa ; died Feb 13, 1885, at
Reading, Pa), son of Jacob and Margaret (Evans) Zell and grandson of Squire John Zell, Churchtown, Pa   Margaret Evans was the
daughter of Maj Samuel and Frances (Lowrey) Evans and grand-
daughter of Col Evans and Margaret (Niven) Evans and of Col
Alexander and Ann (Alricks) Lowrey   Col Alexander Lowrey
was a son of Lazarus Lowrey who was of Scotch-Irish ancestry and
came from the North of Ireland and settled in Donegal, Lancaster
County, Pa , in 1728   In 1729 he was licensed to trade with the
Indians   He died in Philadelphia in 1753   His son Col Alexander
Lowrey was also a celebrated trader   His mansion, half a mile
from the Susquehanna River, near Marietta, was built in 1750-60
The farm contained 391 acres, and was called "Locust Grove." He
was quite celebrated in the early history of Pennsylvania   In July,
1774, he served on the Committee of Correspondence for Lancaster
County, which met in Philadelphia, July 15, 1774, the Committee of
Conference   He was elected Colonel of the Third Battalion of Lancaster County Militia in 1776, and commanded it at the Battle of
Brandywine He served as a delegate from Lancaster County to a
convention at Carpenters   which on June 16, 1776, made a
declaration in favor of Independence and instructed the members

of Continental Congress to vote for it   He was a member of the
committee which framed the first Constitution of the State   He
was a member of the State Legislature for many years   For his
active service see Vol XIII, Second Series, Penna Archives, p.
355, and Vol XIII, Second Series, Penna Archives, p 370   Col.
Evan Evans was Colonel of the Second Battalion, Chester County
Militia   He was commissioned May 7, 1777   He was at Battle of
Brandywine, and member of Carpenters Hall Convention, in June,
1776   He was also member of Committee of Observation, being
chosen Dec 20, 1774   See Second Series, Penna Archives, Vol
XIV, pp 83-94; Second Series, Penna Archives, Vol III, pp 543-
638, Second Series, Penna Archives, Vol XIV, p 65   Major
Samuel Evans was the first Ensign in his father's (Col Evan
Evans) Regiment   He was afterwards Captain of the London
Britain Company, Second Battalion of Chester County   He was
also Major of the Sixth Battalion, under Lieut Col David McKay,
and was in the Battle of Brandywine   See Second Series, Penna
Archives, Vol XIV, p 182 or 102 and p 116 of the same volume
Squire John Zell was a descendant of Johannes Heinrick Zell,
who came from Holland to America in 1684, and whose father
Johannes Heinrich Zell, founded the city of Zell, in Baden on the
river Wiese, and in 1690 organized out of the veterans of the 30
years war the Zell Guards, later the 4th Infantry which has always
been commanded by a Zell   Children of Thomas and Josephine
Patterson (Thompson) Zell (1) Thomas Burd, (2) William
Thompson, (3) Josephine Patterson, (4) Elizabeth Jeannette, (5)
Margaret Lowrey, (6) Theodore Shippen, (7) Lucien Mitchell

33(10)1—**Thomas Burd Zell,** born Nov 4, 1852, at Marietta, Lancaster
County, Pa   Was employed as timekeeper, weighmaster and rail
inspector at the Rolling Mill of the Philadelphia & Reading Railway Co, Reading, Pa, from Sept, 1868, until March, 1885   From
June, 1886, until June, 1893, he had charge of the finishing department of the shape mill of the North Branch Steel Co at Danville,
Pa   In June, 1898, he was appointed under the Civil Service Rules,
Assistant Inspector of Engineering Material for the Bureau of
Steam Engineering, Navy Department, Washington, D C, and
resigned Dec, 1903, to accept the position of Sales Representative
for the Penn Steel Castings & Machine Co, Chester, Pa, and is
at present Sales Agent for the Penn Seaboard Steel Corporation,
Main Office, Philadelphia, Pa   He is a member of the Society of
the Sons of the Revolution   Married on Dec. 12, 1882, at Hummelstown, Dauphin County, Pa, Ada Virginia Nissley (born Feb
6, 1858, died Nov 21, 1885), daughter of John J and Katherine
(Uhl) Nissley, and granddaughter of Christian and Nancy
(   ) Nissley and of John and Hannah (————) Uhl.
Issue (1) John Paul

33(10)11—John Paul Zell, born Aug 30, 1885, at Reading. Pa , died Nov 17, 1885, at Hummelstown, Pa

33(10)2—William Thompson Zell, born July 19, 1854 at Marietta, Lancaster County, Pa Accountant 130 North Second St , Reading, Pa Married on Dec 24, 1889, at Danville, Pa , Alice Beaver Thompson, daughter of Egbert and Sarah Ann (Paulhamous) Thompson and granddaughter of Henry and Letitia (————) Thompson and of John and Catherine (————) Paulhamous Issue (1) Lucian Thompson

33(10)21—Lucian Thompson Zell, born Aug 27, 1896, at Frankford Philadelphia, Pa Address, 130 North Second St , Reading, Pa

33(10)3—Josephine Patterson Zell, born Dec. 23 1855 at Marietta Pa Address, 6510 North Seventh St, Oak Lane, Philadelphia, Pa Married on July 19, 1874, at Reading, Pa Henry Crowther (born Nov 1, 1855, in Reading, Pa), son of Henry and Amelia (Homan) Crowther, grandson of Henry and Mary (Castello) Crowther and of Augustus and Elizabeth (Boyer) Homan, and great-grandson of Hon George Rodney Richard Crowther (Captain in the British Army), a descendant of Henry II of England Mary Castello was the daughter of Rachel (Montefiore) Castello and a granddaughter of Moses Munes Montefiore Issue (1) Henry Lindley, (2) Mary Ethel, (3) Herbert Burd, (4) Helen Ada, (5) Frances Lois, (6) Charlotte Patterson, (7) Edith Florence, (8) Margaret Shippen, (9) Edmond Castello (10) Burd Shippen, (11) Laurance Montefiore, (12) Cecil Richard

33(10)31—Henry Lindley Crowther, born Nov 22, 1875, at Reading, Pa. Address, Conshohocken, Pa Married on June 11, 1902, Mary Beaver, daughter of Dr David R and Mary (Patterson) Beaver of Conshohocken, Pa Issue (1) David Beaver, (2) Mary Rachel

33(10)311—David Beaver Crowther, born Apr 30, 1906, at Philadelphia, Pa

33(10)312—Mary Rachel Crowther, born Dec 24, 1915

33(10)32—Mary Ethel Crowther, born Mar. 24, 1877, at Reading Pa. Address, 6510 North Seventh St , Philadelphia, Pa Married on Sept 8, 1898, at Ridgewood, Pa , Theodore Stengel (died Aug 30 1912 at Ebensburg Pa) son of Godfrey and Fredericka

(1   3)
D
8

33(10)321—Josephine Stengel, born Dec 2, 1899, at Pittsburgh, Pa

33(10)322—Fredericka Mary Stengel, born July 26, 1903, at Pittsburgh, Pa.

33(10)323—Dorothy Stengel, born June 26, 1907, at East Orange, N J., died June 29. 1907

33(10)33—Herbert Burd Crowther, born Dec 4, 1879, at Reading, Pa ; died 1881 at Reading, Pa

33(10)34—Helen Ada Crowther, born Mar 8, 1881, at Reading Pa Address, 2127 Lambert St , Philadelphia, Pa Married on Nov. 14, 1901 at Ridgewood, N J , Charles Andrew Cumings of Tidionte, Pa, son of Henry Harrison and Charlotte (Sink) Cumings and grandson of Charles and Emma (Amsden) Cumings and of Andrew and Sarah (La Rue) Sink C A Cumings is in the automobile business Issue (1) Margaret Shippen

33(10)341—Margaret Shippen Cumings, born Apr. 26, 1908, at Philadelphia, Pa

33(10)35—Frances Lois Crowther, born Oct 14, 1883 at Reading, Pa. Address, 327 East Second St , Bloomfield, Ind Married on June 28, 1905 at Montclair, N J , Edgar Roscoe Cumings (born Feb 20, 1874 at Madison, Ohio) son of Charles and Rebecca A———— (Sullivan) Cumings Edgar Roscoe Cumings received the degree of A B from Union College in 1897 and Ph D from Yale in 1903 He is professor of geology at Indiana University, Bloomington, Ind Fellow of the Amer Assoc Adv Science See "Who's Who in America" and "American Men of Science" Issue (1) Edith Katherine, (2) Edgar Crowther

33(10)351—Edith Katherine Crowther Cumings, born May 12, 1906, at Bloomington, Ind

33(10)352—Edgar Crowther Cumings, born Nov 27, 1909, at Bloomington, Ind

33(10)36—Charlotte Patterson Crowther, born May 20, 1883. in Reading, Pa Married June 5, 1912, Edward Shippen Thomson (3383) son of Theodore Samuel Thompson and Annie (Cassell) Thompson, grandson of William Thompson, Jr , and Charlotte (Patterson) Thomson, who were the great-grandparents of his wife Address, 1912, Thompsontown, Pa See 3383

33(10)37—Edith Florence Crowther, born May 26, 1885. at Reading, Pa Married Sept 29 1914, at Philadelphia, Edward Everett Thompson (10) 113

33(10)38—**Margaret Shippen Crowther,** born Sept 24. 1888, in Philadelphia, Pa Unmarried Address, 6510 North Seventh St, Oak Lane, Philadelphia, Pa

33(10)39—**Edmond Castello Crowther,** born Jan 17. 1891, in Philadelphia, Pa Unmarried Address, Philadelphia, Pa

33(10)3(10)—**Burd Shippen Crowther,** born May 9. 1893. in Boston Unmarried Address, Philadelphia, Pa

33(10)3(11)—**Laurance Montifiore Crowther,** born Jan 24. 1895. in Boston Unmarried Address, Philadelphia, Pa

33(10)3(12)—**Cecil Richard Crowther,** born June 7. 1897, in Pittsburgh Address, Philadelphia, Pa

33(10)4—**Elizabeth Jeannette Zell,** born Feb 8. 1866, at Marietta, Pa. Address Cranberry, N J, R F D Married on April 23. 1898, at Reading, Pa, Thomas Thursby (born July 18. 1855, at London, England) son of James Randall and Martha (Bodell) Thursby and grandson of John and Mary Ann Elizabeth (Harvey) Thursby and of William Bodell For many years Thomas Thursby was Superintendent of the American Gem & Pearl Co, New York City Now engaged in scientific farming Issue (1) Thomas Burd

33(10)41—**Thomas Burd Thursby,** born Nov. 2, 1900, at Dorchester, Mass.

33(10)5—**Margaret Lowery Zell,** born Jan 13 1868, at Reading, Pa Married Dec 14, 1904 at Passaic, N J, Charles Morford Hallman (born Jan 9. 1870, at Allentown, Pa), son of Stephen Jacob and Emma (Morford) Hallman and grandson of Jesse and Susan (————) Hallman and of George and Maria (Hohn) Morford C M Hallman was president of the Kentucky Refinery Co with headquarters at Louisville, Ky Address Reading, Pa

33(10)6—**Theodore Shippen Zell,** born June 15. 1870, at Reading Pa., died June 20, 1896 Married on Dec 5, 1893, Theresa Collins (born Sept 27. 1868 at Wolverhampton, England) daughter of John and Sarah (Harbland) Collins Issue (1) Gladys May

33(10)61—**Gladys May Zell,** born Oct 14. 1894, at Philadelphia. Address, 1623 North Fifty-fifth St, Philadelphia, Pa

33(10)7—**Lucian Mitchell Zell,** born Sept. 15. 1873, at Reading, Pa Address, ... 28, ... othy ... ...

33(10)71—**Dorothy May Zell,** born May 1, 1903, at Philadelphia

33(10)72—**Lucian Mitchel Zell, Jr.,** born Apr. 9, 1906, at East Orange, N J

34—**Sarah Thompson,** born 1783, in Pfoutz Valley, in what is now Perry County, Pa , died March 7, 1862 in the 79th year of her age; buried beside her husband in the Lost Creek Cemetery near McAlisterville, Juniata County, Pa She married on Nov 2, 1802, William McAlister (born Aug, 1775, in Lost Creek Valley, Juniata County, Pa , died Dec. 21, 1847 in the 73rd year of his age), son of Hugh and Sarah (Nelson) McAlister and grandson of Hugh and ————— (Harbison) McAlister, Scotch Protestants, who emigrated from the north of Ireland to America in 1732 settling first in Little Britain Township, Lancaster County, Pa, and later in Tyrone Township in what was then Cumberland and is now Perry County, Pa Hugh McAlister, Jr, was born in 1736 in Little Britain Township, Lancaster County, Pa In 1758 he enlisted in Forbes campaign for the capture of Fort DuQuesne—on the present site of Pittsburgh After his return home from that campaign he married Sarah Nelson of Lancaster County, Pa, and settled first on a farm, near what is now Icksburg, in Sherman's Valley, which he sold to his brother John In 1762 he moved to land he had bought in Lost Creek Valley, Juniata County, Pa, named by him, "Hugh's Fancy" He fought against the Indians in Pontiac's War in 1763 He served as private soldier, sergeant, lieutenant and captain at different times during the Revolution and at about the close of the war was commissioned major—see 34524 Major Hugh McAlister died Sept 22, 1810, and was buried beside his wife in the Lost Creek Cemetery. His record in the Colonial Wars and in the Revolutionary War has been compiled by his great-granddaughter, Mrs Henrietta Graham (McAllister) Baldwin —3452 To her are indebted not only the descendants of Sarah (Thompson) McAllister, but also those of the other branches of the Thompson family, for much pains-taking care in the collection of a great amount of thoroughly reliable information relating to the Thompson and kindred families living along the Juniata and the adjacent country in the "Old Colonial Days," 1754-1764 William McAlister, son of Hugh and Sarah (Nelson) McAlister, was born at "Hugh's Fancy" in Juniata County, in Aug, 1775 Papers now in the possession of his descendants show that he served as paymaster of the 83rd Pennsylvania Regiment in 1812 and 1814 On March 4, 1842 he was appointed one of the two associate Judges of Juniata County, and he served as a trustee of the Lost Creek Presbyterian Church for forty years Children of William and Sarah (Thompson) McAlister, (1) Jane Thompson, (2) Nancy, (3) Hugh Nelson, (4) Thompson, (5) Robert, (6) Elizabeth (7) William, (8) son unnamed, (9) George Washington

341—**Jane Thompson McAllister (' Jean")**, born Dec. 27, 1803, at the McAllister homestead near McAllisterville, Pa , died July 29, 1880 She was
married by Rev John Hutchinson, on Apr 10, 1827, to David Banks,
of Juniata County Pa, son of Andrew and Elizabeth (Lintner)
Banks and grandson of James and Anna (Small) Banks, and of
Christian Lintner, all of Fermanagh Township, near Mifflintown, Pa.
James Banks was born 1732, probably in the town of Ayr, the son of
Hugh Banks, of Ayrshire Scotland. He emigrated to America with
his wife Anna (Small) Banks, settling at New London Cross Roads
Chester County, Pa. James Banks served for two years, 1756-7, in
Captain William Clinton's company of volunteers under the command
of Colonel George Washington In 1758 he enlisted in the army of
General Forbes against Fort Duquesne In 1772 he purchased a tract
of 172 acres in Lost Creek Valley, Juniata County, Pa, from William
Sharon Andrew Banks, his son, who was born in York County, Pa
Jan 12, 1767, and died Dec. 28, 1855 in Lost Creek Valley, was for
many years ruling elder in the Lost Creek Presbyterian Church.
David Banks, his son, who was born May 23 1798 in Juniata County,
and died Mar. 6, 1870, served from 1856 to 1861 as one of the associate judges for Juniata County See "History of Juniata and Susquehanna Valleys in Pennsylvania." p 824-830 Issue (1) James Andrew, (2) William (3) David Stewart, (4) John Edmund, (5) Robert
Edwin, (6) John Nelson, (7) Lucien.

3411—**James Andrew Banks**, born Jan 17, 1828 Went to California in
1853 Served in the Legislature of that State two terms and in the
State Senate one term Came within one vote of being elected U S
Senator He was elected first president of the Young Men's Christian
Association of San Francisco He was killed by Indians in Nevada,
Aug. 1, 1867, while managing mining interests there Never married

3412—**William Banks**, born Mar 12, 1830, died Oct 18, 1914, aged 85
years at Mifflintown, Pa He was for many years an elder in the
Mifflintown Presbyterian Church Married on Oct 1, 1861 Jane
Elizabeth Hamlin, daughter of Dr Philo and Rebecca (North) Hamlin and granddaughter of Darling and Elizabeth (Doty) Hamlin, all
of Mifflintown, Pa. Issue (1) William Hamlin, (2) James Alonza,
(3) Andrew, (4) Ella Kate, (5) Philo Hamlin, (6) Rebecca Jane,
(7) Annie May.

34121—**William Hamlin Banks**, born in Fermanagh Township, Juniata
County, Pa, Nov 16, 1862. Graduated from the medical course at
the University of Pennsylvania, 1889 Under President Cleveland's
second administration he held the office of examining surgeon for
United States pensions Dr Banks is a director of the Mifflintown
& P   the

organizers, and is a director of the Fermanagh Building and Loan Association He is a practicing physician in Mifflintown, Pa. Married Oct 27, 1892 Bessie Jacobs Parker, daughter of Robert E and Catharine (Jacobs) Parker and granddaughter of Caleb Parker, all of Mifflintown, Pa Issue (1) Robert Parker, (2) Jane, (3) William Hamlin, (4) Catharine Jacobs, (5) Hugh McAllister.

341211—Robert Parker Banks, born Oct. 20, 1893

341212—Jane Banks, born Nov 15, 1894

341213—William Hamlin Banks, born July 17, 1896.

341214—Catharine Jacobs Banks, born Feb 6, 1899

341215—Hugh McAllister Banks, born June 5, 1901

34122—James Alonza Banks, born Oct 15, 1864 Druggist, Mifflintown, Pa

34123—Andrew Banks, born Mar 21, 1866 Graduated from Princeton University, 1889 Corporal U S. A., Philippines Co. I, Tenth Pa Vols Infantry. Enlisted April, 1898, honorably discharged, San Francisco, May, 1899 Lawyer District Attorney two terms He is secretary of the Thompson Family Association Address, Mifflintown, Pa

34124—Ella Kate Banks, born May 6, 1868 Married Dec 31, 1891, at Mifflintown, Pa John Howard Neely (born Sept 7, 1858 in Tuscarora Township, Juniata County, Pa), son of John Neely (born June 6, 1814, died May 30, 1892) and Margaret Jane (Ewing) Neely (born Nov 20, 1831, in Perry County, Pa). The grandparents of J Howard Neely were John and Margaret (McFeaters) Neely and William and Sarah (Allison) Ewing His great-grandfather, William Neely lived in his boyhood near the present town of Roxbury, Franklin County, Pa, but later settled in Lack Township, Juniata County, Pa He married Sallie Harvey of Path Valley, Franklin County, Pa William Neely, was a member of the Presbyterian Church at Waterloo, Juniata County, Pa His land in Lack Township, which he had purchased from the Indians, was held in the Neely family until 1873 His son John Neely, born in Lack Township, Juniata (then Cumberland) Co, Pa, June 20, 1774, died Aug. 5, 1846, on a farm in Tuscarora Township, same county, which is now owned by one of his descendants John Neely, Jr, the father of John Howard Neely, was born and died on a farm in Tuscarora Township, Juniata County, Pa He was a member of the Middle

Tuscarora Presbyterian Church J Howard Neely graduated from Princeton University in 1884, and was given the advanced degree of H M by this university in 1887 Since July, 1886, he has been practicing law at Mifflintown, Pa From 1891 to 1894 he served as district attorney Issue (1) Lucien Banks, (2) John Howard, (3) William Hamlin, (4) Helen, (5) Elizabeth Banks (6) Margaret Banks

341241—**Lucien Banks Neely,** born Mar 3, 1893, died Nov 29, 1893, Mifflintown, Pa

341242—**John Howard Neely,** born Nov 22, 1894, Mifflintown, Pa. Graduated from Princeton University degree, A B, 1916

341243—**William Hamlin Neely,** born Feb 2, 1896, Mifflintown, Pa Graduated from the Harrisburg Academy, 1913 Princeton University, 1917

341244—**Helen Neely,** born Dec. 27, 1899, Mifflintown, Pa

341245—**Elizabeth Banks Neely** (twin), born Sept 21, 1902, Mifflintown, Pa

341246—**Margaret Banks Neely** (twin), born Sept 21, 1902, Mifflintown, Pa

34125—**Philo Hamlin Banks,** born Sept 30, 1870, in Fermanaugh Township, Juniata County, Pa, died Nov 23, 1901, at New Orleans, La, buried at Mifflintown, Pa After a course at the Mifflin Academy, he entered the Jefferson Medical College of Philadelphia, Pa, and graduated from that institution in the class of 1901 After graduation, he served for a short time as resident physician at the Jefferson Hospital The Boer war was going on at this time and he was appointed as physician and surgeon on the "Montcalm," an English merchant vessel plying between New Orleans and South Africa On the return trip of his first voyage, he contracted typhoid fever and died at New Orleans

34126—**Rebecca Jane Banks,** born July 18, 1872 Married June 30, 1896, Ezra Doty Parker, son of E Southard and Isabella (Wilson) Parker of Washington, D C, and grandson of Andrew and Ann E. (Doty) Parker of Mifflintown, Pa Ezra D Parker is a banker at Washington, D C Issue (1) Edmund Southard, (2) Helen Wilson.

341261—**Edmund Southard Parker,** born May 30, 1897

341262—**Helen Wilson Parker,**

34127—**Annie May Banks,** born July 14, 1879, died May 10, 1880

3413—**David Stewart Banks,** born Jan 10, 1832, died July 13, 1898, at
Santa Cruz, Cal   B A. Lafayette College, Pa, 1856, and Princeton
Theological Seminary 1859   Presbyterian minister, held pastorates at
Saxton near Altoona, Pa, Easton, Pa, Marquette, Mich, Santa
Cruz, Cal, and elsewhere   Unmarried

3414—**John Edmund Banks,** born Oct 31, 1834, died April 7, 1837.

3415—**Robert Edwin Banks,** born June 29, 1837, died of typhoid fever at
Jefferson College, Pa, April 17, 1858

3416—**John Nelson Banks,** born May 3, 1839   Received the degree of
Bachelor of Scientific Agriculture from the Agricultural College of
Pennsylvania in 1861 and the degree of Master of Scientific Agricul-
ture in 1865   His room-mate at college was his first cousin William
Miller McAllister (3443) who left school to join the Southern army
while J N Banks entered the Northern army   J N Banks has been
a practicing lawyer since 1866   Address, Indiana, Pa   He married
on Jan 23, 1873, Huella Willson, daughter of David and Lucinda
(DeVane) Willson of Allegheny County, Pa, and granddaughter of
Hugh and Margaret (Pearce) Willson   Issue (1) William, (2)
Annie

34161—**William Banks,** born Jan. 23, 1874   Lawyer, Indiana, Penn   Married on Aug. 3, 1904, Carrie Zelma Sweeny, daughter of William
A———————— and Caroline (Lucas) Sweeny of Indiana, Pa, and
granddaughter of John and ———————— (Piffle) Sweeny. Issue
(1) William Nelson, (2) Roxanne, (3) Lucile

341611—**William Nelson Banks,** born Jan 11, 1906.

341612—**Roxanne Banks,** born Aug 31, 1909

341613—**Lucille Banks,** born Jan 25, 1911

34162—**Annie Banks,** born July 8, 1877   Married Sept 19, 1906, Charles
Austin Cunningham, son of David Austin and Emma Moore (Smith)
Cunningham, Indiana, Pa, and grandson of George B————————
and Nancy (George) Cunningham   Address, Banker, Cresson, Pa
Issue (1) John Banks

341621   John Banks Cunningham, born Feb 8, 1908

3417—Lucien Banks, born Jan 13, 1841, died Aug 3, 1907, at Mifflintown, Pa He attended Tuscarora and Airy View Academies and graduated at the University of Pennsylvania Medical College in the class of 1868 and located at Mifflintown, Pa, remaining there in active practice until his death He served as surgeon of the Pennsylvania Railroad Co throughout substantially his professional career. In 1887, he was elected President of the Juniata Valley Medical Society He always took an active part in the politics of his native county and was elected to the State Legislature in 1879 At the time of his death, he was a director of the Juniata Valley National Bank of Mifflintown, Pa, and a stock holder of the First National Bank of the same place and was also president of the Mifflintown-Patterson Water Co

342—Nancy McAlister, born Jan 17, 1807, died Sept. 28, 1807.

343—Hugh Nelson McAllister, born at the homestead in Lost Creek Valley, Pa, June 28, 1809 Graduated from Jefferson College, Pa, 1833 Attended the law school of Judge Reed at Carlisle, Pa Distinguished lawyer of Bellefonte, Pa Member of law firm of Potter & McAllister (1835-1850) and McAllister & Beaver (1850-1873) He first wed Henrietta Ashman Orbison, daughter of William and Eleanor (Elliott) Orbison, Huntington, Pa William Orbison (born June 27, 1777, in York County, Pa, died Aug 23, 1857, in Huntingdon, Pa) was a son of Thomas and Elizabeth (Bailey) Orbison and a grandson of Thomas and Elizabeth (Miller) Orbison and of Benjamin and Elizabeth Bailey Thomas Orbison, Sr, who was born near Lurgan, Ireland, about 1715, came to America about 1741 settling first in Franklin County, Pa, and later in Peter's Township, Cumberland County, Pa, where he died in March, 1779 His wife whom he married on Oct. 19, 1744, was a daughter of James Miller of New Castle, Del Eleanor (Elliott) Orbison was a daughter of Benjamin Elliott by his second wife Sarah Ashman and a grandson of Robert Elliott and of George and Jemima (Murray) Ashman Robert Elliott who was of Irish ancestry died in Peters Township, Cumberland County, Pa, in 1768 George Ashman was a son of John and Constance (Hawkins) Ashman and a grandson of George Ashman who was born prior to 1660 in Lymington County, Wiltshire, England, and came to America about 1670, settling first in Calvert County, Md On Nov 30, 1694, he received a grant from King William III of 500 acres in what was then Cecil County, which he called "Ashman's Hope" About 1687 he married Elizabeth Trahearne, widow of William Cromwell When he died in 1699 he willed "Ashman's Hope" to his son John—see Biographical Encyclopedia of Juniata Valley, Pennsylvania, pp 1-16 By his first wife, Mrs Henrietta Ashman (Orbison) McAllister, Hugh Nelson McAlli~ . . . . The first M . W. A . . . . he married Margaret Hamilton, of Harrisburg, daughter of Hugh and Rosanna (Whiteside) Hamilton, Harrisburg, Pa, and granddaughter of Captain John Hamilton, under whom his grandfather, "Major Hugh" McAllister, had served in the Revolution During the War of 1861-5 Mr McAllister did more than any one man to raise and organize the many companies which left his (Centre) county He finally raised a full company (Co F, 231d Pa Militia), was elected its captain and went with it to the field, serving faithfully until his place could be filled by a younger man He was one of the projectors and constant supporters of the (now) Pennsylvania State College ("McAllister Hall" there is named in his honor), elder in the Bellefonte Presbyterian Church and one of the most learned of the fourteen delegates at large of the Pennsylvania Constitutional Convention. He died in Philadelphia as a member of that body May 5, 1873 (see "Constitutional Convention, McAllister Memorial") Children of H N and Henrietta Ashman (Orbison) McAllister, (1) Mary Allison, (2) Ellen Elliott, (3) son, (4) William Orbison, (5) Sarah Banks, (6) Laura, (7) Nelson

3431—**Mary Allison McAllister,** born at Bellefonte, Pa, Sept 26, 1842 Married on Dec 26, 1865, James Addams Beaver (born at Millerstown, Pa, Oct 21, 1837, died at Bellefonte, Pa, Jan 31, 1914), son of Jacob and Ann Eliza (Addams) Beaver and grandson of Rev. Peter and Elizabeth (Gilbert) Beaver and of Abraham and Lydia (Miller) Addams Abraham Addams was a son of Isaac and Barbara (Ruth) Addams, a grandson of William and Anna (Lane) Adams and of Peter and Catherine (——————) Ruth, and a great-grandson of Richard Adams and of Edward and Ann (Richardson) Lane Lydia Miller was the daughter of Jacob and Elizabeth (Feather) Miller, granddaughter of Peter and Marie (Levan) Feather, a great-granddaughter of Isaac and Mary Margaret Levan and great-great-granddaughter of Daniel and Marie (Beau) Levan—see 344 Rev Peter Beaver's father was George Beaver, a soldier in the Revolution and a member of Anthony Wayne's fourth battalion of the Pennsylvania line, he served in the Revolutionary war in 1776 and 1777 and afterwards as a captain of Associators in Berks County, in 1778 He was a son of George Beaver, a German of French-Huguenot influence who came to America in 1740 with his father Peter Beaver from Elsess, Germany, and settled in Berks County, Pa George Beaver, Jr, married Katharine Kieffer, a daughter of Dewalt and Hannah (Fox) Kieffer, and lived and died at Upper Strasburg, Franklin County, Pa, after the war See "Biographical Encyclopedia of Juniata Valley," pp 1283 and 1291 James Addams Beaver was the junior law partner of his wife's father—343 He graduated from Jefferson College, Cannonsburg, Pa, 1856 (LL D. Dickinson, Pa, and Hanover, Ind, 1889, and University of Edinburgh, Scotland) Admitted to bar in 1858 Practiced at Bellefonte, Pa, 1859-1861 Second

Lieutenant, Second Pennsylvania Infantry, April 21, 1861; Lieutenant
Colonel Forty-fifth Infantry, Oct 21, 1861, Colonel One Hundred
and Forty-eighth Pennsylvania Infantry, Sept 6, 1862 Brevet Brigadier General Volunteers "for highly meritorious and distinguished
conduct throughout the campaign, particularly for valuable service at
Cold Harbor while commanding a brigade, honorably discharged
Dec 22, 1864, shot through body Chancellorsville, May 3, 1863, shot
in side Petersburg, Va, June, 1864; lost a leg at Ream's Station
Aug 24, 1864" Resumed law practice at Bellefonte Was Major
General Pennsylvania National Guards 1870-78 Governor of Pennsylvania 1887-91 Judge of Superior Court of Pennsylvania, 1896-
1914 President, Board of Trustees Pennsylvania State College, Vice-
Moderator Presbyterian General Assembly 1888 and 1895 Member
of the President's Commission for investigating the War Department, 1898 Delegate to the General Missionary Conference, Edin-
burgh, 1910—See "Who's Who in America," "International Who's
Who in the World" Address of Mrs James A Beaver, Bellefonte,
Pa Issue (1) Nelson McAllister, (2) Gilbert Addams, (3) Hugh
McAllister, (4) Thomas, (5) James Addams, Jr

34311—Nelson McAllister Beaver, born Nov. 11, 1866; died Jan 8, 1867

34312—Gilbert Addams Beaver, born Jan 1, 1869 B S Penn State Col-
lege 1893 Served for years as secretary of the International Com-
mittee of the Y M C A, and later as secretary of the College Board
of the Presbyterian Church, U S A Address, Yorktown Heights,
N Y Married on May 12, 1896, Anne Simonton, daughter of John
Wiggins and Sarah (Kunkel) Simonton John W Simonton was
Judge of the Court of Dauphin County, Pa He was a son of
William and Martha (Snodgrass) Simonton and grandson of Dr
William and Jean (Wiggins) Simonton of West Hanover Township,
Dauphin County, Pa Issue (1) Katharine Simonton

343121—Katharine Simonton Beaver, born Nov 10, 1897.

34313—Hugh McAllister Beaver, born Mar 29, 1873. Graduated from
Pennsylvania State College, B. S 1895 He was college secretary
of the Y M C. A of the State of Pennsylvania, serving with
marked distinction Died at Bellefonte, Pa, August 2, 1897 Unmarried —See "A Memorial of a True Life,' by Robert E Speer

34314—Thomas Beaver, born Apr. 8, 1875 Business and farming, Belle-
fonte, Pa Married on Feb 1, 1913 at Bellenfonte, Pa, Millicent
Prince (born March 21, 1890), daughter of Wyrley William and
Rachel (McAfee) Prince and granddaughter of Stephen Fair
Prince and William Vance Iar A in

343141—James Addams Beaver, son of Thomas Beaver, born Mar 11, 1914, at Bellefonte, Pa

34315—James Addams Beaver, Jr, son of James Addams Beaver, Sr., born Dec 26, 1883, died at the Executive Mansion, Harrisburg, Pa, Jan 22, 1887

3432—Ellen Elliott McAllister, born Apr 18, 1846, at Bellefonte, Pa, died Aug 18, 1866

3433—Son, unnamed, born Bellefonte, Pa, Apr. 1, 1848; died the same day

3434—William Orbison McAllister, born June 9, 1849, at Bellefonte, Pa; died Feb 26, 1850

3435—Sarah Banks McAllister, born Apr 2, 1851, at Bellefonte, Pa Married Dec 28, 1871. Dr Thomas Renick Hayes, of Bellefonte, Pa, son of Robert Goodloe Harper and Esther Renick (Foster) Hayes and grandson of John and Margaret (Gray) Hayes and great-grandson of Robert and Margaret (Wray) Hayes and of Capt Gray of the Revolution, and great-great-grandson of Patrick Hayes who came to Dauphin County, Pa, from County Donegal, Ireland in 1725 Dr Thomas R Hayes died Dec. 27, 1913 at Atlantic City, N J Residence of Mrs Sarah (McAllister) Hayes, Bellefonte, Pa No children

3436—Laura McAllister, born Jan 5, 1855, at Bellefonte, Pa., died Apr. 11, 1855

3437—Nelson McAllister, born Apr. 12, 1857, at Philadelphia, died Apr. 15, 1857

344—Thompson McAllister, born Aug 30, 1811, at the old homestead in Lost Creek Valley, Juniata County, Pa; died March 13, 1871 at "Rose Dale" Covington, Va Married on Feb 14, 1839, Lydia Miller Addams (born Feb 11, 1819, at Millerstown, Pa, died Feb 3, 1902 at "Rose Dale") daughter of Abraham and Lydia (Miller) Addams of Millerstown, Perry County, Pa —see pamphlet on "Eightieth Anniversary of Lydia Miller (Addams) McAllister" and "In Memoriam—Lydia Miller (Addams) McAllister," by J Gray McAllister The ancestor of the present America family of Addams (name originally spelled Adams) came to this country from England about 200 years ago and acquired ownership of land in Pennsylvania The records show that on Dec 22, 1681, William Penn deeded 500 acres in the Province of Pennsyl-
. . . . of Ledwell in Oxfordshire, England " (The

name was spelled Addams on the map of the territory) The will of
Robert Adams, dated July 27, 1717 and probated June 6, 1719 refers
to his nephew Richard Adams. Richard Adams was a son of John
Adams, who was living in 1717 In the will of Richard Adams of
what was then Philadelphia County, but is now Montgomery County,
Pa, dated Feb 1, 1747-8, and probated March 24, 1747-8, mention
was made of ten children including William, who was referred to
in the papers of the executors as of Brecknock Township, Lancaster
County, Pa This son William Adams founded Adamstown in Lancaster County, Pa, in 1761 He married Anna Lane, a daughter of Edward and Ann (Richardson) Lane Edward Lane was an Englishman
who came from Jamaica in 1684 and purchased on Dec 12, 1698-9, 25,-
000 acres from Thomas Fairman which was confirmed to him by patent
in 1701 by William Penn When he died in 1710, leaving seven children
including William and Ann—not then married—his son William became owner of that part of the property lying east of the Perkiomen,
218 acres of which he deeded to Richard Adams on Feb 9, 1722 The
youngest son of William and Anna (Lane) Adams was Issac Addams
(the additional having been reinserted, it is said, to distinguish him
from a cousin of the same name), who married Barbara Ruth, daughter of Peter (died Sept, 1771) and Catherine Ruth, of German ancestry Isaac Addams was captain of the Fourth Company of Associators in the Ninth Battalion under Col John Huber The youngest
of the six sons of Isaac and Barbara (Ruth) Addams was Abraham
Addams As a young man he was a merchant in Reading, Pa He
moved, about 1811, to Perry County, Pa, and bought the land on
which Millerstown is built He was a member of one of the most
important courts of the State He was thrice married First, to Lydia,
daughter of Jacob and Elizabeth (Feather) Miller, of Reading Elizabeth Feather was the daughter of Peter and Marie (Levan) Feather,
granddaughter of Isaac and Mary Margaret Levan and great-granddaughter of Daniel and Marie (Beau) Levan, Huguenots who fled from
France to Amsterdam, Holland, and subsequently, in 1715, came to
America and settled in Exeter Township, Berks County, Pa See "The
Addams Family in America," "The Ruth Family" and "The Levan
Family," by Addams S McAllister After his marriage to Lydia M
Addams, Thompson McAllister moved to the farm "Spring Dale," in
Franklin County, Pa, seven miles from Chambersburg, later deeded to
him by his father He was elected member of the Pennsylvania Legislature in 1847 He moved to Covington, Va, in Dec, 1849 having purchased a 2,200-acre tract and built "Rosedale" the Virginia homestead
in 1856-7 He and his younger brother Robert—345—spent much time
together "studying military tactics, were always connected with military
companies, and were both fond of drilling" Thompson formed, and
was made captain of an artillery company near the homestead in Juniata Coun
tain of an

the brothers, under the firm name of T McAllister & Co, were building the approach to Lewis tunnel (section 18 on what was then the Covington & Ohio, now the Chesapeake and Ohio Railroad) between Lewis and Alleghany tunnels on the crest of the Alleghanies, Thompson being in charge of the work In March, 1861, Thompson raised and at his own expense, largely equipped the first volunteer company, for the impending war, in Alleghany County or in that part of Virginia, and was made its captain This company, organized and drilled for the purpose of being placed at the disposal of Virginia, whatever side the State might espouse, became Company A, Twenty-seventh Infantry, of the original "Stonewall Brigade"; Captain McAllister was the oldest (and his son William the youngest) member of the company At the First Manassas battle both were wounded His favorite brother and business associate, Colonel (afterwards General) Robert McAllister commanded the First New Jersey in the same battle, one of two regiments (First and Second New Jersey) that threw their columns across the road at Centerville and finally arrested the retreat that the Stonewall Brigade, more than any other, had brought to pass (See "Sketch of Captain Thompson McAllister," by J Gray McAllister) Camp fever and large, unsettled business interests necessitated, in August, 1861, the resignation of his command (furlough being denied) In the fall of 1861 he was placed in command of all the home-guards and reserves in the Alleghany section, continuing in this service throughout the Civil War He was for many years an elder of the Covington Presbyterian Church Children of Thompson and Lydia M (Addams) McAllister (1) Clara Biddle, (2) Abraham Addams, (3) William Miller, (4) Edgar Thompson, (5) Annie Elizabeth

3441—Clara Biddle McAllister, born Dec. 8, 1839, at "Spring Dale," Franklin County, Pa ; died May 28, 1869 at Covington, Va Married on Sept 29, 1859 at "Rose Dale" Covington, Va, Dr Gabriel McDonald (born May 10, 1827 at Lynchburg, Va, died Sept 22, 1889, near Union, Monroe County, W. Va, buried beside his wife at Covington, Va), son of James and Mary (Jordan) McDonald and grandson of Daniel McDonald and of Thomas and Ann (Withers) Jordan Gabriel McDonald graduated from Hampden Sidney College and subsequently studied medicine at Jefferson College, Philadelphia, receiving the degree of M D He entered the confederate service in 1861, as surgeon of the Twenty-second Virginia Regiment and served for four years, being at the close, division surgeon under General Breckenridge He served continuously as a member of the West Virginia State Board of Health and the State Board of Examiners from the enactment of the laws creating these bodies He was a practicing physician with office at Union, Monroe County, W Va, at the time of his death Children of Dr Gabriel and Clara (McAllister) McDonald (1) Mary Jordan, (2) Willie May, (3) James Addams, (4) Abram Graham

34411—Mary Jordan McDonald, born Nov 12, 1860, died Feb 15, 1862.

34412—Willie May McDonald, born Sept. 19, 1864   Married at "Rosedale,"
Covington, Va, Oct 27, 1915 Capt Samuel Wilberforce Anderson
(born Apr 8, 1836 in Nelson County, Va) son of Robert H and
Susan (Kimbrough) Anderson, grandson of Robert Nelson and
——————— (Spencer) Anderson, and of Joseph and Mary (Nancy)
Kimbrough and great-grandson of John Anderson, Scotchman who
was a Colonel in the Revolutionary War   Samuel Wilberforce
Anderson was commissioned, by Governor Letcher of Virginia, cap-
tain to organize troops for the state line   See 34421   Address of
Samuel W and W May (McDonald) Anderson, Warm Springs,
Va

34413—James Addams McDonald, born Sept 22, 1867, died Aug 6 1868

34414—Clara Gabriella McDonald, born May 11, 1869   Married Nov 2,
1892, at "Rosedale," Covington, Va, Thomas Evred Buck (born Jan
9, 1860, at Front Royal, Va, died Jan 21, 1911, at Lenoir City,
Tenn), son of William Mason and Elizabeth Ann (Ashby) Buck
of Front Royal, Va, and a grandson of William Richardson and
Lucy Neville (Blackmore) Buck   William Richardson Buck was
a son of Capt Thomas and Ann (Richardson) Buck, a grandson of
Charles and Lettitia (Lord) Buck of England, and of William and
Isabella (Calmes) Richardson of Maryland and a great-grandson
of the Marquis De La Calmes, a Huguenot refugee who settled on
the Shenandoah in Virginia   Lucy Neville (Blakemore) Buck was
a daughter of Capt George Neville and Elizabeth (Mauzey) Blakemore, a granddaughter of Thomas and Annie (Neville) Blakemore
and of John Mauzey, a great-granddaughter of George and Mary
(Gibbs) Neville and of Col Henry Mauzey   Thomas Buck, who
was captain of a volunteer company at the close of the Revolution,
was twice high sheriff of Frederick County, Va   He built and
occupied Bel Air homestead on the Shenandoah   Col Henry Mauzey
was Washington's companion in surveying the Northern Neck of
Virginia   Elizabeth Ann (Ashby) Buck was a daughter of William
R and Rebecca Richardson (Buck) Ashby, a granddaughter of
Rev Nathaniel Ashby of Fanquier County, Va, and Lexington, Ky,
and of Thomas and Ann (Richardson) Buck, and a great-granddaughter of Capt John Ashby, Indian fighter   T Evred Buck was a
merchant at Lenoir City, Tenn   Address, Mrs Clara McDonald
Buck, Covington, Va   Children, (1) William McDonald, (2) Evred
Johnson, (3) Frank Speed, (4) Thomas Ashby, (5) Lawrence
Neville.

344141—William McDonald Buck
        Address W McD

344142—Evred Johnson Buck (twin), born June 11, 1895, died Aug. 1, 1896, at Radford, Va.

344143—Frank Speed Buck (twin), born June 11, 1895, died July 27, 1896, at Radford, Va.

344144—Thomas Ashby Buck, born Dec, 1903, at Lenoir City, Tenn

344145—Lawrence Neville Buck, born Aug 28, 1905, at Lenoir City, Tenn

3442—Abraham Addams McAllister, born Aug. 25, 1841, at "Springdale," Franklin County, Pa; died Sept. 4, 1916 at Covington, Va He enlisted 1862 in the Confederate Army in "The Monroe Artillery," soon known as "Bryans Battery, later a part of the Thirteenth Battalion of Virginia Artillery He was successively corporal and sergeant of the Battery, participating in every battle in which the battery was engaged except that of Cedar Creek, Oct 19, 1864, when he was absent on sick leave He was mustered out with the battery at Christiansburg, Va, on Apr 12, 1865 A Addams McAllister was the senior partner of the milling firm of McAllister & Bell, Inc, and president of the firm of A A McAllister and Sons Company, Inc, Covington, Va He was for many years president of the Covington Improvement Company and was president of the Citizens' National Bank, Covington, Va, 1908-12, and director of the Covington National Bank He was a successful and scientific farmer, and owned a controlling interest in a number of enterprises in and near Covington He was an elder in the Covington Presbyterian Church See "McAllister Family Records," by J Gray McAllister On May 10, 1865, at Covington, Va A Addams McAllister married Julia Ellen Stratton (born June, 1838, in Malden, Kanawha County, Va, died Nov 23, 1906 at "Rosedale," Covington, Va), daughter of Joseph Dickinson and Mary Ann (Buster) Stratton, and granddaughter of Archibald and Edna (Dickinson) Stratton and of Claudius and Nancy (Moffet) Buster, the great-granddaughter of Henry and Sarah (Hampton) Stratton, of Joseph and Elizabeth (Wooldridge) Dickinson, of Claudius and Dorcas (Sumpter) Buster and of Thomas and Elizabeth (Johnson) Moffet; the great-great-granddaughter of Thomas and Elizabeth (Elam) Stratton, of William and Jane (Woods) Buster, of Col Philip and Ann (—————) Johnson. See "The Buster Family" and "The Dickinson Family," by Addams Stratton McAllister The Stratton line has been traced back to England through Edward Stratton (1) of Bermuda Hundred, Va, whose son Edward (II) married Martha Shippey daughter of Thomas Shippey Edward Stratton (III) who married Anna Batte, daughter of Henry Batte was the father of Thomas Stratton, who married Elizabeth Elam, daughter of Robert Elam, and the grand-

father of Henry Stratton (a lieutenant in the naval service during
the Revolutionary War), who married Sarah Hampton, mentioned
above See "A Book of Strattons," by Hattie R Stratton Jane
(Woods) Buster was a daughter of Michael and Ann Woods, a
granddaughter of Michael and Mary (Campbell) Woods, and a
great-granddaughter of John and Elizabeth (Worsop) Woods Elizabeth Worsop was a daughter of Thomas and Elizabeth (Parsons)
Worsop and a granddaughter of Richard and Letitia (Loftus) Parsons Letitia Loftus was a daughter of Sir Adam Loftus and his
wife Jane Vaughn, a daughter of Walter Vaughn, of Coldingrove
Sir Adam Loftus was a son of Sir Dudley Loftus and his wife Ann
Bagnal, daughter of Henry Bagnal, of Newry Sir Dudley Loftus
was a son of Archbishop Adam Loftus and his wife Jane Purdon,
daughter of T Purdon Adam Loftus, born 1534 in Yorkshire, England, the son of Right Reverend Edward Loftus, of Levinhead, was
ordained Archbishop of Dublin and made Lord Chancellor of Ireland during Queen Elizabeth's reign See the "Woods-McAfee
Memorial," by Rev Neander Woods See 3445I. On Aug 18, 1908,
A Addams McAllister married, second, Nettie B Handley (born
Dec. 2, 1857 near Kansas City, Mo , died Oct 24 1912 at Covington, Va), daughter of Harrison and Susan Margaret (Mann) Handley, of Covington, Va, granddaughter of John and Elizabeth (Shanklin) Handley, and of Moses Hamilton and Alice (McClintic) Mann,
of Alleghany County, Va, and great-great-granddaughter of Moses
and Mary (Kincaid) Mann, and of William and Keziah (Cailes)
Handley, great-great-granddaughter of William and Jane (Hamilton) Mann and of David and Alberdina Cailes The will of William
Mann, dated Feb. 3, 1778, was recorded in Botetourt County, Va,
Nov , 1778 The will of David Cailes, dated Apr 25, 1786, was recorded July 17, 1787, in Augusta County, Va No issue. Mr McAllister married, third, on May 2, 1916, at Milboro, Va, Mrs Mary Lewis
(Handley) Tyree, widow of Edward Tyree and a cousin of his
second wife. She is a daughter of Austin and Elizabeth (Bell)
Handley, a granddaughter of John and Elizabeth (Shanklin) Handley, and of Joseph G W and Harriet (Dickinson) Bell, a great-
granddaughter of William and Keziah (Cailes) Handley, of Joseph
and Mary Ann (Nelson) Bell and of Adam and Martha (Brown)
Dickinson; a great-great-granddaughter of David and Alberdina
Cailes, of Joseph and Elizabeth (Henderson) Bell, of Alexander
and Ann (Matthews) Nelson; of John and Martha (Usher) Dickinson, and of Samuel and Elizabeth (Gratton) Brown, and a great-
great-great-granddaughter of Joseph Bell of Lancaster County, Pa ;
Sampson and Catherine Matthews of Ireland, of Adam and Catherine (Stevenson) Dickenson, of Lancaster County, Pa , of Edward
and Aminta (Perry) Usher, of England, of William and Jean
Brown, A   .   ·   _ a
County \   M M   ı   -   ʒ ı ... · -   · of

9

Mrs Margaret Ann (Erwin) McAllister—3443. Children of A Addams and Julia E (Stratton) McAllister (1) Joseph Thompson, (2) Mary Lydia, (3) William McDonald, (4) James Gray, (5) Addams Stratton, (6) Clara Annie, (7) Hugh Moffet, (8) Julian Robert

34421—**Joseph Thompson McAllister**, born Feb 27, 1866, at Malden, W. Va Graduated from Hampden-Sidney College, B A, 1889, University of Virginia, LL B, 1891 He is a lawyer with office at Hot Springs, Va He is president of the Hot Springs Valley Investment Co, the Alleghany Land Co, etc He has made a large collection of material on the Virginia militia in the Revolutionary War and is recognized as the best authority on that subject in America This material has been issued in book form under title "Virginia Militia in Revolutionary War" He assisted Secretary Reuben G Thwaite, of the Wisconsin Historical Society, in collecting data for "The Dunmore War," and has been a contributor to the "Virginia Magazine of History," and to the "West Virginia Historical Magazine" He issued his "Historical Sketches of Hot Springs and Bath County, Va." in 1908, and character sketches, "Humor in Ebony," in 1911, "Virginia Militia in the Revolution," 1913, and Index to Saffell and Palmer, 1913 He was a trustee of Hampden-Sidney College from 1896 to 1910 See "Who's Who in America" Married first on Apr 18, 1893, at Warm Springs, Va, Virginia Richards Anderson, daughter of Captain Samuel Wilberforce and Virginia (Richards) Anderson of Warm Springs, Va Captain Anderson, born in Nelson County, Va, Apr 5, 1836, organized the first company that left Nelson County for the Civil War, but turned the actual command of it over to a friend, and was soon elected Captain of the Nineteenth Virginia Infantry His father was Robert H Anderson, of Nelson County, Va, son of Robert Nelson Anderson and ———— (Spencer) Anderson, and his mother was Susan Kimbrough, daughter of Joseph and Mary (Yancey) Kimbrough—See 34412 Children of Joseph T and Virginia (Anderson) McAllister (1) Joseph Thompson, Jr, (2) Jean Graham Joseph T McAllister, Sr, married, second, on Apr 8, 1916, at Caldwell, N. J, Marjorie Roosevelt Leaycraft (born Feb 6, 1886, New York City), daughter of Charles Russell and Mary Leontine (Roosevelt) Leaycraft, granddaughter of Jeremiah and Sarah (Griffin) Leaycraft and of Samuel and Mary Jane (Horton) Roosevelt, a great-granddaughter of Nicholas and Lydia (Latrobe) Roosevelt and of Stephen Horton, a great-great-granddaughter of Jacobus and Annatje (Bogert) Roosevelt and of John Henry Latrobe Annatje Bogert was a daughter of John and Hannah (Peck) Bogert; a granddaughter of Claas and Beeltje (Van Schaick) Bogert and of John and Elizabeth (Van Imbroch) Peck, a great-granddaughter of Jan and Cornelia (Everts) Bogert, and of Dr Gysbert and

Rachel (Montauge) Van Imbrock, a great-great-granddaughter of
Lowens Bogert, of Schoenderwoert, a small village in the south of
Holland. Jacobus Roosevelt (who was the father of Jacobus Roosevelt, Jr, the grandfather of Theodore Roosevelt, Sr, the father
of Ex-President Theodore Roosevelt, Jr.), was the son of Johannes
Roosevelt and his wife Heyltje Sjoerts, daughter of Capt Albert
and Margaret (Clopper) Sjoerts, a grandson of Nicholas Roosevelt and his wife Heyltje Jans Kunst, daughter of Cornelius and
Jan (Barentsen) Kunst, and a great grandson of Claes Martensen
Van Rosenvelt, who with his wife Jannetje Samuels Thomas came
from Zeeland to New Amsterdam in 1649 Child of J T and Marjorie Roosevelt (Leaycraft) McAllister, (3) Meriel Roosevelt

344211—*Joseph Thompson McAllister, Jr*, born Mar 24 1894, at Warm
Springs, Va Attended Cluster Springs Academy 1911-14 and 1915-
16 He died Feb 4, 1917, at Denver, Col, buried at Warm Springs,
Va

344212—*Jean Graham McAllister*, born Dec 6, 1897, at Warm Springs,
Va Graduated from Saint Anne's School, Charlottesville, Va,
1917 Address Hot Springs, Va

344213—*Meriel Roosevelt McAllister*, born July 3, 1917, at Hot Springs,
Va

34422—*Mary Lydia McAllister*, born Sept. 7, 1868, at Covington, Va,
died Oct 9, 1888, at Covington, Va. She attended the Lewisburg
(W Va) Seminary. Married on Nov 29 1887, at Covington, Va.,
Frank Holloway Hammond, son of Col George Wilson Hammond
(C. S A) and Emma Mason (Scott) Hammond, of Covington, Va

34423—*William McDonald McAllister*, born Jan 15, 1871, at Covington,
Va Attended Fishburne Military School President of the Covington Hardware & Furniture Company, Inc, president of the
Virginia Hot Springs Valley Orchard Company, vice-president of
the Virginia Fruit Growers' Association, Vice-president of the Covington National Bank, and President of the Covington Grocery Company. He married first on Sept 23, 1895, at Lewisburg, W Va.
Annie Virginia Harlow, daughter of Benjamin Franklin and Henrietta Clay (Renick) Harlow Benjamin F Harlow, son of Henry
Martin Harlow, was for some years one of the editors of the
"Farmer's Friend," at Union, Monroe County, W Va ; from 1855
to 1858 was editor of the "Greenbrier Era," and was for about a
year in Memphis, Tenn, on the "Daily Bulletin" of that place He
returned to Lewisburg in 1858 . . . . which
he continued until the break . . . . war, when he enlisted

in the Greenbrier Cavalry. On May 11, 1862, he was taken prisoner and confined in Camp Chase until the following fall, when he was exchanged, returned to his regiment, and was in service until the close of the war From June, 1866, to Sept. 2, 1887, he was editor and publisher of the "Greenbriar Independent," of Lewisburg After selling out the "Independent," he gave his attention to farming and stockraising. He was elected mayor of Lewisburg many times, three times a delegate to the Democratic National Convention, twice a member of the State Legislature, holding the latter position at the time of his death He served on the staff of Gov Wilson with the title of Colonel Children of William McD and Virginia (Harlow) McAllister (1) Franklin Addams, (2) Mary Lydia William McD McAllister married, second, on May 16, 1915, at Washington, D C, Mrs Willa Catharine (Skeen) Garrett, widow of Harvey Lincoln Garrett, of Covington, Va, daughter of Robert and Lucy Ellen (Montague) Skeen, and granddaughter of General William Skeen and of Justice James M Montague, of Alleghany County, Va Gen Wm Skeen, who was born in Rockbridge County, Va, and resided in Covington, Va, for many years prior to his death in 1893, aged 75 years, was a son of Robert and Polly (Hart) Skeen James M Montague was a son of William and Judith (Street) Montague of Cumberland County, Va, and a grandson of Thomas and Jane (Daniel) Montague of Powhatan County, Va Thomas Montague was a descendant of Peter Montague, who came to James City, Va, in 1621 and served as a member of the House of Burgesses, 1651-8 Child of William McD and Willa Catherine (Skeen), McAllister, (3) Ellen Montague

344231—**Franklin Addams McAllister,** born July 17, 1896, at Covington, Va "Frank" McAllister attended school at Lewisburg, W. Va.

344232—**Mary Lydia McAllister,** born Nov 13, 1897, at Covington, Va She attended school at Lewisburg, W Va, and Brownsburg, Rockbridge County, Va, and Mary Baldwin Seminary, Staunton, Va, contralto soloist

344233—**Ellen Montague McAllister,** born Feb. 20, 1916, at Philadelphia, Pa

34424—**James Gray McAllister,** born Nov. 27, 1872, at Covington, Va Graduated from Hampden Sidney College, B A, 1894, Union Theological Seminary, Richmond, B D, 1901 He was given the degree of D D by Washington and Jefferson College, Pa, and the Central University of Kentucky in 1906 He was editor of the *Bath County News* at Warm Springs, Va, 1894 5, business manager of the *Central ... from* Richmond, Va 1897 8, assistant professor of

Hebrew at the Union Theological Seminary, 1902-3, pastor of Farm-
ville (Va) Presbyterian Church, 1903-4; adjunct professor of
Hebrew, Union Theological Seminary, 1904-5, president of Hampden-
Sidney College, 1905-8, supplied Hot Springs (Va) Presbyterian
Church 1908-9 Since 1909 he has been teaching in the Presby-
terian Theological Seminary of Kentucky, Louisville, of which since
1911 he has been professor of Biblical Introduction, English Bible
and Biblical Theology Residence, 1133 Cherokee Road, Louisville,
Ky (See "Men of Mark in Virginia"; "Men of America",
"National Cyclopedia of American Biography", "Who's Who in
Louisville," and "Who's Who in America" He married on May 18,
1904, in Winchester, Va, Meta Eggleston Russell, daughter of Isaac
William and Sarah Henrietta Elizabeth (Eggleston) Russell, granddaughter of Isaac and Eliza (Baker) Russell and of Rev William
George and Frances Sanford (Muse) Eggleston, and great-granddaughter of David and Hannah (Greenway) Russell, of James and
Magdalen (Warden) Baker, and of Robert and Elizabeth Muse
The wife of David Russell (who was a son of Richard Russell who
left Holland, 1732, in the "City of London" and purchased land from
the Indians in the Wyoming Valley in Pennsylvania) was a daughter
of William and Mary (Stevens) Greenway who came to America
from Scotland and lived at Greenway Manor, Va See "Family
Records Compiled for the Descendants of I W and S E Russel,"
by J Gray McAllister. Children of J Gray and Meta (Russell)
McAllister, (1) James Gray, (2) Russell Greenway, (3) Sarah
Louise.

344241—James Gray McAllister, Jr, born Nov. 1, 1907, at Hampden-Sidney, Va

344242—Russell Greenway McAllister, born July 20, 1911, at Winchester,
Va

344243—Sarah Louise McAllister, born Apr 7, 1913, at Louisville, Ky

34425—Addams Stratton McAllister, born Feb 24 1875, at Covington, Va
Graduated from the Pennsylvania State College, B S 1898, and
E E 1900; Cornell University, M M. E 1901 and Ph D 1905 Instructor in the departments of physics and electrical engineering,
Cornell University, 1901-5, professorial lecturer on electrical engineering, Pennsylvania State College, 1909-12, associate editor of the
Electrical World, New York City, from 1905 to 1912; editor 1912-15,
consulting engineer 1915— Inventor of alternating-current machin-
ery, author of "Alternating-Current Motors," an electrical engineering college text-book, and of Chapters 6 and 8 of the "Standard
Hand ck ʃ E⟩ . T⟩ . ." Ti s 1-? C m⟩.r of
geneaﬞ tes for M Mﬞ. , ⟩ V ⟩ L D ⟩ ﬞ.ter

and associated families; member of the National Genealogical Society, the Pennsylvania Historical Society, president of the New York Electrical Society 1917-8, president of the Illuminating Engineering Society, 1914-15; vice-president of the American Institute of Electrical Engineers, 1917-8 See "Cyclopedia of Virginia Biography," "National Cyclopedia of American Biography," "Who's Who in Science," "Who's Who in New York" and "Who's Who, in America" Unmarried Address, 261 West 23rd St, New York, N Y

34426—Clara Annie McAllister, born Mar 17, 1877, at Covington, Va, died Aug 12, 1903, at Covington, Va Attended the Lewisburg (W Va) Seminary and the Cincinnati (Ohio) Conservatory of Music Married on Oct 16, 1901, at Covington, Va, George Wellford Call, son of Manfred and Sallie Elizabeth (Watt) Call of Richmond, Va, and grandson of Moses Call of New Hampshire and Sarah Elizabeth (Bryant) Call of Maine No issue

34427—Hugh Moffet McAllister, born Apr. 7, 1879, at Covington, Va Graduated from Hampden-Sidney College, B A 1902 He was associate editor of the *Clifton Forge* (Va) *Review,* June to October, 1902, reporter for the Newport News (Va) *Times-Herald,* July to November, 1903, and April to November, 1904, associate editor *Petersburg Trade Journal,* now *The American Fruit and Nut Journal,* November, 1903 to April, 1904 From November, 1904, to August, 1907, he was bookkeeper for the McAllister Hardware & Furniture Co, Covington, Va, August, 1907, to December, 1909, cashier, Covington Savings Bank, December, 1909, to October, 1910, bookkeeper for the McAllister (now the Covington) Hardware & Furniture Co Since October, 1910, he has been partner and secretary-treasurer of the firm of Julian R McAllister & Co, Covington, Va He is also secretary of the A A McAllister & Sons Co He was for some years a deacon of the Covington Presbyterian Church and its treasurer He married on Jan 3, 1907, at Southside, Mason County, W Va, Evalene Long, daughter of James Washington and Catherine Ann (Hannan) Long The pioneer Long ancestor was Philip Long who came from Lorraine, Germany, settling first in Pennsylvania and after a short time locating permanently, 1720, in Page County, Va His estate has been handed down to Lee Long of the sixth generation Philip Long's son was named Paul, his son was named Philip His son, Adam, married Anna Rosenberger of Rockingham County, Va Their son George Long married Emily Kirk Sterrett of Point Pleasant, W Va, and their son was James Washington Long, father of Evalene (Long) McAllister The father of Emily Kirk Sterrett was William Sterrett, of Point Pleasant, W Va, and her mother was Agnes Bell, of Augusta County, Va The Sterrett ancestors came from Pennsylvania and originally

from Scotland The Hannans came from Cork, Ireland Thomas
Hannan, of Augusta County, Va, married Elizabeth Henry of the
family of Patrick Henry Their son Henry married Rhoda Henderson, of Henderson, W Va, and their daughter Catherine Ann
Hannan is the mother of Evalene (Long) McAllister Henry, son
of Thomas Hannan, was born in the Fort at Point Pleasant William
Henderson married Margaret Bruce Both lived in Scotland Their
son James Henderson, born in Scotland, married Martha Hamilton,
of Virginia Their son Lieutenant John Henderson, of Augusta
County, Va, fought in the battle of Point Pleasant, October 10,
1774 His wife was Anne Givens Their son, Colonel John Henderson of Greenbrier County, (now) W Va, married Elizabeth Stad-
gill, of Greenbrier County, W Va, and their daughter, Rhoda Henderson married Henry Hannan Colonel John Henderson served in
various offices of the county and state He represented his district
for eighteen years consecutively in the State Legislature Children
of Hugh M and Evalene (Long) McAllister, (1) Catherine Ellen,
(2) Clara Long, (3) Emily Ann, (4) Hugh Nelson, (5) James
Addams

344271—Catherine Ellen McAllister, born Aug 31, 1908, at Covington, Va.

344272—Clara Long McAllister, born Jan 23 1910, at Covington, Va.

344273—Emily Ann McAllister, born Aug 28, 1911, at Covington, Va

344274—Hugh Nelson McAllister, born Oct 18, 1913 at Covington Va

344275—James Addams McAllister, born Dec 16 1915, at Covington, Va

34428—Julian Robert McAllister, born Nov 21, 1881 at Covington, Va
He was for several years a member of the firm of McAllister & Call,
general merchants, Covington, Va, and is now of the firm of Julian
R McAllister & Co and treasurer of A A McAllister & Sons Co,
Inc He married on Oct 7, 1908, at Oak Grove near Savannah, Al-
leghany County, Va, Anna Gertrude Massie, daughter of Captain
Hezekiah William and Emma Judson (Ryals) Massie This branch
of the Massie family goes back to Captain Thomas Massie (Col-
onist) who married a Miss Bland and died before 1740 Their son
William married Lucy Macon The son of William and Lucy
(Macon) Massie was Major Thomas Massie (born Aug 11, 1747, at
"Bottoms Bridge," New Kent County, Va) married Sallie Cocke
(born March 8, 1761, at "Turkey Island," on the James River; died
April 20, 1838, at "Level Green," Nelson County, Va) In the spring
of 1775 Major Massie was chosen Captain of a large Company of
Voh   ·   ··   _   ons
agai -ı   ·   ·   · | ·   vas

commissioned captain to recruit regulars to serve in the Virginia Regiment of the line on continued establishment and marched it to Williamsburg in the Spring of 1776 He then went with its regiment to the North, where he saw service under General Washington, he himself for two succeeding years being usually on detached or particular service On Feb 20, 1778, he was promoted to the rank of major "He acted alternately under the commands of Generals Scott, Weedon, Sullivan, Morgan, Woodford, Lord Sterling and others, and was afterwards under the command of General Nelson as aid-de-camp in the winter of 1780-81, when Arnold invaded Virginia and destroyed the public stores and houses at Richmond He was at the siege of Yorktown and the surrender of that post with the British army, in October, 1781 " (See affidavit of Major Thomas Massie, Feb 15, 1833) He died Feb 2, 1834, at his home "Level Green," Nelson County, Va. His son Captain Henry Massie was born Oct 16, 1784, he married on May 18, 1826, Elizabeth Rutherford Daggs, of Hot Springs, Va, and died at "Oak Grove," Jan 12, 1841 Their son Captain Hezekiah William Massie, the father of Gertrude (Massie) McAllister, was born on Oct 21, 1834, at "Oak Grove," where he died Aug 23, 1905 He was captain of Company G, Twenty-second Virginia Infantry Child of Julian R and Gertrude (Massie) McAllister (1) Gertrude Massie

344281—Gertrude Massie McAllister, born Oct 6, 1909, at "Rose Dale," Covington, Va.

3443—William Miller McAllister, born Mar 6, 1843, at "Spring Dale," Franklin County, Pa Leaving the (now) Pennsylvania State College at the outbreak of the Civil War, he enlisted on April, 1861, as youngest in his father's company (Company A, 27th Virginia, Stonewall Brigade) This company was later transformed into the famous "Carpenters Battery" and in this he served until the close of the war (See his "War Diary," typewritten) Graduated in law at University of Virginia, 1869 Married on October 27, 1869, Margaret Ann Erwin, daughter of James Robertson and Martha (Dickinson) Erwin, of Bath County, Va, and granddaughter of William and Margaret (Robertson) Erwin, of Augusta County, Va, and of Col Adam Dickinson and of Martha (Brown) Dickinson, daughter of Col. Samuel Brown of Greenbrier County, W. Va, by his wife Elizabeth, daughter of John Gratton The parents of Col Samuel Brown were William and Jean Brown Martha Robertson was the daughter of Col James Robertson and Margaret (Poage) Robertson and a granddaughter of Robert and Elizabeth Poage who came from Ireland about 1737 and settled near Staunton, Augusta County, Va Robert Poage was a member of the first county court of Augusta County. Col Adam Dickinson was a son of Col. John Dickinson (born, 1731; died, 1790) and Martha (Usher), daughter of Edward and Amitha

(Perry) Usher, and grandson of Adam Dickinson (by his wife Catherine, daughter of Adam Stevenson) who moved from Lancaster County, Pa, to Virginia in 1742 and became one of the first justices for Augusta County, and died in 1760 William M McAllister is a lawyer, business man and farmer He was an attorney for the Commonwealth of Bath County, 1874-1884, special attorney for the U. S. Department of Justice, headquarters Tennessee, 1893-8, member of the Board of Directors Western State Hospital, Staunton, Va 1886-90, and of the Board of Visitors, Virginia Military Institute Member of the Virginia Legislature Dec, 1899-Jan 1, 1902 and active in securing the Constitutional Convention (and thus a progressive constitution) for Virginia Bank Director and officer, president Bath Telephone Company since its organization in 1899 Has been engaged in farming and stock-raising since 1876 Commander Bath Camp Confederate Veterans, elder, Warm Springs Presbyterian Church since 1869—see "Men of Mark in Virginia," 1908 Adress Warm Springs, Va

3444—**Edgar Thompson McAllister**, born Oct. 30 1848, at "Spring Dale," Franklin County, Pa He was a member of the Home Guards during the Civil War, being too young to enter the regular army Married twice, first on Oct 20, 1874 in Alleghany County, Va, Alice Cavendish Mann; died Oct 18, 1895, in Alleghany County, Va, daughter of Moses Hamilton and Alice (McClintic) Mann and granddaughter of Moses and Mary (Kincaid) Mann and great-granddaughter of William and Jane (Hamilton) Mann who married in Scotland and emigrated to America in 1730—See 3442 Children of Edgar T and Alice (Mann) McAllister (1) Alice Miller, (2) William Addams. Edgar T McAllister married, second, on Jan 26, 1898, at Covington, Va, Clementine Dysard of Greenbrier County, W Va. No issue Edgar T McAllister lived for years on his farm near Master's, Alleghany County, Va He died at Covington, Va, Oct 20, 1914

34441—**Alice Miller McAllister**, born Apr. 16, 1877, in Alleghany County, Va

34442—**William Addams McAllister** ("Will Add"), born May 16, 1879, in Alleghany County, Va Graduated from Hampden-Sidney College, B A 1901 Address, W A McAllister, Ivor Stone Company, Carntown, Ky Married on June 7, 1909 at Danville, W Va, Archie Bessie Hopkins, daughter of John William and Nannie (McNeely) Hopkins and granddaughter of Henry Halbert and Julia Ann (Hill) Hopkins and great-granddaughter of Henry Sheldon and Sallie (Edwards) Hopkins of Halifax County, Va The father of Henry Sheldon H prins or '_ ' ', n E _'..! a' 1t 1750. Ch,'l of W A and Ach (Hopkin- M. M....(1) Eliza'eth Hopkins

344421—Elizabeth Hopkins McAllister, born June 3, 1910, at Danville, W.
Va

3445—Annie Elizabeth McAllister, born June 6, 1850, at Covington, Va
Married on Dec 17, 1873, at "Rosedale," Covington, Va , Joseph Root
England (born Nov 29, 1842 in Frederick County, Md , died Jan 22,
1912 at Covington, Va), son of Nathan and Harriett (Root) England
of Carroll County, Md and grandson of John and ————— (Townson) England of Carroll County, Md and great-grandson of Nathan
and ————— (Hargrave) England of Frederick County, Md and
of Dr. Townson of Baltimore, Md   John England was a lieutenant
in the Revolutionary Army   Nathan England was a member of the
committee to welcome Lafayette at Frederick City, Md   Joseph R
England was educated at the Mount Hope Academy, Frederick
County, Md , and took the degree of D D. S in Baltimore, 1866   He
practiced dentistry in Virginia and West Virginia   He enlisted in
June, 1863 at Hagerstown, Md in Company D, Fourteenth Virginia
Cavalry, Jenkins Brigade, Confederate Army, serving until his com-
pany was disbanded in April, 1865   He was elder in the Covington
(Va) Presbyterian Church   For many years until his death he en-
gaged in farming at Covington, Va   Children of Joseph R , and
Annie (McAllister) England (1) Lydia Miller, (2) Harriet Elizabeth,
(3) Charles Thompson, (4) William McAllister, (5) Clarence Mc-
Donald, (6) Twin daughter, (7) Frank Addams, (8) Mary Kyle

34451—Lydia Miller England, born June 21, 1875, at "Rosedale," Covington, Va   Married on Oct 3, 1899 at "Rosedale," John William Ruff,
son of William Alexander Anderson and Mary Elizabeth (Moore)
Ruff and grandson of John Milschleggel and Martha (Wallace) Ruff
of Lexington, Va , and great-grandson of Jacob and Barbara (Milschleggel) Ruff and of Samuel and Rebecca (Anderson) Wallace
Samuel Wallace (born 1745; died March, 1786) was a colonel in the
Revolutionary Army   He was in command of Fort Young on the
Virginia frontier during the French and Indian War   He was a son
of Peter and Martha (Woods) Wallace and a grandson of Peter
and Elizabeth (Woods) Wallace and of Michael and Mary (Campbell) Woods   The parents of both Elizabeth Woods and Michael
Woods were John and Elizabeth (Worsop) Woods   Elizabeth Worsop was a daughter of Thomas and Elizabeth (Parsons) Worsop and
a granddaughter of Richard and Letitia (Loftus) Parsons   Letitia
Loftus was a daughter of Sir Adam Loftus and his wife Jane
Vaughn, daughter of Walter Vaughn   Sir Adam Loftus was a son
of Sir Dudley Loftus of County Dublin, Ireland and his wife Ann
Bagnal, daughter of Henry Bagnal of Newry   Sir Dudley Loftus
was a son of Archbishop Adam Loftus and his wife Jane Purdon,
daughter of J Purdon   Archbishop Loftus was born in York-

shire, England, in 1534, the son of the Right-Reverend Edward
Loftus He was ordained in 1559, and was rapidly promoted by
Queen Elizabeth, being made Archbishop of Armagh when only 27
years old, and subsequently Archbishop of Dublin and Lord Chancellor of Ireland—see the "Woods-McAfee Memorial" by Rev Neander
der M Woods—see 3442 J William Ruff is president of the Bluefield Hardware Company, and the Logan Hardware Company Address, Bluefield, W Va. Children of J William and Lydia (England) Ruff, (1) Lydia Miller, (2) John William, (3) Annie Elizabeth, (4) Louise Kyle, (5) Joseph England, (6) Charles Sheffey,
(7) Wallace McAllister.

344511—Lydia Miller Ruff, born Jan 3, 1901, at Covington, Va , died July
17, 1904 at Covington

344512—John William Ruff, Jr, born Mar. 30, 1905, at Bluefield, W Va.

344513—Annie Elizabeth Ruff, born Oct 22, 1906, at Bluefield, W Va.

344514—Louise Kyle Ruff, born Apr 2, 1908, at Bluefield, W. Va

344515—Joseph England Ruff, born Aug 6, 1909, at Bluefield, W. Va.

344516—Charles Sheffey Ruff, born Nov 19, 1910, at Bluefield. W. Va.

344517—Wallace McAllister ("Mack") Ruff, born June 4, 1912, at Bluefield, W Va

34452—Harriet Elizabeth (Hattie) England, born Sept. 8, 1876, at "Rosedale," Covington, Va Married on Nov 22, 1906, at Covington, William Franklin Bevill, son of Benjamin Wyatt and Sarah Elizabeth
(Kea) Bevill and grandson of William Franklin and Sarah Anne
(Glover) Bevill of Alabama, and of Zacharia Kea of North Carolina, and great-grandson of Thomas Kea of England William F
Bevill, Jr, is secretary and treasurer of the Logan (W. Va) Hardware Co

34453—Charles Thompson England, born Apr 1, 1878, at Covington, Va
Engaged in railway contracting work, Washington, D C Married
on Dec. 15, 1912, at Washington, D C, his cousin Hattie England,
daughter of James W and ————— (Hendry) England and
granddaughter of Nathan and Harriett (Root) England, a great-
granddaughter of John England and a great-great-granddaughter of
Natl an Engl nd of Frederick County Md Sec 3..5 Address
1437 Irving St W sh n i C

34454—William McAllister ("Mack") England, born Apr 3, 1880, at Covington, Va   Attended Hampden-Sidney College 1899-1900   With the Covington Machine Co from 1902 until 1910   With the Oliver Chilled Plow Co. 1910-11.   Died May 7, 1912, at Covington, Va   Unmarried

34455—Clarence McDonald England (twin), born Mar 19, 1882, at Covington, Va   Vice-president of the Logan (W Va) Hardware Co   Married on Dec 22, 1909, Alma Hines, daughter of William Adolphus and Lucy Catherine (Hatchett) Hines of Danville, Va, granddaughter of Henry Davidson Hines of Hinesville, Va, and Celestia Mandwell (Robertson) Hines, originally of Pleasant Gap, Va, and great-granddaughter of Colonel Thomas J Hines of Whilewell, Va, and Frances (Petty) Hines, originally of Halifax County, Va   Children of Clarence and Alma (Hines) England, (1) Katherine McAllister, (2) Annie Elizabeth, (3) Clarence McDonald

344551—Katherine McAllister England, born May 29, 1911, at Logan, W Va.

344552—Annie Elizabeth England, born Feb 19, 1913, at Logan, W Va

344553—Clarence McDonald England, Jr., born May 2, 1916, at Logan, W Va

34456—Daughter, ———— England (twin), born Mar 19, 1882, at Covington, Va , died that day unnamed

34457—Frank Addams England, born Apr. 18, 1884, at Covington, Va   office manager, Oliver Chilled Plow Co, Memphis, Tenn   Married on June 5, 1912, at Clifton Forge, Va, Eva Nair, daughter of Charles Perry and Frances (Burger) Nair and granddaughter of George William and Margaret Jane (Tardy) Nair of Rockbridge County, Va, and great-granddaughter of William Nair from Germany, who located first at Germantown, Pa., and later in Rockbridge County, Va   Issue (1) Eva Nair, (2) Mary Margaret

344571—Eva Nair England, born July 14, 1915, at Chattanooga, Tenn.

344572—Mary Margaret England, born Sept. 7, 1916, at Clifton Forge, Va.

34458—Mary Kyle England, born July 16, 1886, at Covington, Va   Graduated Lewisburg (W. Va) Female Seminary   Married on June 25, 1913, at Covington, Va, Burns Oscar Severson (born Dec 9, 1887), son of Henry Severson (born Jan 21, 1857) and of Mary Olive (Halverson) Severson (born April 2, 1856, at Stoughton, Wis) and grandson of Helga Severson (1796-1856) who came to America

from Norway in 1842 and was one of the pioneer settlers near
Stoughton with his wife Berget (Osen) Severson (born 1818 in
Telemarken, Norway, and grandson of Steven Halverson (born
1822 in Telmarken, Norway) who came to America in 1845 with
his wife Ducas (Evans) Halverson (born 1823 in Telmarken, Norway). B O Stevenson received the degree of B S. from the University of Wisconsin, 1910, and M S from the Pennsylvania State
College, 1915   He is associate professor of Animal Husbandry at
the Pennsylvania State College, State College, Pa.

345—**Robert McAllister,** born June 1, 1813, at "Hugh's Fancy," the old
homestead in Lost Creek Valley, Juniata County, Pa   Married on
Nov 9, 1841 Ellen Jane Wilson (of Mercersburg, Franklin County,
Pa), daughter of Moses Wilson of Hanover Township, Dauphin
County, Pa, and his second wife Elizabeth (Boyd) Wilson, daughter
of Benjamin Boyd, of Derry Township, same county, a farmer of
Scotch-Irish descent, and a member of the Derry Presbyterian Church
The parents of Moses Wilson were Hugh Wilson and Mary (Wilson)
Wilson, daughter of Moses Wilson of Lancaster County, Pa   The
founder of this Wilson family in America was William Wilson, who
emigrated about 1730 from the north of Ireland (whither his ancestors
had emigrated from Scotland) and settled at the junction of the
Swatana and Manarda Creeks, Hanover Township, in what is now
Dauphin County, Pa, but was then Lancaster County   He died in
1736 and is buried in the graveyard of the historic Derry Presbyterian Church, as are also his son, Hugh Wilson, his grandson Hugh
Wilson, and his great-grandson Moses Wilson, father of Ellen Jane
Wilson, in the line given above   They were all farmers and Presbyterians   Moses Wilson was an elder in the Derry Presbyterian
Church   Robert and Ellen (Wilson) McAllister moved in 1842 into
the new house he had built on part of the old "Hugh's Fancy" homestead farm.   He engaged in farming until he began railroad construction work in 1847, and even then supervised the farm until 1854,
when he moved to Bethlehem, Pa, thence in 1857, to Oxford, N J,
where he was building a tunnel three thousand feet long for the Delaware, Lackawanna & Western Railroad (and he was also partner in
railway construction work with his brother Thompson McAllister—
344—in Virginia) at the outbreak of the Civil War. Always interested
in military affairs, he had held while living in Pennsylvania several
commissions in the militia service of that state, the last of which was
from 1854 to 1859 as Brigadier-General in command of the Brady
Brigade, of the uniformed militia of Pennsylvania. When the Civil
War broke out he raised a company at Oxford, N J, went to Trenton,
was commissioned by Governor Olden a Lieutenant-Colonel in the
First New Jersey Regiment and commanded it with rare distinction
at Firs M   . .   ed
Colone   \   .   ng

Colonel to the command of the First Brigade, Second Division, Third
Corps, to which his regiment was attached" He was one of the very
few men who went through the war from its inception to its close,
being present at Bull Run and Appomattox Court House, respectively,
without missing any of the pitched battles (except South Mountain
and Antietam) of the Army of the Potomac, to which he was attached from first to last. He was brevetted Brigadier-General for his
behavior at Boydton Plankroad, Oct 27, 1864, and Major-General for
meritorious conduct throughout the war. A monument was erected
to his command at Gettysburg, the Eleventh Regiment, New Jersey
Volunteers, where he was severely wounded, a minie ball going through
the left leg and a piece of shell hitting the right foot In the second
day of the Battle in the Wilderness, in 1864, two horses were killed
under him and he was hit by a fragment of a spent shell. General
De Trobriand says of him "As punctual in his religious habits as he
was sincere in his belief, he had Protestant religious services regularly
on Sunday at his headquarters The most pleasant attention we
could pay him on that day was to listen to the sermon of his Chaplain" (See sketch of Gen. Robert McAllister, by General John Watts
De Peyster, from "Representative Men") After the war General
McAllister was general manager of the Ironton Railroad Company,
and resided from 1866-1883 in Allentown, Pa Thence he returned
to Belvidere, N. J., where he died Feb. 23, 1891 His widow died in
Mifflintown, Pa, July 8, 1905 Children of Robert and Ellen (Wilson)
McAllister (1) Sarah Elizabeth, (2) Henrietta Graham

3451—**Sarah Elizabeth McAllister,** born Jan 6, 1843, at "Hugh's Fancy,"
Lost Creek Valley, in Juniata County Pa Married on Aug 13,
1863, at Belvidere, N J (where Col McAllister was recuperating
from wounds received at Gettysburg), Wilson Loyd (born Jan. 7,
1841, in Philadelphia, died Sept 9, 1914, in Mifflintown, Pa. Buried
in the Mifflintown Presbyterian Cemetery) son of William and
Elizabeth Bellerby (Spackman) Loyd, of Philadelphia, and grandson of Thomas and Sarah (Smith) Loyd, and of Samuel Spackman
and Ann (Bellerby) Spackman The Loyds were Quakers. (The
other l in the name, dropped by Thomas Loyd to avoid confusion
with a cousin of the same name, has been resumed by the children
of Wilson and Sarah Loyd Wilson Loyd attended Penn Charter
School and Nazareth Hall He conducted a banking and brokerage
business in Philadelphia until 1882, when impaired health necessitated
a change and in 1883 Wilson and Sarah (McAllister Loyd moved
from Germantown, Philadelphia, to "Hugh's Fancy," where they
lived until the Fall of 1911, when they sold the farm and moved to
Mifflintown, Pa Children of Wilson and Sarah (McAllister) Loyd
(1) Robert McAllister, (2) Elizabeth Spackman, (3) Thomas Wilson, (4) Nelson McAllister, (5) William Henry

34511—**Robert McAllister Lloyd**, born June 14, 1864, at Elizabeth, N J Attended Germantown (Pa) Academy, and took a special course in electrical engineering at Lehigh University, 1885 He organized and managed a number of manufacturing enterprises and has held positions in the following companies President of the Plante Co, subsequently sold to the Electric Storage Battery Co, of Philadelphia, President of the Electric Vehicle Co, President of Siemens & Halske Co of America, sold to the General Electric Co, Treasurer of the Electric Boat Co, the Electric Launch Co and the Electro-Dynamic Co, President of the Vehicle Equipment Co, Vice-President of the Appert Glass Co; Vice-President and General Manager of the General Vehicle Co, Long Island, N Y Since 1913 he has been a consulting engineer with office at 1700 Broadway, New York City He served in Squadron A, N G N Y, from 1895 to 1900 He is a member of the Institution of Electrical Engineers in Great Britain, the Society of Automobile Engineers of the United States, the Automobile Club of America, the Dum Tum Club of New York, and the Piping Rock Club at Locust Valley, Long Island He married on Sept 30, 1896, at Huntington Bay, L I, Janet Maitland Belknap, daughter of Robert Lenox and Mary Phoenix (Remsen) Belknap, and granddaughter of Aaron Better and Jennet Lenox (Maitland) Belknap, and of Henry Rutgers and Elizabeth Waldron (Phoenix) Remsen Issue (1) Robert McAllister, (2) Jennet Remsen, (3) Gwendolyn

345111—**Robert McAllister Lloyd, Jr**, born Jan 12, 1898, at New York City

345112—**Jennet Remsen Lloyd**, born Oct 10, 1905, at Cold Spring Harbor, L I

345113—**Gwendolyn Lloyd**, born Sept 12, 1907, at Syosset, L. I

34512—**Elizabeth Spackman Lloyd**, born Nov 27, 1866, at Germantown, Pa Married on Sept 6, 1898 at "Hugh's Fancy" near McAllister-ville, Pa, George Calbraith Clarke (born on Jan 16 at Pittsburgh, Pa) son of Robert Alexander and Henrietta Maria (Calbraith) Clarke and grandson of Rev David Duncan Clarke, D D and Mary Eleanor (Cochrane) Clarke and of George Harris and Maria Cromwell (Reynolds) Calbraith, great-grandson of Samuel and Mary (Duncan) Clarke and great-great-grandson of Robert and ——— (Wier) Clarke Mary Eleanor Cochrane was a daughter of Robert and Margaret (Blackford) Cochrane and granddaughter of Patric and Mary (Eachus) Cochrane George Harris Calbraith was a son of George and Hannah (Harris) Calbraith Maria Cromwell Reynolds . . . . of R . . and Henrietta Maria (Cromwell) Reynolds . . . . . C C . . . . C E . . r . . he

Pennsylvania State College in 1902 He was employed as a civil
engineer by the Pennsylvania Railroad Company for 20 years, and
was resident engineer for the Union Station, Pittsburgh, and the
Pennsylvania Terminal, New York, when they were being built He
is now secretary-treasurer of Fraser, Brace & Co, 1328 Broadway,
New York; Vice-president of Fraser, Brace & Co, Ltd, of Montreal,
and president of the Hydrolithic Waterproofing Co Inc Residence,
Richmond Hill, Long Island, N Y Issue (1) Elizabeth, Lloyd, (2)
George Calbraith

345121—Elizabeth Lloyd Clarke, born Apr 25, 1900, at Philadelphia, Pa

345122—George Calbraith Clarke, Jr., born Feb. 2, 1902, at Pittsburgh, Pa.

34513—Thomas Wilson Lloyd, born June 16, 1869, at Germantown, Philadelphia, Pa Vice-president of the importing firm of Jonas &
Naumberg, furriers, New York City Residence, Short Hills, N J
Married on May 16, 1900 at Chapel of General Theological Seminary, New York, Elizabeth Wheatly Jewett, daughter of Rev Edward
Hurt Jewett, D. D, LL D—Professor of Pastoral Theology at
the General Theological Seminary, New York—and Sophia Seymour
(Miller) Jewett, granddaughter of John Hurt and Katharine (Stanley) Jewett of Nottingham, England, and of Judge Rutger Bleecker
and Mary Forman (Seymour) Miller of Utica, N Y, great-granddaughter of Judge Morris Seymour and Maria (Bleecker) Miller of
New York City Maria Bleecker was the daughter of Rutger and
Catharine (Elmendorf) Bleecker of Albany, N Y Mary Foreman
Seymour was the daughter of Henry and Mary Ledyard (Foreman)
Seymour; granddaughter of Maj Moses and Mollie (Marsh) Sey-
mour, great-granddaughter of John and Rachael (Goodwin) Seymour, great-great-granddaughter of John and Elizabeth (Webster)
Seymour; great-great-great-granddaughter of John and Mary (Wat-
son) Seymour, great-great-great-great-granddaughter of Robert and
Mercy (————) Seymour Major Moses Seymour (born in
Hartford, Conn, July 23, 1742) was present at the surrender of Bur-
goyne in Oct, 1777. Issue (1) Thomas Wilson.

345131—Thomas Wilson Lloyd, Jr, born Jan 31, 1906, at Short Hills, N. J.

34514—Nelson McAllister Lloyd, born Dec 18, 1872, at Germantown, Phil-
adelphia, Pa Graduated from the Pennsylvania State College, 1892
For several years he was city editor of the New York *Evening Sun.*
Author of numerous short stories in the leading magazines and of
the following books "A Chronic Loafer," "A Drone and a
Dreamer," "The Soldier of the Valley," "Mrs Radigan," "The Rob-

berries Company, Ltd.," "Six Stars." See "Who's Who in New York," "Who's Who in America." Residence, Syossett, L I, N Y Married on April 4, 1908, in Florence, Italy, Susanne Livingstone Green (born 1879; died Feb 25, 1913 in New York City) daughter of Charles Ewing and Mary Livingston (Potter) Green of Trenton, N J Granddaughter of Henry Woodhull and Susan Mary (Ewing) Green and of William Woodburn and Margaret (Fox) Potter. Henry Woodhull Green was chancellor and chief justice of the State of New Jersey for 25 years Susan Mary Ewing was a daughter of Chief Justice Ewing Mrs Susanne Livingston (Green) Lloyd was a member of the Colonial Dames of America Issue (1) Nelson McAllister, (2) Charles Ewing Green

345141—**Nelson McAllister Lloyd, Jr**, born Apr 7 1909, at New York City

345142—**Charles Ewing Green Lloyd**, born Feb 25, 1913 in New York City

34515—**William Henry Lloyd**, born June 16, 1877, at Germantown, Pa When the Spanish-American War started he was studying medicine in New York City and was a member of the First Battalion, New York Naval Reserves In April, 1898, he enlisted with his battalion in the U S Navy and served five months on a five-inch gun on the "Yankee" at Santiago, Trinida, Guantonamo and Corsilda He graduated at University of New York and Bellevue Hospital Medical College, 1900 Six months post-graduate study in Paris Appointed to Medical Staff, Correction Department, Blackwell's Island, Jan, 1901, and served two years Went to Mexico in 1903 Was surgeon for two gold mining companies in Durango till 1908, when he went to the Hahualilo Cotton Co as physician and surgeon till 1912. Then practiced in Sante Fe, N M Commissioned First Lieutenant, Medical Reserve Corps, U S Army, 1911 Was on duty with the 20th Infantry Regiment at Fort Bliss, Tex, when in 1916 the 6th Regiment Infantry was sent to Mexico and he was ordered to go with them He married Dec 16, 1909, at Leredo, Republic of Mexico, Edith Vincent Butler, daughter of Benjamin Franklin and Katherine Storm (Vincent) Butler and granddaughter of Capt Benjamin Franklin and Ellen Granville (Parker) Butler and of Rev. Marvin Richardson and Hulda Fowler (Seagrave) Vincent Capt B F Butler, a member of the Twenty-second New York Regiment, was a son of Benjamin Franklin Butler, Secretary of War under President Andrew Jackson and Attorney General under President Martin Van Buren Ellen Granville Parker was a daughter of Dr Willard Parker for whom the Willard Parker Hospital was named Rev. Marvin Richardson Vincent was a professor at the Union Theolo   S.   (B   N. Y C   I.   ')
Sarah

10

345151—Sarah Elizabeth Lloyd, born Dec 24, 1912, at Santa Fe, N M

345152—Edith Vincent Lloyd, born May 26, 1915, at El Paso, Tex

3452—**Henrietta Graham McAllister,** born May 11, 1845, at "Hugh's Fancy" in Lost Creek Valley, Juniata County, Pa Married on Oct 30, 1873 in Allentown, Pa, Johnson Hewitt Baldwin (born April 23, 1832 at Durham, Greene County, N Y ; died Jan 13, 1908 in Mifflintown, Pa), son of James and Loisa (Hall) Baldwin and grandson of Abiel and Eunice (Coe) Baldwin The line of this Baldwin family in America begins with Joseph, son of Richard and Isabell Baldwin of Cholesbury, Bucks County, England Joseph Baldwin and his two brothers Timothy and Nathaniel, came with Herefordshire people to America, (Cholesbury was near the Hereford County line) under the guidance of their pastor, the Rev Peter Prudden This company formed part of Rev John Davenport's Colony, which arrived in Boston, A D, 1037 In 1638 the Davenport Colony settled in New Haven, Conn and in 1639 the Herefordshire people left that Colony, and with people from Wethersfield Conn, formed the Colony which settled at Milford, Conn, with the Rev Peter Prudden as their pastor They were Puritans, Joseph Baldwin, the first American ancestor and his first wife Hannah were among the first settlers of Milford, Conn, in 1639 His son Jonathan was born 1649 in Milford, Conn., and died there in 1739 He married 2nd, Thankful Strong of Windsor, Conn and their son Ezra Baldwin (born 1706 in Milford, Conn, died 1782, in Durham, Conn) married Ruth Curtiss in 1728 He served as a state representative in 1754 Abiel Baldwin, first son of Ezra and Ruth (Curtiss) Baldwin (born 1730 in Milford, Conn ; died 1802 in Durham, Middlesex County, Conn) married in 1756, Mehitable Johnson Their son Abiel Baldwin, 2nd, was born in 1762 in Durham, Conn, died in 1847 in Durham, Greene County, N Y He was a Revolutionary soldier He married first, Eunice Coe and their son James was born 1793 at Durham, N Y and died there in 1848 James married first, Loisa Hall of Bridgeport, Conn (born 1798; died 1838) and their son Johnson Hewitt Baldwin was born 1832 in Durham, Greene County, N Y He practiced law in Pittsburgh, Pa from 1861-1900 He was an elder in the Bellefield Presbyterian Church, Pittsburgh, repeatedly a commissioner to the General Assembly and a member of important ecclesiastical committees His widow resides at Mifflintown, Pa To Mrs Henrietta (McAllister) Baldwin must be given full credit for the highly satisfactory and complete form in which appear the records herewith presented of her own and associated branches of the Thomson family—see 34, and 6 Children of Johnson H and Henrietta (McAllister) Baldwin (1) Eleanor McAllister, (2) James Hewitt, (3) Robert McAllister, (4) Henrietta

34521—Eleanor McAllister Baldwin, born Aug 12, 1874, at Pittsburgh, Pa , died May 3, 1907, in Philadelphia, Pa Married on Aug 9, 1900, at Mifflintown, Pa , James Hayward Harlow, Jr (born Sept 22, 1873 in Allegheny, Allegheny County, Pa), son of James Hayward Harlow (born Sept 30, 1846, at Westminster, Mass) and Thursa Alice (Butler) Harlow and grandson of Noah Richardson Harlow (born April 1, 1815 at Cambridge, Mass , died March 14, 1862 at Lowell, Mass) and Sarah Ann (Hunt) Harlow The founder of the Harlow family in America was Sergeant William Harlow (born in England in 1624, died Aug 2, 1691) who emigrated to America when a boy and in 1638 was given a grant of four acres of land in Plymouth, Mass , where he lived the rest of his life "As Sergeant of the South Company, William Harlow had charge of the old Fort on Burial Hill for many years, and after King Philip's War in 1675 he bought, and used for his home, the old timbers of the fort This house is still standing in Plymouth He was engaged in the Indian warfare, of which the chief event was the great Naragansett fight, when both the Plymouth companies were present under command of Major William Bradford James Hayward Harlow, Jr. graduated from the Western University of Pennsylvania, June, 1896, in the course of Civil Engineering, continued to reside in Edgewood, Alleghany County, Pa , being assistant engineer for the Pennsylvania Water Co June, 1902, removed to Conowingo, Md In the year following till 1911 was assistant engineer for several different companies interested in the development of the water power of the Susquehanna river In 1911 became President and manager of the Havre de Grace Electric Co , which position he now holds Children of J. Hayward and Eleanor (Baldwin) Harlow (1) James Hayward, 3rd, (2) Robert Baldwin

345211—James Hayward Harlow, 3rd, born Oct 1, 1901, in Edgewood, Allegheny County, Pa Address, Havre de Grace, Md , care of J Hayward Harlow

345212—Robert Baldwin Harlow, born June 2, 1904, at Conowingo, Cecil County, Md Address, Havre de Grace, Md , care of J Hayward Harlow

34522—James Hewitt Baldwin, born July 23, 1876 at Pittsburgh Pa. Attended the East Liberty Academy and studied law in his father's office In 1899 entered the employ of the Electric Boat Co, New York In 1902 he became private secretary to William Dulles, New York. From 1903 to 1906 he was western agent for A S Hyde & Sons of New York, with headquarters in St Louis, Mo In 1906 he again became associated with Mr Dulles in various enterprises, princ .   .   t   )13
he w .   .   _   .   ent

Bottle Co, and in 1915 managing director of that company, located in London, England   He served for seven years in the N. Y N G   He married on Nov 19, 1901, at St. Joseph, Mo, Anna Belle Frazer, daughter of Benjamin Boyd Frazer (born Mar, 1826, near Shippensburg, Pa, died Aug 31, 1899, at St. Joseph, Mo) and Ann Eliza (Sterrett) Frazer, granddaughter of Andrew and Ann (Wilson) Frazer, of near Chambersburg, Pa, and of Robert and Jane (Clarke) Sterrett, of near Carlisle, Pa, great-granddaughter of William and Mary (Boyd) Frazier, of Derry Township, Dauphin County, Pa, of Moses and Mary (Snodgrass) Wilson, of Hanover Township, Dauphin County, Pa, and of John and Agnes (Chambers) Sterrett— see 345   Children of James H and Belle (Frazer) Baldwin, (1) Eleanor Frazer, (2) Ann Elizabeth

345221—**Eleanor Frazer Baldwin**, born Sept 11, 1905, at St. Louis, Mo

345222—**Ann Elizabeth Baldwin**, born Sept 16, 1907, at Englewood, N. J

34523—**Robert McAllister Baldwin**, born Sept 13 1877, at Pittsburgh, Pa, died May 31, 1892, at Edgewood, Allegheny County, Pa

34524—**Henrietta Baldwin**, born Nov 22, 1885, at Pittsburgh, Pa. She is a member of the Thomas Mifflin Chapter (Mifflintown, Pa) of the Daughters of the American Revolution having been accepted on the services of three of her ancestors, namely, William Thompson as lieutenant and captain, Hugh McAllister as sergeant, lieutenant, captain and major, and Abiel Baldwin, 2nd, as private soldier

346—**Elizabeth McAllister**, born Jan 7, 1815, died Nov. 21, 1835   Married on June 3, 1834, David Stewart, Esq, son of John and Elizabeth (Walker) Stewart, a grandson of William and Elizabeth Stewart and of David Walker of Mifflin County, Pa, and a great-grandson of Archibald and Margaret Stewart who came to America from Newry, Ireland, and settled in 1753 on what was later known as the "Bark Tavern Tract" in Perry County, Pa   See History of Juniata and Susquehanna Valley, pp 854, 866 and 1084   No issue   See 52—572 and (10).

347—**William McAllister**, born July 5, 1817, died Aug 6, 1822.

348—**Son**, ———— McAllister, born Oct 10, 1820, died unnamed Nov, 1820

349—**George Washington McAlister**, born Feb 9, 1823, at the old homestead, "Hugh's Fancy," in Lost Creek Valley, Juniata County, Pa, where he died Sept 6, 1902, aged 79 years, 6 months and 27 days   He was a farmer and owned and lived on one-half of the old "Hugh's

Fancy" tract   He married on Jan 15, 1850, Mary Myers (born Jan 13, 1827, died Jan 8, 1903, aged 75 years, 1 month and 25 days), daughter of Rev David and Elizabeth (Holtzapple) Myers of McAlisterville, Pa, and granddaughter of Michael Myers of Mifflintown, Pa, and of Adam and Catherine (Mertz) Holtzapple of Lebanon County, Pa   See "Biographical Encyclopedia of Juniata Valley," p 383   Rev David Myers bought the old Mitchell farm west of where his father lived in Fayette Township, Juniata County, Pa   See "History of Juniata and Susquehanna Valleys," p 839   Children of G Washington and Mary (Myers) McAlister, (1) Frances Elizabeth, (2) William Clinton, (3) Laura Jean, (4) David Stewart, (5) Banks Clayton

3491—Frances Elizabeth McAlister, born Dec 8, 1850; died July 3, 1853

3492—William Clinton McAlister, born July 6, 1853, died July 13 1854.

3493—Laura Jean McAlister, born Oct 26, 1855, at the homestead in Juniata County, Pa   She attended the following schools   Bellefonte Academy, 1869-71, Moravian Seminary, 1871-2, Supplee's Institute, Philadelphia, 1872-3   Address, Miss Laura McAlister, Mifflintown, Pa

3494—David Stewart McAlister, born Nov 6, 1856, died Feb 21, 1859

3495—Banks Clayton McAllister, born Oct 5 1859 at the homestead in Juniata County, Pa   From 1892-97 he was a merchant at McAlisterville, Pa, and was postmaster during President Cleveland's second term   From 1897 to 1900 he lived at Montoursville, Lycoming Co, Pa   During this time he was president of the Montoursville Passenger Railway Co, and also of the Montoursville Electric Light Co   He is now farming at the homestead   Address, Mifflintown Pa   Married on April 18, 1888, in Culpeper, Va, Emma Clorinda Irvine, daughter of John and Mary Ellen (Elliott) Irvine of Culpeper, Va (formerly of Perry County, Pa) and granddaughter of William and Sarah (Milligan) Irvine and of James and Jane (Linn) Elliott, great-granddaughter of William and Sarah (McCullough) Elliott and of John and Mary (Ross) Linn, great-great-granddaughter of Edward and Margaret (Kincaid) Elliott, of John and Susanna Ross, and of William and Martha Linn, great-great-great-granddaughter of Robert and Mary (Rainey) Elliott   Robert Elliott was a Scotchman who emigrated to this country from Ireland in 1737 and settled about seven miles north of what is now Carlisle, Pa   See "History of Juniata and Susquehanna Valleys in Pennsylvania," p 1034   Issue (1) George Irvine

34951—George Irvine McAll ster   ᵻ   S---t ₂8 ₁8₀₀ ᵻᵤ ᵻ ᵻᵢ--ᵻ₋ ᵻ₋ nty,
Pa   V   -- ' ᵥ ᵥ·   · ᵤᵧ   ᵤ5 ᵢar

McAlisterville, Pa, Isadore Elsie Reynolds, daughter of Frank Wallace and Annie L (Bentley) Reynolds of McAlisterville, Pa, and granddaughter of Levi and Hannah (Van Ormer) Reynolds and of Caleb and Elizabeth (Criswell) Bentley Levi Reynolds was a son of Stephen Reynolds and his wife who had been the widow, Mrs Elizabeth (Hartman) Kreider Stephen Reynolds was a son of Benjamin and Mary (Job) Reynolds, and a grandson of Henry Reynolds, a preacher of the Society of Friends who came from Nottingham, England, at an early period in our Colonial history and settled in Cecil County, Md See "Biographical Encyclopedia of Juniata Valley in Pennsylvania," p 75

35—**Robert Thompson,** born 1790; died Jan. 3, 1866, at Thompsontown, Pa, in the old stone house built in 1798 by his father, William Thompson—3 After the death of his father, he and his brother William—33— conducted the business at Thompsontown for many years, purchasing much additional land in different localities They purchased at different times the Cuba Mills, the Oakland Mills and other mill properties About 1829 they built a storehouse on the "Diamond" subsequently occupied by Wickersham Shelley; a storehouse was erected on the canal bank, and in 1835 the old mill was torn down and the present mill erected He was a very exact man and upon his notes have been built the later records of the earlier members of the Thompson family He accumulated a large estate, the bulk of which he left to the sons of his brother and business partner, William Thompson, with whom he made his home He died unmarried at his father's homestead, then occupied by the family of his brother William—33

36—**Isaac Thompson,** born Jan 23, 1790, died May 3, 1835, aged 45 years, 3 months, 10 days He inherited from his father a farm in Lost Creek Valley "adjoining the Hugh McAlister property called 'Hugh's Fancy.'" He served in the War of 1812, and was at the Black Rock encampment during that war He carried on business at Newton Hamilton and Hollidaysburg He married twice first his cousin (77) Jane Boal (born June 16, 1801; died Nov. 20, 1833, aged 32 years, 5 months, 4 days), daughter of David and Sarah (Thomson) Boal and granddaughter of John Thomson, Sr Issue (1) son He married secondly Nancy Patterson of Butler County, Pa No issue

361—Son ——————— Thompson, born ———————, died ———————, aged 12 years, drowned in the canal at Mexico, Pa

37—**Jane Mitchell Thompson,** born ———————, died Feb 7, 1847, at Harrisburg, Pa Married Henry Walters (born 1795, died Nov 14, 1854, aged 59; buried at Harrisburg, Pa), son of Jacob and ——————— (Otto) Walter of Liverpool, Perry County, Pa Jacob Walters was a miller and civil engineer of English ancestry Henry Walters was a

35—Robert Thompson, Merchant

372—William Thompson Walters

merchant at Liverpool He left there in 1820 and subsequently became
cashier of the Harrisburg (Pa) National Bank Issue (1) Louise
Martha, (2) William Thompson, (3) Margaret Stuart, (4) Edwin,
(5) Thaddeus, (6) Mary Jane, (7) Jane Mitchell, (8) Charles

371—Louise Martha Walters, born 1823, died Sept 7, 1901, at Millersburg,
Pa , buried at Harrisburg. Unmarried

372—William Thompson Walters, born May 23, 1819, at Harrisburg, Pa.;
died Nov 22, 1894, at Baltimore, Md Attended the University of
Pennsylvania At the age of 19, he was given charge of an iron furnace at Farrandsville, Clinton County, Pa , where he produced, for the
first time in America, iron by the use of coked bituminous coal He
was a merchant, railway director, patron and connoisseur of art. He
did much to develop transportation facilities in the South and was the
president of first steamship line between Baltimore and Savannah,
was Vice-President, Northern Central Railway when it was extended
to Baltimore With his life-long friend, Thos K Scott, President
Pennsylvania Railroad, formed the Southern Security Co, which in
the years 1866 and 1873 borrowed the money to rebuild the railroads
between Richmond and Charleston, Richmond and Danville and Bristol
to Chattanooga, Tenn , and built the Charlotte and Atlanta Air Line
After the panic of 1873 all these roads were sold except what now
forms the Atlantic Coast Line, of which he was the Chairman of the
Executive Committee until his death For ten years he was Chairman
of the Executive Committee of the Texas and Pacific Railroad, which
he and his friend Thos K Scott had projected from the Mississippi
River to San Diego, Cal , but which they sold to Jay Gould, who completed it to a connection at the Rio Grande with the Southern Pacific
He was one of the early art collectors in the United States and Chairman for many years of the Purchasing Committee of the Corcoran
Art Gallery in Washington, D C He was also President of the Peabody Institute of Baltimore He translated from the French, Charles
Du Hays authoritative treatise on the Percheon horse and for 20
years was an importer and breeder of this draught horse to introduce
it into this country From 1867 to 1869 he was Finance Commissioner
of Baltimore City and in 1873 Commissioner to the Vienna Exposition.
See Appleton's Encyclopedia of American Biography The Walters
Art Gallery, Baltimore, Md , is considered one of the finest in existence W T Walters married in 1845, Ellen Harper (born ————,
died 1862), daughter of Charles A and Anna D (————) Harper.
Issue (1) Henry, (2) Jennie, (3) William Thompson

3721—Henry Walters, born Sept 26, 1848, in Baltimore, Md. Educated
at Loyola College, Baltimore, and George Washington University, and
Lawren S   S   t e
U S Ste Corporation   Coast

Line Chairman of the Board of Directors of the Atlantic Coast Line
and of the Louisville & Nashville Railroad Railroads in which he
is financially interested reach every Southern state except West Virginia He is an extensive art collector After his father's death he
rebuilt the Walters Art Gallery, North Charles St, Baltimore Has
built a number of public baths in Baltimore Yachtsman, capitalist,
head of W T Walters & Co, 916 Empire Building, N Y, and 5
South St, Baltimore, Md See "Who's Who in America," etc Unmarried

3722—Jennie Walters, born April, 1854 Married July 11, 1876, Warren
Delano, Jr. Residence, 39 E 36th St, New York Issue (1) Jean,
(2) Sarah, (3) Warren, (4) Lyman, (5) Ellen, (6) Laura

37221—Jean Delano, born —————. Married on June 13, 1914, at
Steen Veletze, Barrytown N Y, the country home of Mr and Mrs
Warren Delano. Prof Harold Edgell of the Art School, Harvard
University, Boston.

37222—Sarah Delano, born ————— Married on June 5, 1915, at
the Roman Catholic Church, Tivoli, N Y., Roland Livingston Redmond, son of Mrs Geraldyn (Livingston) Redmond, New York,
grandson of ———— Johnston Livingston and nephew of the
Countess Henri de Langier-Villars Address, 535 Park Ave, New
York

37223—Warren Delano, 3rd, born ————————, died in infancy

37224—Lyman Delano, born —————

37225—Ellen Delano, born —————

37226—Laura Delano, born —————

3723—William Thompson Walters, Jr., born —————; died very young.

373—Margaret Stuart Walters, born May 27, 1833, in Liverpool, Perry
County, Pa, died on May 25, 1911, at Pittsburgh, Pa Married on
Dec 15, 1852, in Harrisburg, Pa, William Henderson Moore (born
Mar, 1829, died Feb 14, 1889), son of Silas and Lucretia (Henderson)
Moore and grandson of Samuel and Ruth (Blair) Moore and of
Major William and Mercy (Little) Henderson and great-grandson of
Captain John Blair W H Moore was a banker at Lockhaven, Pa
Issue (1) Maria Louise, (2) Henderson Walters

3731—Maria Louisa Moore, born Mar. 2, 1854, at Hollidaysburg, Pa Married on Dec 24, 1885, in Lockhaven, Pa, Walter Lee Merwin (born Mar. 23, 1854, in Durham, Conn., died Feb 5, 1905, in Pittsburgh, Pa), son of Miles Talcott and Ellen A (Foote) Merwin, and grandson of Miles and Phoebe (Camp) Merwin W L Merwin was an attorney-at-law Address of Mrs W L Merwin, 6328 Howe St, Pittsburgh, Pa Issue (1) William Walters, (2) Miles Henderson, (3) Margaret Russell

37311—William Walters Merwin, born July 11, 1887, at Lockhaven, Pa Mining engineer at Paintsville, Ky.

37312—Miles Henderson Mervin, born July 23, 1892, at Pittsburgh, Pa Graduated Lehigh University, 1914 Metallurgist with Pittsburgh Steel Co, Monessen, Pa Married Sept 27, 1913, Lauretta Louise Simon (born July 3, 1892, at Allentown, Pa) Issue (1) Robert Russell

373121—Robert Russell Mervin, born May 12, 1915, at Charleroi, Pa

37313—Margaret Russell Merwin, born July 30, 1895, at Pittsburgh, Pa Address, 6328 Howe St, Pittsburgh, Pa

3732—Henderson Walters Moore, born Oct 15, 1856, at Upper Paxton Mills, Pa Address, 41 Saint Nicholas Terrace, New York City Married on Feb 17, 1910, at New York City, Theresa Eichhorn (born in Germany), daughter of General George Eichhorn of the Bavarian Army Issue (1) Charles Henderson

37321—Charles Henderson Moore, born 1915

374—Edwin Walters, born Dec. 14, 1834. He was a merchant at Baltimore, Md Married on April 4, 1866, Virginia C Torian of Parrish St Mary, La No children

375—Thaddeus Walters, born —————; died ————— in infancy

376—Mary Jane Walters, born —————, died in infancy, buried at Harrisburg, Pa.

377—Jane Mitchell Walters, born —————, died in infancy, buried at Harrisburg, Pa

378—Charles Walters, born ———— —— — N ... t.

38—Elizabeth Thompson, born 1795, at Thompsontown, Pa , died Feb.
11, 1866, in her 71st year, buried in the Thompson family graveyard,
Thompsontown, Pa She married on Dec 14, 1820, at Thompsontown,
Pa, Dr William Waterhouse (born Mar 30, 1794, at Kingwood, N J ,
died Nov 28, 1822, at Millerstown, Pa), son of Ingham and Jean
(Dean) Waterhouse and grandson of Joshua and Elizabeth (Ingham)
Waterhouse and great-grandson of James Ingham who came from
Yorkshire, England, to America between 1700 and 1705 Di William
Waterhouse studied medicine with Dr. Dewees of Philadelphia and
graduated from the Jefferson Medical College Issue (1) Jane Mitchell
Deane.

381—Jane Mitchell Deane Waterhouse, born Sept 15, 1821, at Millerstown, Pa , died May 23, 1867, at Oakland Mills, Juniata County, Pa
Married on Mar 17, 1842, near McAlisterville, Pa , Lucien Wilson
(born Oct 20, 1818, died Sept 23, 1889, at Oakland Mills, Pa), son
of Hugh and Martha (Banks) Wilson, grandson of Robert and Elizabeth (Haines) Wilson and of James and (Catherine) Nelson Banks,
great-grandson of James and Anna (Small) Banks and Robert and
Martha (Patterson) Nelson, great-great-grandson of Hugh Banks
from Aryshire, Scotland See "History of Juniata and Susquehanna
Valleys in Pennsylvania," pp 816, 824 and 838, and "Biographical Encyclopedia of Juniata Valley," pp 343 and 898 James Banks, the ancestor of the American branch, was born about 1732 in Ayr, Scotland,
and emigrated to America with his wife locating first at New London,
Cross Roads, Chester County, Pa , later in York County, Pa , and
finally in 1773 in Lost Creek Valley, Juniata County, Pa , where he
died June, 1793, aged 61 years Of his six children, James the eldest
son, was born 1765 in York County, Pa , and was 24 years old when
he married Catherine Nelson He died near Memphis, Tenn , at the
age of 72 years Robert Nelson is said to have been a nephew of
Thomas Nelson by his second wife Fannie (Houston) Tucker, widow
of a Mr. Tucker of Bermuda Islands whom he married in 1721, whose
son William Nelson—by his first wife Margaret (Read) Nelson—was
president of the Virginia Council and was father of Governor Thomas
Nelson of Virginia —See *Baltimore Sun*, May 13, 1906 —Thomas
Nelson who emigrated to Virginia in 1690, was born Feb 20, 1677, at
Penrith, England, son of Hugh and Sarah Nelson, of Cumberland
County, England Robert Nelson (born 1725, died 1805, aged about
83, at Bowling Green, Ky), settled in Maryland before 1755 and
before 1763 purchased from his cousin William Houston a tract of
land in what is now Lancaster County, Pa He married in 1751
Martha Patterson, daughter of Robert and Elizabeth (Gray) Patter-
son and granddaughter of Walker and Margaret (Scott) Patterson
James Banks who married Catherine Nelson was Major General of
the Eleventh Battalion, U S Army, in the War of 1812 Children of
Lucien and Jane Mitchell (Waterhouse) Wilson, (1) Martha Eliza-

38 Elizabeth (Thompson) Waterhouse

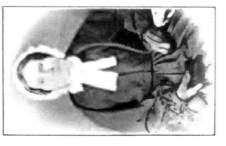

3814 Catherine Wilson Iann

beth, (2) Hugh Horace, (3) William Waterhouse, (4) Catherine
Nelson, (5) Ella Thompson, (6) John Lequear, (7) Lucian Banks,
(8) Julia Marion, (9) Laura Jane, (10) Allen Latimer, (11) Edgar
Waterhouse, (12) Juniata Mary, (13) Southard Doty

3811—Martha Elizabeth Wilson, born Dec. 27, 1842, at Minersville, Pa ;
died Jan 27, 1851 at Oakland

3812—Hugh Horace Wilson, born Mar 28, 1844, at Oakland Mills, Pa.,
died Dec 6, 1874

3813—William Waterhouse Wilson, born Apr 20, 1845, at Oakland Mills,
Pa.; died Jan 20, 1851

3814—Catherine Nelson Wilson, born Jan 6 1847, at Oakland Mills, Pa.
Died March 16, 1917, at Oakland Mills   Married on June 20, 1872 at
Oakland Mills Pa, Howard Stansbury Janney (born Oct 24 1847,
Philadelphia, died July 20, 1900 at Asbury Park, buried at Lost Creek
Valley), son of Benjamin and Georgiana (Janney) Janney and grand-
son of Dr Israel Pemberton Janney and Isabel (Garrettson) Janney
and of George Fox and Sarah (House) Janney   Dr Israel P Janney
was a son of Lewis and Mary (Pennock) Janney and a grandson of
Jacob and Elizabeth (Lewis) Janney   Mrs Catherine (Wilson)
Janney, took an active interest in the Thompson family reunion and
was largely instrumental in insuring the publication of the present
volume of Thompson records   Issue (1) Edgar Pemberton, (2)
Benjamin Stansbury, (3) Nelson Wilson.

38141—Edgar Pemberton Janney, born Apr. 20, 1873, at Philadelphia, Pa ,
died Feb 24, 1902 at Philadelphia

38142—Benjamin Stansbury Janney, born Sept 21, 1874, at Philadelphia,
Pa   Late of the grocery firm of B S Janney, Jr & Co, of Philadelphia   Unmarried   Address, Oakland Mills, Pa

38143—Nelson Wilson Janney, born Sept 13, 1881, at Philadelphia, Pa.
Graduated B. S, University of Pennsylvania, 1902, M. D, University
of Pennsylvania, 1906, M D, University of Muncin, 1911; Ph D,
University of Marburg, 1912.   Resident physician, hospital of University of Pennsylvania 1906-8.   Director of Physiological Chemical
Laboratory of the Montefiore Home, New York, N Y   In 1917, he
was appointed Professor of Medicine at the New York Post Graduate Medical School Hospital and Adjunct Attending Physician to
the M   S   k.
Unm.

3815—Ella Thompson Wilson, born June 7, 1848, at Oakland Mills, Pa
Married first at Oakland Mills, Nov 24, 1875, Rev. Thomas Alexander
Robinson (born at Academia 1847, died Nov 7, 1901)   Graduated
Washington and Jefferson College 1872; Theological Seminary, Alle-
gheny, Pa , 1875, son of John and Sara (Armstrong) Robinson   Is-
sue (1) Lucian Wilson, (2) Sarah Katherine   Married second time,
Oct 15, 1909, Edward Harris   Address, Mrs Ella Thompson Harris,
Marengo, Ill

38151—Lucian Wilson Robinson, born Sept 22, 1876, at Potter's Mills,
Center County, Pa ; died Aug 28, 1910 at Marengo, Ill

38152—Katherine Robinson, born Aug 22, 1882, at Winnebago, Ill   Mar-
ried on Oct 16, 1907 at Marengo, Ill , Edward James Tupper (born
Feb 14, 1876 at Des Moines, Ia) son of Melbourne and Phoebe
(Currier) Tupper and grandson of Calvin and ———— (Loverin)
Tupper and great-grandson of James Currier   Abstractor. Address,
Galesburg, Ill   Issue (1) Helen Katherine, (2) Marguerite Robin-
son, (3) Robert Lucien   ·

381521—Helen Katherine Tupper, born Dec 30, 1908, Clark, S Dakota

381522—Marguerite Robinson Tupper, born Dec. 13, 1910, Galesburg, Ill.

381523—Robert Lucien Tupper, born ————————, Galesburg, Ill

3816—John Lequear Wilson, born Mar 26, 1850, died Aug ——, 1850

3817—Lucian Banks Wilson, born Nov. 24, 1851, at Oakland Mills, Pa ;
died Sept 24, 1912 at Creston, Iowa   For many years of the grocery
firm of Janney & Andrews, Philadelphia   Married on Oct 27, 1898
at Clarion, Pa , Mary Stewart Montgomery   Issue (1) James Montgomery, (2) Margaretha Katherine.

38171—James Montgomery Wilson (twin), born Mar 31, 1901, at Creston,
Ia

38172—Margaretha Katherine Wilson (twin), born Mar. 31, 1901, at Creston, Ia

3818—Julia Marion Wilson, born Mar 23, 1853, at Oakland Mills, Pa ;
died Dec. 2, 1853

3819—Laura Jane Wilson, born June 12, 1854, at Oakland Mills, Pa.; died
Aug 9, 1854

381(10)—Allen Latimer Wilson, born June 30, 1855, at Oakland Mills, Pa.
Stock dealer. Address, Creston, Ia   Married on April 27, 1879 at
Walnut, Ill, Emelon Lindsey, daughter of Isaiah and Eliza (Sill)
Lindsey. Issue (1) Howard Lindsey, (2) Ruth Sill, (3) Myra,
(4) Lucian, (5) Ralph, (6) Harriett Maron

381(10)1—Howard Lindsey Wilson, born May 16, 1880, at Walnut, Ill ,
died Jan 7, 1897 at Creston, Ia   Drowned after saving the life of
a schoolmate

381(10)2—Ruth Sill Wilson, born Apr 8, 1882, at Walnut, Ill ; died Apr
28, 1882

381(10)3—Myra Wilson, born Sept 15, 1883, at Walnut, Ill   Married on
April 20, 1910 at Creston, Union County, Ia , Frederic Waterman
Ide (born Aug 6, 1877 in Grant Township, Union County, Ia)
son of George Abel and Ellen Frances (Allen) Ide and grandson
of William Tiffany and Sarah Ann (Stone) Ide, and of Samuel
Bowen and Mary (Chaffee) Allen   Address, Creston, Ia   Junior
partner in the firm of Geo A Ide & Son, real estate and insurance   Children (1) Lucien Ide, (2) Helen   No record

381(10)4—Lucian Wilson, born July 26, 1886, at Bedford Ill., died June
26, 1909 at Creston, Ia

381(10)5—Ralph Wilson, born Apr. 26, 1889, at Creston, Ia

381(10)6—Harriett Maron Wilson, born May 18, 1893, at Creston, Ill

381(11)—Edgar Waterhouse Wilson, born Nov 2, 1857, at Oakland Mills,
Pa ; died Nov 27, 1915 at Creston, Ill   Unmarried

381(12)—Juniata Mary Wilson, born at Oakland Mills, Pa   Unmarried
Address, Oakland Mills, Pa

381(13)—Southard Doty Wilson, born July 7, 1861, at Oakland Mills, Pa.
Traveling representative of Sprague Warner & Co, Chicago, Ill
Address, 1674 Steele St, Denver, Col   Married on June 30, 1898,
Alberta Maude Johns, daughter of Spencer and Ida Mary (Dur-
fey) Johns and granddaughter of Seth H and Sybil Mary (Pop-
pleton) Durfey   No children

39—Samuel Thompson, born 1792 in Juniata County, Pa ; died Mar 7,
1851 in the 58th year of his age at Pottsville, Schuylkill County, Pa
"Possessed of wealth, energy and public spirit, he did much for the im-
provme   ·   ·   ·   he
Building c···   ·   · (· he

was prompt, active and efficient, while as a member of the town council,
his cool dispassionate judgment and discretion gave him a large share
of influence"—From the *Pottsville Emporium*, March 13, 1851   He
married twice, first, on Nov 6, 1827 at Newton Hamilton, Pa , Ann
West Alricks (born Oct , 1798, died Aug 27, 1828, aged 29 years, 10
months) daughter of James and Martha (Hamilton) Alricks and granddaughter of John and Margaret (Alexander) Hamilton of Shermans
Valley, and of James Alricks, son of Herman Alricks, son of Wessells
Alricks, son of Peter Alricks of Holland   No children   He married
second, on Aug 6, 1833, Elizabeth Cunningham of Newtown Hamilton,
who was born March 3, 1805 and died Oct 5, 1874 at Pottsville, Pa
Issue (1) William, (2) Lewis Cunningham, (3) Emily Jane, (4) Heber
Samuel

391—William Thompson, born May 22, 1834, at Pottsville, Pa ; died July
9, 1905   Prior to the Civil War when 27 years of age he was the
head of a well established and profitable banking concern   In September, 1862, War Governor Andrew Gregg Curtin gave him authority to
recruit a cavalry company in Schuylkill County, and on Nov 1st he
was mustered into the service as captain of Company H, 17th Pennsylvania Cavalry, which belonged to the 2nd Brigade, 1st Cavalry Division,
and served under the successive commands of Generals Pleasanton,
Buford, Merritt and Devin, with the greatest efficiency and distinction
For several months, commencing in May, 1863, Captain Thompson
commanded Gen George G Meade's escort, Companies D and H, and
later was with Gen P H. Sheridan in his battles; his active service,
in fact, included participation in nearly every engagement in which the
Union Cavalry took part in the operations of the Army of the Potomac
during the last two years of the war   He was severely wounded in
the right shoulder at Kearneystown, Va , when three divisions of the
Union Cavalry made a charge upon Gen. Early's entire force, to
divulge its strength and plans   He was elected major Feb 13, 1865,
and a month later, Mar 13th, was brevetted lieutenant-colonel "for
meritorious and distinguished services"   It was only when incapaci-
tated by his wounds that he was ever absent from the front; and with
these exceptions, he never lost a day's duty while he was in the service   He was mustered out on June 20, 1865   Colonel Thompson's
interest in his companions in the army did not end with the war   His
regiment had the honor of firing the first gun in the great conflict at
Gettysburg, and to him to a great extent is due the erection, on that
historic field, of a grand monument to the memory of those who gave
up their lives in the struggle   Upon the close of his service in the
field, Colonel Thompson again turned his attention to the calling for
which his early education and experience had so thoroughly fitted him.
Possessed of a fair competence by inheritance from his father, he
became a large stockholder in the Miners' National Bank of Pottsville,
one of the oldest and most substantial banks in the state   He was

39—Samuel Thompson

392—Lewis C. Thompson

391 — William Thompson

elected a director of this institution on Jan 13, 1882, and thereafter made its interests his life work, his long and honorable connection with it ending only with his death   He served as a cashier from May 23, 1882, until Jan 25, 1893, when he became vice-president   He became president on Jan 12, 1894   His property holdings included some of the finest business blocks in Pottsville   An attendant at the Presbyterian Church, Colonel Thompson was one of its most open-handed supporters   Colonel Thompson never married   He died July 9, 1903, at Pottsville, Pa, and was buried there in the Thompson family plot in the Charles Baber cemetery

392—Lewis Cunningham Thompson, born Nov 7, 1835, at Pottsville, Pa Address, Pottsville, Pa   He attended school at Chambersburg, Franklin County, and continuing his studies at the Bolmar Academy, West Chester, Pa   His business life began early   In April, 1855, in partnership with Harry P Stichter, he established a wholesale and retail hardware business at the corner of Centre and Market Sts, Pottsville, the firm of Stichter & Thompson being the pioneer in the town in that line This association lasted until the spring of 1865, when Mr Thompson purchased Mr Stichter's interest and associated with him his brother, Heber S Thompson, the firm becoming L C Thompson & Co   Later Heber S Thompson withdrew, and from that time the business was carried on by Lewis C Thompson himself until May 1, 1911, when it became incorporated, as previously stated, with the following officers Lewis C. Thompson, president, Wm M Thompson, vice-president, J. Harry Benner, secretary and treasurer; and L C Thompson, William M Thompson, J. Harry Benner, and W K Woodbury, directors Though Mr Thompson's time and attention have been directed principally to the affairs of this concern, he has formed other associations, and is, at present, director of the Miners' National Bank of Pottsville, and a director of the Union Hall Association   He has always taken an active interest in the life of the city, as a member of the Pottsville Club, and a prominent worker in the First Presbyterian Church, he served as president of its Board of Trustees when the present church building on Mahantongo Street was erected, in 1874   During the Civil War, Mr Thompson enlisted in Company A, 27th Emergency Regiment, raised when Lee invaded the State in 1863   He married on June 10, 1862, in Chester County, Rebecca Frances Bruner (born in Chester County, Pa, near the line of Berks County), daughter of John and Maria (Jones) Bruner   Issue (1) Elizabeth May, (2) Marie Louise, (3) Carrie Frances, (4) William Mitchell, (5) Elsie

3921—Elizabeth May Thompson, born March 15, 1863, at Pottsville, Pa. Attended school at Bradford, Mass   Married Feb 20, 1890, at Pottsville, Pa, Frank Bailey Parsons (born ————, died March 16, 1911), son of C
Address of Mrs Elizabeth M Parsons

3922—Marie Louise Thompson, born Aug 9, 1864, at Pottsville, Pa   Married Jan 24, 1900, Henry Townsend Blodget of New York City   Address, East Paget, Bermuda.

3923—Carrie Frances Thompson, born 1866, died in infancy

3924—William Mitchell Thompson, born Dec 15, 1871, at Pottsville, Pa.   Attended school at Pottsville and the Phillips Academy at Andover   Since 1892 he has been in business with his father at Pottsville.   Married on Jan 7, 1902, at Pottsville, Mary Jane Sturman, daughter of   Joseph T and Sarah E (Golightly) Sturman

3925—Elsie Thompson, born July 27, 1875, at Pottsville, Pa.   Address,   801 W Mahantongo St , Pottsville, Pa

393--Emily Jane Thompson, born July 21, 1838; died Nov. 17, 1880, at   Pottsville, Pa   Married on Oct 11, 1866, Major Edward Carey Baird   (born at Pottsville, Pa , Apr 3, 1836; died near Ashland, Va , Nov.   14, 1874), son of Captain J————— Baird of the U S Army and   Eliza Catherine (Carey) Baird and grandson of Henry S—————   and Louisa (—————) Baird and of Matthew and Bridget (Fla-   haven) Carey. Issue (1) Bessie Carey

3931—Bessie Carey Baird, born Sept 1, 1867, at De Pere, Wis   Married   on Oct 3, 1894, at Pottsville, Pa , Joseph Albright Archbald, son of   James and Hannah Maria (Albright) Archbald and grandson of   James and Sarah Augusta Temple (Frothingham) Archbald and of   Joseph Jacob and Elizabeth (Sellers) Albright   Joseph Albright   Archbald is a brother of James Albright, who married Margaretta   Thompson (3943)   He is a manufacturer, 107 Hodge Ave , Buffalo,   N. Y. Issue (1) Joseph Albright, (2) Edward Baird, (3) Heber   Thompson, (4) Emily Baird

39311—Joseph Albright Archbald, Jr , born at Pottsville, Pa , Aug 5,   1897   Address, 107 Hodge Ave , Buffalo, N Y

39312—Edward Baird Archbald, born at Buffalo, N. Y., Aug. 13, 1898.   Address, 107 Hodge Ave , Buffalo, N Y

39313—Heber Thompson Archbald, born at Buffalo, N Y , Nov 12, 1900   Address, 107 Hodge Ave , Buffalo, N Y

39314—Emily Baird Archbald, born at Buffalo, N. Y., Jan 23, 1904. Ad-   dress, 107 Hod Ave , Buffalo, N Y

394—Heber Samuel Thompson, born Aug 14. 1840, at Pottsville, Pa , died Mar 9, 1911 A B Yale 1861, A M Yale 1871 He enlisted as private in the "First Defenders" on Apr 16, 1861, the first troop in the Civil War to enter Washington Later he served as captain of the Seventh Pennsylvania Cavalry He was President of the Board of Trustees of the State Hospital for Injured at Ashland, Pa , and president of the Edison Electric Illuminating Co He was a member of the Pennsylvania State "Coal Waste Commission" See "Who's Who in America," Vol I, 1910-11 It was he who co-operated with his first cousin Theodore Samuel Thompson (338) in the preparation of the "Thompson Family" booklet upon which the present family records have been based He married on Jan 23, 1866, at Pottsville, Pa , Sara Eliza Beck (born Jan 16, 1840, at Pottsville, Pa), daughter of Isaac and Margaretta (Pitman) Beck, and granddaughter of Joseph and Eleanor (Copeland) Beck, and of Ephraim and Mary (Patterson) Pitman Address, Pottsville, Pa Issue (1) Emily Baird, (2) Samuel Clifton, (3) Margaretta, (4) Eleanor, (5) Heber Harris

3941—Emily Baird Thompson, born Nov 10, 1866, at Pottsville, Pa Address, 7432 Sprague St , Mt. Airy, Philadelphia, Pa Married on Apr 15, 1891, John Parke Hood of Philadelphia (born ——————, died Mar 17, 1904), nephew of Franklin B Gowen Hood Issue (1) John Parke, (2) Sidney, (3) James Gowen, (4) Heber Thompson

39411—John Parke Hood, Jr, born Apr. 21. 1893, Mt. Airy, Philadelphia, Pa

39412—Sidney Hood, born Jan 2, 1896, Mt Airy. Philadelphia. Pa

39413—James Gowen Hood, born Dec 27. 1899, Mt Airy, Philadelphia, Pa

39414—Heber Thompson Hood, born Apr 13, 1904, Mt Airy, Philadelphia, Pa

3942—Samuel Clifton Thompson, born May 7, 1869, at Pottsville, Pa. Address, New York City Graduated Yale and Columbia Universities in mining engineering Married at Johannesburg, South Africa, Victoria Stanton Issue (1) Samuel Clifton, Jr—no record

3943—Margaretta Thompson, born May 5, 1871, Pottsville, Pa Married on Oct. 21, 1897, at Pottsville, Pa , James Archbald, Jr (6th), son of James Archbald (5th) and Hannah Maria (Albright) Archbald and grandson of James (4th) and Sarah Augusta Temple (Frothingham) Archbald and of Joseph Jacob and Elizabeth (Sellers) Albright. James Archbald son   of Joseph Albright Archbald who married Bessie Carey   he is engineer of the Girard
11

Estate and General Manager of the Girard Water Co (succeeded his father-in-law Heber S Thompson) with offices in Thompson Building, Pottsville, Pa Issue (1) Margaretta Thompson, (2) Sara Thompson, (3) James Archbald, (4) Wodrow.

39431—**Margaretta Thompson Archbald,** born Apr. 29, 1899, Pottsville, Pa

39432—**Sara Thompson Archbald,** born Sept 13, 1900, Pottsville, Pa

39433—**James Archbald, 7th,** born Aug 7, 1905, Pottsville, Pa

39434—**Wodrow Archbald,** born Oct 18, 1907, Pottsville, Pa

3944—**Eleanor Thompson,** born ————————, Pottsville, Pa ; died on ————————, at ————————

3945—**Heber Harris Thompson,** born Sept 12, 1880, Pottsville, Pa   Married Florence Westbrook, daughter of Dr Cherrick Westbrook. Address, Tamaqua, Pa

BRANCH NO. 4

4—**Elizabeth Thomson**, born ——————, died ——————. On ——
——— she married Robert McAlister (born ————————; died May 26,
1828; probably buried in Tuscarora Valley, Juniata County, Pa), son of
Hugh and Sarah (Nelson) McAlister and grandson of Hugh and ———
(Harbison) McAlister, Scotch protestants, who came from Ireland to
America in 1732, settling in Lancaster County, Pa See 34, 56 and 6
The will of Hugh McAlister, Sr, was dated Apr 19, 1769, and probated
Aug 15, 1769, at Carlisle, Pa Hugh McAlister, Jr (born 1736 in Lan-
caster County, Pa, died Sept 22, 1810) joined the forces of Forbes in
the French and Indian War He served as sergeant, lieutenant and cap-
tain in the army of the Revolution, and was commissioned major of the
Seventh Battalion of the Militia in Cumberland County, Pa, May 1,
1783 See "History of the Susquehanna and Juniata Valleys in Pennsylvania," pp 123 and 831 After their marriage, Robert and Elizabeth
(Thomson) McAlister settled at Nook, in Tuscarora Valley, in Juniata
County, Pa, where doubtless he and she died and were buried, although
their graves have not been located From May 5 to Nov 5, 1813,
Robert McAlister served as corporal in Captain Matthew Rodgers Company of Pennsylvania Militia belonging to the regiment commanded by
Colonel Reese Hill Robert and Elizabeth (Thomson) McAlister died
without issue

BRANCH NO. 5

5—**Robert Thomson**, born ——————; died on the farm three miles below Thompsontown, Pa, on the Juniata River. Doubtless he was the Robert Thompson of Fermanagh Township, in what is now Juniata County, Pa, whose will dated Feb 24, 1787, and probated April 5, 1787, at Carlisle, Pa., gives his estate to his son William (51), a minor, and other minor children and to his wife—not mentioned by name He appointed as his executors his wife and David Boal—probably the husband of his sister Susanna (7) This will is recorded in Cumberland County Will Book E P 105 It was witnessed by Gerard Ferrill; Samuel Willy, possibly a relative of the husband of his sister Jean Thomson (2), and Thomas Palley, probably the person who witnessed the will of Pioneer John Thomson Robert Thompson was taxed on a saw-mill in Fermanagh Township, Juniata County, Pa, in 1785-6, the two years preceding his death He may or may not have been the Robert Thompson who served as a private in Captain John Clarke's company of Associators of Northumberland County in 1776 In this company was William Greenlee, presumably the husband of his sister Mary Thomson (1) Robert Thompson married Sarah Mitchell, a sister to Jane Mitchell who married William Thompson (3) By some the father of Sarah and Jane Mitchell was said to have been David Mitchell of Chestnut Level, Lancaster County, Pa, and by others James Mitchell of Cumberland County, Pa A certain David Mitchell whose will—witnessed by William Mitchell—was dated 1756, Chestnut Level, Lancaster County, Pa, left children Samuel, Jean, Abram, Margaret Eleanor, Sarah, George and David He may have been a son or a brother of John Mitchell of Drumore Township, Lancaster County, Pa, who died in 1759 leaving sons Samuel, William, John, George and David See "Notes and Queries," Vol III, Third Series, by W H Egle, page 483 It is possible that John Mitchell who came from Ireland to Lancaster County, Pa, served as colonel of the Cumberland Militia at Lancaster, and died about 1785 in what is now Perry County, was of this family See "History of Susquehanna and Juniata Valleys in Pennsylvania," p 1130 According to Robert Thompson (35), son of William and Jane (Mitchell) Thompson, his mother was a daughter of "James Mitchell of Cumberland Valley, near Chambersburg" According to Hugh Nelson McAllister (343) grandson of Jane (Mitchell) Thompson, she "was born within one mile of Strasbury, now Franklin (then Cumberland) County Her father was killed by the Indians in a harvest field during the French and Indian War (1754-60) near what is now called St Thomas, seven miles west of Chambersburg" Among the early land titles in Letterkenny Township, in which Strasburg is located was one granted July 10, 1752, to James Mitchell Joseph and William Mitchell also owned land there in 1754 Among the persons killed by Indians in a harvest field near Shippensburg on July 19, 1757, were James, Joseph and William Mitchell   It is not improbable that the father of Jane and Sarah was James rather than David Mitchell and that he was of the Lancaster County Mitchells who were progenitors of many of the Mitchell families throughout the Cumberland Valley   See No 3   Children of Robert and Sarah (Mitchell) Thompson, (1) William, (2) John, (3) Robert, (4) James, (5) Andrew, (6) Jane, (7) Mitchell

51—William Thompson (called Little), born ————, 1774, died July 7, 1847, in his 73rd year, buried at Thompson's Lock, Pa   Married on April 16, 1818, in Juniata County, Pa, Hannah Mincer (born 1790, died Sept 29, 1840, in her 51st year buried at Thompson's Lock, Pa)   He lived in Thomsontown, Pa   Issue (1) Josiah, (2) Isaac Ambrose, (3) Sarah Mincer, (4) Mary, (5) Rebecca

511—Josiah Thompson, born ———— at Thompsontown, Pa , died ———— at Covington, Ky , buried at Covington, Ky   Married ————Pauley.   Issue (1) Mary

5111—Mary Thompson, born ————   Married ———— Shaner   Issue (1) son   No record

512—Isaac Ambrose Thompson, born Feb 23, 1823; died May 30 1860, aged 33 years, 3 months and 5 days, buried at Thompson's Lock, Pa

513—Sarah Mincer Thompson, born Feb 25, 1826, died Sept 26, 1869, aged 43 years, 7 months and 1 day, buried at McAlisterville, Pa   Married her cousin (665) Isaac Thompson McAllister (born April 30, 1830; died Nov 19, 1894 at West Newton, Pa) son of Robert Harbison and Mary (Crawford) McAllister and grandson of William and Sarah (Thomson) McAlister   Issue (1) William, (2) Mary Thompson—see 665

514—Mary Thompson, born Dec 8 1824; died Apr 6, 1896, at Mifflintown, Pa   Married on June 20, 1861, her cousin John Hutchinson McAlister (born March 10, 1818, died May 16, 1890, buried at Mifflintown, Pa), son of John Bell and Jane (Thompson) McAllister and grandson of William and Sarah (Thomson) McAlister   They lived at Mifflintown, Pa   No issue   See 56 and 637

515—Rebecca Thompson, born 1830; died Sept 19, 1840, in her 10th year; buried at Thompson's Lock, Pa

52—John Thompson, born Oct 30, 1776, died Jan 6, 1830, aged 58 years, buried at Locks, Pa   He and his brother James—54—settled in Lost Creek Valley   . . . Michael Bashore and purchased the . . . land originally granted to James

Micheltree. In connection with his brother Robert—53—John Thompson purchased in Nov., 1811, an adjoining tract which had also been granted to James Micheltree—see "History of Juniata and Susquehanna Valleys in Pennsylvania," p 871   John Thompson was a farmer, but he is said to have acted as a pilot for arks and rafts on the Juniata River. He owned two boats, built by himself, which he used to convey his produce to Harrisburg and other points. He is said to have erected one of the first brick houses in this section of Pennsylvania, the bricks for its construction having been made on his own farm—see "Biographical Encyclopedia of Juniata Valley, Pa," p 997   He was a member of the United Presbyterian Church   He was twice married   His first wife was Rachel Stewart (born May 8, 1780, died May 9, 1813, in Delaware Township, Juniata County, Pa), daughter of William and Elizabeth Stewart and granddaughter of Archibald and Margaret Stewart—see (10)   Issue (1) Jane, (2) Mary, (3) Martha   John Thompson married secondly on Oct 14, 1816, in Perry County, Pa, Jane Gilfillen (born Sept 25, 1797, died Feb 16, 1855), daughter of James Gilfillen—see 72   Children of John and Jane (Gilfillen) Thompson (4) William Gilfillen, (5) James, (6) Robert Mitchell, (7) John, (8) Rebecca

521—Jane Thompson, born on ——————, at ——————, died on ——————, at ——————; buried at ——————   Married on ——————, at ——————, Gideon Claybaugh, of Red Oak, Brown County, Ohio   They subsequently moved to Henderson County, Ill. Issue (1) William

5211—William Claybaugh, born ——————. Address, Red Oak, Brown County, Ohio   Married ——————

522—Mary Thompson, born on ——————, at ——————, died on ——————, at ——————, buried at ——————   Married on ——————, at ——————, Michael Benner, of Brown County, Ohio Issue ——————

523—Martha Thompson, born ——————, died in early life.

524—William Gilfilen Thompson, born July 20, 1817; died on July 23, 1892   Married twice, first on Jan 18, 1842, at Thompsontown, Pa, Lucinda Caroline Kinsloe (born 1823, died Feb 10, 1855, aged 32 years)   Issue (1) Alice Adelia, (2) Jane Pamelia   Married second, on April 5, 1859, at Harrisburg, Pa, Mary Elizabeth Bomgardner, daughter of William and Sarah (Egle) Bomgardner, granddaughter of Valentine and Elizabeth (Thomas) Egle, great-granddaughter of Casper and Elizabeth (Mentges) Egle and of Martin Thomas Jr, son of Martin Thomas, Sr. Valentine Egle, Martin Thomas, Jr, and Casper Egle were Revolutionary soldiers   Martin Thomas, Sr., was a

Home of John Thompson 52, on the Juniata, Delaware Township.
Juniata Co., Pa., now owned by his grand-daughter,
Mrs. Arthur Trexler 5243.

Home of John Thompson (527), " Bridge John " and Sarah (Rodgers)
Thompson, Delaware Township, Juniata Co., Pa.

lieutenant on the frontier during the French and Indian War   Children of William G and Mary Elizabeth (Bomgardner) Thompson (3) Lillian Olivia, (4) Ralph Bomgardner

5241—Alice Adelia Thompson, born Dec. 4, 1846, on Thompson's farm, near Thompsontown, Pa , died —————— Married on June 6, 1871, at Harrisburg, Pa , James Allison. Address, 104 R St, N E, Washington, D C   Issue (1) James Burns

52411—James Burns Allison, born ——————. Married Dec. 4, 1906, at Washington, D C , Maude Henrietta Bean   Issue (1) Florence Burns, (2) Maude Elizabeth

524111—Florence Burns Allison, born July 23, 1908

524112—Maude Elizabeth Allison, born Nov 6, 1910

5242—Jane Pamelia Thompson, born Oct 28, 1852, on Thompson's farm, near Thompsontown, Pa , died June 1, 1907, at Washington, D C , buried at Harrisburg, Pa   Married Jan - , 1871,at Harrisburg, Pa , Grafton Fox (born   -   , died June, 1909) Issue (1) Mary Grafton

52421—Mary Grafton Fox, born Jan 10, 1872, at Harrisburg, Pa

5243—Lillian Olivia Thompson, born June 9 1861, Harrisburg, Pa   Married on Jan 8, 1884, at Thompsontown, Pa , Arthur R———— Trexler, son of Jonas and Elizabeth (Good) Trexler and grandson of Jonas and Sarah (——————) Trexler   A R Trexler was a merchant at Sunbury, Pa   Issue (1) Thompson Arthur, (2) Mary Elizabeth

52431—Thomas Arthur Trexler, born Oct. 10, 1884, at Thompson's Lock, Pa   Address, Sunbury, Pa

52432—Mary Elizabeth Trexler, born Nov 9 1887, at Sunbury, Pa   Married, June, 1913, at Sunbury, Pa , Robert Glover, of Mifflinburg, Pa   Address, Scranton, Pa

5244—Ralph Bomgardner Thompson, born June 29, 1863, at Harrisburg, Pa   Hardware merchant at Millerstown, Perry County, Pa   Married on Dec 16, 1896, at Thompsontown, Pa , Clara Pauline Rippman, daughter of Charles Adolphus and Mary (Walz) Rippman and granddaughter of John Godfrey and Mary (Stutz) (——————) Rippman   1) Mary K

52441—Mary Kathleen Thompson, born Jan 9, 1898, at the William Gilfillen Thompson homestead, one mile east of Thompsontown, Pa
Address 1916, Millerstown, Pa

525—James Thompson, born at Thompson's Lock, Pa, 1819; died June 18,
1854, aged 35 years, buried at Locks, Pa (Some confusion as to which
children belong to the different wives) Married twice, first on March
17, 1842, at Thompson's Lock, his cousin—(11)7 Eleanor Thompson
(born 1819, died Feb 22, 1844, aged 25 years), daughter of Peter and
Mary (Patterson) Thomson and granddaughter of John Thomson, the
Pioneer and of Andrew Patterson—see (11) Issue (1) Ellen Cecelie
He married the second time on March 20, 1845, at Van Dyke, Pa, his
cousin Wilhelmina Thompson—314—daughter of John Goshen and
Abigail (North) Thompson and granddaughter of William and Jane
(Mitchell) Thompson Issue (2) Mary Evaline (Eva), (3) Heber,
(4) James Addison

5251—Ellen Cecelie Thompson, born Feb 13, 1844, at Thompson's Lock,
Pa Address, 221 North Second St, Harrisburg, Pa Married on
Dec 1, 1865, at Harrisburg, Pa, James Porter Harris, son of John
Porter Harris (born Aug 1836, died Feb 27, 1900), grandson of
John and Maria (Parsons) Harris Issue (1) William Domer.

52511—William Domer Harris, born Sept 11, 1866, at Harrisburg, Pa
Address, 221 North Second St, Harrisburg, Pa Married on Sept
15, 1893, at Harrisburg, Pa, Emelie Pauline Sieber, daughter of
Charles Frederick and Mary Elizabeth (Bessenger) Sieber and
granddaughter of George and Elizabeth (————) Bessenger
Issue (1) James Porter, (2) Mary Elizabeth, (3) Ellen Cecelia.

525111—James Porter Harris, 2nd, born Nov 11, 1894, Harrisburg, Pa.

525112—Mary Elizabeth Harris, born Jan 27, 1902, Harrisburg, Pa

525113—Ellen Cecelia Harris, born Nov 18, 1903, Harrisburg, Pa.

5252—Mary Evaline (Eva) Thompson, born Aug 18, 1852, at Thompson's
Lock, Pa, died Feb 1, 1915 at McAlisterville, Pa, buried at Mifflintown, Pa

5253—Heber Thompson, born Aug 1, 1847, at Thompson's Lock, died
Aug 8, 1849

5254—James Addison Thompson, born ————, died in infancy.

526—**Robert Mitchell Thompson,** born at Thompsontown, Pa., Feb. 14,
1822, died Dec 24, 1879, at Thompson's Lock, Pa. He was a farmer
and owned land below Thompsontown in Juniata County, Pa., which
had originally been patented by Isaac Yost. He married twice, first
on Dec. 20, 1853, Amelia Evans North (born Jan 25, 1831, died April
10, 1859), daughter of John and Jane Huston (McAlister) North of
McAlisterville, Pa., a granddaughter of Joshua and Mary (Murry)
North and of Hugh and Catherine (Elliott) McAlister a great-granddaughter of Roger and Ann (Rambo) North, of Hugh and Sarah
(Nelson) McAlister and of John and Jane (Huston) Elliott; a great-
great-granddaughter of Caleb North and of Peter and Ann (Cock)
Rambo, and of Hugh and   (Harbison) McAlister   Roger
North, who came to this country with his parents in 1730, entered the
army in 1748 and was made lieutenant in the Provincial Service   Hugh
McAlister, Jr., was a private in the French and Indian War, and
served as sergeant, lieutenant, captain and major in the Revolutionary
War   John Elliott was a major in the Revolutionary War   The
mother of his wife, Jane (Huston) Elliott was Catherine Buchan-
an, sister to the grandfather of President Buchanan—see "His-
tory of Juniata and Susquehanna Valleys in Pennsylvania," pp 753
and 1035   Children of Robert Mitchell and Amelia Evans (North)
Thompson (1) Clara Jane, (2) Mary Agnes, (3) Ida Belle, (4) Dallas
Clinton, (5) Amelia North, (6) Calvin North   He married second
time on Sept 11, 1860, at New Bloomfield, Perry County, Pa., Sarah
Ellen Toomey (born in Juniata Township, Perry County, Pa., died
Aug 2, 1905), daughter of Henry and Henrietta (Brown) Toomey
Issue (7) Ida Mary, (8) Rettie May, (9) Annie Laura (10) Robert
Mitchell, (11) Nora Ellen, (12) Harry Toomey, (13) Domer Roy,
(14) Lottie Alice

5261—**Clara Jane Thompson,** born Sept. 28, 1854, died Mar 11, 1855,
at Thompsontown, Pa

5262—**Mary Agnes Thompson** (twin), born Aug 7 1856; died same day,
at Thompsontown, Pa

5263—**Ida Belle R. Thompson** (twin) born Aug 7, 1856, died same day,
at Thompsontown, Pa

5264—**Dallas Clinton Thompson,** born Dec. 7, 1857, at Thompsontown, Pa
Address, Topeka Kan, R F D. No 2   Married on March 11, 1884,
at Valley Falls, Kan, Clara Tait (born Apr 24, 1862, at Madison,
Ind), daughter of James F and Jennet (Brown) Tait, granddaughter
of John and Jean (McKay) Tait and of Alexander and Bell (Martin)
Brow   · ·   · · North,
(4) k · · ·

52641—**Bertha Jane Thompson,** born June 30, 1887, at Valley Falls, Kans Address, Topeka, Kans, R F D No 2

52642—**Lottie Belle Thompson,** born Dec. 25, 1891, at Denison, Kans , died Aug 1, 1912 at Topeka, Kans

52643—**Hugh North Thompson,** born Oct. 8, 1894, at Denison, Kans. Address, Topeka, Kans, R F. D No 2

52644—**Robert Roy Thompson,** born Sept. 15, 1897, at Denison, Kans Address, Topeka, Kans, R F D No 2

5265—**Amelia North Thompson** (twin), born Apr. 1, 1859; died Sept. 3, 1859, buried at Thompson's Lock, Pa

5266—**Calvin North Thompson** (twin), born Apr 1, 1859, died Sept. 3, 1859, buried at Thompson's Lock, Pa

5267—**Ida Mary Thompson,** born June 9, 1861, at Thompson's Lock, Pa Address, 2255 N 6th St, Harrisburg, Pa. Married at Thompsontown, Pa, Apr 18, 1893, Elmer Elsworth McCauley, son of James and Mary (Ewig) McCauley Issue (1) Mary Ellen

52671—**Mary Ellen McCauley,** born May 19, 1895, at Harrisburg, Pa Address, 2255 N 6th St, Harrisburg, Pa

5268—**Rettie May Thompson,** born Nov. 18, 1862, at Thompson's Lock, Pa Address, 334 S Brown St, Lewistown, Pa Married Dec 27, 1881 at Thompson's Lock, Pa , Reuben Wendell Grubb, son of Reuben and Rebecca (Orner) Grubb and grandson of Henry and Mary (————) Grubb Issue (1) Reuben Clair, (2) Domer Martin, (3) Roy Thompson, (4) Cormel Park, (5) Robert Burns, (6) Rebecca Joy

52681—**Reuben Clair Grubb,** born Aug. 24, 1882, in Greenwood Township, Perry County, Pa Married on April 19, 1906, at Elkhart, Ind , Greachen Rufner of Elkhart, Ind Address, Jones, Mich. Issue (1) Delas Blair

526811—**Delas Blair Grubb,** born July 22, 1907, at Elkhart, Ind

52682—**Domer Martin Grubb,** born 1884, at Reward, Perry County, Pa., died 1894 of diphtheria

52683—**Roy Thompson Grubb,** born 1886, at Reward, Perry County, Pa ; died 1894 of diphtheria

52684—Cormel Park Grubb, born 1888, at Thompson's Lock, Pa ; died 1894 of diphtheria.

52685—Robert Burns Grubb, born Sept. —, 1899, at Thompson's Lock, Pa. Address 334 S Brown St, Lewistown, Pa   Law student

52686—Rebecca Joy Grubb, born May 14, 1898, at Raccoon Valley, Pa Address, 334 S Brown St, Lewistown, Pa

5269—Annie Laura Thompson, born Sept 7, 1864, at Thompson's Lock, Pa   Address, 2255 N 6th St, Harrisburg, Pa

526(10)—Robert Mitchell Thompson, Jr, born June 5, 1866, at Thompson-town, Pa   Address, 401 N 4th St, Huntington, Pa   Married on Oct 5, 1886 at New Bloomfield, Pa, Mary Ann Vincent, daughter of David R and Hannah Maria (Kauffman) Vincent   Now in the employ of Penn R R Co in electrical signal department   Issue (1) Nellie Pauline, (2) Robert Preston, (3) Alton Cochran, (4) Nora Lozetta, (5) Pearl Ellen

526(10)1—Nellie Pauline Thompson, born Mar 27, 1887, at Millerstown, Pa   Address, 410 N 4th St, Huntingdon, Pa

526(10)2—Robert Preston Thompson, born Nov 2, 1888; died Aug 7, 1899, Millerstown, Pa.

526(10)3—Alton Cochran Thompson, born Jan 2, 1891, at Millerstown, Pa   Address, 410 N 4th St, Huntingdon, Pa

526(10)4—Nora Lozetta Thompson, born May 4, 1892, at Millerstown, Pa. Married Oct 18, 1916, at Huntingdon, Pa, Lester Haupt Strickler, of Huntingdon, son of Henry Dill and Mary Etta (Maulls) Strickler, and grandson of Thomas G and Martha (—————) Strickler   Address, 1157 Cleveland Ave, Niagara Falls, N Y

526(10)5—Pearl Ellen Thompson, born Sept 22, 1894, at Millerstown, Pa Address, 410 N 4th St, Huntingdon, Pa

526(11)—Nora Ellen Thompson, born Dec 15, 1867, at Thompsontown, Pa ; died Jan 30, 1891 at Thompsontown, Pa

526(12)—Harry Toomey Thompson, born Apr. 1, 1871   Address, Williamsburg, Pa   Married on ————— at McAllisterville, Pa, Effie Nora Van Ormer of McAlisterville, Pa   Issue (1) Effie M... ... ... (4) Lawrence Lamont, (5) Harold Alton to James Raymond, (7) Richard Leland

526(12)1—**Effie Maria Thompson**, born June 25, 1899, at Roaring Spring, Pa

526(12)2—**Harry Robert Thompson**, born Dec 10, 1900, at Bedford, Pa.

526(12)3—**Burns Elmer Thompson**, born Oct 4, 1903, at Lewistown, Pa.

526(12)4—**Lawrence Lamont Thompson**, born June 24, 1905, at Williamsburg, Pa, died Aug 4, 1905.

526(12)5—**Harold Alton Thompson**, born Mar 26, 1909, at Williamsburg, Pa

526(12)6—**James Raymond Thompson**, born Sept. 21, 1914, at Williamsburg, Pa

526(12)7—**Richard Leland Thompson**, born Apr 30, 1916, at Williamsburg, Pa

526(13)—**Domer Roy Thompson**, born Apr 3, 1876, at Thompsontown, Pa, died Feb 5, 1903, at Harrisburg, Pa, buried at Thompson's Lock, Pa

526(14)—**Lottie Alice Thompson**, born July 28, 1877, at Thompsontown, Pa Address, Thompsontown, Pa Married on Apr 6, 1899 at Harrisburg, Pa, William Frederick Rippman, shirt manufacturer, son of Charles Adolphus and Mary (Walz) Rippman and grandson of John Godfrey and Mary (Stutz) Rippman and of Henry Martin and Anna Christina Walz Issue (1) Erma Elizabeth, (2) Mabel Pauline, (3) Mary

526(14)1—**Erma Elizabeth Rippman**, born Feb. 26, 1900, at Millerstown, Pa Address, Thompsontown, Pa

526(14)2—**Mabel Pauline Rippman**, born Dec. 12, 1902, at Millerstown, Pa Address, Thompsontown, Pa

526(14)3—**Mary Rippman**, born Apr 24, 1916, at Harrisburg, Pa

527—**John Thompson** (called "Bridge John," to distinguish him from Goshen John—31), born Sept. 9, 1824, in Delaware Township, Juniata County, Pa, one mile east of Thompsontown, died Dec 31, 1908 at Thompsontown, Pa After the death of his mother in 1855, John Thompson purchased a portion of the homestead property and erected thereon a stone dwelling house which was destroyed by fire in 1891 For eleven years John Thompson conducted the Thompson House, a hotel at Mechanicsburg, Cumberland County, Pa see Biographical

Encyclopedia of Juniata Valley in Pennsylvania, p 997   He married on Dec 20, 1847, near Mexico, Pa, Sarah Rodgers (born Jan 24, 1824, died July 8, 1886) daughter of Colonel Matthew and Mary (Kennedy) Rodgers and granddaguhter of William and Mary (Kelly) Rodgers—see (11)5, (11)7, and (11)9   Matthew Rodgers (born 1770, died Apr 14, 1837) was Captain and afterwards Colonel in the War of 1812.   His wife was born in Ireland in 1792 and died May 28, 1854   William Rodgers came from England, he served as a private in Capt Lacey's 4th Battalion in the Revolution   Children of John and Sarah (Rodgers) Thompson, (1) Floyd, (2) Jane Rebecca, (3) Girl, (4) Girl, (5) James Luther, (6) John Rodgers, (7) Charillie, (8) William Cloyd

5271—Floyd Thompson, born ————, 1849; died ————. Unmarried

5272—Jane Rebecca Thompson, born Jan 10, 1851, one mile east of Thompsontown, Pa   Address, Mechanicsburg, Pa   Married on Oct 18, 1871 at Mechanicsburg, Pa, John Jacob Milleisen (born Apr. 20, 1851, at Mechanicsburg, Pa) son of Joseph and Barbara (Martin) Milleisen and grandson of George and Mary (Fritchey) Milleisen and of Rev Mr Martin and Mary (Brookhart) Martin   John Jacob Milleisen is a coal and lumber merchant at Mechanicsburg, Pa   No children

5273—Girl—twin, born ————, 1853, died ————.

5274—Girl—twin, born ————, 1853, died ————.

5275—James Luther Thompson, born Jan 12, 1855, one mile east of Thompsontown, Pa   Address, Mifflintown, Pa, R F D No 2, Box 12   Married on Feb 16, 1882, four miles east of Mifflintown, Juniata County, Pa, Anna Adams (born ————, died Sept 8, 1890) daughter of William Adams, by his second wife Caroline (Jacobs) Adams, granddaughter of Jacob and Catherine (Lintner) Adams and great-great-granddaughter of James and Isabella (Welden) Adams, from Chester, England—see (11)5, (11)8, and (11)9   Issue (1) Mary, (2) Laura Curran, (3) Anna Adams, (4) Sarah Rodgers, (5) John, (6) Rebecca

52751—Mary Thompson, born Oct 14, 1883, east of Mifflin, Pa   Address, 1941 Market St, Philadelphia, Pa   After teaching four years in public schools of Juniata County she entered the Pierce Business College of Philadelphia, and is now head bookkeeper for an electrical company in that city

52752—Laura Curran Thompson,   Ma (1885   Address Mifflintown, Pa, R. F D No 2, Box 1

52753—**Anna Adams Thompson,** born Aug 16, 1886 Address, 419 South Ave, Wilkinsburg, Pa She graduated as a trained nurse from the Columbia Hospital (United Presbyterian) of Wilkinsburg, Pa, Oct 30, 1911, after a very successful three-year course and has been engaged in her profession since her graduations

52754—**Sarah Rodgers Thompson,** born May 25, 1888 Address, Children's Hospital, Pittsburgh, Pa. She graduated from the High School of Mechanicsburg in May, 1908, and is a member of the class of 1914 of trained nurses of The Children's Hospital of Pittsburgh, Pa

52755—**John Thompson,** born June 26, 1889 Address, Mechanicsburg, Cumberland County, Pa He graduated with honors from the Electrical Engineering Course in Carnegie Technical Schools, of Pittsburgh, Pa, in 1912.

52756—**Rebecca Thompson,** born Sept 8, 1890, three miles east of Mifflintown, Pa Address, Mifflintown, Pa, R F D No 2, Box 12 She spent two years in Westminster College of Music, New Wilmington, Pa Married, Dec 20, 1916, Walter Smith, of Walker township, Juniata Co., Pa.

5276—**John Rodgers Thompson,** born Nov 17, 1859, one mile east of Thompsontown, Pa Address, 701 Lincoln St, Topeka, Kans Married on —————— at Sidney, Ohio, Anna S———— Stevenson daughter of Samuel S———— and Margaret G (McClure) Stevenson and grandson of Thomas and Mary Jane (————) Stevenson and of Andrew S———— and Jane M (————) McClure. Issue (1) Marguerite Joy

52761—**Marguerite Joy Thompson,** born Dec. 26, 1887, at Topeka, Kans. Graduated 1913, from Muskingum College, New Concord, Ohio

5277—**Charllie Thompson,** born Nov. 17, 1859, one mile east of Thompsontown, Pa Address, Mifflintown, Pa, R F D No 2, Box 12.

5278—**William Cloyd Thompson,** born Aug. —, 1861, one mile east of Thompsontown, Pa Married on —————— at ——————, Martha Johnson Issue (1) Jennie Grace, (2) Maude Ellen

52781—**Jennie Grace Thompson,** born ——————. Married Sept. 9, 1908 at ——————, Kans., Joseph Knipp Address, Palco, Kans Issue (1) Evelyn Lucile

527811—**Evelyn Lucile Knipp,** born —— ——

52782—Maude Ellen Thompson, born ——————, at ——————. Address, Hill City, Kans

528—Rebecca Thompson, born ——————; died ——————.

53—Robert Thompson, born Sept —, 1780, died Dec. 5, 1854, aged 74 years, 3 months   He was called "Farmer Robert" although he was a tanner as well as a farmer.   In Nov, 1811, he and his brother John Thompson—52—purchased a tract of land in Lost Creek Valley, originally granted to James Micheltree in 1767   He also purchased part of the land of Andrew Thompson—(10)—where he lived and died—"History of Juniata and Susquehanna Valleys," p 871   He married twice first Elcy Pauly (born April 16, 1788, died Nov 28, 1829, aged 41 years, 7 months and 12 days   Issue (1) Montgomery, (2) John Ewing, (3) Elizabeth, (4) James Addison, (5) Jane, (6) Mitchell   He married second, Mary Lukens (born 1797; died Oct 5, 1865; aged 68 years, buried at Thompson's Lock, Pa)   Issue (7) Nelson, (8) Henry, (9) Maria Louise, (10) Sarah Isabella

531—Montgomery Thompson, born ——————   He lived 12 miles from Davenport, Iowa, in 1883   Died before 1908

532—John Ewing Thompson, born ——————   He lived in Henderson County, Ill   Died before 1908

533—Elizabeth Thompson, born ——————; died before 1908.   Married William Lukens of Ohio, widower of her cousin Nancy Thompson (542), daughter of James Thompson.   No data   See 572

534—James Addison Thompson, born Dec 21, 1826; died Mar 7, 1850, aged 23 years, 2 months and 14 days

535—Jane Thompson, born May 31, 1813, died Aug 15, 1893, aged 80 years, 3 months and 15 days; buried at Galatia, Barton County, Ohio   Married her cousin—(11)4—Samuel Thompson (born July 9, 1810, died Nov. 2, 1857), son of Peter and Mary (Patterson) Thompson and grandson of Pioneer John Thomson   Issue (1) Perthenia, (2) George Addison—see (11)4

536—Mitchell Thompson, born ——————; died before 1908   He emigrated to Oregon when a young man, settling in Willamette Valley   Married Agnes —————— of Oregon   His descendants live in Portland

537—Nelson Thompson, born 1837   died Jan. 31, 1838, aged 1 year; buried at Thompson's Lock, Pa.

538—Henry Thompson, born 1839, died Oct. 5, 1839, aged 8 months, 8 days; buried at Thompson's Lock, Pa

539—Maria Louise Thompson, born ——————, was living in 1908.

53(10)—Sarah Isabella Thompson, born —————— Married William Nelson Issue (1) Edgar Thompson, (2) Chester Roy

53(10)1—Edgar Thompson Nelson, born —————— Married —————— Branthoffer. Issue (1) Elizabeth, (2) Mary Amanda No data

53(10)2—Chester Roy Nelson. No data.

54—James Thompson, born ——————, died —————— He and his brother John Thompson—52—settled in Lost Creek Valley In 1803 they sold their property to Michael Bashore and purchased a tract of land originally granted to James Micheltree He subsequently sold his interest to his brother Robert—53—and moved to Ohio, locating at Chillicothe in 1824 and later in Brown County. He married near Mexico, Pa , Margaret Carson Issue (1) Samuel, (2) Nancy, (3) Robert, (4) Theodore, (5) John, (6) Margaret, (7) William

541—Samuel Thompson, born —————— Went to San Francisco about 1850 No data on his descendants

542—Nancy Thompson, born ——————; died ——————. Married William Lukens, who after her death married Jane Thompson (533), daughter of Robert and Elcy (Pauly) Thompson No data.

543—Robert Thompson, born —————— Lived at Red Oak, Brown County, Ohio Married —————— McLenehan Issue ——————.

544—Theodore Thompson, born ——————, died ——————, 1849, killed by an explosion on a steamer on his way home from California

545—John Thompson, born ——————; died ——————, 1849, on the Gulf of Mexico on his way to California

546—Margaret Thompson, born ——————, died ——————. Married Mitchell A—————— Thompson (554), son of Andrew and Rebecca (Stuart) Thompson M A Thompson was killed during the Civil War. Issue ——————.

547—William Thompson No data

"Greendale," Home of Andrew Thompson (55) and Rebecca (Stuart) Thompson, on the Juniata, Delaware Township, Juniata Co., Pa.

55—**Andrew Thompson,** born ————————; died ———————— He was called "Farmer" to distinguish him from his uncle Andrew Thompson (10) who was called "Tailor" He settled on his father's place and bought other lands adjoining In March, 1817, he purchased from John Thompson land originally granted to James Micheltree in March, 1761 He married twice; first Rebecca Stewart (born Dec 15, 1782, died Jan 24, 1852), daughter of William and Elizabeth Stewart and granddaughter of Archibald and Margaret Stewart who came to this country from Newry, Ireland, and in Sept, 1753, settled on what was known as the Bark Tavern Tract in Perry County, Pa—See (10) Children of Andrew and Rebecca (Stewart) Thompson, (1) David, (2) William Stewart, (3) Robert Newton, (4) Mitchell A , (5) Addison, (6) Sarah, (7) Andrew Andrew Thompson married secondly in 1840 the widow of his cousin (33) William Thompson, Jr, Mrs Charlotte Chambers (Patterson) Thompson No issue

551—**David Thompson,** born ———————— He was a physician living in Ohio in 1883 He married ———————— Brownlow No data

552—**William Stuart Thompson,** born April 11, 1818, at Thompsontown, Pa , died July 4, 1897 He moved to Illinois in the fall of 1890 Married on Apr 15 1841 in Greenfield, Ohio, Nancy Ann Smith (born July 17, ——, died July 5, 1880) daughter of Isaac and Ann (Mitchel) Smith Issue (1) Sarah Ann, (2) Andrew Adolphus, (3) Rebecca, (4) Elizabeth Smith, (5) J———————— P————————, (6) Harriett Jane, (7) William M————————, (8) Charles O————————

5521—**Sarah Ann Thompson,** born ————————, 1842, in Brown County, Ohio Married on ———————— at ————————, George A———————— Johnson, son of William and Margaret (Baird) Johnson Address, E Colorado St, Passadena, Cal, R F D No 1, Box 147a Issue (1) Addie M————————, (2) Frank W————————

55211—**Addie M————————** Johnson, born ————————, at Piper City, Ill. Address, Los Animas, Cal Unmarried

55212—**Frank W————————** Johnson, born ————————, at Piper City, Ill Farmer Address, Los Animas, Cal Unmarried

5522—**Andrew Adolphus Thompson,** born April 10, 1848, in Juniata County, Pa., died Oct 3, 1908. Address, 312 S 17th St , New Castle, Ind Married on Sept 22, 1874 at Piper City, Ill , Eliza Campbell, daughter of Aaron Lyle and Maria (McAdam) Campbell and granddaughter of George and H M McAdam Issue 1 Charles C————————, (2) Lida M ———— ——, (3) Eliza

12

55221—Charles C——— Thompson, born Sept 3, 1875. Unmarried Secretary-Treasurer of the C C Thompson Lumber Company, New Castle, Ind

55222—Lida M——— Thompson, born June 27, 1881 Married on ——— at ———, W——— R——— Snodgrass Address, 2825 8th St, Kansas City, Mo No children

55223—Ella Thompson, born Nov. 19, 1878; died in infancy

5523—Rebecca Thompson, born —————— Married on ——————, at ———, —————— McKinney Issue (1) Annie, and others

55231—Annie McKinney, born ——————, at ————— Married —————— North Address, Chicago, Ill

5524—Elizabeth Smith Thompson, born June 11, 1851, near Monmouth, Ill Married Sept 9, 1872, near Piper City, Ill, Joseph Priestly Glenn, son of James and Nancy (———) Glenn Retired from business Address, Stockton, Ill Issue (1) Hugh, died, (2) Elmer, (3) Oran, (4) Ella M———, (5) Edna E———, (6) Charles No data

5525—J——— P——— Thompson (twin), born Nov. 2, 1854, at Monmouth, Ill, died 1904 at Forrest, Ill

5526—Harriett Jane Thompson (twin), born Nov 2, 1854, at Monmouth, Ill Address, Huntsville, Ala Married on April 20, 1880, at Piper City, Ill, John B——— Stevenson (born, Nov. 5, 1857; ——————), son of James M and Jaby B (Whitworth) Stevenson and grandson of Russel and Jane (———) Whitworth Issue (1) Charles W———, (2) Frank P———, (3) Harry M———, (4) George M———, (5) Hattie Elizabeth, (6) Clara Elizabeth

55261—Charles W——— Stevenson, born Jan 28, 1881, at Thawville, Ill Address, Huntsville, Ala Manager of the Pintch Compressing Company Married on Nov 26, 1903, at Sheffield, Ala, Alice Barcus Issue (1) John Melvin, (2) Clara Elizabeth, (3) Bertha May

552611—John Melvin Stevenson, born Dec 22, 1904, at Sheffield, Ala Died, Aug 22, 1915 Buried in Maple Hill Cemetery, Huntsville, Ala

552612—Clara Elizabeth Stevenson, born Aug 23, 1906, at Meridian, Miss. Address, Huntsville, Ala

552613—Bertha May Stevenson, born Mar 11, 1908, at Meridian, Miss. Address, Huntsville, Ala

55262—Frank P——————— Stevenson, born Feb. 2, 1882, at Thawville, Ill. Address, 2633 Lyle Ave, Maplewood, Mo In the railway mail service Married on Oct 5, 1910, Frances Elizabeth Johnson of Meridian, Miss Issue (1) James William

552621—James William Stevenson, born July 24, 1911, at St Louis, Mo

55263—Harry M Stevenson, born May 11, 1884, at Piper City, Ill Address, Huntsville, Ala Manager of cleaning establishment Married Jan 25, 1910, Margaret Lee Detwiler Issue (1) Victor Lee, (2) Dorothy Virginia, (3) Madge

552631—Victor Lee Stevenson, born Dec 3, 1911 Address, West Huntsville, Ala

552632—Dorothy Virginia Stevenson, born Sept 13, 1913, at West Huntsville, Ala

552633—Madge Stevenson, born May 13, 1915, at St Louis, Mo.

55264—George M——————— Stevenson, born April 28, 1886, at Piper City, Ill Address Huntsville, Ala Electrical engineer Married on Jan 14, 1908, in St Louis, Mo , Mary Ella Fitzwater (born ———; died at Chattanooga, Tenn , July 5, 1912). No children

55265—Hattie Elizabeth Stevenson, born March 12, 1888, at Lincoln, Tenn Married on Oct 21, 1910, at Madison, Ala , Arthur S——————— Gilbert, owner and manager of a cotton compress, Amory, Miss. Issue (1) Mary Nell, (2) Arthur S, (3) George Owen

552651—Mary Nell Gilbert, born May 24, 1912, at Amory, Miss

552652—Arthur S Gilbert, Jr., born Oct 7, 1913

552653—George Owen Gilbert, born Oct 13, 1915

55266—Clara Elizabeth Stevenson, born Aug 25, 1890, at Fairbury, Ill Married, Feb 24, 1912, William B Ward, overseer of cotton mill, West Huntsville, Ala Issue (1) Clara Ella, (2) William Larry.— No record

5527—William M—   Thompson, ' rn June 8 1857. Address, Los Animos, Cal

5528—Charles O———————— Thompson, born Apr 20, 1860; died Sept 13, 1912, aged 52 years, buried in Maple Hill Cemetery, Huntsville, Ala Unmarried

553—Robert Newton Thompson, born Aug 28, 1812 in Juniata County Pa , died April 27, 1881   He served nine months in the 83rd regiment, Illinois Infantry Married in Chillicothe, Ohio, 1835, his cousin—(10)9 —Rebecca Stewart Thompson (born July 21, 1816, died Feb 15, 1908), daughter of Andrew and Jane (Stewart) Thompson and granddaughter of John Thompson, the Pioneer. Issue (1) Jane Stewart, (2) Rebecca, (3) Andrew Mitchell, (4) Mary Elizabeth, (5) Rebecca Jane, (6) Sarah Inez, (7) Thomas Smith, (8) Florence Alma, (9) Julia Ann, (10) David Stewart, (11) Ida Agnes.

5531—Jane Stewart Thompson, born Aug. 28, 1836, died Nov. 23, 1842 in Russelville, Ohio

5532—Rebecca Thompson, born June 22, 1838, died June 29, 1838 in Russelville, Ohio

5533—Andrew Mitchell Thompson, born at Thompsontown, Pa , Aug 19, 1839, died at Piper City, Ill , June 15, 1913   He served four years in the 50th Regiment Illinois Volunteers   He was in the march with Sherman to the sea   He was a charter member of the United Presbyterian Church of Piper City, Ill. Married on May 24, 1876 at Bloomington, Ind , Mary Elizabeth Johnson, daughter of David and Mary (Adams) Johnson who moved from South Carolina to Bloomington, Ind , about 1853   No children

5534—Mary Elizabeth Thompson, born Feb 22, 1842, died June 29, 1869 in Piper City, Ill

5535—Rebecca Jane Thompson, born Apr 3, 1844, died Aug 10, 1909 in Sterling, Kans   Married on ———————— at ———————— Jasper J———— Greenlee, son of ———————— of ———————— Address, Arlington, Col   Issue (1) William Oliver, (2) John Newton, (3) Stewart Clifford, (4) Silas Thompson, (5) Ida May, (6) Florence Ann, (7) Emmett, (8) Idella Myrtle, (9) Lizzie Elnora, (10) Frank Mitchell

55351—William Oliver Greenlee, born May 15, 1867   Address, Amy, Kan

55352—John Newton Greenlee, born May 5, 1869   Address, Scott City, Kan

55353—Stewart Clifford Greenlee, born April 5, 1871. Address, Shattuck, Okla

55354—Silas Thompson Greenlee, born July 27, 1872, died Aug 4 1873

55355—Ida May Greenlee, born May 11, 1874, died July 14, 1875

55356—Florence Ann Greenlee, born Mar. 8, 1877 Married on ———— at ——————, ———— Norton Address, Pittsburgh, Kan

55357—Emmet Greenlee, born Oct 30, 1879 Address, Radium, Kan

55358—Idella Myrtle Greenlee, born Oct. 16, 1882 Wed ———— Johnson Address, Mankato, Kan

55359—Lizzie Elnora Greenlee, born Sept 3, 1884, died July 15, 1886

5535(10)—Frank Mitchell Greenlee, born June 30, 1886 Address, Ness City, Kan

5536—Sarah Inez Thompson, born Feb. 11, 1846, died Aug. 30, 1894 in Bird City Kan Married Cyrus W Williamson (born ————, died ————————) Issue (1) Mary Jane, (2) Helen Bell, (3) Albert Stewart, (4) Florence Pearl, (5) Julia Adelia, (6) David Samuel, (7) Ida Grace Elnora

55361—Mary Jane Williamson, born Mar 30, 1875 Address, Rock Island, Tex Married on ———— at Bird City, Kan, Edgar Curry.

55362—Helen Bell Williamson, born Mar 17, 1876 Address, Clyde, Kan Married on Feb 27, 1901, at Bird City, Kan, ———— Hayes

55363—Albert Stewart Williamson, born Sept 16, 1878 Address, Sheridan, Wyoming

55364—Florence Pearl Williamson, born June 9, 1880 Address, Los Angeles, Cal Married on ———— at ————Joseph Parodos

55365—Julia Adelia Williamson, born Jan 11, 1882 Address, Eureka, Kan Married on ———— at Eureka, Kan, Clem Cook

55366—David Samuel Williamson, born Oct. 14, 1883 Address, Arcadia, Fla

55367—Ida Grace Elnora Williamson, born Jan 8, 1884 Wed ———— Gardner Address, Neodasha, Kan

5537—Thomas Smith Thompson, born May 23, 1848; died Dec 24, 1909 at Garnett, Kan He served for two years in the 46th Regiment Illinois Volunteer Infantry He married on April 25, 1877 at Monmouth, Ill. Sue Elnora Jamison No Issue

5538—Florence Alma Thompson, born June 24, 1851 at Russelville, Ohio.
Address, Campbell, Cal Married on Mar 13, 1890 at Idana, Kan,
Samuel Shotwell (born ——————; died Feb 23, 1904) son of
Benjamin and Katherine Shotwell No issue

5539—Julia Ann Thompson, born Dec 7, 1853, died July 16, 1893 in Piper
City, Ill

553(10)—David Stewart Thompson, born Apr 11, 1856 at Monmouth, Ill.
Address, Campbell, Cal, R F D No 10, Box 40, fruit grower.
Married twice. first on June 20, 1882 at Del Rey, Ill, Hattie
F———— Van Neste (born Sept. 1862, died Jan 30, 1890),
daughter of George H———— and Eliza (Shottenkirk) Van
Neste Issue (1) George Newton, (2) Nellie Alma, (3) Harry
Stewart He married second time on Oct 3, 1890, Mattie Brown
Issue (4) John David, (5) Robert Roy, (6) Mary Luella

553(10)1—George Newton Thompson, born May 28, 1883. Address, San
Jose, Cal, R F D No 6, Box 339c Married Sept 15, 1906
in Louisiana, Allie Fulenmider. Issue (1) Audrey Lualma, (2)
George Newton.

553(10)11—Audrey Lualma Thompson, born Sept. 16, 1907, San Jose, Cal

553(10)12—George Newton Thompson, Jr., born June 19, 1907, San Jose,
Cal

553(10)2—Nellie Alma Thompson, born at Idana, Kan on Mar 16, 1885 at
Campbell, Cal Married James Theadon Jennings Address,
2901 N Broadway, Los Angeles, Cal Issue (1) James Theodore

553(10)21—James Theodore Jennings, Jr, born Mar 25, 1911, Los Angeles,
Cal

553(10)3—Harry Stewart Thompson, born Mar 30, 1888, at Idana, Kan.
In U S Marines

553(10)4—John David Thompson, born June 30, 1892; died Dec. 5, 1892, at
Greeley, Col

553(10)5—Robert Roy Thompson, born at Piper City, Ill, Feb 24, 1893
Clerk in Commandants Office, U S Navy, San Francisco, Cal

553(10)6—Mary Luella Thompson, born Apr 11, 1896 at Piper City, Ill.
Address, Campbell, Cal

553(11)—Ida Agnes Thompson, born May 12, 1860, died Nov. 10, 1900, at
Piper City, Ill

554—Mitchell A———— Thompson, born ———— at ————
Killed during the Civil War   Married three times first on ————
at ————, his cousin Margaret Thompson—546—daughter of
James and Margaret (Carson) Thompson Issue ? Married second
time, Elizabeth McQuisten Issue (1) Montfort Married third time,
Eliza Thorn Issue (2) Cora

5541—Montfort Thompson, born ————, died in early manhood

5542—Cora Thompson, born ———— Married ———— McCain.

555—Addison Thompson, born ————, died young.

556—Sarah Thompson, born ————; died young.

557—Andrew Thompson, born ————, died young

56—Jane Thompson, born 1777; died Feb 23, 1850 in her 73rd year, buried
at Brown's Mills, Juniata County, Pa   Married on Oct 28, 1806, her
cousin (63) "Squire John," John Bell McAlister (born Apr 12, 1782;
died Apr 14, 1847, aged 65 years) son of William and Sarah (Thompson) McAlister and grandson of Pioneer Hugh McAlister and Pioneer
John Thompson   John B McAlister was admitted to the Perry County
bar in 1856   He was for many years a Justice of the Peace and an
elder in the Lost Creek Presbyterian Church Issue (1) Sarah, (2)
David, (3) Eliza, (4) Mary, (5) Mitchell, (6) Lucinda, (7) John
Hutchinson, (8) Jane Thompson—see 63

57—Mitchell Thompson, born 1789, died Dec 27, 1830 in his 41st year.
Married on Mar 22, 1813, Jane Allen (born Aug 7, 1795, died Apr 5,
1841 daughter of David and Mary (Nelson) Allen and granddaughter
of Robert Nelson—see 32   David Allen was a soldier in the Revolutionary Army   Robert Nelson (born ————, 1725; died 1805 at Bowling Green, Ky) was said to have been a nephew of Thomas Nelson, Sr,
by his second wife Fannie (Houston) Tucker Nelson, widow of Mr
————, Tucker of Bermuda Islands, whom he married about 1721
Thomas Nelson and his first wife, Margaret (Reed) Nelson were the
parents of William Nelson of Yorktown, Va, president of the Virginia
Council, and was secretary Thomas Nelson, Jr (born 1716, died
1782) who married Armistead Thomas Nelson, Sr, born Feb 20, 1677
at Penrith, England, was the son of Hugh and Sarah Nelson of Penrith, County of Cumberland, England He emigrated to the Colony of
Virginia in 1690 and the Robert ——— Sarah, May 12, 1696 Robert Nelson
married ——— Na——— ———, who

became Mme Jerome Bonapart) daughter of Robert and Elizabeth Gray Patterson and granddaughter of Walker and Margaret (Scott) Patterson of the Parish Hawwich. Martha (Patterson) Nelson died at Cedar Springs, Pa, July 26, 1794, aged about 63 years Children of Mitchell and Jane (Allen) Thompson (1) Lavinia Allen, (2) Adeline Nelson

571—**Lavinia Allen Thompson**, born June 13, 1814, died June 16, 1864. Married on June 6, 1835 in Millerstown, Pa, James Madison Cochran (born Nov 17, 1810 at Millerstown, Pa, died Aug 9, 1861 at Liverpool, Perry County, Pa) son of Thomas and Sophia Maria (Porter) Cochran, and grandson of Robert Porter—see 421 and 42134 Thomas Cochran was born 1776 in Redcastle, near Londonderry, Ireland, and came to this country with his brothers Samuel, Robert and William, settling in Chester County, Pa, at a place now known as Cochranville Thomas Cochran moved in 1801 to Millerstown, Pa, where he and his wife were the principal promoters of the Presbyterian Church erected in 1831, and where he died in 1847 His wife, who was born 1776 in Redcastle, near Londonderry, Ireland, and died in 1848 at Millerstown, Pa, was the daughter of Robert Porter, an uncle of Governor Porter of Pennsylvania, who served as colonel in the Revolution and participated in the Battle of Brandywine—see Biographical Encyclopedia of Juniata Valley in Pennsylvania, p 1272 Children of James Madison and Lavinia Allen (Thompson) Cochran (1) Mary Ann, (2) Elmira Jane, (3) Thomas Porter, (4) Eliza Adaline, (5) Ada Marion

5711—**Mary Ann Cochran**, born Nov. 9, 1835 in Buffalo Township, Hunters Valley, Pa, died July 14, 1913 at Liverpool, Pa ; buried there Married twice first on Oct 29, 1851 at Liverpool, Pa, George Harrison Martin, of Liverpool, Pa Issue (1) Jerome Lukens, (2) Mary Alice, (3) George Allen, (4) Annie Lavinia She married secondly in 1866, W L Lenhart (born Mar 26, 1837, at Shamokin Dam, Pa) son of Lewis and Deborah (Snyder) Lenhart and grandson of George Lenhart. W L Lenhart owns a saw-mill at Liverpool, Perry County, Pa He has served as councilman, school director and burgess Issue (5) Lewis Thompson, (6) John Wesley, (7) Florence Marion, (8) Stewart L————, (9) Porter C————

57111—**Jerome Lukens Martin,** born May 6, 1853 in Hunters Valley, Pa ; died Nov 6, 1854

57112—**Mary Alice Martin,** born Feb 20, 1855 in Liverpool, Pa. Married on Mar 14, 1878 in ————, John Westley Williamson Address, 2108 E Fork St, Philadelphia, Pa Issue (1) John Porter

571121—**John Porter Williamson,** born Jan 11, 1875

57113—George Allen Martin, born May 26, 1857, in Liverpool, Pa President Pittsburgh Tube Co, Pittsburgh, Pa Married June 27, 1883, at Chicago, Ill, Hattie O'Neill No children

57114—Annie Lavinia Martin, born March 9, 1859, at Liverpool, Pa. Married Nov 27, 1877, at Liverpool, Pa, George Tharp Address, Liverpool, Pa Issue (1) Allen Corey, (2) Stewart LeRoy, (3) Mary Helen No record

57115—Lewis Thompson Lenhart, born March 12, 1867, in Liverpool, Pa, died June 14, 1910 He was cashier in the Continental Hotel, Philadelphia Married, June 6, 1906, in Philadelphia, Ann B Cattenberger No children

57116—John Wesley Lenhart (twin), born Aug. 2, 1876, in Liverpool, Pa ; died June 1, 1906 Married, 1900, Annie Freed Issue (1) Lester Freed No record

57117—Florence Marion Lenhart, (twin), born Aug 2, 1876, in Liverpool, Pa Married, 1900, Ira Wert Address, Liverpool, Pa Issue (1) Lenhart, (2) Mary Alice

5711171—Lenhart Wert, born April 2, 1901, died April 24, 1907, in Harrisburg, Pa

571172—Mary Alice Wert, born May 9, 1907

57118—Stewart L———— Lenhart (twin), born July 2, 1873, died ————
————.

57119—Porter C———— Lenhart (twin), born July 2, 1873; died ————
————

5712—Elmira Jane Cochran, born July 8, Hunters Valley, Pa

5713—Thomas Porter Cochran, born Feb 8, 1839, at Hunters Valley, Pa

5714—Eliza Adeline Cochran, born July 8, 1841, Hunters Valley, Pa.

5715—Ada Marion Cochran, born Oct 10, 1849 at Liverpool, Pa Married on Aug 8, 1870, Capt Daniel Meshan, Bradford, Pa Issue (1) Theresa Piollet

57151—Theresa Piollet Meshan, ... 28, 18-- Address 210 Pine St, Harrisburg, Pa

572—**Adeline Nelson Thompson,** born Feb. 29, 1824, in Delaware Township, Juniata County, Pa, died -————. Married on Sept 30, 1839 at Thompsontown, Pa, John Stewart Lukens (born Aug 1, 1819 near Thompsontown, Pa ; died May 21, 1895), son of Abraham and Annie (Stewart) Lukens, grandson of Henry and Gracy (Stewart) Lukens and of Squire John and Elizabeth (Miller) Stewart, a great-grandson of Abraham Lukens, of David Walker and of William and Elizabeth Stewart, parents of both Gracy and John Stewart, a great-great-grandson of John and Elizabeth Lukens and of Archibald and Margaret Stewart His grandfather, Henry Lukens, who settled in 1802 on what was subsequently known as the Bradford Fruit Farm in Juniata County, Pa, was a son of Abraham Lukens who warranted 232 acres of land in Juniata County, Pa, Mar 7, 1775, and a grandson of John and Elizabeth Lukens who patented 243 acres on Jan 2, 1767 and 366 acres on Apr 13, 1774 in Juniata County, Pa The great-great-grandparents of J. Stewart Lukens, Archibald and Margaret Stewart, came to this country in Oct, 1752 from Newry, Ireland, and in Sept, 1753 settled on what was known as the "Bark Tavern Tract" in Perry County, Pa J Stewart Lukens was a Justice of the Peace for 22 years Issue (1) Martha Jane Stewart, (2) Lavenia Annie, (3) Ada Marion

5721—**Martha Jane Stewart Lukens,** born Jan 11, 1848, at ————— Elijah P.——— Hudson of Minnesota Issue (1) Lewis Leonard, (2) Willie Seward

57211—**Lewis Leonard Hudson,** born Mar 12, 1864

57212—**Willie Seward Hudson,** born May 25, 1867 Address, Thompsontown, Pa

5722—**Lavenia Annie Lukens,** born —————, died young.

5723—**Ada Marion Lukens,** born —————; died young.

BRANCH NO. 6.

6—Sarah Thomson, born ——, 1748, died Jan 3, 1814, aged 66 years; buried with her husband at Brown's Mills, in what was then Mifflin and is now Juniata County, Pa Married on June 30, 1772, William Mc-Alister (born ——, 1745, died July 7, 1819, aged 74 years), son of Hugh McAlister, Scotch Protestant who married a Miss Harbison and emigrated from the north of Ireland to this country, settling first in Lancaster County and later in what is now Perry County, Pa, where he died in 1769—see 3, 44, and 56 At the age of 18 years in July, 1763 he was one of a party of twelve who pursued and fought a band of twenty-five Indians who invaded Tuscarora Valley—see "History of Juniata and Susquehanna Valleys in Pennsylvania," p 75 On page 835 it is stated that "William McAlister, with his older brother Hugh and others returned to Juniata Valley after the Indian troubles had ceased in 1766 and he settled on a tract at the head of the Cocolamus which was taken up by John Gallagher, June 4, 1762 On (Aug 13,) 1766 he purchased and (on Oct. 29, 1766) he obtained an order of survey for a (107-acre) tract called the 'Addition' (in Fermanagh and Greenwood Township, Mifflin County, Pa, for which the warrant of acceptance was issued on Nov 11, 1790) In 1812 he obtained a warrant for 73 acres south and west He also purchased other tracts of land in the neighborhood On the Gallagher tract he settled, and, on June 30, 1772, married Sarah Thompson He joined Captain John Hamilton's Company during the Revolution Before leaving home he made his will, dated Dec 21, 1776, leaving his estate to his wife Sarah, and only son Hugh (61) then three years old He went to the army and returned in safety He cut his name out of the will he had written with his own hand It is now in the possession of his grandson John B McAlister (624) He was one of the party who gathered May 21, 1780 to organize to protect the frontier In 1789 he built at the place now known as Brown's Mills, a grist-mill, saw-mill and distillery, and in 1790 was assessed on 150 acres of land, the mills, distillery and a slave He lived at the farm until his death July 7, 1819, aged 74 years, his wife, Sarah, had died a few years previous The grist-mill was burned in later years and rebuilt by John McAlister (63) It was about one mile below the Mansion House, and later was sold by the McAlisters to the Stitzer Brothers (632) who sold the property to Peter Brown William McAlister built a fulling-mill on the main road, at what is now Cocolamus, in 1814, which was completed, however, by his son William (62), who fitted it up for fulling and put in carding machines The mill was torn down in 1848 and a tannery built which was run by John McAlister until 1862" As a result of the labors of Mrs Henrietta (McAlister) Baldwin (3452), who is doubly related to the descendants of William and Sarah (Thompson) McAlister, although not herself a descendant, there has been collected a complete

record of William McAlister's Revolutionary Service, and as a result of
the labors of Miss Jane Elliott McAlister a relative but not a descendant,
much information has been collected concerning the descendants The
will made by William McAlister prior to going to war is now in the
possession of the family of John Edmund Jamison (6441) It bears the
date of Dec, 1776 in which month the company under Captain John
Hamilton was raised in and left Lost Creek Valley On pp 248, 249,
Penn Archives, Fifth Series, Vol VI, appear the names of William
McAlister and his brother Hugh, as members of the Associators and
Militia, County of Cumberland, Fourth Battalion, in service Jan, 1778
In Jan, 1779 their names appear on the muster roll of Capt. James
Gibson's Company of Militia of the Fourth Battalion of Cumberland
County, commanded by Col James Wilson—see Penn Archives, Fifth
Series, Vol VI, pp 259 and 243 He was a member of Capt Hugh
McAlister s Company, Seventh Battalion, Cumberland County Militia,
commanded by Col Purdy, May 1, 1780—Fifth Series, Vol VI, p 478
also pp 483, 484 His name appears on the pay roll of Capt Daniel
McClellan's Company of Cumberland County Associators and Militia in
service from Sept 1, 1780 to Nov 2, 1780—Vol VI, Fifth Series, pp 614,
619 also pp 471, 472 William McAlister received depreciation pay for
service in the Cumberland County Militia—Vol IV, Fifth Series, p 294
The descendants of William McAlister are eligible to membership in the
"Sons of the Revolution" or the "Daughters of the Revolution " In his
last will, dated May 31, 1819 in Greenwood Township, Mifflin County,
Pa, William McAlister makes no mention of the only persons referred
to in his earlier will, namely, his wife and son Hugh, both of whom
had died before the later date He devises to his sons John, son William,
son Robert H, grandson William Harrison McAlister, son John's children, grandson William son of Isaac, son Isaac's children, grandson William Bell son of daughter Mary, sons William John and Robert; children
William, John, Isaac and Mary who married Thomas Bell He appointed
his "sons William and John, both of Greenwood Township" his executors
with David Boal (7) and Robert Thompson (3) as arbitrators in case
of dispute The children of William and Sarah (Thomson) McAlister
were (1) Hugh, (2) William, (3) John, (4) Isaac Thompson, (5) Mary,
(6) Robert Harbison

61—Hugh McAlister, born 1773, died young, after Dec 2, 1776

62—William McAlister, born Aug 28, 1780; died April 14, 1861, aged 80
years, 7 months and 18 days, buried with wife at McAlisterville, Pa.
He was a surveyor and a farmer, lived near Cocolamus He married
on Jan. 30, 1810, Mary (Polly) McCully, born Aug 23, 1787, died July
2, 1847, aged 59 years, 10 months and 10 days, buried at McAlisterville,
Pa She was the daughter of Thomas McCully (died Aug 30, 1826,
in the 64th year of his age) and Jane (————) McCully (died

Aug. 10, 1826 in the 65th year of her age). Issue (1) Sarah, (2) Jane
E————, (3) William Harrison, (4) James, (5) John Bell, (6)
Annie.

621—Sarah (Sallie) McAlister, born Jan 6, 1811, died June 29, 1897, aged
86 years, 5 months and 23 days Lived in McAlisterville, Pa Never
married

622—Jane E McAlister, born May 7, 1813; died Oct 11, 1891, aged 78
years, 7 months and 4 days. Married on April 10, 1862, William
Cunningham (born 1826, died Feb 16, 1886, aged 66 years; buried
with his wife at Mifflintown, Pa.) son of David and Jane (————)
Cunningham. No issue.

623—William Harrison McAlister, born Nov. 26, 1815; died Nov 1, 1897,
(buried at McAlisterville) He was a merchant at Cocolamus Mar-
ried on June 8, 1859, in Tuscarora Valley, Rebecca Jane Kelly (born
Oct 7, 1825, in Tuscarora Valley), daughter of Moses and Elizabeth
Lyon (Patterson) Kelly and granddaughter of John and Rebecca
(Clark) Kelly and of John and Nancy (Lyon) Patterson, and great-
granddaughter of Alexander Patterson who was born in Ireland in
1724 (See Biographical Encyclopedia of Juniata Valley, pp 816, 825)
She was a sister of Elizabeth Kelly, who married John Moore Died
Sept 28, 1913 at McAlisterville, Pa No children

624—James McAlister, born Nov. 22, 1818, at Cocolamus, Pa.; died July
25, 1876, aged 57 years, 8 months and 3 days buried at McAlisterville,
Pa Married on March 16, 1875, in Mifflin County, Pa , Rebecca
Armstrong Lyon of Mifflin County, Pa (born Nov. 18, 1831, died ——
at Lewistown, Pa), daughter of Hon George Armstrong Lyon of
Mifflin County, Pa (born 1801, died Oct 23, 1873) and Jessie (Alexander) Lyon (born Jan 17 1806, died May 12, 1835). Granddaughter
of James Alexander (born Feb 16, 1772, died April 17, 1847) and
Jane (Adams) Alexander (born in Philadelphia Pa , Sept. 15, 1776,
died July 27, 1834). Great granddaughter of James Alexander and
Rosey (Reed) Alexander, great. great-granddaughter of John and
Margaret (Glasson) Alexander, who came to America 1736, and settled
in Chester County, Pa. No issue. Mrs Mary Lyon McAlister, married
second, Prof. David Wilson, Ph D (born April 7, 1813). Principal
of Tuscarora Academy from 1839 to 1852, of Airy View Port Royal
from 1852 to 1890 Died April 19, 1890. Buried at Church Hill, Port
Royal, Pa Mrs Wilson died at Lewistown, Pa and is buried at
Belleville, Pa

625—John Bell McAlister, born Oct 11, 1821, at Cocolamus, Pa., died at
McAlisterville Pa, June 29 aged 61 years 8 months and 18
days. Lived at McAlisterville, Pa Never married.

626—Annie McAlister, born March 26, 1825, died Sept 17, 1891, aged 66 years, 5 months and 22 days   Married on May 9, 1871, James Gilfillen of Millerstown, Pa   James Gilfillen (born 1806, died Oct 26, 1879, aged 73 years) had formerly married Margaretta Hollingsworth Alexander   He was a son of James and Sarah (Jones) Gilfillen   No issue

63—"Squire John" McAlister, born April 12, 1782, died April 14, 1847. Married on Oct. 28, 1806, his first cousin, Jane Thomson (born 1777; died Feb 23, 1850, in her 73rd year, buried at Brown's Mills, Pa), daughter of Robert Thomson (56) and Sarah (Mitchell) Thomson and granddaughter of John Thomson, the grandfather of John McAlister   See Biographical History of Juniata Valley Pa., p. 835 and 915   The father of Sarah Mitchell was probably James Mitchell, who was killed by the Indians   Issue (1) Sarah, (2) David, (3) Eliza, (4) Mary, (5) Mitchell, (6) Lucinda, (7) John Hutchison, (8) Jane Thompson

631—Sarah McAlister, born Aug 4, 1807, at Cocolamus, Pa.; died Aug 18, 1880, at McAlisterville, Pa   Married on Feb. 6, 1849, at Cocolamus, Pa , John Stitzer (born 1809, died April 1, 1879, aged 70 years, at Mifflinburg, Pa)   They lived for several years in Juniata County and also in Union County, Pa   They lived for some years on a farm near Washington, D C , and later moved to Port Royal where both died   No issue

632—David McAlister, born ——————; died young.

633—Eliza McAlister, born 1812 at Cocolamus, Pa.; died Oct. 22, 1877, at Doyles Mill, Pa   Married on Jan. 12, 1847, at Cocolamus, Pa , Isaac Hawn (born 1809; died April 4, 1874, aged 65 years, buried above Port Royal, Pa)   No issue

634—Mary McAlister, born 1815, died July 23, 1868, aged 53 years). Married on Nov 10, 1846, David Montgomery Jamison (see 6623) (born July 10, 1811; died Feb 11, 1901), son of John and Sarah (Watson) Jamison and grandson of John Watson (born March 12, 1776) and Jane Wilson (born March 19, 1758, died Sept 11, 1803) (see 644)   See page 382 of Stewart Family. No issue

635—Mitchell McAlister, born ——————, died young.

636—Lucinda McAlister, born Feb 20, 1820, in McAlisterville, Pa , died Oct 27, 1885. Married on Nov. 17, 1846, John Patterson Kelly (born in Milford Township Juniata County, Pa , Nov 20, 1821; died March 22, 1902 at Doyle's Mills, Pa , son of Moses and Elizabeth Lyon

(Patterson) Kelly, and grandson of John and Rebecca (Clark) Kelly and of John and Nancy (Lyon) Patterson (see Biographical Encyclopedia of Juniata Valley, 1897, J M Runk & Co, Chambersburg, Pa, pages 816, 825 and 1274) Farmer and merchant at Doyles Mills, Pa Issue (1) Edward McAlister, (2) Jennie Elizabeth, (3) James Austin, (4) Mary Laura

6361—Edward McAlister Kelly, born Oct 18, 1850 Married on Nov 14, 1872, Jennie Wilson McDonald (she died June 30. 1912 at Port Royal, Pa.) daughter of John and Catherine (Allen) McDonald No issue Address, 1912 Spruce Hill, Pa See Biographical Encyclopedia of Juniata Valley, page 1274

6362—Jennie Elizabeth Kelly, born June 13. 1852. in Juniata County, Pa Married on Feb 1, 1883, Samuel Alexander Graham (born Dec 21, 1845 in Spruce Hill Township), son of Samuel and Isabell Young (Patton) Graham, grandson of William and Fannie (Lyon) Graham (see Biographical Encyclopedia of Juniata Valley, Pa, pages 964 and 791) Farmer, Port Royal, Pa. Issue (1) Charles Kelly. (2) Lucinda Bell, (3) Infant, (4) Edgar Thompson, (4) Henry Alexander

63621—Charles Kelly Graham, born March 1, 1886; died Aug 27, 1886

63622—Lucinda Bell Graham, born Nov 18, 1887, at Spruce Hill, Juniata County, Pa. Married on June 5, 1907, at Spruce Hill, Robert McClellan Barton, son of Josiah McClellan and Ida Collins (Crouce) Barton and grandson of Robert W——— and Sarah Jane (McWilliams) Barton High School Principal, Middleburg, Snyder County, Pa Issue (1) Harry Graham, (2) Karl McClellan, (3) *daughter.*

636221—Harry Graham Barton, born Sept. 16, 1907, at Spruce Hill, Pa

636222—Karl McClellan Barton, born April 20, 1911, at Spruce Hill, Pa.

636223—Daughter Barton, born Dec. 1913

63623—Infant Graham, born Aug. 18, 1889, at Spruce Hill, Pa.; died Sept 1, 1889 at Spruce Hill.

63624—Edgar Thompson Graham, born Feb 23, 1894 in Spruce Township, Juniata Co, Pa Unmarried Address, Port Royal, Pa.

63625—Harry Alexander Graham, b July 7 1895 at Spruce Hill, Pa.; died April 12, 1900 at Spruce Hill Buried at Academia, Pa.

6363—James Austin Kelly, born April 2, 1856, died March 28, 1883. Unmarried Buried at Academia, Pa

6364—Mary Laura (Melinda) Kelly, born March 8, 1865, at Mifflin, Juniata Co., Pa., died Jan 24, 1905 Married Feb. 3, 1887 at Doyles Mills, Pa George Henry Moyer, son of Nathaniel and Mary Catherine (Kepner) Moyer, grandson of Samuel and Catherine (Schwink) Moyer and great grandson of George and Catherine (Kline) Moyer see Biographical Encyclopedia of Juniata Valley, Page 820 Issue (1) Charles Edward, (2) Harry Nathaniel, (3) Elizabeth Jane, (4) Albert Kelly, (5) George Norman, (6) Mary Rebecca, (7) Pearl Emeline. Mrs Mary (Kelly) Moyer is buried at Academia, Pa

63641—Charles Edward Moyer, born June 27, 1888, in Mifflin, Juniata Co, Pa Address, 5923 Howard Street, East Pittsburgh, Pa

63642—Harry Nathaniel Moyer, born Jan 11, 1890, in Mifflin Address, Mifflin, Pa

63643—Elizabeth Jane Moyer, born Sept. 1, 1891, in Mifflin, Pa Address, Mifflin, Pa

63644—Albert Kelly Moyer, born Aug. 5, 1893, in Mifflin, Pa. Address, Mifflin, Pa

63645—George Norman Moyer, born Jan. 12, 1895, in Mifflin, Pa. Address, Mifflin, Pa

63646—Mary Rebecca Moyer, born July 21, 1897, in Milford Township, Juniata Co, Pa Died Jan 25, 1907

63647—Pearl Emeline Moyer, born March 3, 1903, in Milford Township Address, Mifflin, Pa.

637—John Hutchison McAlister, born March 10, 1818, at Cocolamus, Pa, died May 16, 1890, at Mifflintown, buried at Mifflintown, Pa Married on June 20, 1861, Mary Thomson (born Dec 8, 1824; died April 6, 1896, at Mifflintown, Pa), daughter of William and Hannah (Mincer) Thomson and a granddaughter of Robert and Sarah (Mitchell) Thomson, the grandparents of both the father and the mother of John Hutchinson McAlister (see 665). Lived at Mifflintown, Pa No issue

638—Jane Thomson McAlister, born March 11 1822, died Sept 27, 1890, at McAlisterville, Pa. Unmarried

64—Isaac Thompson McAlister, born May 7, 1784, died Jan 5, 1829 Married on May 21, 1815, Eleanor Wilson, daughter of Nathaniel and Eleanor (——————) Wilson of Columbia County. They moved near Cincinnati, Ohio where he died Issue (1) William, (2) Eleanor, (3) Nathaniel Wilson, (4) Sarah Thomson, (5) Hester Maria

641—William McAlister, born Feb 25, 1816, died in infancy.

642—Eleanor McAlister, born Sept 14, 1818, at Pleasant Ridge—now Cincinnati, Ohio; died 1842, buried at Pleasant Ridge, Pa Married on July 1, 1835 at McAlisterville, Pa , Lewis North, son of James and Rachel (Jordan) North grandson of William North—see Biographical Encyclopedia of Juniata Valley, Page 795—brother of John North who married Jane Huston McAlister, first cousin of Eleanor McAlister Lewis North was a carpenter and undertaker at Pleasant Ridge, Ohio, where he died Jan 1842 aged 58 years Buried at Pleasant Ridge. Issue (1) Theodore, (2) Euphemia Strouse, (3) Ellen, (4) Sarah Maria

6421—Theodore North, born Aug. 5, 1836, at Pleasant Ridge, Ohio, died in Thompsontown, Pa , Aug 16, 1855. Aged 19 years and 11 months , buried at McAlisterville

6422—Euphemia Strouse North, born April 20, 1839 at Pleasant Ridge, Ohio, died May 11, 1864; aged 25 years, 6 months and 15 days Buried at Mifflintown, Pa Married on Nov 10, 1858 at Mifflin, Pa William B—————— Forester of Harrisburg, Pa , machinist at Mifflin shops of P R R Issue (1) Caleb Lewis, (2) Minnie L——————.

64221—Caleb Lewis Forester, born —————— , at Mifflintown, Pa ; died 1913, at Kansas City, Mo Undertaker at Kansas City Married on —————— , Miss Kipp Address, Mrs C L Forester, 918 Brooklyn Ave , Kansas City, Mo Issue (1) Hazel Kipp

642211—Hazel Kipp Forester, born at Kansas City, Mo

64222—Minnie L—————— Forester, born Feb 21, 1863, at Mifflin, Pa.; died Dec 9, 1879, aged 16 years, 9 months and 18 days, buried at Mifflintown, Pa

6423—Ellen North, born 1840 or 1841 at Pleasant Ridge, Ohio; died about 1866; buried at Cincinnati, Ohio. Married on —————— —————— at Pleasant Ridge John Pearson son of —————— —————— Issue, two sons ud to be in California

13

6424—Sarah Maria North, born 1842 at Pleasant Ridge, Ohio, died about 1856, buried at Pleasant Ridge, Ohio.

643—Nathaniel Wilson McAlister, born Aug 12, 1820, at Cincinnati, Ohio; died during summer of 1867 at Washingtonville, Pa Married on May 21, 1850 Mary W———— Barber, daughter of Rev Daniel Barber, a Presbyterian Minister. N W. McAlister lived at Washingtonville, Pa Issue (1) Eleanor, (2) Alice, (3) Thomas, (4) Jessie.

6431—Eleanor McAlister, born near McAlisterville, Pa., died on ———— ———————————— at Philadelphia, Pa , buried at Williamsport, Pa. Married on ———————————— at ———————————— J———————— B———————— Rank, a lumber dealer, Philadelphia, Pa No issue. After his first wife's death, Mr. Rank married———— ————————Kerr and lived and died at Washington, D C

6432—Alice McAlister, born near McAlisterville, Pa , died ———————— young, at Washingtonville, Pa

6433—Thomas McAlister, born ———————————————————— · · at ————————; died ————————, in 1882, aged about 20 years, at Philadelphia, buried at Washingtonville, Pa

6434—Jessie McAlister, born at Washingtonville, Pa , died ————————; ———————— young at Washingtonville, Pa.; buried at Washingtonville, Pa

644—Sarah Thompson McAlister, born June 24, 1823, at Pleasant Ridge, now Cincinnati, Ohio (died Nov 20, 1896, buried at McAlisterville, Pa) Married on March 9, 1840, at McAlisterville. Pa , Robert Wilson Jamison (born Sept 24, 1816; died June 1, 1875), son of John and Sarah (Watson) Jamison and grand-son of John Watson (born March 12, 1776) and Jane (Wilson) Watson (born March 19, 1758, died Sept 11, 1803) of Juniata County, Pa See Page 381 of the "Stewart Family" See 634 and 6623 Issue (1) John Edmund, (2) Henry Clay, (3) William Watson, (4) David Montgomery, (5) Lucien Wilson, (6) Sarah Watson, (7) Isaac McAlister, (8) Jennie Eleanor, (9) Clara May

6441—John Edmund Jamison, born on Sept. 7, 1841, near McAlisterville, Pa He served in Co D, 35 Penn Inft Farmer, retired, elder in Presbyterian Church, McAlisterville, Pa Married on Jan 8, 1867, Catherine Graybill (born April 3, 1842, near Mexico, Pa , died May 27, 1914; buried at McAlisterville, Pa , daughter of Peter and Hannah Graybill, and granddaughter of John and Mary (Eppler) Graybill Issue (1) William Grant, (2) Mary Laura, (3) Sadie Elizabeth, (4) Robert Wilson, (5) Hannah Graybill, (6) John Cloyd, (7) Olive Catherine, (8) Thaddeus Stevens, (9) Jacob Oscar

64411—William Grant Jamison, born July 8, 1868, near McAlisterville, Pa Address, 2405 North Sixth Street, Harrisburg, Pa Married on April 6, 1898 at Newport, Pa Olive May Bixler (born July 15, 1868 Bixler's Mills, Perry County, Pa) daughter of Joseph McKendree and Almira (Behel) Bixler and grand-daughter of Jacob and Sarah (Lesh) Bixler. Issue (1) Catherine Bixler

644111—Catherine Bixler Jamison, born July 20, 1899 at Harrisburg, Pa Address, 2405 North Sixth Street, Harrisburg, Pa

64412—Mary Laura Jamison, born Jan 24 1871, at McAlisterville, Pa Married on Sept. 28, 1893 at McAlisterville, Pa Reuben Bandy Firkins, son of Leonard and Mary (Abbott) Firkins and grandson of Edwin and Lydia (Chappel) Firkins of England Farmer Shabbona, De Kalb Co , Ill R R. No 2 Issue (1) Robert Jamison, (2) Dorothy Catherine, (3) John Henry, (4) Beulah May, (5) Curtis James

644121—Robert Jamison Firkins, born March 17, 1895, at Shabbona, Ill.

644122—Dorothy Catherine Firkins, born April 16, 1897, at Shabbona, Ill

644123—John Henry Firkins, born May 28, 1899, at Shabbona, Ill

644124—Beulah May Firkins, born April 14 1902, at Shabbona, Ill

644125—Curtis James Firkins, born Oct 20, 1906, at Shabbona, Ill

64413—Sadie Elizabeth Jamison, born March 9 1873, at McAlisterville, Pa Married on Oct 22, 1895 at Swales, Pa Henry Clinton Sausman, son of John Kauffman and Barbara (Smith) Sausman and grandson of John and Sarah (Kauffman) Sausman and of Daniel and Christiana (Koons) Smith Merchant at McAlisterville, Pa Issue (1) John Jamison.

644131—John Jamison Sausman, born April 18, 1907, at Swales Pa

64414—Robert Wilson Jameson, born Sept 21 1875, at McAlisterville, Pa Address, Amboy, Ill Insurance Agent. Married on Dec. 24, 1907 at McAlisterville Pa Lottie May Leister, daughter of Jonas and Sabine (Argobast) Leister and granddaughter of Abraham and Eliza   ies Robe

644141—**James Robert Jameson,** born July 23, 1910, at Amboy, Ill.

64415—**Hannah Graybill Jamison,** born Feb 25, 1878, at McAlisterville, Pa.
Married on March 31, 1903 at Mifflintown, Pa B Frank Vanormer
(born July 20, 1873), son of Williamson and Elizabeth (Shields)
Vanormer and grandson of Amos and Hannah (Houghawout) Vanormer. Rural Mail Carrier, McAlisterville, Pa Issue (1) Elizabeth, (2) Catherine, (3) Sarah, (4) Charles Jamison, (5) Alice
Isabel

644151—**Elizabeth Vanormer,** born Jan. 5, 1905, at McAlisterville, Pa

644152—**Catherine Vanormer** (twin), born Dec 14, 1906, at McAlisterville,
Pa, died April 18, 1909 at McAlisterville, Pa, buried at Mc-
Alisterville, Pa

644153—**Sarah Vanormer** (twin), born Dec. 14, 1906, at McAlisterville, Pa.

644154—**Charles Jamison Vanormer,** born April 20, 1909, at McAlisterville,
Pa.

644155—**Alice Isabel Vanormer,** born Oct. 11, 1911, at McAlisterville, Pa

64416—**John Cloyd Jamison,** born on July 1, 1881, died Mar 1, 1882, aged
8 months

64417—**Olive Catherine Jamison,** born Jan. 26 1882, at McAlisterville, Pa.
Married on Sept 26, 1913 at East Salem, Pa, John Longaker, son
of Elias and Barbara (Hart) Longaker Address, Wabasso, Fla.
Issue (1) John Grabill

644171—**John Grabill Longaker,** born Apr 4, 1915, at Jacksonville, Fla

64418—**Thaddeus Stevens Jamison,** born March 21, 1885 at McAlisterville,
Juniata County, Pa Address McAlisterville, Pa, R F D. Married on Oct 27, 1911 at Oakland Mills, Juniata County, Pa. Alma
Florence Kinzer, daughter of Luther and Emma (Smith) Kinzer
and granddaughter of Samuel and Mary (Liedy) Kinzer Issue
(1) Mildred Emma, (2) Olive Catherine

644181—**Mildred Emma Jamison,** born May 16, 1912, at Oakland Mills, Pa.
died June 26, 1913 at Wabasso, Fla Buried there

644182—**Olive Catherine Jamison,** born Jan. 5, 1914, at Wabasso, Fla

64419—Jacob Oscar Jamison, born on April 25, 1888, at McAlisterville, Pa
Merchant, Wabasso, Fla   Unmarried

6442—Henry Clay Jamison, born May 28, 1844, died Dec. 8, 1884

6443—William Watson Jamison, born Sept 30, 1848 (died July 24, 1882,
aged 33 years, 9 months and 24 days, buried at McAlisterville, Pa)
Married on Dec 24, 1875 Lizzie S Landis, daughter of Benjamin and
Susan (Stuck) Landis (born 1858, died Nov 17, 1878, aged 20
years)   Issue (1) Benjamin Wilson and (2) Lillian May.

64431—Benjamin Wilson Jamison, born Sept 2, 1876, died Nov 1, 1878

64432—Lillian May Jamison, born Jan 17, 1879, died Mar. 5, 1879

6444—David Montgomery Jamison, born May 15, 1852, near McAlisterville,
Pa ; died April 22, 1809 at Amboy, Ill   Married on July 16, 1878 at
Limerick, Bureau Co, Ill   Jennie Lenora Ryder, daughter of Jacob
and Emeline (Black) Ryder and granddaughter of William and
Rachael (————————) Ryder and of Rebecca Black   Mrs Jamison
lives 1913 in Amboy, Ill   Issue (1) Harry Wilson, (2) Robert Her-
man, (3) Boyd Leroy, (4) Ida Bernice, (5) William Harrison, (6)
David Montgomery.

64441—Harry Wilson Jamison, born April 5, 1879, at Republican City,
Nebraska   Address, Nanton, Alberta, Can   Married on Nov. 4,
1902 at Franklin Grove, Ill   Lulu Viola Buck, daughter of George
Washington and Belinda (Feldkirchner) Buck, and granddaughter
of George and Susan (————————) Feldkirchner. No children.

64442—Robert Herman Jamison, born Dec 28, 1880 at Harlane, Neb , died
Sept 7, 1883 in De Kalb Co, Ill.

64443—Boyd Leroy Jamison, born June 7, 1883 at Paw Paw, Ill ; died Sept.
26, 1884 at Paw Paw, Ill

64444—Ida Bernice Jamison, born July 27, 1885 at Paw Paw, Ill   Married
Jan 1 1908 at Amboy, Ill   Charles Wilbur June (born April 1, 1881
at Amboy, Ill), son of Walter Edmund June (born June 26, 1846 at
Binghampton, N Y ; died Aug. 1, 1902 at Amboy, Ill) and Elizabeth Ann (Binns) June (born Sept. 9, 1853 at Manchester, England),
grandson of Walter June (born Feb 2, 1796, died Aug 18, 1872 at
Am··s I'' an Hannah ▔ ·· 'Palmer) June (born March 12,
1803 in Pau eld C··, C nn   ied Dec. 26, 1890 at Amboy, Ill) and

grandson of George Binns (born Dec. 27, 1825 at Staly, England;
died May 17, 1902 at Amboy, Ill) and of Ann (Johnson) Binns
(born March 11, 1825 at Stockport, England, died July 9, 1907 at
Amboy, Ill. Charles W. June is a farmer at Amboy, Lee Co, Ill.
Issue (1) Leroy Albert

644441—Leroy Albert June, born Sept 18, 1912, at Amboy, Ill

64445—William Harrison Jamison, born May 16, 1892, at Harmon, Lee
County, Ill Storekeeper for Northern Utilities Company, Morrison,
Ill.

64446—David Montgomery Jamison, born Sept 9, 1894, at Lee Center, Ill ,
died June 26, 1898 at Amboy, Ill

6445—Lucien Wilson Jamison, born July 23, 1854, near McAlisterville, Pa.
died Aug 30, 1913 at Lamoni, Iowa For 19 years he lived on a farm
near Paw Paw, Ill Married on Jan 27, 1886, at Sandwich, Ill, Louise
Nicholson from near Elmira, N Y, daughter of Charles and Fannie
(Cady) Nicholson, of New England ancestry Issue (1) Fannie Cady,
(2) Sarah Minnie, (3) Delos Nicholson, (4) Harrison McAlister,
(5) Charles Victor Dewey

64451—Fannie Cady Jamison, born on May 19, 1887, at Paw Paw, Ill.
Married on Dec. 25, 1912 at Lamoni, Iowa Arthur Leonel Martin
(born Sept. 3, 1889), son of Rasmus and Rebecca (Wadley) Martin
and grandson of William and Mariani (Bozarth) Wadley, Rasmus
Martin was born in Denmark. A. L. Martin is a farmer at Lamoni,
Iowa No issue.

64452—Sarah Minnie Jamison, born Sept 21, 1889, at Paw Paw, DeKalb
Co, Ill She taught in the rural schools of Decatur and Ringgold
Counties, Ill, for four years Married, Feb 22, 1911, at Lamoni,
Iowa, Benjamin H. Barnes (born Jan 6, 1887), son of William
Henry and Margaret (Sincoe) Barnes William Henry Barnes was
a pioneer settler of Southern Iowa, and a soldier in the Civil War
Benjamin H Barnes is a farmer Address, Clark, S D Issue (1)
Margaret Louise, (2) Ruth Elberta

644521—Margaret Louise Barnes, born Jan 25, 1914, at Clark, S. D

644522—Ruth Elberta Barnes, born Dec 30, 1915, at Lamoni, Iowa

64453—Delos Nicholson Jamison, born on March 20, 1892, at Paw Paw, Ill.
Manager of farm at Davidson, Saskatchewan, Can. Unmarried

64454—Harrison McAlister Jamison, born on Oct 25, 1896, at Paw Paw, Ill Address, Lamoni, Iowa.

64455—Charles Victor Dewey Jamison, born on May 2, 1899, at Paw Paw, Ill. Address, Lamoni, Iowa

6446—Sarah Watson Jamison, born June 1, 1857, died June 9, 1857

6447—Isaac McAlister Jamison, born July 3, 1859 Married on July 31, 1884 at Millerstown, Pa, Catherine Alice Schreffler, daughter of Jacob and Catherine (Hepner) Schreffler Farmer, McAlisterville, Pa Issue (1) Edgar Wilson, (2) Annie May.

64471—Edgar Wilson Jamison, born Feb 8, 1886, near McAlisterville, Pa Farmer Address, R R No 1, McAlisterville, Pa Married on March 31, 1910 at McAlisterville, Effie Elizabeth Long (born Dec. 16, 1885, near Oakland Mills, Pa), daughter of Franklin and Josephine (Dunn) Long and granddaughter of Eli and Martha (Vanormer) Dunn Issue (1) Freede May, (2) Mildred Kathryn

644711—Freeda May Jamison, born May 26, 1913, near McAlisterville, Pa

644712—Mildred Kathryn Jamison, born Sept. 1, 1914, at Washingtonville, Pa

64472—Annie May Jamison, born on Aug. 23 1889, near McAlisterville, Pa. Married on Dec 20, 1911 at Wilmington, Del Irwin Walter Bashore, son of Irwin and Martha (Stouffer) Bashore and grandson of David and Elizabeth (Brennaman) Bashore Farmer Address, Mifflintown, Pa, R R No children

6448—Jennie Eleanor Jamison, born June 11, 1861, near McAlisterville, Pa Married twice, first on March 24, 1886 at McAlisterville, Pa Jacob Rauch Goshert (born Feb 23, 1847; died Nov. 4, 1895), son of John and Catharine (Rauch) Goshert Issue (1) Clara Jamison, (2) Leroy Wilson, (3) Bernice. Married second time, on Jan 31, 1903, at Burket, Ind John Theodore Cunningham, son of James Thompson and Mary (Miller) Cunningham, grandson of————————and——————————(Thompson) Cunningham of Eastern Pa Address Burket, Kosincko Co., Ind No issue.

64481—Clara Jamison Goshert, born May 2_ 189_ at Burket Ind Address Burket Ind Teacher Valparis University

64482—**Leroy Wilson Goshert,** born March 25, 1892, at Burket, Ind. Address, Burket, Ind Graduated from the Winona College of Agriculture, Winona Lake, Ind.

64483—**Bernice Goshert,** born May 7, 1894, at Burket, Ind Address, Burket Ind Teacher

6449—**Clara May Jamison,** born Aug 12, 1864, at Swales, Pa. Farmer Address, Bunkerstown, Juniata Co, Pa Married on March 16, 1898 at Swales William Henry Rempfer, son of George and Nancy (Mickey) Rempfer and grandson of George and Margaret (Wagner) Rempfer. Issue (1) Mary Margaret.

64491—**Mary Margaret Rempfer,** born May 11, 1903. Address, Bunkerstown, Pa.

645—**Hester Maria McAlister,** born on June 7, 1827, at Pleasant Ridge, Ohio, died on——— at ————. Married on Oct 19, 1848, at McAlisterville, Pa John Curran Moore (born on———— at Shirleysburg, Huntington County, Pa), son of Dr James Moore and Harriet (Barton) Moore, grandson of John Moore and Rebecca (Curran) Moore and of Kimber Barton—a hero of the Revolution, who died in 1835, aged 92—and Mary (Eason) Barton John Moore was a major under Washington in the Revolution See Biographical Encyclopedia of Juniata Valley, page 612 After the death of Hester Maria (McAlister) Moore, J C Moore married Mary George (born about 1823) a descendant of Jane (McAlister) George. Children of J C and H M (McA) Moore Issue (1) Harrietta Louisa, (2) Clara, (3) Julia, (4) Isaac Ulysses.

6451—**Harriette Louisa Moore,** born ————; died 1850.

6452—**Clara Moore,** born on ————, at Shippensburg, Pa. Unmarried Address, Camp Hill, Pa

6453—**Julia Moore,** born on Nov 8, 1854, at New Grenada, Fulton County, Pa (died ————) Married on Dec 6, 1876 at Mount Joy, Pa. William Winebrenner Cassel, son of Jacob Ennisman and Mary Jane (Winebrenner) Cassel. Address, Mount Joy, Lancaster Co, Pa Issue (1) Maude Moore, (2) Clara Wynne, (3) Charles Moore

64531—**Maude Moore Cassel,** born on July 26, 1878, at Mount Joy, Lancaster Co, Pa. Married on June 15, 1905, at Mount Joy, Pa William Clayton Zeiders, son of John and Lucy (Allen) Zeiders Address, 40 N 13th Street, Harrisburg, Pa Issue—— ———

64532—Clara Wynne Cassel, born April 20, 1880, at Mount Joy, Lancaster Co., Pa. Graduated from Mount Joy High School, 1896. Employed in Division of Public Records, Pa. State Capitol, Harrisburg. Unmarried. Address, 616 North Second Street, Harrisburg, Pa.

64533—Charles Moore Cassel, born on Oct. 11, 1888, at Sterling, Neb. Address, Mount Joy, Pa.

6454—Isaac Ulysses Moore, born at Grenad, Fulton County, Pa. Died in childhood 1862.

65—Mary McAlister, born Aug. 4, 1786. Married on ——————. Thomas Bell, born ——————; died (see 662). Thomas Bell was a boat builder for the Ohio River trade at Pittsburgh. Issue (1) John B——————, (2) Elizabeth, (3) Sara, (4) William McAlister, (5) Thompson, (6) Thomas Sharon, (7) Robert Boyd, (8) Mary.

651—John B—————— Bell, born on —————— at ——————; died ——————. Married on —————— at ——————. Mary McFarland, daughter of —————— of ——————. Issue (1) Mary, (2) William, (3) John, (4) Emily, (5) Thomas, (6) Sarah.

6511—Mary Bell, born ——————. Address, Sewickley, Pa.

6512—William Bell, born ——————. Address, ——————.

6513—John Bell, born ——————; died —————— in infancy.

6514—Emily Bell, born ——————; died —————— in infancy.

6515—Thomas Bell, born ——————. Address, Chicago, Ill. Married on —————— at —————— —————— of —————— of —————— ——————. Issue two children.

65151—————— Bell, born ——————————.

65152—————— Bell, born ——————————.

6516—Sarah Bell, born ——————.

652—Elizabeth Bell, born ——————. Married on —————— at ——————. John McCullough. Address, ——————. Issue (1) Sharon, (2) Mau ine, (3) Elizabeth, (4) Warren, (5) Webster, (6) Jane.

6521—Sharon McCullough, born —————————. Address ————————————.

6522—Madeline McCullough, born ————————————. Married ——————
———————— at —————————, De Witt, son of ————————
of ———————— Issue, 9 children

6523—Elizabeth McCullough, born ———————— Married on————————
at ———————————— De Witt, son of ———————————— of
———————————— Issue, 3 children

6524—Warren McCullough, born —————— Address, ————————————

6525—Webster McCullough, born —————— Address, ——————————

6526—Jane McCullough, born ————————— Address, ————————— .

653—Sara Bell, born ——————. Married on ————— at ————
——————, James Marshall, son of James and Mary (Peebles) Marshall　No issue

654—William McAlister Bell, born —————————, 1813; died —————————,
1893　Married —————————, 1839, Elizabeth Stuart McFadden, (born
1813, died 1900) daughter of James and Margaret (Stuart) McFadden
and granddaughter of Galbraith Stuart and Elizabeth (Scott) Stuart,
a cousin of Sir Walter Scott.　William McAlister and Elizabeth
Stuart (McFadden) Bell lived at Buena Vista, Westmoreland
County, Pa　Issue (1) James McFadden, (2) Mary Margaret, (3)
Emma Ellen, (4) Laura Jane, (5) Thomas.

6541—James McFadden Bell, born 1840; died July 7, 1906.　Banker at
Pittsburgh, Pa　Unmarried.

6542—Mary Margaret Bell, born July 27, 1842.　Married on Dec. 25, 1864
Captain Calib Greenawault　They lived at Buena Vista, Pa
Captain Greenawault died Dec 23, 1883.　No issue　Address of
Mrs. Mary (Bell) Greenawault, West Newton, Pa.

6543—Emma Ella Bell, born June 24, 1845 (died Dec. 26, 1900, buried at
West Newton, Pa)　Married on Nov —————, 1870 at —————
James Secrist, son of Page and ————— (Blackburn) Secrist
Address, West Newton, Pa　Issue (1) Laura Page, (2) William
Bell.

65431—Laura Page Secrist, born on May 24, 1872, at ——————————.
Graduated from the Pittsburgh Female College, 1892　Address,
West Newton, Pa

65432—William Bell Secrist, born on Oct 27, 1880, at ————— Graduated from Allegheny College, 1900 Attorney-at-law, Frick Annex, Pittsburgh, Pa.

6544—Laura Jane Bell, born on May 17, 1847 Married on Oct 7, 1875, at Buena Vista, Pa Isaac Thompson McAlister, born April 30, 1830 Lived in McAlisterville, Pa., where he kept store. Isaac T McAlister died Nov 4, 1894, at West Newton, Pa., where his widow now resides (1914) Issue (1) Elizabeth Bell, (2) Sara Eleanor, (3) William Stuart (see 6653-4-5)

6545—Thomas Bell, born on April, 1849, at Buena Vista, Allegheny County, Pa (died Aug 1904) Married May 27 1891, Nancy Rebecca Thompson, daughter of Harvey and Anna (McWilliams) Thompson and grandson of Matthew and Annie (—————) Thompson and of James and Deborah (—————) McWilliams Issue (1) William McFadden, (2) Jay Thompson, (3) Thomas Harvey.

65451—William McFadden Bell, born 1892, at Buena Vista Pa Address, Buena Vista, Pa

65452—Jay Thompson Bell, born —————, 1894, at Buena Vista, Pa. Student at Penn State College, State College, Pa

65453—Thomas Harvey Bell, born —————, 1899, at Buena Vista, Pa Address, Buena Vista, Pa

655—Thompson Bell, born at Pittsburgh, Pa ; died in Pittsburgh Pa, ————— 1885, buried in Allegheny Cemetery, Pittsburgh Banker. Unmarried

656—Thomas Sharon Bell, born on ————— at —————; died in Pittsburgh, Pa, —————, 1856 Unmarried.

657—Robert Boyd Bell, born on ————— at —————; died in Chicago Unmarried

658—Mary Jane Bell, born on —————, 1824, at ————— (died 1889). Married on —————, 1846 at Pittsburgh, Pa Archibald M————— Marshall, son of James and Jean (Peebles) Marshall of Allegheny City Pa. Issue (1) Mary Emma, (2) Walter, (3) Jennie, (4) Elizabeth Bell (5) Alice.

6581—Mary Emma Marshall, born on Jan 26, 1847, at Allegheny, Pa
(died Aug 8, 1896)   Married on Sept. 1, 1870, at Allegheny, Pa.
Arthur Wellington Bell son of Thomas and Charlotte (Harvey) Bell
and grandson of William and Esther (Foxhall) Bell and of Ambrose
and Charlotte (Hunterville) Harvey   (Issue (1) Mary Marshall, (2)
Arthur Wellington, (3) Archibald Marshall.

65811—Mary Marshall Bell, born Aug 17, 1873, at Allegheny, Pa   Married
on April 22, 1897, at Allegheny, Pa   Carroll Hamilton Fitzhugh,
son of Col Charles Lane and Emma (Shoenberger) Fitzhugh and
grandson of Henry and Elizabeth (Carroll) Fitzhugh and of George
K——————— and Sarah (Hamilton) Shoenberger   Address, 807
Ridge Avenue, Pittsburgh, Pa.   No Children.

65812—Arthur Wellington Bell, born March 2, 1875   Graduated from
Yale University, 1899   Broker % Holmes Wardrop & Co, Pittsburgh, Pa   Unmarried.

65813—Archibald Marshall Bell, born July 15, 1877, in Alleghany, Pa
Graduated at Yale University, 1900   Address, care of Spang Chal-
fant & Co. Fayette Coal Company, Pittsburgh, Pa   Married April
11, 1901, at Baltimore, Md   Genevieve Lord, daughter of Charles
King and Elizabeth (Walterhouse) Lord   Issue (1) Archibald
Marshall, (2) Charles Lord, (3) Genevieve Lord.

658131—Archibald Marshall Bell, Jr, born Jan 9, 1902.

658132—Charles Lord Bell, born April 3, 1905.

658133—Genevieve Lord Bell, born May 22, 1908

6582—Walter Marshall, born —————; died —————, about 1852,
aged 4 years

6583—Jennie Marshall, born —————, died —————, 1854, aged
7 years

6584—Elizabeth Bell Marshall, born Oct 24, 1854   Married June 5, 1884
Harmer Denny.   Address, 811 Ridge Avenue, North Side, Pittsburgh,
Pa.   Issue (1) Harmer, (2) Archibald Marshall.

65841—Harmer Denny, Jr, born July 2, 1886, at Pittsburgh, Pa.   Unmarried

65842—Archibald Marshall Denny, born Nov 6, 1887, at Pittsburgh, Pa
Married on Sept 28, 1907, at New York, Katharine Varnum Ken-
dall, daughter of William Beals and Kate (Whitney) Kendall
Issue (1) Archibald Marshall, (2) Katharine Kendall, (3) Kendall
Whitney

658421—Archibald Marshall Denny, Jr, born Aug 22, 1908, at Bay Head,
N J.

658422—Katharine Kendall Denny, born Jan. 27, 1910, New York

658423—Kendall Whitney Denny, born Dec 9, 1912.

6585—Alice Marshall, born ——————, died aged 5 years, about 1856

66—Robert Harbison McAlister, born Jan 19, 1797, died ————, 1859,
buried at Browns Mills, Pa Married on ———— at ————
Mariah "Mary" Crawford, a sister of Dr Crawford, probably Dr
Samuel B Crawford, son of David and Margaret (Brown) Crawford
(She died May 4, 1858, aged 57 years) Issue (1) Elizabeth, (2)
Agnes, (3) James W., (4) Hamilton, (5) Isaac Thompson, (6) James
Allen, (7) Catherine, (8) Elliott, (9) Herbison

661—Elizabeth McAlister, born Aug 11, 1819, at Cocolamus, Pa on the
farm of (6) William McAlister, died Jan 23 1881, at McAlisterville,
Pa. Married on Jan 3, 1865 at Cocolamus, Pa, Daniel Westfall
(born Jan 10, 1805, in Germany, died May 27, 1892, aged 87 years, 4
months and 17 days Buried at McAlisterville, Pa), son of Godfrey
Westfall of Westphalia, Germany. Daniel Westfall had formerly
married Edythe Emily Oles (who died in 1870), the mother of Hannah
Catherine Westfall, who married James Allen McAlister (666) No
issue

662—Agnes "'Nancy" McAlister, born May 26, 1821, died at McAlisterville,
Pa, Oct 25, 1895, aged 74 years, and 5 months, buried at Browns Mills,
Pa Never married

663—James W. McAlister, born Dec 24, 1822; died Dec 31, 1823, buried
at Browns Mills, Pa.

664—Hamilton McAllister, born Aug 24, 1824, at Swales, Juniata County,
Pa (died Sept 24, 1899 at Morrisdale Mines, buried at Warrior's
Mark). Married on ———— Amanda Foster (born June 11,
1834, died April 19, 1880), daughter of William and Elizabeth (Nash)
Foster. Issue (1) James Allen, (2) Lucinda Jane, (3) Andrew
Smith, (4) Silas Cresswell, (5) Agnes Ann, (6) Annie Mary, (7)
William Harrison (8) Isaac Thompson.

6641—James Allen McAllister, born Jan 30, 1856, at Manor Hill, Pa (died July 18, 1888), killed in West Virginia Pulp & Paper Company mill at Tyrone, Pa. Married on Sept 23, 1878 at Warrior's Mark, Pa, Jennie Elizabeth Kanour, daughter of John and Catharine Kanour Issue (1) Bertha Naomi, (2) Lilly May, (3) Minnie Edith, (4) Pearl Amanda

66411—Bertha Naomi McAllister, born Sept 7, 1879, at Warrior's Mark, Pa. Unmarried

66412—Lilly May McAllister, born May 26, 1881, in Tyrone, Blair County Pa Unmarried Address, Tyrone, Pa

66413—Minnie Edith McAllister, born March 11, 1883, in Tyrone, Pa Unmarried Address, Tyrone, Pa

66414—Pearl Amanda McAllister, born Aug. 13, 1886, Tyrone, Pa Unmarried Address, Tyrone, Pa

6642—Lucinda Jane McAllister, born March 7, 1857, at Manor Hill, Huntington, Pa Married at Lewistown, Pa, on Sept 8, 1881, John Fry Schirm (see 6615), son of George and Dorothy (Rabold) Schirm Address, 581 Washington Avenue, Tyrone, Pa Issue (1) James William (2) Harvey Edgar, (3) George Blair, (4) Anna May, (5) Albert, (6) Carrie Elizabeth, (7) Viola (8) Eva Rosalin, (9) Dorothy Jane, (10) Ivaloo, (11) Frederick McAlister

66421—James William Schirm, born July 11, 1882, at Hunt Furnace, died Aug 25, 1882

66422—Harvey Edgar Schirm, born June 27, 1883 Address, 809 26th St, Altoona, Pa Married on Nov 7, 1907, at Sinking Valley, Susanna Rebecca Dickson, daughter of Adam and Mary Ellen (Morrow) Dickson Issue (1) Lucille, (2) Eleanor Elizabeth, (3) Richard Dickson

664221—Lucille Schirm, born Jan 1, 1909, at Altoona, died Jan 2, 1909

664222—Eleanor Elizabeth Schirm, born Feb 13, 1910, at Altoona, Pa

664223—Richard Dickson Schirn, born Dec 25, 1912, at Altoona, Pa

66423—George Blair Schirm, born Dec 23, 1884, at Sinking Valley, died Aug 14, 1885.

66424—**Anna May Schirm,** born Dec. 30, 1885. Married on June 21, 1910, Winfield Scott Sensor Address, 607 Washington Avenue, Tyrone, Pa. Issue (1) Margaret Louise.

664241—Margaret Louise Sensor, born Feb 18, 1911, at Tyrone, Pa

66425—**Albert Schirm,** born April 4, 1887, at Tyrone, Pa ; died Feb. 9 1888 at Tyrone

66426—**Carrie Elizabeth Schirm,** born May 7, 1888. Address, 581 Washington Avenue, Tyrone, Pa

66427—**Viola Schirm,** born Jan 1, 1890, at Tyrone, Pa., died May 3, 1890 at Tyrone, Pa.

66428—**Eva Rosalin Schirm,** born March 30, 1891, at Tyrone, Pa., died Sept 25, 1891

66429—**Dorothy Jane Schirm,** born Oct 23, 1893 Address, 581 Washington Avenue Tyrone, Pa

6642 (10)—**Ivaloo Schirm,** born Oct 10, 1897 Address, 581 Washington Avenue, Tyrone, Pa

6642 (11)—**Frederick McAlister Schirm,** born Feb 29 1904, at Tyrone, Pa , died Jan 22, 1905 at Tyrone.

6643—**Andrew Smith McAllister,** born on Sept 28, 1858, at Manor Hill, Pa Married on Dec 17, 1884 at Vermillion, Ohio, Mary Elizabeth Pelton, daughter of Franklin and Mary Elizabeth (Davis) Pelton and granddaughter of Josiah and Lucy Pelton No issue. Address, 238 Howe Street, Elyria, Ohio.

6644—**Silas Cresswell McAllister,** born June 1, 1860, at Manor Hill Pa. Married on Oct. 18, 1881, at Belle Wood, Pa, Harriet Weaver (born at Dix Station, Pa, Oct 25, 1861), daughter of John and Nancy (Nearhoof) Weaver, granddaughter of John and Sally Weaver and of Andrew and Mary Nearhoof Address, 306 Glover Street, Jersey Shore, Lycoming Co, Pa Issue (1) Nancy Beatrice, (2) Orvis Charles, (3) Oscar James, (4) Willard Cail, (5) Laura Mae.

66441—Nancy Beatrice McAllister,   , _ _ _t Dix Station Pa Address Jersey Shore, Pa

66442—**Orvis Charles McAllister,** born Oct 30, 1888, at Morrisdale, Pa. Address, Jersey Shore, Pa.

66443—**Oscar James McAllister,** born April 24, 1894, at Morrisdale, Pa. Address, Jersey Shore, Pa.

66444—**Willard Carl McAllister,** born Sept 6, 1898, at Morrisdale, Pa Address, Jersey Shore, Pa.

66445—**Laura Mae McAllister,** born Dec 28, 1909, at Jersey Shore, Pa

6645—**Agnes Ann McAllister,** born May 17, 1862, at Manor Hill, Huntington County, Pa   Married on Feb. 12, 1885, at Birmingham, Huntington County, Pa, George H Schirm, son of George and Dorothy (Rabold) Schirm   Address, 1913   Coal Dealer, 308 East Tenth Street, Tyrone, Pa.   Issue (1) Charles William, (2) Edith May, (3) Ella Grace, (4) Helen Beatrice

66451—**Charles William Schirm,** born Aug. 27, 1889, at Tyrone, Pa.

66452—**Edith May Schirm,** born Jan 24, 1891, at Tyrone, Pa.

66453—**Ella Grace Schirm,** born July 12, 1893, died Jan 2, 1895, Tyrone, Pa.

66454—**Helen Beatrice Schirm,** born July 8, 1900, at Tyrone, Pa

6646—**Annie Mary McAllister,** born on March 2, 1865, at Manor Hill, Pa. Married on May 24, 1887, at Tyrone, Pa, Asbury Weston Johnson (born Sept 13, 1864 at Warrior's Mark, Pa) son of Asbury and Catherine (Weston) Johnson, grandson of Philip and Ruth (————) Johnson and of Elijah and Mary (————) Weston. Address, 762 Park Ave, Tyrone, Pa   Issue (1) Charles Chester, (2) Frances Catherine, (3) James Weston.

66461—**Charles Chester Johnson,** born May 25, 1892, at Tyrone, Pa   Address, Tyrone, Pa

66462—**Frances Catherine Johnson,** born Feb. 1, 1895; died Feb 3, 1895, Tyrone, Pa.

66463—**James Weston Johnson,** born June 25, 1899, at Tyrone, Pa.

6647—William Harrison McAlister, born Jan 10, 1870, at Manor Hill, Huntington County, Pa Address, 1913 Locust Street, Jersey Shore, Pa Married April 7, 1891 at Tyrone, Pa, Ella Weaver, daughter of John and Nancy (Nearhoof) Weaver and granddaughter of John and Sally (————) Weaver and of Andrew and Mary (————), Nearhoof. Issue (1) Ella Marie, (2) Esther, (3) Hazel Beatrice

66471—Ella Maria McAlister, born Jan 27, 1895, at Jersey Shore, Pa Address, Jersey Shore, Pa.

66472—Esther McAlister, born April 15, at Jersey Shore, Pa

66473—Hazel Beatrice McAlister, born Sept 1, 1900, at Jersey Shore, Pa.

6648—Isaac Thompson McAlister, born July 27, 1872, at Manor Hill, Pa, died Sept 30, 1907 in railway yards at St Marys, Elk County, Pa. Married Feb 16, 1893 at Morrisdale, Pa, Elizabeth Clouser of Morrisdale, Pa, daughter of John and Frances (Beihels) Clouser. Issue (1) James Westfall, (2) Howard Clair

66481—James Westfall McAlister, born July 24, 1888 Address, 117

66482—Howard Clair McAlister, born July 8, 1890 Address, 117 Neubert Street, St Marys, Pa.

665—Isaac Thompson McAlister, born April 30, 1830; died Nov 19, 1894, West Newton, Pa. Married twice; first on ————, his cousin, Sarah Mitchell Thompson (born Feb 25, 1826, died Sept 26, 1869, aged 43 years, 7 months and 1 day), daughter of William and Hannah (Mincer) Thompson (See 513) William Thompson was the son of Robert and Sarah (Mitchell) Thompson and grandson of John Thompson, Sr, the greatgrandfather of Isaac Thompson McAlister, and grandson of James Mitchell of Cumberland Co, Pa Issue (1) William A, (2) Mary Thompson As his second wife, Isaac Thompson McAlister married on Oct. 7, 1875, his cousin Laura Jane Bell (See 6544), a granddaughter of Thomas and Mary (McAlister) Bell Issue (3) Elizabeth Bell, (4) William Stuart, (5) Sara Eleanor.

6651—William A. McAlister, born Sept 14, 1863, died Sept 27, 1863, aged 4 months and 13 days

6652—Mary Thompson "Minnie" McAlister, born Dec. 17, 1864, at McAlisterville, Pa. Married on May 23, 1893, at Mifflintown, Pa, George Howard Martin, son of Anderson and Sarah Louise (Jamison) Martin and grand . . . . . l . . . . and Sarah (Watson) Jamison, daughter . . . . and Jane (. . . . . . .) Watson. (See 634 and 644)

14

No issue   Address, El Monte, Los Angeles, Co , Cal   George Howard Martin died Oct. 16, 1913 at Sunbury, Pa., buried at Mifflintown,
Pa

6653—**Elizabeth Bell McAlister,** born Sept 6, 1878 (A B. Allegheny
College, 1900)   Married Nov. 28, 1905, William Charles Donnelly
of Mifflintown, Pa son of James Marshall and Hannah Maria (Brat-
ton) Donnelly and of Charles and Eliza (Grumman) Bratton. W. C.
Donnelly is a U S Customs Officer   Address Katherine Road,
Brookline, Pa Issue (1) James Marshall, (2) Mary Elizabeth

66531—James Marshall Donnelly, born March 27, 1907, at Mifflintown, Pa

66532—Mary Elizabeth Donnelly, born June 16, 1910, at Philadelphia, Pa.

6654—**William Stuart McAlister,** born Nov. 8, 1881   Address, 247 Milwaukee St , Detroit, Mich

6655—**Sara Eleanor McAlister,** born Sept 30, 1885   Married on Dec 20,
1910, John "Jack" Carpenter Thomas of Pottstown, Pa   Address,
Vivian, Louisiana.

666—**James Allen McAlister,** born Sept. 20, 1826, at Cocolamus, Pa.; died
July 16, 1891 at McAlisterville, Pa , aged 64 years 9 months and 26
days. Married on Jan 2, 1870 at East Salem, Pa , Hannah Catherine
Westfall (born Jan 10, 1834, died March 26, 1900 at McAlisterville,
Pa , daughter of Daniel and Edythe Emily (Oles) Westfall and
great granddaughter of Davis and Edythe (Eyler) Oles of Scotland
and of Godfrey Westfall of Westphalia, Germany   (See 663) Issue
(1) Robert Elliott, (2) Mary Emily

6661—**Robert Elliott McAlister,** born at Cocolamus, Pa., Dec 19, 1870
Farmer   Address, Dodge, Neb   Married on Nov 27, 1890,
at McAlisterville, Pa , Beckie Ammerman, daughter of Robert W——
Ammerman and Leah (Eminhizer), granddaughter of Daniel and
Rachel Ammerman and of Abraham and Catherine Eminhizer Issue
(1) Karl Westfall, (2) Lena Blanche, (3) Allen Wesley, (4) Donald
Earl, (5) Edythe Catherine, (6) Robert Elliott.

66611—Karl Westfall McAlister, born in Tyrone, Blair County, Pa ,
Sept 24, 1891. Unmarried Address, Dodge, Neb

66612—Lena Blanche McAlister, born McAlisterville, Pa , June 18, 1893.
Married on Nov 27, 1900, George F——————— Siedemann. Address, Dodge, Neb. Issue (1) Georgetta Emily

666121—Georgetta Emily Siedermann, born Dec 17, 1911, at Dodge,
Dodge County, Nebr.

66613—**Allen Wesley McAlister,** born May 21, 1897, at McAlistervelle, Pa. Address, Dodge, Neb

66614—**Donald Earl McAlister,** born July 21, 1900, at Dodge, Dodge County, Neb   Address, Dodge, Neb

66615—**Edythe Catherine McAlister,** born Jan 4, 1906, at Dodge, Dodge County, Neb   Address, Dodge, Neb

66616—**Robert Elliott McAlister, Jr,** born Mar 27, 1913, at Wilhoit, Ozark County, Mo

6662—**Mary Emily McAlister,** born Nov 24 1872 at Cocolamus, Pa Married on Sept 5 1900, at McAllistervelle, Pa.   Charles Robert Soder, (born May 2, 1873), son of John and Lydia Ann (Bushey) Soder and grandson of Conrad and Mary (——————) Soder, of Germany, and of Samuel Bushey of Berks County, Pa   Farmer Address, Mifflintown, Juniata County, Pa, R F D No 2   John Soder (born Dec. 13, 1832 in Baden Baden Germany) came to America in 1861 and enlisted in Co K 98 Penn Volunteers. After marriage in 1863 he located in Juniata County Pa. near Oakland Mills   Children of Charles Robert and Mary Emily (McAlister) Soder   Issue (1) John Allen, (2) Samuel James, (3) William Mann, (4) Lydia Catherine, (5) Mary Eleanor

6621—**John Allen McAlister Soder,** born June 25 1901, at McAlistervelle, Pa

6662z—**Samuel James Soder,** born Nov 16, 1902, at McAlistervelle, Pa

66623—**William Mann Soder,** born Sept 17, 1904, died March 25, 1905 at McAlistervelle, Pa

66624—**Lydia Catherine Soder,** born June 21, 1909, at McAlistervelle, Pa

66625—**Mary Eleanor Soder,** born Aug 16, 1915, at McAlistervelle, Pa.

667—**Catherine McAlister,** born July 12, 1831, died July 25, 1845, buried at Browns Mills, Pa

668—**Elliott McAlister,** born Dec. 8, 1834, died Dec 12, 1845; buried at Browns Mills, Pa

669—**Herbison McAlister,** born ——————; died ——————; buried at Brow · ·

BRANCH NO. 7.

7—Susanna Thomson, born ————; died Oct 11, 1824 Married on ———————— at ————————, Capt David Boal of Pfontz Valley, Perry County, Pa (born 1739, died Aug 11, 1814 in the 75th year of his age, buried near Thompsontown, Pa). That it is unsafe to depend upon the spelling of family names, and especially that of the Boal family, is shown by the following item on page 784 of the "History of Juniata and Susquehanna Valleys in Pennsylvania," referring to Beale Township, "David Bowel warranted sixty-seven acres Mar 23, 1767, now owned by James Beale   The names David and Thomas Bowel (the latter having land near the old forge) may be supposed to be varied spellings for Beale; but they belonged to a family after whom Boalsburg, Pa, was named" On Nov 5, 1795, Nathaniel Dickey conveyed a tract of 239 acres in Fayette Township, Juniata County, Pa to "David Bole of Pfoutz Valley (now Perry County), Thomas Bole, son of David settled upon the place and upon the death of his father in 1824 he inherited it and in 1840 sold it to William McMeen" This tract was near the site of McAlisterville In 1797 "Major Hugh McAlister and David Boles each donated a plot of ground on their farms adjoining" for the Lost Creek Presbyterian Church—"History of Juniata and Susquehanna Valleys," pp 809, 834, 838, and 840 David Bole (spelled also "Bowel" in public documents) was appointed one of the trustees to organize Mifflin County in 1789, but he declined to serve because he resided below the Narrows in Greenwood Township, then Cumberland, now Perry County, and hence did "not reside within the limits of the said Mifflin" Pfoutz Valley, the home of the husband of Susanna Thomson was in Greenwood Township, which is now partly in Perry and partly in Juniata County, Pa in both of which are to be found descendants of David and Susanna (Thomson) Boal David Boal served in the Revolutionary War under Colonel Purdy of Cumberland County, as a private in 1776 and as a captain in 1780 His company of Cumberland County Militia was reported in service with him as captain from June 22 to Aug 22, 1782 In 1787 he was appointed one of the executors of the will of his brother-in-law (7) Robert Thompson of what was then Fermanaugh Township, Cumberland County, Pa and is now Greenwood Township, Juniata and Perry Counties, and Fermanaugh Township, Juniata County, Pa Children of David and Susanna (Thomson) Boal (1) Sarah, (2) John, (3) Nancy, (4) Elizabeth, (5) Thomas, (6) William Alexander, (7) Jane

71—Sarah Boal, born ————, 1770, died after 1860 (?), in Juniata County, Pa Married on Nov 15, 1810, Paul Cox (born July 22, 1781; died Mar 3, 1861) son of William Cox William Cox was a brother of Paul Cox, a merchant of Philadelphia, who took up lands in what of the "Seven Star Tavern' in Greenwood Township in what is now Juniata County, before the Revolution, upon which William Cox settled In 1790 Paul Cox, son of William Cox was assessed on the land and owned a distillery—"History of Juniata and Susquehanna Valleys," p 890 Issue (1) Lewis, (2) William, (3) David Boal, (4) Thomas, (5) John, (6) Susanna, (7) Mary.

711—**Lewis Cox,** born April 19, 1811, in Juniata County, Pa.; died ————. Married twice, one of his wives being a Miss Rumbaugh Issue by first wife (1) William, (2) Thomas, (3) Elizabeth

7111—**William Cox,** born ——————— Never married

7112—**Thomas Cox,** born ——————— Lived in Missouri

7113—**Elizabeth Cox,** born —————— Married John Mack and moved to Canada after 1860

712—**William Alexander Cox,** born Oct 22, 1821, at the old homestead in Greenwood Township, Juniata County, Pa He was a school teacher and building contractor. Lived in Mifflintown, Pa, until 1860, when he moved with his family to a farm near Bristol, Ind, where he died Aug 14, 1895, aged 73 years, 9 months and 22 days. He married on Feb 1, 1844, Mary Elizabeth Knepp (born July 28, 1820, near Mc-Kees Falls of the Susquehanna River, died Nov 27, 1908, at Bristol, Ind), daughter of John and Sarah (Clemmens) Knepp Among the wedding presents was a quilt made by Miss Nancy Boal (No 73), now in the possession of Mrs. Martha Minerva (Cox) Light (No 7125). Children of William Alexander and Mary Elizabeth (Knepp) Cox (1) Luther Titus, (2) David Boal, (3) Hebron Thompson, (4) Mary Susanna, (5) Martha Minerva

7121—**Luthur Titus Cox,** born Nov 4, 1844, at the Paul Cox homestead in Greenwood Township, Juniata Co, Pa, died, Dec 8, 1854, on his farm two miles northwest of Bristol, Ind Attended Michigan College, and a normal college at Lebanon, Ohio He taught school for several years until his failing health compelled a change in occupation, when he took up farming He was married Jan 14, 1874, at Bristol, Ind, by Rev. John Meaffitt, to Sarah Jane Hilbish, daughter of Peter and Catherine (Bickhart) Hilbish. Issue (1) Lena Endora

71211—**Lena Endora Cox,** born Oct 16, 1876, at Bristol, Ind Married on Sept 16, 1897, at Bristol, Ind, Walter Scott Oberholtzer (born May 22, 1866, in Mifflintown, Pa), son of Joseph and Elizabeth (Kauffman) Oberholtzer and grandson of Jacob and Mary (Walter) Oberholtzer and of Jonathan and Elizabeth (Cleck) Kauffman Rev W

S. Oberholtzer graduated from the Pennsylvania College at Gettysburg, Pa, in 1893, and received degree of A M from the Gettysburg Theological Seminary in 1896 Pastor of the English Trinity Lutheran Church Address, 406 So Logan St, Denver, Colo Issue (1) Walter Dwight

712111—Walter Dwight Oberholtzer, born Jan 2, 1908, at Dakota City, Neb

7122—David Boal Cox, born Jan 17, 1846, at the Paul Cox homestead in Juniata Co, Pa, died Aug 11, 1910, aged 64 years, 7 months, 24 days He attended the Ft Wayne (Ind) College, and the Normal School at Valparaiso, Ind, and taught school for many years At the death of his father in 1895, David Boal Cox bought the farm that his father had owned since 1859 He was married on Jan 21, 1869 at Bristol, Ind, by the Rev Mr Lantz of the Reformed Church, Elmira Zeigler (born Jan 4, 1847, near Selinsgrove, Snyder Co, Pa ; died April 21, 1916), daughter of Harrison and Katherine (Snyder) Zeigler Issue (1) Ida Minerva, (2) girl, (3) Mabel, (4) Mary Elizabeth, (5) Elma Grace, (6) Elsie Alberta

71221—Ida Minerva Cox, born Dec. 10, 1870, at Bristol, Ind ; died Nov 22, 1901. Unmarried

71222——————— Cox, a twin sister, born and died Dec 10, 1870

71223—Mabel Cox, born May 6, 1876, at Bristol, Ind., died May 16, 1876.

71224—Mary Elizabeth Cox, born Nov 13, 1877 Graduated from the Bristol High School, 1894 Married on Dec. 27, 1909, Ralph Theron Dausman (born Dec 24, 1887, at Maxwell, Tenn), son of Rezin and Lowetta (Dutrow) Dausman, grandson of Jacob Dausman, of Germany, and Margaret (Snyder) Dausman, of Pennsydvania, and of Emanuel and Sarah Elizabeth (Bumgardner) Dutrow, great-grandson of Jacob and Margaret Snyder, of Snyder Co, Pa, and Huntington Co, Ind, of Andrew and Lydia (Yingling) Dutrow, of Germany and Frederick Co, Md, and of Isaac and Eliza (Benhaus) Bumgardner, of Dayton, Ohio Rizin Dausman, who was born Jan 15, 1859, married on Mar 16, 1887, Lowetta Dutrow, who was born Nov 20, 1860, in Green Co, Ohio, and died Apr 6, 1904, at Bristol, Ind Their son Ralph Theron Dausman, attended the Bristol High School and spent one year in the preparatory department of West Virginia University, at Morgantown, W Va He is agent for the New York Central at Bristol, Ind Issue (1) Paul Edward, (2) John Dutrow

71 Paul Edward Dausman, born Au ... ... Kalamazoo, Mich

712242—John Dutrow Dausman, born Nov. 4, 1914 at Otsego, Mich

71225—Elma Grace Cox, born Dec. 11, 1880, at Bristol, Ind , died Dec 27, 1908 Graduated from the Elkhart Business College in 1903 Married Sep 20, 1905, William B Sudborough, of Bristol, Ind No issue

71226—Elsie Alberta Cox, born Oct 8, 1884, at Bristol, Ind Attended the High School in Bristol, Ind , and the Tri-State Normal School at Angola, Ind Address, Bristol, Ind

7123—Hebron Thompson Cox, born March 4, 1848, at the Paul Cox homestead in Juniata Co , Pa , died Aug 20, 1857, aged 9 years, 5 months and 16 days

7124—Mary Susanna Cox, born Feb 25, 1852, at the Paul Cox homestead, died Aug 19, 1857, aged 5 years, 5 months and 24 days, of scarlet fever, from which her brother died the day following

7125—Martha Minerva Cox, born Nov 11, 1858, at the Paul Cox homestead in Juniata Co , Pa Attended the Bristol, Ind High School and taught school for a number of years She married on Apr 14, 1889, at Bristol, Ind , Rev Somerville Light, D D (born Dec. 6, 1860, in Avilla, Noble Co , Ind), son of James Dorsey and Frances Loraine (Burnham) Light Somerville Light graduated from the Ft Wayne (Ind) College in 1881 He received the degrees of A B and A M from DePauw University, and the degree of S T B from the DePauw School of Theology In 1905 DePauw University conferred upon him the honorary degree of Doctor of Divinity, D D In 1884 he became a member of the North Indiana Conference of the Methodist Episcopal Church In 1909 he was appointed to the Goshen District over which he presided for the legal term of six years, when he was transferred to the superintendency of the Richmond District, of which he is now superintendent, with headquarters at Richmond, Ind Mrs Martha Minerva (Cox) Light has collected many household articles of interest to the descendants of Susan (Thompson) Boal, and to her these descendants are indebted for a large part of the records herewith presented No children

713—David Boal Cox, born Jan. 21, 1816, in Juniata County, Pa , died Aug 11, 1889 at Greenwood Township, Juniata County, Pa Married three times, first on —————— at ——————, Rebecca Jones, daughter of Edmund and Catherine (Webster) Jones Second marriage on —————— at ——————, Elen Okeson Third marriage on —————— at Harrisburg, Pa , Anna Maria Roush, daughter of Henry and Mary (Kleffman) Roush Issue—no children by his first wife, 2 by his second wife and 5 by his third wife. (1) Minerva, (2) Randolph, (3) Mineola Jane, (4) Samuel Diven, (5) Emma, (6) Irwin

7131—**Minerva Catherine Cox,** born Oct 14, 1848, in Juniata County, Pa
Married on Feb 25, 1873 at the home of her father in Juniata County,
Isaac Newton Rinehart, son of Frederick and Mary Ann (Ulsh)
Rinehart, and grandson of Frederick and Mary (Tibbens) Rinehart
and of Joseph and Susanna (Kline) Ulsh, and great-grandson of
Henry Ulsh and of Leonard and ———— (Wagner) Kline   I. N.
Rinehart is a farmer   Address, Bellflower, Ill   See 7133 and 74
Issue (1) Emma Clara, (2) Frederick David, (3) Joseph Banks, (4)
Isaac Newton, (5) Anna Pearl, (6) Stella June, (7) Randolph Ridge-
ley, (8) John Prizer Henry, (9) Nellie Fay   See "Biographical
Encyclopedia of Juniata Valley, Pa ," pp 1289 and 1315

7131:—**Emma Clara Rinehart,** born July 17, 1873, at Millerstown, Pa.
Married twice. First at Wartsburg, Wash , Charles R. Kennedy,
(born ————, died ————, in Walla Walla, Wash)
Issue (1) Henry, (2) Hazel, (3) Floyd—no record   She married
(second) at Nez Perce, Ida , William McLennan   Issue (4) William—no record

71312—**Frederick David Rinehart,** born Mar 16, 1875, at Millerstown, Pa.
Address, Enterprise, Oregon   Married on ———— at ————,
Hattie Dunlap

71313—**Joseph Banks Rinehart,** born Sept 11, 1877, at Millerstown, Pa.
Address, Mansfield, Ill. Married on ———— at ————,
Ada Haines

71314—**Isaac Newton Rinehart, Jr ,** born Oct. 27, 1879, at Millerstown, Pa
Farmer at Farmer City, Ill   Married on Oct 19, 1904 at Millerstown, Pa , Elizabeth Beaver (born Dec 1, 1880), daughter of Samuel
Long and Mary Elizabeth (Kipp) Beaver and granddaughter of
George and Maria Catherine (Long) Beaver and of Jacob and Elizabeth (Harmon) Kipp, great-granddaughter of Rev Peter and Elizabeth (Gilbert) Beaver—see 3431—and of Johnathan Long, great-
great-granddaughter of Capt George and Katherine (Keiffer) Beaver
See "Biographical Encyclopedia of Juniata Valley," pp. 1283 and 1291
and "History of Juniata and Susquehanna Valleys," p 1326   Capt
George Beaver was the son of George Bieber Beaver who left Rotterdam in the ship "Friendship" and landed in Philadelphia, Pa Nov
2, 1744   Katherine Keiffer was the daughter of Dewalt Keiffer and
the granddaughter of Abraham Keiffer who sailed from Rotterdam
in the ship "Two Brothers" in 1748   See "Colonial and Revolutionary Families" by J W Jordan   Children of J N and Elizabeth (Beaver) Rinehart (1) Mary Elizabeth, (2) Harry Beaver,
(3) Minerva Catherine, (4) Willard Gilbert, (5) Frances Margaret,
(6) Ethel Mae

713141—Mary Elizabeth Rinehart, born Nov 27, 1905, at Farmer City, Ill.

713142—Harry Beaver Rinehart, born Sept. 6, 1907, at Farmer City, Ill.

713143—Minerva Catherine Rinehart, born Oct. 7, 1909, at Farmer City, Ill

713144—Willard Gilbert Rinehart, born Mar. 17, 1912, at Farmer City, Ill.

713145—Frances Margaret Rinehart, born Nov 23 1913, died Sept. 20, 1914

713146—Ethel Mae Rinehart, born Aug 29, 1915

71315—Anna Pearl Rinehart, born Jan 28, 1833, at Millerstown, Pa. Married A R Kirk Address, Bellflower, Ill

71316—Stella June Rinehart, born June 25, 1885, at Ottawa, Kans. Married on Dec 25, 1906, at Bellflower, Ill, George Hunter Kumber, son of Gilea Lee and Hannah (Gillespie) Kumber Farmer, Bellflower, Ill Issue (1) Mary Kathryn, (2) John Newton, (3) Arthur Lee, (4) Ruth Helen

713161—Mary Kathryn Kumber, born July 16, 1908

713162—John Newton Kumber, born Nov. 21, 1909

713163—Arthur Lee Kumber, born Dec 25, 1910

713164—Ruth Helen Kumber, born Oct 8, 1912

71317—Randolph Ridgeley Rinehart, born Aug. 9, 1888, in Ottawa, Kans. Address, Wartsburg, Wash Unmarried

71318—John Prizer Henry Rinehart, born July 2, 1891, at Waitsburg, Wash. Address, Waitsburg, Wash. Unmarried

71319—Nellie Fay Rinehart, born Sept. 9, 1894, at Waitsburg, Wash Address, Bellflower, Ill Unmarried

7132—Randolph Cox, born July 31, 1851, in Juniata County, Pa , died in Redling, Cal, Mar ——, 1912 Married on ———— at Ottawa, Kan, his cousin (7151) Elizabeth Cox, daughter of John and Matilda (Reed) Cox and granddaughter of Paul and Sarah (Boal) Cox No issue

7133—**Mineola Jane Cox,** born Sept 15, 1862, at Dimmville, Juniata County,
Pa   Married on Jan 25, 1883 at Dimmville, Willis Washington Ulsh,
son of Leonard Kline and Caroline (Rickabaugh) Ulsh, grandson of
Joseph and Susanna (Kline) Ulsh, a car builder—see 7131 and 74
Address 420 Willon Ave, Altoona, Pa   Issue one son born Feb
28, 1885, died Mar 3, 1885

7134—**Samuel Diven Cox,** born Apr 20, 1863, in Juniata County, Pa   Ad-
dress, 1511 Eighth St, Altoona, Pa   Married on June 27, 1900, at
Altoona, Pa, Mary Sechler Ishler, daughter of Emanuel and Mary
Ann (Sechler) Ishler and granddaughter of John and Mary (Wolfe)
Sechler   A car builder   Issue (1) Sara Elizabeth

71341—**Sara Elizabeth Cox,** born Dec 16, 1901, at Altoona, Pa, died Dec.
12, 1914

7135—**Emma Cox,** born Jan 17, 1865, in Juniata County, Pa   Married
on Dec 23, 1886, in Juniata County, Pa, William Henry Zeiders (born
Jan 13, 1860), son of Henry and Sarah Jane (Seiders) Zeiders and
grandson of George and Susanna (Fitting) Zeiders and of John
Seiders   William H Zeiders taught school for ten years   He was
elected prothonotary of Juniata County, Pa, in 1893 and 1896, and
since 1902 he has been a furniture dealer at Mifflintown, Pa   Issue
(1) Cullen Bryant, (2) Willis Holmes, (3) Samuel David, (4) Maybelle Anna, (5) Harold Henry

71351—**Cullen Bryant Zeiders,** born in Greenwood Township, Juniata
County, Pa, June 20, 1888   Married on May 12, 1914, at Hazelton,
Pa, Mary Leonard, daughter of Thomas and Lizzie (Harman)
Leonard   Address, Mifflintown, Pa

71352—**Willis Holmes Zeiders,** born Nov 20, 1889, in Pfoutz Valley, Perry
County, Pa, died June 8, 1894

71353—**Samuel David Zeiders,** born May 30 1894, at Mifflintown, Pa   Address, Mifflintown, Pa

71354—**Maybelle Anna Zeiders,** born Mar 3, 1896, at Mifflintown, Pa

71355—**Harold Henry Zeiders,** born May 18, 1901, at Mifflintown, Pa
Address, Mifflintown, Pa

7136—**Irwin Justis Cox,** born June 6, 1867, in Juniata County, Pa   Address, Pfoutz Valley, Perry County, Pa   Married on Oct 19, 1890,
in Juniata County, Pa, Almeda Barner, daughter of Henry Barner
Farmer, Pfoutz Valley, Pa   Issue (1) Emeline, (2) Lillian Maria,

71361—Emeline Cox, born Nov 2, 1891, at Altoona, Pa   Married ————
Sarver. Address, Millerstown, Perry County, Pa, R F D No 1

71362—Lillian Maria Cox, born Sept. 6, 1895, in Juniata County, Pa   Address, Thompsontown, Pa, R F D No 2

71363—Charles David Cox, born Aug 12, 1902, at Altoona, Pa   Address, Thompsontown, Pa, R F D No 2

7137—Charles Cox, born Jan 12, 1873, in Juniata County, Pa.; died Aug 17, 1873

714—Thomas Cox, born ————————, died ————————   Married Frances Reed   Issue six children   No data

715—John Cox, born ————————, in Greenwood Township, Juniata County, Pa., died at Ottawa, Kas   Married Matilda Reed   Issue seven children including (1) Elizabeth, (2) Clara

7151—Elizabeth Cox, born ————————, died ————————.   Married Randolph Cox   See 7132.

7152—Clara Cox, born ————————, in Greenwood Township, Juniata County, Pa   Married on ————————, 1881, John S Harley (born Jan 20, 1848, in Fayette Township, Juniata County, Pa), son of Philip and Deborah (Anderson) Harley and grandson of John Anderson and of Joseph and Sarah (Markley) Harley, great-grandson of Samuel and Catherine (Sowers) Harley and great-great-grandson of Christopher Sowers, the first German printer to come to America, who conducted a printing establishment in Philadelphia   John S Harley has filled the offices of assessor and auditor of Delaware Township, Juniata County, Pa, since 1880   See "Biographical Encyclopedia of Juniata Valley, Pa," page 998   Issue (1) James Blaine, (2) Leroy, (3) Ernest

71521—James Blaine Harley, born ————————

71522—Leroy Harley, born ————————

71523—Ernest Harley, born ————————, died Oct. 31, 1895

716—Susanna Cox, born Nov. 5 1812. in Juniata County Pa ; died before 1841. Married on Dec 13, 1831, in Juniata County, Pa, John Dimm (born 1803, in Greenwood Township, Juniata County, Pa., died 1864 in Dimmsville Pa), son of Henry and Catherine (Wilt) Dimm, a grandso———   on of John Dimm and of Michael Wilt On Jan 25, 1772, Michael Wilt purchased the old Leonard Pfoutz tract of land in what is now Greenwood Township, Juniata County, Pa, and conveyed it on Sept 7, 1773, to Adam Wilt of Bethel Township, Lancaster County, Pa A portion of the property afterwards passed to Catherine (Wilt) Dimm, wife of Henry Dimm who settled thereupon in 1805 and died there Oct 10, 1846, aged 70 years About 1835 his sons John, James and Samuel purchased the Cargill grist-mill, afterwards owned and operated by John Thompson Dimm—7161 The pioneer of the Dimm family in Pennsylvania was John Dimm who was said to have come from Germany about the year 1650 and settled in Philadelphia and later in Berks County where he died His son Christopher Dimm settled in Luzerne County, Pa, near the present site of Wilkes-Barre His son Henry Dimm married Catherine Wilt and settled in what is now Greenwood Township, Juniata County, Pa John Dimm, the son of Henry and Catherine (Wilt) Dimm, operated a farm and a saw-mill in Greenwood Township and was appointed the first postmaster at Dimmsville, a village in that township named for the family From 1852 to 1857 he served as associate judge of the court of common pleas in Juniata County —"History of Juniata and Susquehanna Valleys," p 885 and 890, and "Biographical Encyclopedia of Juniata Valley," pp 774, 936 and 992 Children of John and Susanna (Cox) Dimm (1) John Thompson, (2) David Boal, (3) Nancy Jane, (4) Thomas P After the death of his first wife, John Dimm married her sister Mary Cox —See 717

7161—**John Thompson Dimm,** born Dec 8, 1832, near Dimmsville, in Greenwood Township, Juniata County, Pa ; died Dec. 28, 1912 He was a merchant, miller and postmaster at Dimmsville, Pa, and in 1884 was elected county commissioner He married Sarah Ann Castle (born Apr, 1831, at Dimmsville ; died May 21, 1906, at Dimmsville), daughter of David and Mary (Sellers) Castle, and granddaughter of Joseph and ———— (Sharon) Sellers Issue (1) Ada Mary, (2) Laura Annie, (3) David Sharon, (4) James Sellers, (5) Edith May, (6) John Calvin, (7) Carrie Castle, (8) Charles Milton, (9) Myra Clementine, (10) Wayne Thompson.

71611—**Ada Mary Dimm,** born Feb. 18, 1857, at Dimmsville, Pa., died July 22, 1908 Married on Jan 27, 1878, at ————, J M Ulsh. Address, Lancaster, Pa Issue ————

71612—**Laura Annie Dimm,** born Feb 3, 1859, died June 2, 1859

71613—**David Sharon Dimm,** born June 29, 1860; died Aug 20, 1882

71614- James Sellers Dimm, born March 5 1862, died July 23, 1877

71615—Edith May Dimm, born Oct 18, 1863, at —————. Married on March 13, 1890, at —————, William R Ulsh Address, 2225 Sixth St, Harrisburg, Pa Issue ———

71616—John Calvin Dimm, born Oct 8, 1865, in Greenwood Township, Juniata County, Pa He established the *Juniata Star* in 1892 In 1895 he was appointed a member of the council of Mifflintown, Pa See "Biographical Encyclopedia of Juniata Valley," p 774 He married on March 9, 1892, Mary Gertrude Bratton, daughter of Charles Bratton, of Bratton Township, Mifflin County, Pa—See 6653 Issue three children No data

71617—Carrie Castle Dimm, born Aug 10, 1867, died Oct 16, 1867

71618—Charles Milton Dimm, horn Nov 28, 1868 at Dimmsville, Pa With Munson Steamship Line Address, 262 Clinton Ave, Brooklyn, N Y. Married Nov 26, 1904, Laura Vernon Issue (1) Marjorie Vernon, (2) George Vernon.

716181—Marjorie Vernon Dimm, horn Dec. 10, 1909

716182—George Vernon Dimm, born Feb 4, 1911

71619—Myra Clementine Dimm, born Dec 15 1870 at Dimmsville, Pa Married on Dec 15, 1897, Harry Allen Luck Address, Lewistown, Pa Issue —————.

7161(10)—Wayne Thompson Dimm, born Oct 28, 1876, at Dimmsville, Pa. Married on Jan 30, 1909, Frances Spencer Carr Address, 326 Fifty-first St, Newport News, Va Issue —————.

7162—David Boal Dimm, born Feb 9 1835, near Dimmsville, in Greenwood Township, Juniata County, Pa, died 1915, aged 80 years Farmer at Thompsontown, Pa He served three terms as a school director and one term as county commissioner See "Biographical Encyclopedia of Juniata Valley," p. 992 He married twice, first on June 2, 1857, in Greenwood Township, Juniata County, Pa, Hannah Puntius (born ———, in Greenwood Township; died —————, 1877), daughter of Joseph Henry Puntius Issue (1) Emma Jane, (2) David Harvey, (3) Clara Amelia, (4) Elmer Ellsworth, (5) Mary Elizabeth, (6) William Luther, (7) Margaret Katherine, (8) John C———, (9) Cora Ella, (10) Anna Minerva, (11) Ibra Lewis, (12) Albert Puntius David Boal Dimm married, second, on Nov. 11, 1879, Amanda Spicher (born —————), daughter of Daniel and Sarah (Ikes) Spicher and granddaughter of ————— and Mary (Kauffman) Spicher See 71621 Issue (13) Laura Augusta, (14) Myrtle Lucret, 15 Ch ', R,

71621—Emma Jane Dimm, born May 9, 1858, in Thompsontown, Pa.
Married on Dec 28, 1876, at Thompsontown, Pa, David E———
Spicher (born June 15, 1854, in Delaware Township, Juniata County,
Pa), son of Daniel and Sarah (Ikes) Spicher and grandson of
——————— and Mary (Kauffman) Spicher, brother of Amanda
Spicher—7162 Daniel Spicher was a school teacher for twelve
years He is now a farmer in Delaware Township, Juniata County
See "Biographical Encyclopedia of Juniata Valley," p 993 Issue (1)
David Floyd, (2) Edna Pearle, (3) Charles Roy, (4) Chester Cleve-
land, (5) Marjorie Anna, (6) Ruth Elizabeth

716211—David Floyd Spicher, born June 14, 1878, at Thompsontown Pa ;
died April 2, 1899, at Harrisburg, Pa

716212—Edna Pearle Spicher, born Oct 13, 1879, in Juniata County, Pa.
Married on Feb 26, 1901, Roy George Reynolds, son of Frank
Reynolds R G Reynolds enlisted in the Spanish-American War.
Address, 119 Pennbaker Ave, Lewistown, Mifflin County, Pa.
Issue (1) Evelyn, (2) Armond Lamar, (3) Frederick George, (4)
Rudolph, (5) Kenneth

7162121—Evelyn Reynolds, born Sept 12, 1901, at Lewistown, Pa

7162122—Armond Lamar Reynolds, born Oct. 12, 1902, at Lewistown, Pa

7162123—Frederick George Reynolds, born Feb. 28, 1909, at Thompsontown,
Pa

7162124—Rudolph Reynolds, born Jan. 27, 1911, at Lewistown, Pa

7162125—Kenneth Reynolds, born Mar 12, 1913. at Lewistown, Pa.

716213—Charles Roy Spicher, born Feb. 7, 1884, at Thompsontown, Pa
Married on June 16, 1907, at ——————, Pearl Rankin Address,
Hingham, Hill County, Mont Issue (1) Clement Rankin, (2)
Charles Rodney.

7162131—Clement Rankin Spicher, born Mar —, 1909.

7162132—Charles Rodney Spicher, born June —, 1911, at Hingham, Mont.

716214—Chester Cleveland Spicher, born Aug 28, 1887, at Thompsontown,
Pa Address, Hingham, Mont

716215—Marjorie Anna Spicher, born Mar. 21, 1889 at Thompsontown, Pa
    ,   Thompsontown, Pa.

716216—**Ruth Elizabeth Spicher**, born Apr 24, 1892, at Thompsontown, Pa Married George Shelley Address, 434 West Joseph St, Mishawaka, Ind Issue (1) Robert Elwood

7162161—**Robert Elwood Shelly**, born Apr 24, 1913, at Mishawaka, Ind.

71622—**David Harvey Dimm**, born Mar. 26, 1859, in Delaware Township, Juniata County, Pa Farmer, R F D No. 1, Mifflintown, Pa Married on Jan 12, 1882, in Fayette Township, Juniata County, Pa, Elizabeth Brown, daughter of Peter and Julia (————) Brown Issue (1) Charles Olen, (2) Julia Anna, (3) Ena Mae, (4) Florence

716221—**Charles Olen Dimm**, born Feb. 12, 1885, in Delaware Township, Juniata County, Pa Address, R F D No 1, Mifflintown, Pa Married on Sept 30, 1908, in Greenwood Township, Perry County, Pa, Pearl Rumbaugh, daughter of Frank and Sarah (————) Rumbaugh Issue (1) Ruth Elizabeth

7162211—**Ruth Elizabeth Dimm**, born July 2, 1911, at Mifflintown, Pa

716222—**Julia Anna Dimm**, born Jan 15, 1887, in Delaware Township, Juniata County, Pa Married on June 4, 1914, David Burton Rumbaugh (born Sept 14, 1885)

716223—**Ena Mae Dimm**, born Feb. 8, 1889, in Delaware Township, Juniata County, Pa Married on Feb 7, 1912, in Delaware Township, Lloyd Heckman, son of George and Cora (————) Heckman. Farmer, Mifflintown, Pa

716224—**Florence Dimm**, born July 10, 1893, in Delaware Township, Juniata County, Pa

71623—**Clara Amelia Dimm**, born May 25, 1860, in Kurtz Valley, Pa ; died Nov. 5, 1892 Married at San Francisco, Cal, Hayes P———— Speakman Issue (1) Mary Ethel, (2) Albert Fredcolm, (3) Florence

716231—**Mary Ethel Speakman**, born ——————— Married James Lee, Address, 122 Seventeenth Ave, San Francisco, Cal

716232—**Albert Fredcolm Speakman**, born ————————.

716233—**Florence Speakman**, born ————————.

71624—**Elmer Ellsworth Dimm**, born Apr 28, 1861, in Kurtz Valley, Pa. Address, Lewistown, Pa Married at Granville, Mifflin County, Pa, Alice William Issue Harry, Roy, (3) Oscar.

716241—David Dimm, born ——————, at ——————. Married Anna
Martin   Issue (1) Paul, (2) Charlotte.

7162411—Paul Dimm, born ——————

7162412—Charlotte Dimm, born ——————

716242—Freda Dimm, born ——————.

716243—Oscar Dimm, born ——————

71625—Mary Elizabeth Dimm, born Oct 5, 1862, in Kurtz Valley, Pa.
Address, Thompsontown, Pa   Unmarried

71626—William Luther Dimm, born ——————

71627—Margaret Katherine Dimm, born Apr 27, 1865, at Thompsontown,
Pa   Address, Somersett, Perry County, Ohio   Married on April 3,
1896, at Carthage, Mo, William Ralph Cline, son of John Randolph
and Henrietta (Finnell) Cline   Issue (1) Ruth Marie

716271—Ruth Marie Cline, born Aug 3, 1899, at Front Royal, Va

71628—John C—————— Dimm, born July 8, 1865, in Kurtz Valley, Pa,
died July 25, 1869

71629—Cora Ella —————— Dimm, born Apr 7, 1868, at Thompson-
town, Pa   Address, Somerset, Ohio   Married on Oct 16, 1890, at
Thompsontown, Pa, Montgomery Bastress, son of Peter and Eva
(Dressler) Bastress   No children

7162(10)—Anna Minerva Dimm, born Oct 15, 1869, in Kurtz Valley, Pa.
Address, Thompsontown, Pa   Unmarried

7162(11)—Ibra Lewis Dimm, born July 3, 1871 in Kurtz Valley, Pa   Address, Bala, Pa.   Married Nettie McAllister   Issue (1) Florence,
(2) Mildred

7162(11)1—Florence Dimm, born ——————, at ——————, died on
——————, at ——————

7162(11)2—Mildred Dimm, born ——————, at ——————

7162(12)—Albert Puntius Dimm, born Mar 16, 1873, in Kurtz Valley,
Pa   Address, Thompsontown, Pa   Married on May 12, 1898, in
Frontz Valley, Perry County, Pa., Mary Martha Jones, daughter

of James Gilson and Catherine Anne (Grubb) Jones and grand-
daughter of Edmund and Catherine (Webster) Jones and of
David and Martha (Stevens) Grubb Issue (1) Margaretta, (2)
Marion

7162(12)1—**Margaretta Dimm,** born Aug 29, 1900, in Kurtz Valley, Juniata
County, Pa Address, Thompsontown, Pa

7162(12)2—**Marion Dimm,** born Jan 18, 1903, in Kurtz Valley, Juniata
County, Pa Address, Thompsontown, Pa

7162(13)—**Laura Augusta Dimm,** born June 30, 1879, at Thompsontown,
Pa Married on June 30, 1906, at Thompsontown, Pa, Parke
Martin Bonebaker, son of Jacob and Amanda (————) Bone-
baker and grandson of Jacob and Susanne (————) Bonebaker
Engineer, Estherville, Iowa Issue (1) Arlene Mae

7162(13)1—**Arlene Mae Bonebaker,** born Aug. 10, 1908, at Estherville, Iowa

7162(14)—**Myrtle Lucretia Dimm,** born June 16, 1880, at Thompsontown,
Pa

7162(15)—**Charles Rosco Dimm,** born Feb 11, 1881, at Thompsontown, Pa.
Traveling salesman Address, Steven Girard Bldg, Philadelphia,
Pa

7163—**Nancy Jane Dimm,** born ————, 1837, in Juniata County, Pa Unmarried Address, Millerstown, Pa, R F D No 3

7164—**Thomas P———— Dimm,** born ————, 1840, in ———— Address, Millerstown, Pa, R F D No 3

717—**Mary Cox,** born May 27 1814, died ———— 1909 in Dimmsville,
Pa Married on ————, 1828, in Greenwood Township,
Juniata County, Pa, John Dimm (the widower of her sister Susanna—
716) John Dimm died in 1864 at Dimmsville, Greenwood Township,
Juniata County, Pa, which was named for his family See "Biograph-
ical Encyclopedia of Juniata Valley," pp 774, 936 and 992, and the
"History of Susquehanna and Juniata Valleys," p 890 Issue (1)
Calvin, (2) Louis A————, (3) Minerva.

7171—**Calvin Dimm,** born ————, at Dimmsville, Pa, died on ——
————, at ————, young

7172—**Louis A———— Dimm,** born on ————, at Dimmsville, Pa
Add . . \
15

7173—**Minerva Dimm,** born ————, at ————, died ————
    ———— Married David Sieber Lived at McAlisterville, Pa

72—**John Boal,** born ————, 1790, at the Boal Homestead in Perry
    County, Pa, died July 27, 1836, in the 45th year of his age Married on
    ————, 1826, at ————, Sarah Ann Gilfillen (born Aug 3,
    1810, died Oct 16, 1883), daughter of James Gilfillen (1781-1852) and
    Sarah (Jones) Gilfillen (1784-1854) and granddaughter of James Gil-
    fillen (1742-1804) and Nancy (Watts) Gilfillen and of Lewis and
    Patience (Londen) Jones, and great-granddaughter of Robert and Jean
    (McConnell) Gilfillen and great-great-granddaughter of James and
    Margaret (Briton) McConnell. See Carlisle, Pa, Wills—1764 James
    Gilfillen, Sr, served in the Revolution under Captain Jonathan Robeson
    of Cumberland County. See Pa Archives, Vol XV, p 592 Lewis
    Jones (born 1752, died 1799) served as a private under Captain Parr
    at the surrender of Fort Washington See Pa Archives, Vol 10,
    Second Series, p 27 He was a grandson of David Jones (who married
    Sarah Bertram, daughter of Rev William Bertram), who came to
    America in 1701 and obtained from William Penn, title to land now
    called Overbrook, Pa, where some of his descendants now live Chil-
    dren of John and Sarah Ann (Gilfillen) Boal (1) Jane, (2) David

721—**Jane Boal,** born Dec. 21, 1833, near Millerstown, Pa, died Dec 5,
    1910, at Topeka, Kan Married on Nov 29, 1860, at the Boal home-
    stead, Perry County, Pa, her cousin—(11)7—Thomas Boal Thompson
    (born March 25, 1820, in Juniata County, Pa, died in Perry County,
    Pa, May 29, 1891), son of Peter and Mary (Patterson) Thompson
    Issue (1) Charles Stuart, (2) Minnie Alforetta, (3) Alberta, (4)
    Frank Carrol, (5) Bessie Marguerita, (6) Henrietta, (7) Mary Mabel,
    (8) Grace Eolena See (11)7

722—**David Boal,** born Sept. 26, 1835, died May 25, 1909, at National City,
    Cal Married on Dec 28, 1858, in Mahontongo, Juniata County, Pa,
    Cordelia Emaline Thompson (born July 18, 1837, in New Buffalo,
    Perry County, Pa, died Nov 3, 1912, National City, Cal), daughter
    of Samuel and Sarah (Boughman) Thompson—not related Issue (1)
    John Edgar, (2) Cochran Thompson, (3) Samuel Herbert

7221—**John Edgar Boal,** born Mar 29, 1860, at Millerstown, Pa Address,
    National City, Cal Vice-president and general manager of the San
    Diego Land Corporation and the San Diego Fruit Co, San Diego,
    Cal, also of Sweet Water Co Married on Dec 15, 1886, at Na-
    tional City, Cal, Mary Eliza Dickinson, daughter of William Green
    · -l Sarah (Kip) Dickinson Issue (1) Helen Dickinson, (2) Mai-
        l   , n   , ld i Dickinson

72211—Helen Dickenson Boal, born Sept 19. 1887, at Topeka, Kan Married Apr 25, 1911, at National City, Cal, Horton LeClere Titus, son of Harris Lewis and Mary (Horton) Titus Issue (1) Dorothy Helen, (2) Harry Lewis

722111—Dorothy Helen Titus, born Mar 20, 1912, at San Diego, Cal

722112—Harry Lewis Titus, born Aug 20, 1913, at San Diego, Cal

72212—Marian Dickinson Boal, born Aug 4, 1894, at National City, Cal.

72213—Edgar Dickinson Boal, born May, 1897, at National City, Cal

7222—Cochran Thompson Boal, born Jan 5, 1864, at Millerstown, Pa Manager of Electrical Properties, Great Falls, Mont Married Apr 13, 1887 at Oil City, Pa, Marie Lillian McAllister, daughter of John B——— and Marguerita E——— (Rice) McAllister, granddaughter of Alexander and Elizabeth (Boughman) McAllister and of John and Margaret E (———) Rice Issue (1) Bessie McAllister

72221—Bessie McAllister Boal, born Jan 23 1891 at Logansport Ind Married on May 1, 1911, Roland Howard Willcomb, son of Wilber and Maybelle (Ordway) Willcomb Roland H Willcomb graduated from the Massachusetts Institute of Technology Civil and mining engineer, Great Falls, Mont Issue (1) Marie Lillian, (2) Maybelle Ordway

722211—Marie Lillian Willcomb, born Mar 13, 1912, at Great Falls, Mont.

722212—Maybelle Ordway Willcomb, born Dec. 10, 1914, at Great Falls, Mont

7223—Samuel Herbert Boal, born Dec 31, 1867, at Millerstown, Pa Bookkeeper San Diego Fruit Co, National City, Cal Married Apr 7, 1897 at Topeka, Kans, Lillian Gemmell, daughter of Robert Brown and Anna Eliza (Campbell) Gemmell No children

73—Nancy Boal, born 1788, died Nov 19, 1857, aged 69 years, at the home of her niece Mary (Cox) Dimm, Dimmsville, Pa Unmarried

74—Elizabeth Boal, born ——— Married John Ulsh No record See 7133

75—Thomas Boal, born 1791 died April 9 1862 aged 68 years buried near

76—William Boal, born 1796, died April 10, 1831, in his 38th year; buried at Thompson's Lock, Pa

77—Jane Boal, born June 16, 1801, at ——————— , died Nov 20, 1833, aged 32 years, 5 months and 4 days   Married on Dec 1, 1825 at ——— ———————, her cousin—36—Isaac Thomson (born Jan 23, 1790 at ———————, died May 3, 1835 aged 45 years, 3 months and 10 days, son of William and Jane (Mitchell) Thomson   Issue one son, drowned in the canal at Mexico, Pa, aged 12 years

BRANCH NO. 8.

8—**Isaac Thomson,** born 1751, in Pennsylvania, died in the summer of 1823 at Middlefield, Ohio, aged 72 years Pension records show that he enlisted in the Revolutionary War first as a private at Carlisle, Pa, county seat of Cumberland which then included what is now Juniata and adjacent counties He re-enlisted as a lieutenant in 1777. It is a tradition in the family that he was accustomed to ride to Harrisburg to collect the money due from the United States Government which the state had assumed to pay When informed that payment would not be made in full, he told the committee that they were a lot of thieves and refused to accept anything Robert Thompson, probably his brother—7—afterwards collected in part, sending the money to Isaac Thompson who had then left Pennsylvania Isaac Thompson owned the farm at the east of the homestead of Pioneer John Thomson in Juniata County, Pa, which he sold to his brother William—3—on Apr 27, 1779, the year and probably the month of his father's death In 1781-3 he was taxed on a saw-mill and in 1782-3 on a grist-mill in Fermanagh Township, Juniata County, Pa It was probably in 1783 that he began his wanderings which took him first to the western part of Pennsylvania, then to New York State and finally to Geauga County, Ohio He was referred to by other members as "Old Uncle Isaac" and by some as "Lost Uncle Isaac" for reasons that will be apparent from the following excerpts from the "Pioneer History of Geauga, Ohio" "The first permanent settlement in Middlefield was made in March, 1799, by Isaac Thompson and his wife Jane, and three sons, James, William and John—the last a child two months old, also a daughter, Eliza, aged 3 years The family was originally from Washington County, Pa, leaving that place about 1795 Their first settlement was on the Genessee River, in the state of New York, where they resided one year From there they started for the unbroken wilds of the west Their route was down the river, to Lake Ontario by boat, up the lake and Niagara River to the falls Hauling their boat around Niagara, with a team, they re-embarked, ascending the river to lake Erie, coasting on the lake as far as Erie harbor, where they were overtaken by a storm, and lost everything except the clothes upon their persons From Erie they hauled their boat across country to a stream called French Creek, coasted down the creek to the Ohio River, and down the river to a little village called Charlestown, on the Virginia side At Allegheny they left Sarah Wells, a daughter of Mrs Thompson by her first husband The family resided in Charlestown about two years, became disgusted with the society, packed up their goods and started up the river, leaving their daughter Polly, aged 13, with an acquaintance on the Ohio side of the river. Arriving at the mouth of Beaver River, they found an empty cabin, in which they stored a part of their goods packing the remainder on in old horse they _____ _____ _____ _____ from Charlestown, and

mounting the wife and child also on the horse, the husband on foot, they
started for the lake, with no road but an Indian trail The son James,
had gone to Mentor the spring before In the January following this
date their son John Thompson was born They remained in Mentor
until the middle of March, and started for the Ohio River They
stopped for the night at a place later known as Johnson's corners, in a
cabin occupied by two men, Hill and Lemoin They selected a site on
the blazed road running from Fairport Harbor, Lake Erie, to the Ma-
honing River at Warren, Ohio, and near the center of the township Hill
and Lemoin helped them build a cabin and soon after left for parts
unknown, leaving them the first permanent settlers in the township
"The first white person born in the limits of the township, was a daughter
of Isaac Thompson (88—Lydda), on the 6th of Apr, 1801 " About two
weeks after the birth of Thompson's daughter, in 1801, he and his son
James, located a lot of land in Richmond, near the mouth of Grand
River While (away), working on this land, two Indians came to their
house in Middlefield, acting in a cowardly, sneaking manner, peering
through the cracks of the house, talking low, and conducting themselves
badly After more ill behavior they left The family was thoroughly
frightened, and the more so for knowing the Indians to be bad char-
acters One was part French and could speak English well Mother
Thompson was not well, and besides herself and babe, she had only her
son William, a lad of 12 years, and a hired girl They expected the
Indians back the coming night The boy and hired girl barricaded every
entrance to the house, and by night, had a pretty strong fortress As
soon as it was dark, they put out the light and fire, and huddled in one
corner and listened, in terrible suspense, for the cat-like tread of the
Indians Soon a step was heard Some one approached the door and
knocked No sound within Then a louder rap Then conversation in
English The inmates began to take courage, and enquired "Who is
there, and what is wanted?" The answer came· "We are travelers, and
want supper and lodging, we are friends" Being satisfied they were
friendly, they quickly unbarred the door, and were overjoyed to see
two stalwart white men walk in They were soon furnished with supper,
the best the house afforded When Mother Thompson told the men of
the visits of the Indians, they put their riffles in order, and laid themselves down before the fire About midnight, one of the Indians came and
opened the door, looking in very cautiously He saw the two men, and
hurriedly withdrew and disappeared in the darkness, and was never seen
afterwards In the summer of 1823, Isaac Thompson sickened and died,
after a residence of a little over 24 years in a new country, and most
of the time in an unbroken wilderness Enduring hardships and priva-
tions almost unheard of in any country, he quietly fell asleep in death,
honored and respected by all who knew him At the time he settled in
the Genessee country, it was very new, as also was his sojourn on the
Ohio River at Charlestown, Va, in an almost unbroken wilderness
The same is true of his stay in Mentor, and of his final settlement in

Thompson Homestead, Middlefield, Ohio

Built in 1818 by James Thompson No. 84 on land where Isaac Thomson No. 8 and his son James settled in 1799

Middlefield, when all things were in a primeval state. Mr Thompson was a lieutenant in the Revolutionary War, and connected with the body guard of General Washington　He drew a pension from the government, and to obtain his money he was obliged to travel all the way to Pittsburg (this should be Harrisburg) for each installment　At the time of his death he was 72 years old　His widow survived him about 19 years　We consider grandmother Thompson, one of the most useful women who ever lived in the township　By the sickness in her own family and amongst neighbors, she acquired considerable knowledge of the medicinal properties of roots and herbs and barks, which grew in the woods　She was useful as a nurse and also as a physician　In those early times, there were but few doctors, and those not the best, grandmother having many calls, both in town and out of town, for her fame as a nurse had extended far and near　Perhaps no woman that ever lived in our town, or ever will live here, so much endeared herself to all the people of the town as this good old lady　She died in 1842, without an enemy in the world, aged seventy-eight　Isaac Thompson was twice married　His first wife, whom he married at about the end of the Revolutionary War, was Martha Larimore of Philadelphia　Issue (1) James, (2) John, (3) Polly, (4) William　He married secondly Mrs Martha Jane (Evans) Wells (born 1764, died 1842, aged 78 years) widow of Benjamin Wells, of Fermanagh Township in what is now Juniata County, Pa.　Issue (5) Robert, (6) Eliza, (7) John, (8) Lydda, (9) Robert E.

81—James Thompson, born 1779 in Pennsylvania, died Oct 15, 1877, at Middlefield, Ohio　He accompanied "Old Uncle Isaac Thompson" on his wanderings through western Pennsylvania and New York into Ohio, and having become tired of the nomadic life, compelled the family to halt in Geauga County, Ohio　He became a man of influence in that community, and organized a company in the War of 1812　He was twice married　first to Sarah Wells, daughter of his step-mother Martha Jane (Evans) and Benjamin Wells　Issue (1) Isaac Newton, (2) Harriet, (3) Martha, (4) James Madison, (5) Edward, (6) Edmond　He married secondly at Mesopotamia, Ohio, Mercy Tracy, daughter of Gilbert and Deborah (Woodworth) Tracy and granddaughter of Ezra and Jemima (Kimball) Tracy and of Jonathan and Mercy (Parker) Woodworth　Gilbert Tracy (born 1761 at Preston, Conn ; died 1841 at Scipio, N Y) was in the army during the entire period of the Revolution, he served in the brigade commanded by Lafayette　He was a descendant of Thomas Tracy, who came to Salem, Mass, in 1636, and in 1659 was one of the four men granted the town of Norwich, Conn, by Uncas, Sachem Mohegans, in gratitude for services rendered when besieged by Sachem Narragansetts　He sat in the Colonial Assembly for twenty sessions, and was lieutenant in the Indian wars　Issue (7) Philander Tracy, (8) Mary, (9) Clarinda, (10) Deborah Susan, (11) Newton ; Adelaide E , Robert

811—Isaac Newton Thompson, born at Middlefield, Ohio, June 18, 1805; died Nov, 1879; buried at Middlefield, Ohio. He engaged in the mercantile business at Middlefield, Ohio, the business now being carried on by his son Henry. I N Thompson never held any public office, and was never affiliated with any fraternal order, being much opposed to secret societies. He was a member of the Methodist Episcopal Church. In August, 1832, at Burton, Ohio, he married Jedidah Anne Foot, a descendant of Nathaniel Foot who located at Wethersfield, Conn, in 1632. She was a daughter of Aaron and Jedidah (Sherman) Foot and a granddaughter of Aaron and Mary (Bronson) Foot and of Elihu Sherman of Williamstown, Mass. All of her ancestral lines are of New England stock, and date back to 1630-5. A full account of the Foot line is given in "The History of the Foots in America." Children of Isaac Newton and Jedidah Anne (Foot) Thompson, (1) John, (2) Henry, (3) Sarah

8111—John Thompson, born at Middlefield, Ohio, 1837, died at the age of 14 years, being killed by lightning together with his cousin Henry Thompson (849)

8112—Henry Thompson, born at Middlefield, Ohio, Oct 10, 1840. Merchant, Middlefield, Ohio. He was educated at the Western Reserve Seminary at Farmington, Ohio. Upon the completion of his studies, he entered upon a mercantile career with his father at Middlefield, Ohio. Upon the death of his father he assumed charge of the business. For twenty-five years after the Civil War, he served as postmaster at Middlefield. He married twice first in Jan, 1863, at Ashland, Ohio, Eliza Jane Poe (born —————, died Dec 25, 1887), daughter of Daniel and Jane West (Ingram) Poe. She was descended from the Maryland Poes. George Jacob Poe was a soldier of fortune, born in the Palatinate, on the upper Rhine. He served under the English Queen Anne, came with his family of several children to Antietam Creek, Md, in 1745. Among the children was Adam (the ancestor), born at sea. Adam married Elizabeth Cochran from the west coast of Ireland. He held a captain's commission in the Revolution, was detailed to border warfare, became an Indian fighter, and was in many battles that are recorded in the histories dealing with that period. The fight of which most has been written was that known as the fight with Big Foot on the banks of the Yellow Creek. In this battle the Wyandotte nation was practically exterminated. In 1910, the citizens of Stark County, Ohio, erected a monument in commemoration of his services. Among his children was Andrew (the ancestor), who married Nancy Hoy, daughter of Charles Hoy, of York County, Pa, and there was born to them 12 children. Daniel (the ancestor) became a Methodist circuit rider and while on an e and for the church found Jane West Ingram, a girl of 21, teaching

among the Indians on the Green Bay, Mich, 200 miles from civiliza-
tion They were married and were sent by the church to the then
republic of Texas, where in the midst of their activities they were
stricken with fever and died within a half hour of each other They
were buried in one grave under the pulpit of the Methodist Church
of San Augustine Jane West Ingram was of Puritan ancestry, each
branch of which came to America in 1630 They all located in
Hadley, Mass, and include Montagues, Smiths, Boltwoods, Hubbards,
Dickinsons, Lewises and Gardners A full history of each family is
given in Judd's "History of Hadley" Issue (1) John Andrew, (2)
Agnes Maria, (3) James Harry, (4) Christine He married secondly,
in Feb, 1889, at Middlefield, Ohio, his cousin—81(11)1—Eugenie
Squibb (born Sept, 1863), daughter of David Bower and Susan
(Thompson) Squibb and granddaughter of Robert and Margaret
(Bower) Squibb of York, Pa Eugenie Squibb was educated at the
Western Reserve Seminary Address, Middlefield, Ohio No issue

81121—**John Andrew Thompson**, born Feb 25, 1866, at Middlefield, Ohio,
died 1916, at Cleveland, Ohio Graduated from the Ohio Wesleyan
University, 1889 He was admitted to the bar in 1891 and practiced
law at Cleveland, Ohio, until his death He was a member of the
Sons of the American Revolution, by virtue of the services of five
ancestors in that conflict He served for two years as president of
the Thompson Family Association He married on July 6, 1896, at
Newton, Mass, Lois Belle Cory, daughter of Rev John Bruce and
Emily (Gates) Cory of Puritan and English ancestry Lois Bell
Cory graduated from the Ohio Wesleyan University in 1889, and
thereafter spent three years studying music in Dresden, Germany
Issue (1) Emily Gates, (2) Deborah Lois

811211—**Emily Gates Thompson**, born at Cleveland, Ohio, died in infancy.

811212—**Deborah Lois Thompson**, born Dec 25, 1900, at Cleveland, Ohio.
Address, Colonial Hall, Grove City, Pa

81122—**Agnes Maria Thompson**, born Nov 7, 1868, at Middlefield, Ohio
She was educated at Oberlin College and taught school for several
years Unmarried Address, Middlefield, Ohio

81123—**James Harry Thompson**, born Oct. 1, 1870, at Middlefield, Ohio
He was educated at the Hiram College Formerly manager of the
Stillman Hotel and now manager of the Hollenden Hotel, Cleveland,
Ohio Married on Nov 1, 1898, in Cleveland, Ohio, Edna Fovargne,
daughter of John and Elizabeth (Wilson) Fovargne John
Fovargne's ancestors were French and Elizabeth Wilson's ancestors
we... English A... of th...

81124—Christine Thompson, born 1875 at Middlefield, Ohio, died Aug, 1884 at Middlefield

8113—Sarah Thompson, born 1843 at Middlefield, Ohio; died 1908 in Oberlin, Ohio   Married twice, first at Middlefield, Ohio, Albert John Tuttle, son of John and Abigail (Tolles) Tuttle—see 819   Issue (1) William Ransom   She married secondly W. R James

81131—William Ransom Tuttle, born Oct 10, 1868, at Burton, Ohio   Graduated with first honors from Olivet College, Mich, 1894   He received the degree of A M. from Columbia University in 1897   He was principal of the Bryan Ohio High School, from 1898 to 1902, head of the department of history and civics at the East St Louis High School from 1902 to 1910 and has been instructor in American and industrial history in the Lake View High School, Chicago, since 1910   He married on Aug 7, 1902 at Buchanan, Mich, Fannie Lesbia Beardsley, (born Oct 17, 1870, in Buchanan, Mich), daughter of David and Rachel (Wheeler) Beardsley and granddaughter of Elizah Hubbell and Matilda (Lehman) Beardsley and of ————— and Edith (Colwell) Wheeler   Fannie Lesbia Beardsley graduated from Otterbein University in 1894 and taught in the Bryan, Ohio public schools from 1898 to 1902   Issue (1) Helen Salome.

811311—Helen Salome Tuttle, born June 28, 1903, in East St Louis, Ill

812—Harriett Thompson, born July 4, 1807; died April 8, 1825.   Married Chauncey Johnson   Issue (1) Harriet

8121—Harriet Johnston, born —————, died in infancy

813—Martha Thompson, born Nov 11, 1808, at Middlefield, Ohio   Married Jan, 1837, Seneca Tracy (brother of her step-mother) son of Gilbert and Deborah (Woodworth) Tracy.   Issue (1) Phoebe D———, (2) Martha Alice, (3) Mary Irene

8131—Phoebe D Tracy, born —————, died —————.

8132—Martha Alice Tracy, born at Middlefield, Ohio, Jan 8, 1840   Graduated from the Cleveland Homeopathic Medical College, 1882   Practiced medicine at Urbana, Ohio, for 18 years   Unmarried   Address, Middlefield, Ohio

8133—Mary Irene Tracy, born July 11, 1848, at Middlefield, Ohio.   Unmarried   Address, Tarrytown-on-Hudson, N Y

814—James Madison Thompson, born Jan 15, 1812, at Middlefield, Ohio, died Sept 23, 1803   Married 1840, Phoebe Tracy, sister of his step-
   [illegible line]

8141—**Adele E Thompson,** born July 7, 1849 Past-President of the Cleveland Women's Press Club Author of "Becks Fortune" 1899, "Betty Sheldon," "Patriot" 1901; "Brave Heart Elizabeth" 1902, "A Lassie of the Isles," 1903, "Polly of the Pines," 1906, "American Patty," 1909, "No-Body's Rose," 1911, see "Who's Who in America" Unmarried. Address, Middlefield, Ohio

815—**Edward Thompson,** born Dec 15, 1813, at Middlefield, Ohio, died Jan, 1894 at Middlefield, Ohio Married Jane Alden, daughter of Enoch and Lucinda (Grey) Alden, a descendant of John and Priscilla Alden Issue (1) Arthssa, (2) Albert S, (3) Roslyn, (4) Emily, (5) Mary, (6) Nellie

8151—**Arthissa Thompson,** born Dec 6, 1848, died —————. Married 1868, Henry W Tracy (who served in the Seventh Ohio Infantry during the Civil War) son of Evander and Almeda (Smith) Tracy, a retired farmer. Issue (1) Lottie

81511—**Lottie Tracy,** born Sept 17, 1869, at Middlefield, Ohio Married her cousin, Ernest W Wright, son of Harvey L and Augusta (Thompson) Wright Issue (1) Edward—see 87111

8152—**Albert S Thompson,** born Feb 26, 1846, at Middlefield, Ohio Farmer, Address, Orwell, R F D No 3, Box 15 Married on Aug 21, 1867 at Windsor, Ada C Heathman, daughter of James A and Amy (Willson) Heathman and granddaughter of James and Almira (—————) Heathman and of Solomon and Lydia (—————) Willson Issue (1) Myrtus E, (2) Edith A

81521—**Myrtus E. Thompson,** born Feb. 2, 1872, at Middlefield, Ohio Address, Huntsburg, Ohio Married on Oct 13, 1897, in Huntsburg, Ohio, Leona Bell Huges No children

81522—**Edith A. Thompson,** born July 22, 1877 Married Oct 16 1902, at Windsor, Herbert L Rice Address, (Triumph) Lockwood, Ohio, R F D. Issue (1) Edwin A, (2) Herbert H, (3) Fanny A, (4) Paul T, (5) Myrtus C. No data

8153—**Roslyn Thompson,** born 1850, died 1909. Married Asa N. Wright. No issue—see 8156

8154—**Emily Thompson,** born Jan, 1848; died Aug., 1848

8155—**Mary Thompson,** born 1853, died 1885 Married Adelbert Southwell Issue (1) Bernice

81551—Bernice Southwell, born May 18, 1877   Address, Middlefield, Ohio

8156—Nellie Thompson, born 1855   Married Asa N. Wright—See 8153
Issue (1) Jane

81561—Jane Wright, born June 1878   Address, Black Rock, Idaho

816—Edmond Thompson, born Feb 1, 1816.   He was a wholesale merchant
at Cleveland, Ohio at the time of his death, Feb ——, 1878   Married
Susan Holiday   Issue (1) William

8161—William Thompson, born 1856; died 1880.

817—Philander Tracy Thompson, born Jan 13, 1820, died 1898.   Unmarried   "A man who led in every good work and whose life was one
of service to others"

818—Mary Thompson, born July 11, 1821, died July, 1848.   Unmarried.

819—Clarinda Thompson, born June 23, 1823, in Geauga County, Ohio·
died Sept 21, 1908   Married on Jan 8, 1850 in Geauga County, Ohio,
Goodwin Stoddard Tolles (died June 28, 1892 at Geneva, Mich), son
of Ransom and Ann (Stoddard) Tolles—see 8113.   Issue (1) Ann,
(2) Goodwin Stoddard, (3) Mary, (4) James Thompson

8191—Ann Tolles, born Oct 23, 1850; died 1858 in Geauga County, Ohio.

8192—Goodwin Stoddard Tolles, Jr, born Feb 6, 1858, in Geauga County,
Ohio   Address, R F D No 5, South Haven, Mich   Married on
Aug. 13, 1882 in Van Buren County, Mich, Clara Warner, daughter
of Anson and Olive (Mead) Warner and granddaughter of Alonson
and Electa (Blowers) Warner and of Hurum and Phoebe (Lewis)
Meade—see 8193   Issue (1) Shirley Earl.

81921—Shirley Earl Tolles, born Dec 9, 1885, in Van Buren County, Mich
Address, R F D No 5, South Haven, Mich   Married on July 1,
1907, Myrtle Wilkins   Issue (1) Mary Marie, (2) Ralph Goodwin,
(3) Leon Earle

819211—Mary Marie Tolles, born Aug 20, 1908, in Van Buren County,
Mich

819212—Ralph Goodwin Tolles, born April 11, 1910, in Van Buren County,
Mich

819213—Leon Earl Tolles, born June 7, 1912, in Van Buren County, Mich.

8193—**Mary Tolles,** born Jan 14. 1861, in Geauga County, Ohio, died Apr 29, 1906 Married on Nov 19, 1882, in Van Buren County, Mich, Frank Warner, son of Anson and Olive (Mead) Warner and grandson of Alonson and Electa (Blowers) Warner and of Hurum and Phoebe (Lewis) Mead—see 8193 Farmer Address, R. F. D No 5, South Haven, Mich. Issue (1) Linn Bernice, (2) Lula Irene, (3) Frank Tolles

81931—**Linn Bernice Warner,** born Aug 27, 1887, in Van Buren County, Mich Unmarried Address, South Haven, Mich, R F D No 5

81932—**Lula Irene Warner,** born Aug 22, 1891, in Van Buren County, Mich. Unmarried Address, South Haven, Mich, R F D No 5.

81933—**Frank Tolles Warner,** born Jan 2 1894, in Van Buren County, Mich Unmarried Address, South Haven, Mich, R F D No 5.

8194—**James Thompson Tolles,** born April 12 1862, in Geauga County, Ohio Farmer Address, South Haven, Mich, R. F D No 5 Married on Mar 25, 1888, in Van Buren County, Mich, Minnie Knowles, daughter of Benjamin and Lucretia (Smith) Knowles and granddaughter of Elijah and Eliza (Demming) Knowles and of Alvah and Lucretia (Van Avery) Smith Issue (1) James Benjamin, (2) Nellie Frances, (3) Goodwin Stoddard, (4) Franklin Knowles, (5) Albert

81941—**James Benjamin Tolles,** born Jan 6 1890 in Van Buren County, Mich Unmarried Address, South Haven, Mich, R F D No 5

81942—**Nellie Frances Tolles,** born Aug 24, 1892, in Van Buren County, Mich Unmarried Address, South Haven, Mich, R F D No 5

81943—**Goodwin Stoddard Tolles,** born Sept 22, 1895, in Van Buren County, Mich Unmarried Address, South Haven, Mich, R F D No 5

81944—**Franklin Knowles Tolles,** born Aug 22, 1899, in Van Buren County, Mich Unmarried Address, South Haven, Mich, R F D No 5

81945—**Albert Tolles,** born May 22, 1906, in Van Buren County, Mich Address, South Haven, Mich, R F D No 5

81(10)—**Delia Thompson,** born June 1, 1825, died 1904 Married Noah Bristol Page, son of Noah Page, a pioneer to Burton, Ohio, from Northford, Conn Issue (1) Carrie

81(10)1—**Carrie Page,** born Feb 1857, died 1800 Married Perry B Reed No issu

81(11)—**Susan Thompson,** born May 2, 1827 Married David Bower Squibb, son of Robert and Margaret (Bower) Squibb of York, Pa Address, Middlefield, Ohio Issue (1) Eugenia

81(11)1—**Eugenia Squibb,** born Sept., 1863 She was educated at the Western Reserve Seminary Married Feb, 1889, her cousin—8112, Henry Thompson, son of Isaac Newton and Pudith Ann (Foot) Thompson Address, Middlefield, Ohio No issue—see 8112

81(12)—**Maria Thompson,** born April 12, 1830, died 1888 Married Jonathan T Elliott Issue (1) Emma, (2) Mercy

81(12)1—**Emma Elliott,** born ——————, died in infancy

81(12)2—**Mercy Elliott,** born 1862, died 1882

81(13)—**Pauline Thompson,** born April 15 1833 Married in 1860, Warren Bishop Address, Middlefield, Ohio

81(14)—**Robert Thompson,** born July 18, 1837, died Nov, 1857 Unmarried

82—**John Thompson,** born Aug 5, 1783; died young

83—**Polly Thompson,** born April 10, 1785, died ———————— Married on July 30, 1806, Stephen Bond Issue (1) Seldon, (2) Lora, (3) Clarinda, (4) Mary Family moved to Illinois —No data

84—**William Thompson,** born March 25, 1789, died Oct 6, 1870 He was a soldier in the War of 1812 Married on Feb 8, 1815, Lucinda Walden Issue (1) Clarrissa, (2) Isaac, (3) Justus, (4) Austin, (5) Augustus, (6) Silas, (7) Elisha, (8) Benjamin Franklin, (9) Henry

841—**Clarissa Thompson,** born Nov 11, 1815, at Middlefield, Ohio, died Jan 15, 1894 Married Eli F Bishop Issue (1) Horace, (2) James M

8411—**Horace Bishop,** born May 2, 1839, died June 10, 1886 Married Sabia Barb Issue (1) Cora, (2) Elmer, (3) Ada

84111—**Cora Bishop,** born ——————— Married Charles Kallenberg. Address, Middlefield, Ohio Issue (1) Della, (2) Ernest

841111—**Della Kallenberg,** born ——————. Married Clarence Leggett. Address Montville, Ohio Issue (1) Ruth (2) James, (3) Charles.

841112—**Ernest Kallenberg**, born ――――――, at Middlefield, Ohio Was student at Mt Union and Wooster Colleges, and later superintendent of the high school at Mecca, Ohio

84112—**Elmer Bishop**, born ――――― No data

84113—**Ada Bishop**, born ――――― No data

8412—**James M. Bishop**, born July 15, 1840, died 1863 in the army during Civil War.

842—**Isaac Thompson**, born Nov 30, 1817, at Middlefield, Ohio, died ―――――― Married Elizabeth Reed, daughter of John and Joania (――――) Reed Issue (1) Maria J, (2) Adelbert O, (3) Susie F, (4) Addie, (5) George

8421—**Maria J. Thompson**, born 1845, died ――――――, at Middlefield, Ohio Married William H Wilbur No data

8422—**Adelbert O Thompson,** born in Middlefield, Ohio Address, Middlefield, Ohio Married Cornelia Stanton

8423—**Susie F Thompson**, born Sept. 28 1858 Married on May 26, 1878, in Chardon, Ohio, Fred M Smiley, son of J R Smiley and grandson of John A Smiley Merchant at Andover, Ohio Issue (1) Genae H, (2) George H, (3) Hal K

84231—**Genae H Smiley**, born Sept 22, 1879 at Andover Ohio Married on June 10, 1901, J J Robinson Address, % Bessemer R R Co, Pittsburgh, Pa Issue (1) Lois E

842311—**Lois E Robinson,** born Aug 8, 1902, at Pittsburgh, Pa

84232—**George H Smiley**, born Nov 18, 1881, at Kinsman, Ohio Merchant, Kinsman, Ohio Married on Aug 8, 1906, Bessie Beckworth No children

84233—**Hal K Smiley**, born Feb 3, 1888 at Kinsman, Ohio Merchant, Andover, Ohio Married on Oct 10, 1910, Bessie Reed Issue (1) Hallie

842331—**Hallie Smiley**, born July 10, 1911

8424—**Addie Thompson**, born April 8, 1869, died about 1871

8425—**George Thompson,**

843—Justus Thompson, born 1819, at Middlefield, Ohio, died at Rock
Creek, Ohio Married Lucy —————— Issue (1) William, (2)
Cora, (3) Edward No data

844—Austin Thompson, born 1822, at Middlefield, Ohio; died in Michigan.
Married Jane Baker Issue (1) Warren, (2) Edward No data

845—Augustus Thompson, born 1824, at Middlefield, Ohio, died in Colorado Was a soldier in the Civil War Married twice first ——————
Fuller, second —————— Issue (1) Henry, (2) Frank No data

846—Silas Thompson, born 1827, at Middlefield, Ohio, died at Middlefield,
Ohio, 1899 Married twice first ——————— Critchett, second Hattie
Rexford Issue (1) Susan

8461—Susan Thompson, born —————— Married Alonz Hutchinson
Address, Los Angeles, Cal

847—Elisha Thompson, born 1830, at Middlefield, Ohio, died 1840; killed
by falling tree

848—Benjamin Franklin Thompson, born March 16, 1832, at Middlefield,
Ohio, died at Claridon, April 13, 1902 Superintendent of the County
Infirmary for many years. Married Anna Bosley Issue (1) Robert,
(2) Charlie

8481—Robert Thompson, born —————— Married —————— Beardslee
Address, Claridon, Ohio

8482—Charlie Thompson (girl), born —————— Married Olen Pfonty
No data

849—Henry Thompson, born 1832, at Middlefield, Ohio, died in childhood,
killed by lightning together with his cousin (8111) John Thompson

85—Robert Thompson, born July 24, 1794, died young

86—Eliza Thompson, born Oct 6, 1796, at Charleston, W Va , died 1820
at Middlefield, Ohio, aged 23 Unmarried

87—John Thompson, born Jan 6, 1799, at Mentor, Ohio; died 1832, aged
33 Justice of the Peace for many years Married on Jan 3, 1822,
Jerusha Russell, daughter of Samuel and Mary (Rice) Russell Issue
(1) Ellsworth K , (2) Zenas, (3) Mary, (4) Caroline

871—Ellsworth R Thompson, born Oct 5 1822 at Middlefield, Ohio, died
( )   (   )   and Caroline Dudley Issue (1) Augusta

8711—Augusta **Thompson,** born Aug. 24, 1850, at Middlefield, Ohio, died 1900 Married 1870, at Middlefield, Ohio, Harvey L Wright, a soldier in the Civil War, and now a retired farmer at Middlefield Issue (1) Ernest W, (2) George, (3) Lillian A

87111—Ernest W. **Wright,** born March 23, 1871, at Middlefield, Ohio He was a school teacher and is now a building contractor at Middlefield Married his cousin (81511) Lottie Tracy, daughter of Henry W and Arthssa (Thompson) Tracy. Issue (1) Edward

871111—Edward **Wright,** born Feb 22, 1899, at Middlefield, Ohio. Address, Middlefield, Ohio

87112—George **Wright,** born ——————, died ——————

87113—Lillian A **Wright,** born May 14, 1877, at Middlefield, Ohio Married Arthur Starling Address, Spokane, Wash Issue (1) Harvey, (2) Esther, (3) Lois

871131—Harvey **Starling,** born ————— Address, —————

871132—Esther **Starling,** born ————— Address —————

871133—Lois **Starling,** born ————— Address —————

872—Zenas **Thompson,** born July 12, 1826, at Middlefield, Ohio; died —————, at South Haven, Mich Married on Oct 20, 1853, at Warren Trumbull County, Ohio, Susan Gates, daughter of William and Harriett (Bundy) Gates and granddaughter of Elisha and Abigail (—————) Bundy Elisha Bundy was a colonel in the Revolutionary War Issue (1) Hattie

8721—Hattie **Thompson,** born July 30, 1858, at Nelson Ledge, Ohio Unmarried She is a school teacher Address, 220 Superior St, South Haven, Mich.

873—Mary **Thompson,** born Aug 31, 1827, at Middlefield, Ohio. Address (1912), Middlefield, Ohio Married twice first on Jan 1, 1854, at Middlefield, Ohio, Israel Reed, son of George and Johanne Reed. Issue (1) John, (2) Ada She married secondly Waterman Hodges. No issue Address, Middlefield, Ohio.

8731—John **Reed,** born —————. Address, Middlefield, Ohio. Married at Middlefield, Ohio, Ellen E Russell, daughter of George and Adaline (Gates) Russell and granddaughter of William Gates No issue

16

8732—**Ada Reed,** born Nov 12, 1860, at Laporte, Ind   Married on Dec 26, 1882, at Middlefield, Ohio, Clifford F Harrison, son of William and Silvia Harrison   Farmer, Middlefield, Ohio   Issue (1) Howard S, (2) son

87321—**Howard S. Harrison,** born ―――――――. Unmarried.

87322—**(Son) Harrison,** born May 10, 1892, died June 23, 1892

874—**Caroline Thompson,** born 1832, at Middlefield, Ohio, died 1873 at Garrettsville, Ohio   Married Clinton Tracy, a nephew of Mercy Tracy—see 81   Issue (1) Lester, (2) Flora

8741—**Lester Tracy,** born at Middlefield, Ohio, died at Denver, Colo Unmarried

8742—**Flora Tracy,** born ――――――――, died ――――――― Unmarried

88—**Lydia (Lydda) Thompson,** born April 6, 1801, at Middlefield, Ohio; died Aug 25, 1875, at Middlefield   Married on Sept 16, 1819, Moses Morse (born Aug 4, 1793, died March 17, 1885, at Middlefield, Ohio), son of Darrius and Experience (Adams) Morse and grandson of Moses and Lydia (Danniels) Morse and of George and Sarah Adams, great-grandson of Benjamin and Sarah (Faleslat) Morse, great-great-grandson of Jeremiah and Elizabeth (Hamant) Morse, great-great-great-grandson of Joseph and Hannah (Phillips) Morse, and great-great-great-great-grandson of Samuel Morse who was born in 1587, came to New England in the ship "Increase" in 1635 with his wife Elizabeth and son Joseph, and died in 1654 at Medfield, Mass   Moses Morse enlisted as a Minute Man in the War of 1812   Children of Moses and Lydda (Thompson) Morse, (1) John, (2) Eliza, (3) Rhoda, (4) Levi, (5) Harriett, (6) Mary, (7) Sarah, (8) Ellen, (9) David Benjamin, (10) Edward L, (11) Albert, (12) Phoebe Caroline

881—**John Morse,** born July 1, 1820, at Mesopotamia, Ohio; died Feb 27, 1889, in Middlefield, Ohio   Farmer   Married in 1842 at Vernon, Pa, Mary Ketchum, daughter of Benjamin and Louisa (Adams) Ketchum of Cattaraugua County, N Y   Issue (1) Louisa Melissa, (2) Elsie Althea, (3) Elbridge Volna, (4) Rhoda Roseltha, (5) Ellen Edna, (6) Charles Alva, (7) Mary, (8) Alva Charles, (9) Captola Ardelle

8811—**Louisa Melissa Morse,** born Nov 26, 1845, at Middlefield, Ohio. Married on March 3, 1862, at Charidon, Ohio, John Marshall Hamilton, son of Charles and Hannah Hamilton of Charidon, Ohio   J M Hamilton served in the Forty-first Ohio Volunteer Infantry in the Civil War   Issue (1) Nettie, (2) Lottie, (3) Otis, (4) Nellie, (5) Hattie, (6) Mamie, (7) Belle, (8) Josie, (9) Carl, (10) Gertie

88111—Nettie Hamilton, born Nov 26, 1866, at Munson, Ohio   Married Frederick Greene, railroad supervisor, Ravenna, Ohio   No children.

88112—Lottie Hamilton, born Aug 27, 1869, at Huntsburg, Ohio   Married Claude Eggleston   Address, Chagrin Falls, Ohio   Issue (1) Claudine, (2) Ruth, (3) Zeno   No data

88113—Otis Hamilton, born Oct. 24, 1871, at Middlefield, Ohio   Married at Dorset, Ohio, Eva Williams.   Issue (1) —————, died in infancy, (2) Joe   No data

88114—Nellie Hamilton, born Jan. 4, 1873, at Middlefield, Ohio   Married Norman Atkins, son of Perry Atkins, Burton, Ohio   Issue (1) Mildred   No data

88115—Hattie Hamilton, born Jan 12, 1873, died Feb 10. 1877

88116—Mamie Hamilton, born Sept 7, 1878; died Oct 17. 1885

88117—Belle Hamilton, born Nov 14, 1880   Married Harry Larson, of Huntsburg, Ohio   Issue (1) Donald, (2) Adelene

881171—Donald Larson, born —————

881172—Adelene Larson, born April 25, 1915.

88118—Josie Hamilton, born Oct. 1, 1883   Address, State Hospital, Cleveland, Ohio   Married Apr 13, 1915, Harry Ashern, of Cleveland, Ohio

88119—Carl Hamilton, born Dec 9, 1885, at Middlefield, Ohio.   Address, Burton, Ohio   Married on Jan 1, 1908, Hattie Freeman   No children

8811(10)—Gertie Hamilton, born April 26, 1888   Married Jay Parks, of Cleveland, Ohio   Issue (1) Virginia, (2) Genevieve

8811(10)1—Virginia Parks, born —————

8811(10)2—Genevieve Parks, born May 4, 1916

8812—Elsie Althea Morse, born Sept. 16, 1847, at Middlefield, Ohio.   Married Cassius M. Pierce (born —————, died Feb 9, 1911, at Middlefield, Ohio), son of Richard and Emily (Hazen) Pierce of Middlefield, Ohio   C M Pierce served in the Eighty-sixth and One Hundred and Seventy-seventh Ohio Volunteer Infantry in the Civil War   He served one term in the Washington State Legislature   Issue   (1) Opal   2 Pearl

88121—Otto Pierce, born May 19, 1873, at Middlefield, Ohio; died Nov 12, 1880

88122—Pearl Pierce, born Aug 6, 1875, at Middlefield, Ohio. Married on Dec 23, 1900, Sherman F Sperry, son of Hezekiah and Ann (Gates) Sperry of Middlefield, Ohio Issue (1) Elsie, (2) Anna, (3) Pierce, (4) Martha No data

8813—Elbridge Volna Morse, born Feb. 28, 1850. Address, Chesterland, Ohio Married twice first on Feb 27, 1875, Mary Ann Sanford (born May 14, 1853; died July 23, 1887), daughter of Ira and Mary Rose) Sanford of Middlefield, Ohio Issue (1) Effie Viola, (2) Myrta Annetta, (3) Lora Ann, (4) Victor Ernest He married secondly on Aug 28, 1888, Mrs Ella Caroline (Kelly) Strahlem, widow of Isaac Strahlem of Toledo, Ohio No children Historian of the Morse-Thompson Family.

88131—Effie Viola Morse, born Dec. 9, 1873 at Middlefield, Ohio Married George Crampton, son of Nolly Crampton of Burton, Ohio Issue (1) Vera.

881311—Vera Crampton, born Nov. 18, 1894, at Burton, Ohio Married Dec, 1914, at Cleveland, Ohio, J. Metzger. Address, Public Library, Cleveland

88132—Myrta Annetta Morse, born July 19, 1876, at Middlefield, Ohio. Unmarried She is a school teacher at Chesterland, Ohio

88133—Lora Anna Morse, born Feb 10, 1881, at Middlefield, Ohio Married on Aug 23, 1906, at Burton, Ohio, Clarence Edmond Jenks, son of Edmond C Jenks, of Middlefield, Ohio Clarence E Jenks is head of Industrial School, Louisville, Ky Issue (1) Edmond Victor, (2) Marjorie (Louisville, Ky) No data

88134—Victor Ernest Morse, born April 13, 1884, at Middlefield, Ohio. Address, Chesterland, Ohio Married Nov 11, 1912, Helen Nettie Taylor Issue (1) Hallie, (2) John Herbert.

881341—Hallie Morse, born Sept 12, 1913.

881342—John Herbert Morse, born Nov. 12, 1915.

8814—Rhoda Roseltha Morse, born 1853, died Feb, 1861

8815—Ellen Edna Morse, born July 12, 1855 Married on Dec 27, 1878, Ezra G Ohl (born Dec 4, 1847), son of David and Betsy (White) Ohl of Ohltown, Ohio He served in the 196th Ohio Volunteer Infantry in the Civil War Address, Middlefield, Ohio Issue (1) ...n, ( ) Teddie

88151—**Bessie Ohl**, born May 8, 1880, at Middlefield, Ohio Married on Sept 17, 1903, at Cleveland, Ohio, Walter Groff Address, 9804 Miles Ave, Cleveland, Ohio Issue (1) Maxwell, (2) Edgar. No data

88152—**Teddie Ohl**, born Nov 30, 1891, at Middlefield, Ohio, died in infancy.

8816—**Charles Alva Morse**, born 1857, died Feb, 1861

8817—**Mary Morse**, born 1860, died 1860, two weeks old

8818—**Alva Charles Morse**, born May 30, 1863, at Middlefield, Ohio. Married on Jan 17, 1888, Etta Newman (born June 21, 1869), daughter of John and Emma Newman, of Burton, Ohio Issue (1) Gracie, (2) Georgia, (3) Gertie, (4) Mildred Mary, (5) Marguerite Treasure, (6) Nina Ester

88181—**Gracie Morse** (triplet), born Sept 3, 1889, at Middlefield, Ohio

88182—**Georgia Morse** (triplet), born Sept. 3, 1889; died Sept 3 1889

88183—**Gertie Morse** (triplet), born Sept 3, 1889 at Middlefield, Ohio

88184—**Mildred Mary Morse**, born Sept 8 1891, at Middlefield, Ohio. Married on May 1, 1912, Elmer Stoneman, son of Elias and Alice (————) Stoneman Address, Chagrin Falls, O

88185—**Marguerite Treasure Morse**, born Dec. 30, 1897, at Newbury, Ohio

88186—**Nina Ester Morse**, born Sept. 14, 1901, at Bainbridge, Ohio

8819—**Captola Ardelle Morse**, born June 5, 1865, at Middlefield, Ohio. Married on Aug 13, 1892, at Centralia, Oregon, Charles J Petit (born in Fredericksburg, Ohio), son of Pierre and Fillicia (Rouies) Petit, of France Address, 3412 Riverside Ave, Cleveland, Ohio Issue (1) Christine Mary, (2) Lucy Cecele, (3) Charles Morse, (4) Chester John, (5) Clarence Vincent, (6) Carol Jean

88191—**Christine Mary Petit**, born Jan. 25, 1894, at Chagrin Falls, Ohio

88192—**Lucy Cecele Petit**, born July 21, 1895 at Chagrin Falls, Ohio

88193—**Charles Morse Petit**, born May 12, 1897, at Chagrin Falls, Ohio.

88194—**Chester John Petit**,   an   u Cleveland Ohio

88195—Clarence Vincent Petit, born Nov. 24, 1907, at Cleveland, Ohio

88196—Carol Jean Petit, born Sept 8, 1911, at Cleveland, Ohio.

882—Eliza Morse, born Dec 21, 1821, at Middlefield, Ohio, died Dec 6,
1878 at Van Wert, Ohio   Married 1842, Charles Jones, son of Deacon
Evander and Cynthia (————————) Jones of Middlefield   Charles
Jones kept a tavern at N Newbury, Ohio, and later lived at Cleveland
and Van Wert, Ohio   Issue (1) Annettie, (2) Infant

8821—Annettie Jones, born 1844 at N Newbury, Ohio, died 1905 in
Chicago, Ill   Married at Van Wert, Ohio, Thomas Saltzgaber (born
————————, died 1890) a soldier of the Civil War, Van Wert, Ohio
Issue (1) Ola, (2) Charles, (3) Carey   No data

883—Rhoda Morse, born Oct 24, 1823, at Middlefield, Ohio   Address,
Middlefield, Ohio   Married 1848, at Hudson, Ohio, Ruben Hollenbeck
(born ————————, died Aug. 3, 1892) son of Gad and Phoebe (Bishop)
Hollenbeck, of Hudson, Ohio   Issue (1) Sylvester D, (2) Harmony,
(3) Charles

8831—Sylvester D Hollenbeck, born Aug 10, 1849   He was County
Auditor for several years   Lived in St Petersburg, Fla   Married twice, first, Jennie Bishop of Middlefield, secondly, Kate Hath-
away   Issue by first wife (1) Harland, (2) Jessie.

88311—Harland Hollenbeck, born March, 1872, died at Toledo, Ohio.
Married Carrie Burt (born Mar 4, 1872, died Oct 8, 1909) of
Toledo, Ohio   No data

88312—Jessie Hollenbeck, born Aug 15, 1876   Married on Dec 6, 1905,
F Vernon Osborne, Buffalo, N. Y.   Issue (1) Helen Elizabeth

8832—Harmony Hollenbeck, born Oct 20, 1852   Married David Chittenden—see 889—Middlefield, Ohio.   Issue (1) Thomas H, (2) Reuben,
(3) Ora C.

88321—Thomas H Chittenden, born Oct. 25, 1875.   Married on Sept 22,
1897, Ola Jewett, Hartsburg, Ohio   Issue (1) Dora May, (2) Odas
Jewett, (3) Sarah Augusta, (4) Carroll Paul   No data

88322—Reuben Chittenden, born Sept 27, 1882   Married on Sept 26, 1906,
Susie G Hirshfield, Mesopotamia, Ohio   Issue (1) Josephine V
No data

88323—Ora C Chittenden, born Oct 4, 1887   Married on Nov. 25, 1910,
. . . . Buckman, Ohio

8833—**Charles Hollenbeck,** born ———— Married Frances Livingston
No children

884—**Levi Morse,** born April 17, 1826, at Middlefield, Ohio, died Jan 13,
1904 at Middlefield Married on Sept 30, 1856, Lucy Hawthorne,
daughter of James and Chloe (Brace) Hawthorne, of Parkman, Ohio
Issue (1) Ernest, (2) Earle, (3) Sherman, (4) Robert

8841—**Ernest Morse,** born Sept 2, 1869, died March 16, 1870.

8842—**Earl Morse,** born ————. Married on Oct 17, 1891. Mary
Lane of Farmington, Ohio Issue (1) Clare —, (2) Clyde P, (3)
Carlysle E

88421—**Clare J Morse,** born April 30, 1891; died July 19, 1896

88422—**Clyde P Morse,** born Feb 21, 1893

88423—**Carlysle E Morse,** born Aug 4, 1896

8843—**Sherman Morse,** born ———— Married Mary Hosmer, Parkman, Ohio. Issue (1) Leita

88431—**Leita Morse,** born Nov 1, 1894

8844—**Robert Morse,** born ———— Unmarried

885—**Harriett Morse,** born Jan 19 1828, died Aug. 21, 1829

886—**Mary Morse,** born Sept 28, 1829 at Middlefield, Ohio   Address,
Detroit, Minn   Married on Mar 4, 1849, William Cowles, died Mar
4, 1883, son of Joseph and Mary Cowles, of Connecticut Issue (1)
Frank W, (2) George R, (3) Edgar A, (4) Edna M, (5) Minnie M,
(6) Wallace A

8861—**Frank W. Cowles,** born March 27, 1851. Address, Elysian, Minn.
Married Louise Robinson Issue (1) Bertha Alice, (2) James Edgar,
(3) Earl Franklin, (4) Arthur W

88611—**Bertha Alice Cowles,** born June 29, 1879. Married on Dec 1, 1897,
Clarence Casey of Elysian Minn Issue (1) Della, (2) Gladys, (3)
Ambrey, (4) Orpha No data

88612—**James Edgar Cowles,** born Aug 25 1881. Address, Elysian, Minn
Married on .. 1, 1908 .. No children

88613—Earl Franklin Cowles, born May 17 1885   Address, Elysian, Minn. Married on Nov 24, 1909, Reno Casbur   Issue (1) Earl C.   No data

88614—Arthur W. Cowles, born Sept 10, 1888   Railroad agent   Unmarried

8862—George R. Cowles, born July 2, 1853   Lived at Janesville, Minn. Married 1908, Emma McKinny   Issue (1) Leon R, (2) Alta Bess

88621—Leon R. Cowles, born March 1, 1883.   Address, 4027 Twelfth Ave, Seattle, Wash   Married   No data

88622—Alta Bess Cowles, born Aug, 1887   Married ——————   No children

8863—Edgar A Cowles, born Feb. 1, 1858.   Address, St Mary's, Ohio. Married Ada Denton   No children

8864—Edna M Cowles, born Aug. 1, 1860; died Aug 5, 1888   Married O L Cooley.   Issue (1) Ethel Louisa, (2) Edith May, (3) Ella Pearl

88641—Ethel Louisa Cooley, born Nov 7, 1882   Married on Dec 2 1903, Maynard Porter, Tiffin, Ohio   Issue (1) Mary Josephine   No data

88642—Edith May Cooley, born July 22, 1884   Married on Dec 20, 1903, Elmer E Reynolds, New York Mills, Minn   Issue (1) Frances V, (2) Gertrude Alice, (3) Leonard E   No data

886421—Frances V Reynolds, born ——————, died Dec 6, 1905

88643—Ella Pearl Cooley, born Jan 8, 1886   Married on Nov 5, 1902, Benjamin C Bailey, Perham, Minn   No data

8865—Minnie M. Cowles, born Jan 1, 1866   Married Charles Wakefield, of Janesville, Minn   Issue (1) Harold Edward, (2) L D C

88651—Harold Edward Wakefield, born Aug 7, 1886   Married on June 15, 1912, Stella Wakefield of Moore Jaw, Saskachewan, Can   No children

88652—L D. C. Wakefield, born May 28, 1893   Address, Elysian, Minn. No children

8866—Wallace A Cowles, born Sept 18 1860   Address, Elysian, Minn. 1   1   1 1. 1   ss (1) Abel Maudie, (2) Olive Constance

88661—**Alta Blanche Cowles,** born 1890   Married William Jensen. Issue
(1) ——————. No data

88662—**Olive Constance Cowles,** born 1892   Married William Moen, of
Minneapolis, Minn   No data

887—**Sarah Morse,** born Nov 14, 1831, at Middlefield, Ohio; died March
27, 1900 at Middlefield   Married on Oct, 1860, Wilhard Plumley (born
April 20, 1820, died June 10, 1897, in Middlefield, Ohio)   Issue (1)
Emma, (2) Edward

8871—**Emma Plumley,** born Feb 23, 1862   Married on June 2, 1890,
Almon Moyer. Address, Warren, Ohio. Issue (1) Grace E, (2)
Christobelle S

88711—**Grace F. Moyer,** born Aug 12, 1893   Attended the Warren (Ohio)
Business College

88712—**Christobelle S Moyer,** born Nov 16, 1899

8872—**Edward Plumley,** born May 25, 1864   Address, Middlefield, Ohio.
Married on Dec 12, 1900, Alvina Havens of Parkman, Ohio   Issue
three children   No data

888—**Ellen Morse,** born Nov 8, 1833, at Middlefield, Ohio   Address, Burton, Ohio   Married on Jan 1, 1861, David Ames (born March 7, 1831
in E Claridon, Ohio; died Dec 3, 1895 at Middlefield, Ohio), son of
Mosier and Polly Ames of Claridon, Ohio   No children

889—**David Benjamin Morse,** born Dec. 6, 1835. at Middlefield Ohio.
Address, Warren, Ohio   He served in the Seventh Ohio Volunteer
Infantry during the Civil War   Married on Sept 25, 1864, Harriett
Crittenden, daughter of Frederick and Deborah (Alden) Crittenden—
see 88(12) and 8832   Issue (1) Frank W, (2) Herbert, (3) Edna,
(4) Edith

8891—**Frank W Morse,** born July 12, 1868, at Middlefield, Ohio   Address
Warren, Ohio   Married Dec 8, 1913, Mabel May Elizabeth Somers,
(born Mar 27, 1881, at Baltonsborough, Somersetshire, England),
daughter of George and Mary Ann (Curtis) Somers

8892—**Herbert Morse,** born Dec 27, 1869, died Sept 1, 1870

8893—**Edna Morse,** born March 14 1874   Address, 5607 Euclid Ave,
Cleveland Ohio   Married on Sept 26, 1896, William Michael, son
of Frederick and Elizabeth Michael   Issue (1) Fred M, (2) Edith
Leone

8893¹—Fred M. Michael, born April 3, 1899

88932—Edith Leone Michael, born Jan 16, 1902

8894—Edith Morse, born April 25, 1879. Married Jan 5, 1914, in Pittsburgh, Pa, John Frederick Walters (born Aug. 20, 1878, at Cambridge Springs, Pa), son of John and Mary Jane (Webster) Walters

88(10)—Edward L, Morse, born June 16, 1838, at Middlefield, Ohio, died
Dec 9, 1906 at Chardon, Ohio He was a practicing physician at
Chardon He served as orderly sergeant in the Forty-first Ohio
Volunteer Infantry during the Civil War Married on Sept 13,
1876, Mrs Lydia (Atwood) Bishop, daughter of Dr Joseph and
Elizabeth Atwood Mrs E L Morse is a practicing physician at
Chardon, Ohio No children

88(11)—Albert Morse, born May 4, 1843, at Middlefield, Ohio; died Sept.
1, 1900 at Middlefield, Ohio Unmarried.

88(12)—Phoebe Caroline Morse, born Sept 9, 1845, died Nov 11, 1913.
Married on Aug 27, 1865, Henry W Crittenden (born Aug 15,
1841) son of Frederick and Deborah (Alden) Crittenden of Middlefield and grandson of William Crittenden from Connecticut—see
8832 and 889—H W. Crittenden was a merchant in Middlefield and
later a druggist in Burton, Ohio He served in the Seventh Ohio
Volunteer Infantry during the Civil War Issue (1) Frederick, (2)
Bird Leon

88(12)1—Frederick Crittenden, born Feb 26, 1868. Address, Burton, Ohio.
Married on Nov 7, 1889, Louise Reed of Detroit, Mich Issue (1)
Cecile E, (2) Arleen H.

88(12)11—Cecile E. Crittenden, born Sept 28, 1898 Music teacher Married June 28, 1916, at Burton, Ohio, Stuart D Strong

88(12)12—Arleen H Crittenden, born Oct 16, 1894

88(12)2—Bird Leon Crittenden, born Feb 10, 1874 Address, Burton, Ohio.
Married twice, first on Feb 10, 1896, Mabel Downing (born ————
————, died 1907 Issue (1) Celestine He married second time
on June 21, 1911, Virginia Kilhus, daughter of George and Bertha
Kilhus of Chardon, Ohio Child, (2) Henry Williams

89—Robert I Thompson, born June 6, 1804 died 1816, aged 12 years

BRANCH NO. 9.

9—John Thomson, born ——————, died May-June, 1846, near Butler, Pa He was said to be a "man of affairs" in 1824 In the "Thompson Family" booklet it is stated that he "married and lived in Juniata County, moved to Butler County, Pa The Thompsons and Pattersons of Butler County are his descendants One of his sons married a sister of David Allen and moved to Covington, Ind ? Ky.? where they lived in 1857" It is said he owned a store and a tannery In Book B, p 383, of Butler County Wills is recorded the will of John Thompson as probated June 22, 1846 In this will, declared by word to Benjamin Miller and Margaret Turk on May 12, 1846, he gives his remaining estate to his wife Martha, his sons and daughters have previously received their shares —See notes on deeds to sons 91, 92, and 99 He married Martha Park, daughter of ——————————, of Chester County, Pa (she was still living at the time of his death, May, 1848) Issue (1) John Park, (2) James, (3) Joseph, (4) Samuel, (5) Isabella, (6) Zelia, (7) Frances, (8) William Clinton, (9) Robert W——————

91—John Park Thompson, born ——————, 1804 near Bedford, Pa, died Oct 1, 1874 His father John Thompson, Sr, and his mother Martha spent their last days at his home, and in consideration thereof he was deeded on March 27, 1837, by his parents a part of the land on which they lived See Butler County, Pa, Wills, Book K, p 205 He was married in 1832, by Rev. Davis at Bedford, Pa, to Eliza Bowman (born Feb 4, 1806, died June 21, 1887), daughter of John and Phebe (McClintock) Bowman John Bowman (born Aug, 1772) was a son of Thomas Bowman (born ——————, died Jan, 1783, in Franklin County, Pa) and Mary (Campbell) Bowman, daughter of Samuel Campbell He married on April 5, 1798, Phebe McClintock (born July 9, 1779, died Dec 28, 1849) Issue (1) Maria Louisa, (2) Phebe, (3) William, (4) Martha, (5) George W——————

911—Maria Louisa Thompson, born June 24, 1833 Married Oct. 11 1855 at Butler, Pa, George Washington Rupp (born 1811 near Mercersburg, Franklin County, Pa, died Aug 4, 1872, in Utica, N Y), son of Jacob (or John) Rupp (born ——————, died 1823) and Susan (Myers) Rupp Issue (1) Cornelia Bowman, (2) Eliza Thompson, (3) Sue Myers, (4) Havelock, (5) Ada V Count

9111—Cornelia Bowman Rupp, born Sept 10, 1859, at Bedford, Pa Address, Mrs R L Holliday, 417 South State St, Dover, Del Married on Dec 26, 1878, at Youngstown, Ohio, Robert Lowry Holliday (born May 6, 1858, at Hollidaysburg, Pa, died May 12, 1906, at Dover, Del), son of ———————————————————————————— of

John and Elizabeth (Boyle) Bell   R L Holliday was superintendent of the Delaware Division of the P S & W R R at time of his death, May 12, 1906   Issue (1) Persifor Smith, (2) Robert Fleming Lowry, Jr

91111—Persifor Smith Holliday, born Feb 10, 1883, at Altoona, Pa. Address, 205 Ninth St, N E, Canton, Ohio   Married on Feb 12, 1908, at Wellsville, Ohio, Sarah Jane Nelson, daughter of James Montgomery and Joanna (Sample) Nelson and grandson of George and Isabella (Montgomery) Nelson and of James Gray and Mary Elizabeth (Stackhouse) Sample. P. S. Holliday attended the Mercersburg Academy, Lehigh University, the University of Pennsylvania, and Drexel Institute   Address, 734 Walnut St, Canton, Ohio   Issue ————————

91112—Robert Fleming Lowry Holliday, Jr, born Feb 8, 1885, at Bedford, Bedford County, Pa   Address, 477 Columbia Ave, Palmerton, Pa   Chief of Estimating Division of New Jersey Zinc Co, Palmerton, N J   Married on March 20, 1909, at New Brighton, Staten Island, Jeanette Van Vechten, daughter of Cuyler and Jessie (Giles) Van Vechten and granddaughter of Cuyler and Hannah (Hammond) Van Vechten   Issue (1) Robert Lowry

911121—Robert Lowry Holliday, born Sept. 11, 1913, at New Brighton, Staten Island, N Y

9112—Eliza Thompson Rupp, born Apr. 20, 1861, at Bedford. Married Humphrey Barton   Address, 650 Goodrich Ave, St Paul, Minn

9113—Sue Myers Rupp, born ———————   Died in infancy

9114—Havelock Rupp, born ———————. Died in infancy.

9115—Ada V Count Rupp, born ———————. Died in infancy

92—James ——————— Thompson, born ———————   On Apr. 1, 1846, he purchased from his father John Thompson and mother Martha for $5 a tract of 183 acres of land in Center Township, Butler County, Pa, granted to the said John Thompson by patent on Jan 23, 1824—see Butler County Deed Book P, p 208   He was a physician at Butler, Pa   Died ———————, at ———————   Unmarried. No other data

93—Joseph Thompson, born Butler County, Pa. Married on ——————— at Mobile, Ala, French lady   Issue daughter

931———————— Thompson, born ———————   Married on ——————— at Mobile, Ala, Mr Shelton   No other data

94—Samuel Thompson, born —————, died ————— Unmarried No other data.

95—Isabella Thompson, born ————— Married ————— No other data

96—Zelia Thompson, born —————, 1810?, in Butler County, Pa , died —————. Married on —————, at Pittsburgh, Pa , James Gilliland (born —————, died —————) No data Issue (1) Mary.

961—Mary Gilliland, born ————— No data

97—Frances Thompson, born in 1807 at Unionville, Butler County, Pa ; died Apr , 1838 at Butler, Pa Married in 1831, James Hull Graham, son of Robert Graham Issue (1) Emmett, (2) James, (3) Sarah Martha, (4) Loyal Young

971—Emmett Graham, born 1832, died in infancy

972—James Graham, born 1834, died in infancy.

973—Sarah Martha Graham, born June 28, 1836, at Butler, Pa Married on Aug 28, 1862, at Bakerstown, Pa , John Moore Thompson, of Kittanning, Pa. (born 1833, died in Seattle, Wash , 1904) Address, 4547 Fourteenth Avenue, N E, Seattle, Wash Issue (1) James Elmer, (2) Fannie Idelette, (3) Mary Adelaide, (4) Loyal Graham, (5) Annie Ray, (6) Thomas Ewing, (7) William Plumer

9731—James Elmer Thompson, born Aug 8, 1863, at Kittanning, Pa. Married, 1894, Katherine Zylmann No issue Address, Seattle, Wash Ordained Evangelist

9732—Fannie Idelette Thompson, born Jan 30, 1865, at Kittanning, Pa. Educated at Gordonsville (Va) Woman's College Married Alvin Rene Graham, 1894 Address, San Diego, Cal

9733—Mary Adelaide Thompson, born Oct 20, 1866 at Kittanning, Pa Graduate of Gordonsville, Va (Central) Woman's College Married Rev. J Black, 1898 (died 1907). High school teacher for 24 years (1916) Address, 4547 Fourteenth Ave , Seattle, Wash

9734—Loyal Graham Thompson, born May 4, 1869, at Kittanning, Pa Farmer Married Nov 4, 1894, Lora E Welch Issue (1) Ev... R... (2) William Clifford, (3) Lloyd Ellsworth, (4) Da... M...

9735—**Annie Ray Thompson,** born 1872 at Kittanning, Pa   Address, 4547 Fourteenth Ave, N E, Seattle, Wash

9736—**Thomas Ewing Thompson,** born 1874 in Kittanning, Pa. Graduate of Grove City College and Western Theological Seminary, Allegheny, Pa, and Ph D (1914)   Married, 1906, Martha McBride, of Imperial, Pa, daughter of John C and Elizabeth McBride, of Midway, Pa   Issue, Thomas Ewing, Jr (born in 1907)   Pastor of Presbyterian Church, Haffey, Pa

9737—**William Plumer Thompson,** born Nov 15, 1879, at Gordonsville, Va   Graduate of the University of Washington, 1908   Chemist   Assistant chemist, Pittsburgh Testing Laboratory, Pittsburgh, Pa   Married, June 28, 1917, at Minshall, Pa, Lelia Dorothy Rankin, daughter of Rev G L and Laura (Miller) Rankin

974—**Loyal Young Graham,** born Oct. 22, 1837, in Butler County, Pa. Address, 1709 Spring Garden St, Philadelphia, Pa   Pastor Emeritus   For fifty years he was active as a minister in the Presbyterian Church   He was pastor of the Olivet Convent Presbyterian Church, Philadelphia, Pa, for thirty-five years   He served as a vice-moderator of the General Assembly and moderator of the Synod of Pennsylvania   Married on April 25, 1861, at Cannonsburg, Pa, Sarah Jane McCoy (born —————; died Aug, 1901), daughter of William and Martha (Chambers) McCoy   Issue (1) William Thompson, (2) Ralph Lowry, (3) Loyal Young, Jr

9741—**William Thompson Graham,** born Nov. 2, 1862, at Somerset, Pa   Address, W T Graham, M D, 5027 Woodland Ave, Philadelphia, Pa

9742—**Ralph Lowry Erskine Graham,** born Jan 17, 1870, in Rehobeth, Westmoreland County, Pa   Served as Minister Presbyterian Church at Wissinoming, Pa   Address, Philadelphia, Pa   Graduate of Preston and Union Theological Seminary, New York   Married on June 7, 1893, at Philadelphia, Pa, Matilda Eccles, daughter of Thomas and Matilda (MacDonald) Eccles and granddaughter of Daniel and Martha (—————) MacDonald   Issue (1) Loyal Young, (2) Ralph MacDonald

97421—**Loyal Young Graham** (3rd), born Mar 15, 1894, at Kane?, Pa   Studied law at the University of Pennsylvania

97422—**Ralph MacDonald Graham,** born Dec 7, 1900, at Chestnut Hill, Philadelphia, Pa

9743—Loyal Young Graham, Jr, born June 6, 1874, at Philadelphia Address, 195 West Grand St, Rahway, N J Minister of First Presbyterian Church Married on June 2, 1910, at Overbrook, Pa, Florence Baker Ketcham, daughter of John K and Emily Gertrude (Baker) Ketcham and granddaughter of Benjamin and Mary Ann (Smith) Ketcham and of Sylvester Jacob and Keturah (King) Baker. Issue (1) Emily McCoy

97431—Emily McCoy Graham, born Jan 12, 1913, at First Presbyterian Manse, Rahway, N J

98—William Clinton Thompson, born Dec 21, 1812, at Lullinople, Butler County, Pa ; died April 19, 1897, at Oxford, Ill He worked his way through Jefferson College at Cannonsburg, Pa, by teaching He finished his medical course at the Ohio Medical College, Cincinnati, and practiced medicine in Vernon, Ind, St Charles, Miss, and Indianapolis, Ind—for fifty years in the latter place. He served as brigade surgeon with the rank of major under General McClelland for three years during the Civil War. He served for sixteen years as state senator, and was for six years a member of the Indianapolis city council On Dec 6, 1837, at Vernon, Ind, he married Mary Chalfant New (born 1821), daughter of John Bowman and Maria (Chalfant) New, and granddaughter of Jethro and Sarah (Bowman) New and of Thomas and Mary (Gray) Chalfant John Bowman New was a Camelite preacher in Delaware. Jethro New was a soldier of the Revolution Sarah Bowman was a granddaughter of Jost Hill, a Dutchman who sailed in his own ships from England, bringing a colony of people who settled near the present site of Jamestown, Pa Address, Mrs. Mary Chalfant Thompson, 1708 Pennsylvania St, Indianapolis, Ind Children of W C and M C Thompson, (1) James, (2) Mary Easton

981—James Thompson, born Feb —, 1839, in Cincinnati, Ohio, where his father was studying at the Ohio Medical College Present address unknown

982—Mary Easton Thompson, born Dec 1, 1856, in Indianapolis, Ind ; died May 27, 1911, in ————. She graduated from the Ogontz School, Ogontz, Pa, near Philadelphia Married on March 4, 1879, Horace Chipman Starr, son of William Cooper and Anna Maria (Chipman) Starr and grandson of Charles West and Elizabeth (Wilson) Starr and of Horace D Chipman and great-grandson of John Cooper Starr of Hadfield, N J. Charles West and Elizabeth (Wilson) Starr, "Friends" from Philadelphia, went west in 1827 in prairie wagons, settling at the present site of Richmond, Ind William Cooper Starr was Lieutenant Colonel of the Ninth West Virginia Volunteer Infantry in the Civil War Address of H C Starr, 1966 South Meridian St Indianapolis Ind Children of H C and M E Starr, (1) William Thompson (2) ... William ...

9821—**William Thompson Starr,** born Dec 2, 1879, at ————— Banker and broker, office 115 Broadway, residence 220 West 110th St, New York Married on April 21, 1907, at —————, Elsie Sara Moore, daughter of Governor General Moore of the Sandwich Islands Address, ————— No children.

9822—**Marie Wilhelmina Starr,** born July 22, 1887, at Indianapolis, Ind Graduated from the Ogontz School, Ogontz, Pa, 1906 Married on June 29, 1911, at "Arrohead," Leland, Mich—the summer home of the Starr family—John Newhall (born March 8, 1883, at Glencoe, Ill), son of Benjamin and Flora (Cooper) Newhall and grandson of Franklin and Harriett (—————) Newhall Franklin Newhall, an early settler in Chicago, was for years a wholesale fruit dealer John Newhall graduated from the agricultural course at Cornell University, 1906 Now assistant manager of the Betsey River Fruit Growers Association, Thompsonville, Mich Issue (1) John

9822—**John Newhall, Jr,** born July 22, 1912, at Thompsonville, Mich

99—**Robert W————— Thompson** According to a deed dated Mar 27, 1837, and recorded in Butler County, Pa, Deed Book K, p 618, he purchased for $1 00 from his parents John and Martha Thompson, a tract of land of 154 acres in Center Township No other data

BRANCH NO. 10.

(10)—**Andrew Thomson**, born —————, died ————— He first
settled at Thompsontown, Juniata County, Pa, but sold his land and
in 1803 went to Ohio, settling at Chillicothe. He married on June
30, 1798, Jane Stewart (born April 17, 1778, in Scotland, died Dec
21, 1874, aged 96 years, 9 months, buried at Monmouth, Ill), daughter
of William and Elizabeth Stewart and granddaughter of Archibald
and Margaret Stewart. William Stewart with his parents came to
America from Newry, Ireland, in Oct, 1752. In 1753 they moved to
Cumberland County, Pa, and occupied a tract of land on what was
later known as Stewart's Branch of the Little Juniata Creek. In
1765 William and Elizabeth Stewart occupied a plantation adjoining
the west end of the Bark tract south of the Mahonoi Mountain, on
both sides of the Little Juniata Creek, in Rye Township, then Tyrone,
Cumberland County, as shown by an affidavit made before Justice
David Walker at Andrew Thompson's in Greenwood Township,
Mifflin County, Pa, Aug 3, 1810. This land was known as the Bark
Tavern tract and contained 348 acres. On Nov 17, 1761, William
Stewart purchased a tract of 300 acres one mile above what is now
Thompsontown and in Sept, 1763, he warranted 43 acres adjoining.
On Aug 13, 1768, he purchased additional land on the opposite side
of the river from his settlement. He served in the Fourth Class of
Cumberland County Militia in 1778. He died July 29, 1784, and his
wife Elizabeth whom he married in 1765 died Aug 12, 1822. Three
of their daughters were married to Thompsons, as follows. Jane
to Andrew Thompson—(10); Rachel to John Thompson—52, and
Rebecca to Andrew Thompson—55. See "History of Juniata and
Susquehanna Valleys in Pennsylvania," pp 866, 867, 871 and 1083.
The family name is spelled at times Stuart, and some of the members
claim descent from the Royal House of England. Children of
Andrew and Jane (Stewart) Thompson, (1) John, (2) Elizabeth,
(3) William, (4) Mary, (5) Stewart, (6) Julia Ann, (7) Andrew
Patterson, (8) Mary Jane, (9) Rebecca Stewart, (10) Margaret
Stewart, (11) Gracy, (12) Thomas Boston. The name is spelled
"Stuart" by many of the descendants

(10)1—**John Thompson**, born May 4, 1799, at Thompsontown, Pa; died
Oct 29, 1862 in Caroline Falls Co, Texas. He was a practicing physician at Russellville, Ohio, and Monmouth, Ill. He married twice
first on July 29, 1824, at Russellville, Brown County, Ohio, Isabella
Johnson (born Sept 11, 1806, at Chillicothe, Ohio, died Jan 26, 1837,
at Russellville, Ohio), daughter of Prof Nathaniel Johnson of Chillicothe, Ohio. Issue (1) William Carson Stewart, (2) Fredonia, (3)
Rufus Andrew (4) Nathaniel Johnson, (5) Elizabeth, (6) Inez

17

He married the second time on Aug 20, 1839, at Russellville, Ohio, Nancy Bayne (born Sept 9, 1814), daughter of Samuel and Helen (West) Bayne Issue (7) Silas Patterson, (8) Isabella, (9) Jane Stuart, (10) Helen West, (11) John Graham, (12) Julia Ann, (13) Agnes.

(10)11—**William Carson Stewart Thompson,** born Nov 7, 1825, at Richmond, Jackson County, Ohio, died Sept 25, 1895, in Waco, Tex Married on July 12, 1859, in Waco, Tex, Mary Virginia Goode (born in Jackson, Miss, died July 5, 1876, in Waco, Tex) W C S Thompson is an architect and builder at Waco, Tex Issue (1) William V, (2) John Richard, (3) Edward Everett, (4) Rufus Newton

(10)111—**William V Thompson,** born Sept. 5, 1861, at Waco, Tex.; died Oct 1, 1861

(10)112—**John Richard Thompson,** born Sept 18, 1862, at Waco, Tex, died Oct 11, 1862

(10)113—**Edward Everett Thompson,** born May 5, 1865, in Matamoras, Mexico Address, Waco, Texas, in merchantile business Married on July 24, 1895 at Detroit, Mich, his double cousin, Maribel Curran (born Nov 17, 1863, at Middletown, Ohio, died Oct 18, 1912, in New York City), daughter of Ulysses Thompson and Elizabeth (Thompson) Curran No issue—see (10)15 and (11)312 He married second, on Sept. 22, 1914, at Oak Lane, Philadelphia, his cousin, Edith Florence Crowther (born May 26, 1885, at Reading, Pa), daughter of Henry and Josephine Patterson (Zell) Crowther See 33(10)37. Issue (1) Mary Virginia

(10)1131—**Mary Virginia Thompson,** born July 30, 1916, at Waco, Tex

(10)114—**Rufus Newton Thompson,** born Aug 21, 1868, in Waco, Tex Address, Contractor, Waco, Texas Married on Nov 13, 1890, Mrs Emma E McClain He is a decorator at Waco, Texas Issue (1) Pearl, (2) Maude Vivian, (3) Thelma

(10)1141—**Pearl Thompson,** born Dec 9, 1892, in Waco, Tex, died same day.

(10)1142—**Maude Vivian Thompson,** born Apr. 23, 1894, at Waco, Tex. Married Apr 22, 1913, at Waco, Tex, Walter Clyde Robinson Address, El Paso, Tex

(10)1143—**Thelma Thompson,** born Mar 27, 1897, at Waco, Tex Address, Waco, Tex Married, Apr. 2, 1914, William Dee Graves Issue (1) Dee Wym II

(10)1—Dr. John Thompson

*(10)13 – Rufus Andrew Thompson, (10)11 – William C. S. Thompson
and (10)14—Nathaniel J. Thompson*

Sons of Dr. John Thomson, meeting in 1889 after a separation of 35 years.

(10)11431—Dee Wynell Graves, born Mar 7, 1915, at Waco, Tex.

(10)12—Fredonia Thompson, born June 26, 1827, at Richmond, Jackson County, Ohio; died Aug 13, 1828, at Chillicothe, Ohio

(10)13—Rufus Andrew Thompson, born Sept 24, 1829, in Chillicothe, Ohio; died in Colorado Springs, Colo, Aug 12, 1906 Married in Greenville, Pa, Feb 13, 1862, Isabella Dunbar Brown (born Apr 15, 1835, died in Colorado Springs, Jan 21, 1905), daughter of James Wilson and Jane (King) Brown Issue (1) William A, (2) Eva Belle, (3) May L, (4) James Rufus, (5) Mary Elizabeth, (6) Helen Dunbar

(10)131—William Anderson Thompson, born Dec. 18, 1863, near Monmouth, Ill Address, Cripple Creek, Colo

(10)132—Eva Belle Thompson, born Apr 3, 1865, near Monmouth, Ill Address, Grand Portage, Minn Teacher in Grand Portage, Indian Day School

(10)133—May L Thompson, born May 1, 1867, at Chenoa, Ill Address, 1401 W. 3rd St, Santa Ana, Cal

(10)134—James Rufus Thompson, born June 16, 1869, at Piper City, Ill Address, 1401 W 3rd St, Santa Ana, Cal

(10)135—Mary Elizabeth Thompson, born Jan 31, 1874, at Piper City, Ill ; died Apr 9, 1874

(10)136—Helen Dunbar Thompson, born June 11, 1875, at Piper City, Ill Address, Women's University Club, 106 E 52nd St, New York City Inspector, Tenement House Dept, N Y. City

(10)14—Nathaniel Johnson Thompson, born July 26, 1831, at Chillicothe, Ohio, died in Denver, Colo, on Oct 6, 1903 He served as principal of public schools in Cincinnati, Ohio, and was later a farmer in Colorado near Denver Married Mary Looker (born, 1844, in Ohio, died 1908 in Denver, Colo), granddaughter of Orthuriel Looker, of New York and Ohio, a soldier in the Revolution, said to have served an unexpired term as governor of Ohio Children of N J and Mary (Looker) Thompson (1) Frank Lincoln, (2) Helen Stuart, (3) George Hough, (4) Harry Looker, (5) Herbert Benner

(10)141—Frank Lincoln Thompson, born Apr 3 1865, at Glendale, Ohio, Col N , 13 at   at   Uni-

(10)142—**Helen Stuart Thompson,** born May 11, 1868, at Cincinnati, Ohio
Address, 2483 Pans St, Cincinnati   Author of "Windy Creek"

(10)143—**George Hough Thompson,** born April, 1872, at Cincinnati, Ohio,
died Sept 26, 1877 at Denver, Colo

(10)144—**Harry Looker Thompson,** born Jan, 1875, at Denver, Colo., died
Oct 2, 1877, at Denver

(10)145—**Herbert Benner Thompson,** born May 1, 1877, at Denver, Colo.
Mayor of Aurora, Colo   In business with the Washburn Jersey
Dairy Company, Aurora, Colo   Married Maude McCoy   Issue
(1) Stuart Eugene, (2) Margaret Helen, (3) George Dudley, (4)
Edna May

(10)1451—**Stuart Eugene Thompson,** born June, 1899

(10)1452—**Margaret Helen Thompson,** born May, 1902.

(10)1453—**George Dudley Thompson,** born June, 1906

(10)1454—**Edna May Thompson,** born Nov, 1908

(10)15—**Elizabeth Thompson,** born May 24, 1833, at Chillicothe, Ohio;
died Jan 9, 1910 in Waco, Tex   Married on Dec. 29, 1859 at Chillicothe, Ohio, her cousin—(11)31—Ulysses Thompson Curran (born
March 7, 1834; died Feb 28, 1914), son of James and Mary
(Thompson) Curran   Issue (1) Charles Courtney, (2) Maribel,
(3) Fannie May, (4) Stanley Arthur—See (11)31

(10)16—**Inez Thompson,** born Oct 26, 1836, at Chillicothe, Ohio

(10)17—**Silas Patterson Thompson,** born Mar 19, 1841, at Russellville,
Ohio   He enlisted in the 77th Illinois Regiment at Metamora,
Ill in 1862 and was discharged at Vicksburg just after the battle
at that place   He did not live to reach home, but died March 12,
1863 on the Mississippi River steamer, buried in Hellman, Ark

(10)18—**Isabella Thompson,** born June 22, 1843, at Russellville, Ohio; died
Jan 31, 1900   Married first on Feb 14, 1861 at Low Point, Ill,
Isaac Crume Hogue, son of Anna (Richardson) Hogue and grand-
son of James and Mary (————————) Hogue   Issue (1) Laura
Agnes, (2) Silas Francis, (3) Annabell, (4) Irene Stuart, (5)
Thirza Helen, (6) Theoph   Married second time on Sept 9, 1885
at Kansas City, Mo, Cassius M Findlay   Issue (7) Jennie Lora,
(8) Julia Flora

(10)181—**Laura Agnes Hogue**, born Jan 29, 1862, in Warren County, Ill
Married on Nov 23, 1880 at Topeka, Kans, John Martin Woodley
(born Nov 21, 1860, at Red Wing, Minn, died Dec 8, 1902 Address, 1717 West St, Topeka, Kans Issue (1) Maude Roena, (2)
Charles Isaac, (3) Arretta May, (4) Mary Helen, (5) John Mahlon, (6) Corrine Agnes, (7) Annie Laurie, (8) Ralph Emerson

(10)1811—**Maude Roena Woodley**, born April 13, 1881, at Wakarusa, Kan
Married Apr. 13, 1903, at Elmont, Kan, Theron Melton (born
Nov. 24, 1879), son of Thomas J and Elizabeth Melton Farmer,
Osborne, Kan Issue (1) Lawrence Woodley, (2) Forrest, (3)
Delmar, (4) Ralph Everett

(10)18111—**Lawrence Woodley Melton**, born Nov 3, 1905, at Tecumseh,
Kan

(10)18112—**Forrest Lyle Melton**, born Feb 19, 1908, at Tecumseh, Kan

(10)18113—**Delmar Melton**, born Jan 2, 1912, at Lura, Kan

(10)18114—**Ralph Everett Melton**, born May 11, 1915

(10)1812—**Charles Isaac Woodley**, born Nov. 27, 1882. at Tevis, Kan.
Married Feb 29, 1909 at Big Spring, Kan, Maude Bunce (born
Aug 13, 1888 at Grover, Kan), daughter of John Jay Bunce of
Grover, Kan Charles Isaac, Farmer, Lecompton, Kan Issue
(1) Clifford Jay

(10)18121—**Clifford Jay Woodley**, born Jan 9, 1910, at Big Spring, Kan.

(10)1813—**Arretta May Woodley**, born Jan 4 1885, at Kingman, Kan
Married Oct 22, 1902, at Elmont, Kan, James Egbert Harrington
(born May 2, 1878), son of John and Ann Harrington of Mayetta
Farmer, Hoyt, Kan Issue (1) Agnes Marie, (2) John Eugene,
(3) Marjorie Bernice

(10)18131—**Agnes Marie Harrington**, born Nov 5, 1903, at Mayetta, Kan.

(10)18132—**John Eugene Harrington**, born April 29, 1907, at Hoyt, Kan

(10)18133—**Marjorie Bernice Harrington**, born Dec 5, 1911, at Hoyt, Kan.

(10)1814—**Mary Helen Woodley**, born Nov 25, 1886. at Ninescah, Kan.
Married on Aug 4, 1909 at Topeka, Kan, Frank Oscar Heyl
(born May 26, 1886 at Topeka, Kan), son of Valentine and Mary
Heyl of Topeka, Kan Piano business, Topeka, Kan Issue (1)
Glen Oscar, (2) D..... ....

(10)18141—Glen Oscar Heyl, born Dec 29, 1910, at Topeka, Kan

(10)18142—Doris Mae Heyl, born July 7, 1913, at Topeka, Kan

(10)1815—John Mahlon Woodley, born Nov 29, 1888, at Topeka, Kan
Address, 1717 West St, Topeka, Kan

(10)1816—Corrine Agnes Woodley, born May 5, 1891, at Tecumseh, Kan
Married March 23, 1910 at Topeka, Kan, Julius August Rose
(born July 1, 1888 at Abilene, Kan), son of Frederick and Susannah Rose of Abilene, Kan   Address, 1825 Lincoln St, Topeka,
Kan   Issue (1) Howard Everett

(10)18161—Howard Everett Rose, born June 15, 1911, at Topeka, Kan.

(10)1817—Annie Laurie Woodley, born Oct. 3, 1894, at Tecumseh, Kan
Address, 1717 West St, Topeka, Kan.

(10)1818—Ralph Emerson Woodley, born Oct. 6, 1900, at Elmont, Kan.
Address, 1717 West St, Topeka, Kan

(10)182—Silas Francis Hogue, born Jan 15, 1864, in Warren County, Ill
Married on Nov 23, 1887 in Topeka, Kan, Carrie Lenora Rey-
nolds, daughter of Charles and Frances Louise (Blake) Reynolds
and granddaughter of George Washington and Mehitabel (Weeks)
Reynolds and of Horace Virgil and Elizabeth C (Waldron) Blake,
of Fall River, Mass   Farmer, Lecompton, Kan   Issue (1) Leta
Frances, (2) Charles Howard   Married, second, Oct 19, 1915, at
Lawrence, Kan, Katharine Virgil Cunningham. No issue.

(10)1821—Leta Frances Hogue, born March 20, 1890, at Topeka, Kan.
Married on June 22, 1910 at Topeka, Kan, Lester Willman
Collins (born June 18, 1890 at Elysian, Minn), son of John
Edward and Alice Collins of Topeka, Kan   L W Collins is as-
sistant to engineer of tests, Santa Fe R R, Chicago   Issue (1)
Margaret Jane.

(10)18211—Margaret Jane Collins, born Jan. 4, 1915, at Topeka, Kan

(10)1822—Charles Howard Hogue, born Nov. 26, 1894, at Topeka, Kan.
Address, 108 E 15th St, Topeka, Kan

(10)183—Annabell Hogue, born Oct. 2, 1867, at Monmouth, Ill   Married
twice; first on April 14, 1885, Ben Woodley, son of George and
Arretta Woodley of Red Wing, Minn   Farmer, Syracuse, Kan
Issue (1) Mable, (2) Homer, (3) Isabell   Married second time
on Dec 27, 1904 at Topeka, Kan, John F Webster. Farmer
Address, Syracuse, Kan   No issue

(10)1831—Mable Woodley, born July 3, 1886, at Kingman, Kan   Married
on May 2, 1906 at Syracuse, Kan , Arthur Stone   Issue (1) Raymond Arthur, (2) Anabel

(10)18311—Raymond Arthur Stone, born Aug 15, 1907, at Syracuse, Kan.

(10):8312—Anabel Stone, born Nov 23, 1912, at Syracuse, Kan

(10)1832—Homer Woodley, born Aug 7, 1889, at Syracuse, Kan.

(10)1833—Isabell Woodley, born Oct 24, 1891 ; died April 2, 1892.

(10)184—Irene Stuart Hogue, born April 9, 1870, at Monmouth, Ill   Married Nov 20, 1893 at Topeka, Kan , Charles Woodley   Farmer
Address, Pana, Kan   Issue (1) Donald

(10)1841—Donald Woodley, born June 16, 1898, at Elmont, Kan.   Address, Johnson City, Kan

(10)185—Thirza Helen Hogue, born Nov 5, 1873, at Topeka, Kan   Married Jan 18, 1893 at Tecumseh, Kan , Sherman Austin (born Aug
18, 1868)   Farmer   Address, E 17th St, Topeka, Kan   Issue
(1) Orvill, (2) Elsie, (3) Reba

(10)1851—Orvill Austin, born July 21, 1894, at Spencer, Kan

(10)1852—Elsie Austin, born Oct 9, 1895, at Spencer, Kan ; died Aug 10,
1896, at Spencer, Kan.

(10)1853—Reba Austin, born Nov. 14, 1896, at Spencer, Kan

(10)186—Theoph Hogue, born Sept 20, 1877, at Topeka Kan , died Feb.
29, 1904 at Topeka, Kan.

(10)187—Jennie Lora Findlay (twin), born July 25, 1886, at Topeka, Kan.
Married on Jan 9, 1907 at Topeka, Kan , Charles Howell (born
Jan 30, 1884)   Farmer   Address, Silver Lake, Kan.   Issue (1)
Harold Leroy, (2) Henry Eugene

(10)1871—Harold Leroy Howell, born Dec 24 1909, at Silver Lake, Kan

(10)1872—Henry Eugene Howell, born May 9, 1913, at Silver Lake, Kan.

(10)188—Julia Flora Findlay (twin), born July 25, 1886, at Topeka, Kan
Married on Feb 17, 1909, at Topeka, Kan , Walter Pyles (born
Sept 28, 1879)   Address, 1619 Fillmore St, Topeka, Kan   Issue
(1 \ᐧᐧ ᴨ , ᴊ ᐧ

(10)1881—Virginia Lucile Pyles, born April 26, 1911, at Topeka, Kan

(10)19—Jane Stewart Thompson, born Oct 15, 1844, at Russellville, Brown County, Ohio Married at Metamora, Woodford County, Ill on Feb 19, 1864, Perry Cornelius Quinn (born July 26, 1838, died July 19, 1911) son of Samuel and Sarah (Hopping) Quinn Address, Mrs J S Quinn, Willow Springs, Howell County, Mo Issue (1) Rose Ella, (2) John Thompson, (3) Sarah Bell, (4) Albert Cornelius, (5) Mitchell J————.

(10)191—Rose Ella Quinn, born at Piper City, Ill, May 10, 1868. Address, Monmouth, Ill, R F D No. 1 Married on Nov 6, 1888 at Monmouth, Ill, Harry Dunn, son of Allen Dunn Issue (1) Maude, (2) Clarence, (3) Charles P————, (4) Roy E————, (5) Ralph H————, (6) Frank L————

(10)1911—Maude Dunn, born March 13, 1890, at Monmouth, Ill.

(10)1912—Clarence Dunn, born Nov. 11, 1894, at Monmouth, Ill

(10)1913—Charles P———— Dunn, born Jan. 15, 1898, at Monmouth, Ill

(10)1914—Roy E———— Dunn, born June 13, 1899, at Monmouth, Ill.

(10)1915—Ralph H———— — Dunn, born Nov 13, 1903, at Monmouth, Ill

(10)1916—Frank L———— Dunn, born July 22, 1906, at Monmouth, Ill

(10)192—John Thompson Quinn, born Sept 4, 1870, at Metamora, Ill Address, Payson, Okla, R F. D. No 2 Married on Dec 24, 1896, at Kirkwood, Ill, Clara May Love, daughter of Thomas Vernon and Mary Martha (Craven) Love, and granddaughter of Hugh Love Issue (1) Thomas Perry, (2) William Clifford, (3) Jesse Silas, (4) Ralph, (5) Georgia May, (6) Dollie Frances

(10)1921—Thomas Perry Quinn, born Nov 25, 1897, at Kirkwood, Ill

(10)1922—William Clifford Quinn, born Sept. 18, 1899, at Payson, Okla

(10)1923—Jesse Silas Quinn, born Nov 5, 1901, at Payson, Okla.

(10)1924—Ralph Quinn, born May 29, 1903, at Payson, Okla

(10)1925—Georgia May Quinn, born Sept 23, 1905, at Payson, Okla.

(10)1926—Dollie Frances Quinn, born Oct. 7, 1908, at Payson, Okla.

(10)193—Sarah Bell Quinn, born Jan 13, 1877; died Sept, 1877

(10)194—Albert Cornelius Quinn, born Dec. 27, 1879, at Monmouth, Ill.;
    died Oct ——, 1881

(10)195—Mitchell J Quinn, born Apr. 22, 1887, at Willow Springs, Mo.
    Married Nov 14, 1912

(10)1(10)—Helen West Thompson, born Sept 5, 1846, at Russellville,
    Ohio, died April 13, 1890. Unmarried

(10)1(11)—John Graham Thompson, born May 23, 1848, died near Ger-
    lan, Ill on Feb 10, 1904 He was a Civil War soldier Married
    twice; first on Aug 26, 1874 at Monmouth, Ill, Sadie Curran
    Issue (1) Roy, (2) Charles Married second time on Aug 20,
    1889, at Metamora, Ill, Annie Johnson (born March 2, 1874, at
    Burkville, Ky) Address, Peoria, Ill Issue (3) Samuel Guy,
    (4) Alice Ethel, (5) Frances Anna, (6) Charlotte Maribel, (7)
    William John, (8) Georgiana Johnson, (9) Joseph Graham.

(10)1(11)1—Roy Thompson, born Jan , 1879, at Monmouth, Ill , died 1897
    Sikeston, Mo

(10)1(11)2—Charles Thompson, born Oct , 1880, at Monmouth, Ill , died
    1883 or 1884 in Sikeston, Clark County, Mo

(10)1(11)3—Samuel Guy Thompson, born Jan 23, 1891, at Metamora, Ill

(10)1(11)4—Alice Ethel Thompson, born Sept 25, 1892, at Metamora, Ill.
    Married on Oct 20, 1910, William Morton Address, R F D
    No 6, Homer, Ill. Issue (1) William Richard, (2) Martha
    Anna, (3) Charles Arthur

(10)1(11)41—William Richard Morton, born Nov 8, 1911, at Homer, Ill

(10)1(11)42—Martha Anna Morton, born Dec. 29, 1912, at Homer, Ill.

(10)1(11)43—Charles Arthur Morton, born Sept 7, 1914, at Homer, Ill

(10)1(11)5—Frances Anna Thompson, born Mar 9, 1894, at Metamora, Ill.
    Married July 13, 1914, Arthur Peacher Address, Benton, Ill

(10)1(11)6—Charlotte Maribel Thompson, born Sept 21, 1896, at Mon-
    mouth, Ill Married Jan 7, 1915, Pope Bates Smith, of Bir-
    mingham, Ala Address, 1843 Park Ave , Chicago, Ill Issue
    (1) Eleanor Charlotte

(10)1(11)61—**Eleanor Charlotte Smith,** born Oct 2, 1915.

(10)1(11)7—**William John Thompson,** born Feb. 7, 1898, at Monmouth, Ill ; died Mar. 11, 1898

(10)1(11)8—**Georgiana Johnson Thompson,** born June 3, 1900, at Monmouth, Ill   Address, 1843 Park Ave, Chicago, Ill

(10)1(11)9—**Joseph Graham Thompson,** born Oct 12, 1903, at Monmouth, Ill   Address, Illinois Soldiers' Orphans Home, Normal, Ill

(10)1(12)—**Julia Ann Thompson,** born Feb 2, 1853, died at Russellville, Ohio, May ——, 1853

(10)1(13)—**Agnes Thompson,** born Oct. 15, 1854, at Russellville, Ohio; died near Peoria, Ill on Nov 15, 1892, buried at Metamora, Ill. Married on Sept 10, 1885 at Metamora, Ill, Charles Johnson (born May 18, 1848, died June 3, 1899)   Issue (1) Helen Elizabeth, (2) William, (3) Marion

(10)1(13)1—**Helen Elizabeth Johnson,** born Oct 29, 1886, at Bloomington, Ill.   Married on Aug 11, 1909 at Bloomington, Ill, Mr ——— Hayslip   Lived at 3022 Edgewood Ave, Chicago, Ill   Issue (1) Mina Elizabeth.

(10)1(13)11—**Mina Elizabeth Hayslip,** born Nov. 20, 1910.

(10)1(13)2—**William Johnson,** born July 2, 1889, at Pekin, Ill ; died Jan. 26, 1890 at Pekin, Ill

(10)1(13)3—**Marion Johnson,** born Nov. 15, 1892, at Canton, Ill.   Address, Marion J Quinn, Willow Springs, Mo   His mother dying at his birth, he was adopted by her sister, Mrs. J. S. Quinn

(10)2—**Elizabeth Thompson,** born Jan 28, 1801, in Juniata County, Pa, died May 18, 1885   Married James Johnson (born ———, died May 18, 1885, at Monmouth, Ill   Issue (1) Agnes, (2) Julia, (3) Nathaniel, (4) Fredonia

(10)21—**Agnes Johnson,** born ———

(10)22—**Julia Johnson,** born ———

(10)23—**Nathaniel Johnson,** born Nov 3, 1829, died Aug 13, 1871

(10)24—**Fredonia Johnson,** born   ——— ~ .

(10)3—William Thompson, born Aug. 4, 1803, in Juniata County, Pa, died Feb 5, 1857 in Warren County, Ill He moved from Brown County, Ohio to Monmouth, Warren County, Ill in 1855 He was a farmer He married in Lancaster County, Ohio, Margaret Wilson (born Jan 17, 1805, died May 3, 1857), daughter of Samuel and Sarah (Martin) Wilson and granddaughter of Nathaniel Wilson—see (10)35 Issue (1) Andrew Patterson, (2) Samuel Wilson, (3) John Stewart, (4) Josiah, (5) Sarah Jane, (6) Elizabeth Ann, (7) Margaret, (8) William Newton.

(10)31—Andrew Patterson Thompson, born May 14, 1830, at Chillicothe, Ohio, died Dec 22, 1889 in Denver, Colo Married on ————, 1860 in Illinois, Harriett Elizabeth Moore Issue (1) Frank David, (2) William Stuart, (3) Anna Blanche

(10)311—Frank David Thompson, born Mar 11, 1861, at Monmouth, Ill. A grocer and manufacturer, 2145 Court Place, Denver, Colo A member of the firm of Thompson & Korfhage and president of the Retail Merchants Association, of Colorado—(1912) Elected Col State Legislature, Nov 1914 for two years He married on Nov. 3, 1886 in Denver, Colo, Ida Marie Korfhage, daughter of Henry C Korfhage of Denver, Colo Issue (1) Earl Emerson, (2) Noel Wellington, (3) Blanche Nathalie, (4) Hazel Daphne, (5) Frank David, Jr

(10)3111—Earl Emerson Thompson, born Sept 3, 1887, died May 25, 1900

(10)3112—Noel Wellington Thompson, born Oct 30, 1889, at Fort Morgan, Colo Printer, Denver, Colo Married, June 17, 1916, Elizabeth Bolton, of Denver, Col

(10)3113—Blanche Nathalie Thompson, born Jan 1, 1891, at Fort Morgan, Colo Address, 2625 Race St, Denver, Colo

(10)3114—Hazel Daphne Thompson, born Mar. 1 ——, at Topolobampo, of Sinalva, Mexico Address, 2625 Race St, Denver, Colo

(10)3115—Frank David Thompson, Jr., born Apr. 14, 1902, in Denver, Colo. Address, 2625 Race St, Denver, Colo

(10)312—William Stuart Thompson, born at Monmouth, Ill Address, Arapahoe and 17th Sts, Denver, Colo

(10)313—Anna Blanche Thompson, born 1805 died 1871

(10)32—Samuel Wilson Thompson, born Oct. 2, 1831, in Ross County,
Ohio, died May 21, 1882, in Dubuque, Iowa Married on Apr 4,
1861, at Aledo, Mercer County, Ill, Sarah A Henderson, daughter
of Colonel William Henderson Address, Mrs Sarah A Thompson,
113 McAlister Ave., St Paul, Minn Issue (1) Bertha H, (2)
Ella W

(10)321—Bertha H———— Thompson, born at Cedar Rapids, Ia, Sept
27, 1867 Married on Oct 2, 1889, in Dubuque, Iowa, Edward W
Grievish, fruit grower, Troutdale, Ore Issue ————— No
data

(10)322—Ella W. Thompson, born Aug. 29, 1870, in Dubuque, Ia Married on Oct 20, 1892, at Chicago, Ill, Frederick H Harm,
merchant jeweler Address, 113 McAlister Ave, St Paul, Minn
Issue (1) Harold Thompson

(10)3221—Harold Thompson Harm, born Apr 23, 1900, at St Paul, Minn

(10)33—John Stewart Thompson, born Dec. 25, 1833, in Ross County,
Ohio, died Dec 19, 1911, in Monmouth, Ill Married —————.
Address, Mrs J S Thompson, Gerlaw, Ill Issue (1) Mack, (2)
Nannie, (3) Katie, (4) Pearl, (5) Charlie

(10)331—Mack Thompson, ————— Address, Iowa.

(10)332—Nannie Thompson, born —————, at ————— Married
on —————, at —————, ————— McIntire, Monmouth, Ill

(10)333—Katie ————— Thompson, born —————, at —————
Married on —————, at —————, ————— Stevens,
Dixon, Mo

(10)334—Pearl Thompson, born —————, at ————— Address,
Gerlaw, Ill

(10)335—Charlie ————— Thompson, born —————, at —————
————— Address, Gerlaw, Ill

(10)34—Josiah Thompson, born Dec. 15, 1835, in Ross County, Ohio, died
Dec 26, 1914, at Monmouth, Ill Married on Aug 22, 1860, in
Warren County, Ill, Nancy Elizabeth McCrery (born Sept 1, 1837,
died Apr 25, 1910), daughter of John Campbell McCrery (born
Sept 26, 1808, died 1856) and Jane (Foster) McCrery (born Sept.
9, 1809; died Dec 17, 1896) His parents were born and married
in Albyville, S C, and moved to Illinois in 1836 Children of
Josiah and Nancy Elizabeth (McCrery) Thompson, (1) William
Fram, (2) Minnie Ann, (3) Kitty Jane, (4) Etta Margaret

(10)341—William **Irvin** Thompson, born in Warren County, Ill, Jan 1,
1863 Address, R. F D No 2, Monmouth, Ill Married on Dec.
7, 1892, in Warren County, Ill, Della Shaw (born Jan 1, 1871,
in Warren County, Ill, died Aug 22, 1899), daughter of David
Jackson Shaw (born in Brown County, Ohio, June 22, 1840, died
Feb 19, 1902, at Alexis, Warren County, Ill) and Nancy Jane
(Armstrong) Shaw (born in Indiana County, Pa, May 19, 1840,
died Aug, 1895), and granddaughter of Robert Shaw who moved
from Brown County, Ohio, to Warren County, Ill, in 1856 W I
Thompson is a director of the Second National Bank, Monmouth,
Ill Issue (1) Martha, (2) Lee Carl, (3) Della Elizabeth

(10)3411—**Martha** Thompson, born Jan 1, 1895, in Warren County, Ill.
Address, Monmouth, Ill

(10)3412—**Lee Carl** Thompson, born Nov 29, 1897, in Warren County, Ill.
Address, Monmouth, Ill

(10)3413—**Della Elizabeth** Thompson, born June 27, 1898, in Warren
County, Ill Address, Monmouth, Ill.

(10)342—**Minnie Ann** Thompson, born Mar 11 1864, in Warren County
Ill Married on Mar 12, 1884, in Warren County, Ill, Michael
Rankin Gallaugher, son of William Gallaugher (born Jan 4, 1825;
died Aug. 9, 1900) and Margaret (Muse) Gallaugher (born May 1,
1827; died Apr 1, 1902) William and Margaret (Muse) Gallaugher were born in Ayrshire, Scotland, where they were married on Oct 22, 1848 Michael Rankin Gallaugher is a farmer at
Monmouth Ill, R. F D No 2 Issue (1) Merle May, (2) Elizabeth Chloe

(10)3421—**Merle May** Gallaugher, born Jan 1, 1885, at Alexis, Warren
County, Ill. Married on Aug 23, 1906, at Monmouth, Ill, Lewis
George Gabby (born Mar 23, 1883), son of John Calvin Gabby
(born Apr 22, 1857, at Little York, Warren County, Ill) and
Mary (Moore) Gabby (born at Little York, 1860, died Mar 12,
1904, at Little York) Lewis George Gabby is a farmer at Little
York, Warren County, Ill. Issue (1) Donald J, (2) James
Gallaugher.

(10)34211—**Donald J.** Gabby, born July 26, 1808, at Little York, Ill

(10)34212—**James Gallaugher** Gabby, born Apr 12 1912 at Little York,
Ill

(10)3422—**Elizabeth Chloe Gallaugher,** born Mar. 23, 1890, at Monmouth, Warren Conuty, Ill. Married on Feb. 3, 1910, at Monmouth, Ill, Harry McConnell (born Oct 22, 1887, at Little York, Ill), son of George McConnell (born Oct 16, 1860, in Ohio) and Agnes (Brambly) McConnell (born Apr 16, 1860)   Harry McConnell is a farmer at Monmouth, Ill   Issue (1) Hugh Rankin, (2) Ruth Louise

(10)34221—**Hugh Rankin McConnell,** born —————.   Address, Monmouth, Ill

(10)34222—**Ruth Louise McConnell,** born Oct. 22, 1912.

(10)343—**Kitty Jane Thompson,** born Dec 14, 1866, at Monmouth, Warren County, Ill   Married on Sept 17, 1890, at Monmouth, Ill, William R Adams (born Sept 19, 1864, at Waterset, Iowa), son of Charles Adams (born in Knox County, Ill, in 1836, died at Greeley, Colo, July, 1904) and Anna (Curry) Adams (born near Springfield, Ill, in 1844, died Jan, 1886, at Freeport, Ill)   William R Adams is president of the Colony Investment Co, Greeley, Colo   Issue (1) Roy, (2) Etta Ruth, (3) George Donald, (4) Mary Anna, (5) Margaret Elizabeth, (6) William Charles, (7) Howard Raymond

(10)3431—**Roy Thompson Adams,** born Jan 5, 1892, at Greely, Colo

(10)3432—**Etta Ruth Adams,** born May 13, 1893, at Greeley, Colo

(10)3433—**George Donald Adams,** born Oct 11, 1894, at Greeley, Colo

(10)3434—**Mary Anna Adams,** born June 10, 1896, at Greeley, Colo

(10)3435—**Margaret Elizabeth Adams,** born Nov. 3, 1897, at Greeley, Colo

(10)3436—**William Charles Adams,** born Apr 21, 1899, at Greeley, Colo.

(10)3437—**Howard Raymond Adams,** born Apr. 6, 1902, at Greeley, Colo

(10)344—**Etta Margaret Thompson,** born July 17, 1869, at Monmouth, Warren County, Ill   Married on Feb 16, 1893, at Monmouth, Ill, Robert M Smith (born Feb 28, 1869, at Gerlaw, Warren County, Ill), son of J Ryan Smith (born in Green County, Ohio, in 1836, died at Gerlaw, Ill, Sept 27, 1907) and Ellen (Buck) Smith (born in Schuyler County, Ill., in 1843).   Robert M Smith is a farmer at Alexis, Warren County, Ill   Issue (1) Helen, (2) Josiah Thompson, (3) Cleo Ryan, (4) Flora Catherine, (5) Elizabeth Mildred, (6) Gerald DeLoyd

(10)3441—Helen Smith, born Feb 16, 1894, at Alexis, Ill

(10)3442—Josiah Thompson Smith, born Mai 5, 1895, at Alexis, Ill.

(10)3443—Cleo Ryan Smith, born Apr. 6, 1896, at Alexis, Ill.

(10)3444—Flora Catherine Smith, born Aug 8, 1901, at Alexis, Ill

(10)3445—Elizabeth Mildred Smith, born Nov. 14, 1903, at Alexis, Ill

(10)3446—Gerald DeLoyd Smith, born Aug. 18, 1908, at Alexis, Ill

(10)35—Sarah Jane Thompson, born July 3, 1838, in Springfield, Ross
County, Ohio Married on Oct 28, 1858, at Spring Grove, Ill, her
cousin John Alexander Wilson, son of John M and Eliza (Duffield)
Wilson and grandson of Samuel and Sarah (Martin) Wilson and
great-grandson of Nathaniel Wilson—see (10)3 Nathaniel Wilson
came from Scotland to America, settling in Cumberland County,
Pa Issue (1) Rozetta (2) Elizabeth Ann, (3) James Andrew,
(4) Sarah Edith, (5) Hiram

(10)351—Rozetta Wilson, born June 17, 1862, at Spring Grove, Ill. Married ———— Brooks Address, Stronghurst, Ill

(10)352—Elizabeth Ann Wilson, born Aug 27 1864, at Spring Grove, Ill
Married on Dec 22, 1886, at Biggsville, Ill, William Andrew
Stewart, son of Samuel and Elizabeth (Rankin) Stewart and
grandson of James and Elizabeth (Brown) Stewart Address,
Biggsville, Ill Issue (1) Samuel Wilson, (2) Theressa, (3) Eliza-
beth, (4) Hazel, (5) Frances Lee, (6) Cyrus Byron

(10)3521—Samuel Wilson Stewart, born June 9 1888, in Cheyenne County,
Kan Address, Biggsville, Ill Married on Oct 15, 1912, at
Monmouth, Ill, Stella Annetta Leggett (born Nov. 15, 1891).

(10)3522—Theressa Stewart, born May 18, 1890, in Cheyenne County,
Kan Address, Biggsville, Ill

(10)3523—Elizabeth Stewart, born Oct. 3, 1891, in Cheyenne County,
Kan ; died ————

(10)3524—Hazel Stewart, born May 6 1893 at Biggsville, Ill Address,
Biggsville, Ill

(10)3525—Francis Lee Stewart,   Address ————

(10)3526—Cyrus Byron Stewart, born June 30, 1899, at Biggsville, Ill
Address, Biggsville, Ill

(10)353—James Andrew Wilson, born May 17, 1867, at Biggsville, Ill.
Farmer, Biggsville, Ill   Married on May 26, 1896, at Biggsville,
Ill, Elizabeth Gibb, daughter of Paul David and Mary (Steven-
son) Gibb, and granddaughter of John and Agnes (McMaster)
Gibb and of John and Elizabeth (Gibb) Stevenson   Issue (1)
Bertha Opal, (2) Ruth Oleva, (3) Walter Glenn

(10)3531—Bertha Opal Wilson, born Dec. 25, 1897, near Biggsville, Ill
Address, Biggsville, Ill

(10)3532—Ruth Oleva Wilson, born Sept. 17, 1902, near Biggsville, Ill.
Address, Biggsville, Ill

(10)3533—Walter Glenn Wilson, born Feb 27, 1906, near Biggsville, Ill
Address, Biggsville, Ill

(10)354—Sarah Edith Wilson, born Aug 14, 1872, at Biggsville, Ill. Address, Biggsville, Ill

(10)355—Hiram Wilson, born Dec 1, 1873, at Biggsville, Ill   Address,
South America

(10)36—Elizabeth Ann Thompson, born Aug. 14, 1840, in Russellville,
Brown County, Ohio, died July 11, 1863, in Monmouth, Ill   She
was a school teacher   Never married

(10)37—Margaret Thompson, born Jan 1, 1843, in Russellville, Brown
County, Ohio   Married on May 10, 1866, at Monmouth, Ill, John
McDougall, son of James and Ellen (Bain) McDougall   Address,
R F D No 2, Biggsville, Ill   No children

(10)38—William Newton Thompson, born Feb. 17, 1845, in Brown County,
Ohio, died Oct 28, 1871, in Fort County, Ohio   Married in 1868,
in Illinois, Anna E. Legget (born Apr 24, 1846, died Jan 17, 1874).
Issue (1) son

(10)381—_____ Thompson, born and died, 1871

(10)4—Mary Thompson, born Apr. 11, 1806, died May 8, 1806

(10)5—Stewart Thompson, born July 11, 1807, died Dec 21, 1834

(10) Julia Ann Thompson, born Sep 11 ? 1809, died Feb. 25, 1834

(10)7—**Andrew Patterson Thompson,** born Nov 9, 1811; died Nov. 24, 1833

(10)8—**Mary Jane Thompson,** born Apr. 13, 1814, in Juniata County, Pa ; died Nov. 20, 1874, at Monmouth, Ill   Married John Barton   No issue

(10)9—**Rebecca Stewart Thompson,** born July 21, 1816, died Feb 15, 1908, in Piper City, Ill, aged 91 years   Married in Chillicothe, Ohio, her cousin Robert Newton Thompson (553), son of Andrew and Rebecca (Stewart) Thompson and grandson of Robert and Sarah (Mitchell) Thompson and of William and Elizabeth Stewart   Issue (1) Jane Stewart, (2) Rebecca, (3) Andrew Mitchell, (4) Mary Elizabeth, (5) Rebecca Jane, (6) Sarah Inez, (7) Thomas Smith, (8) Florence Alma, (9) Julia Ann, (10) David Stewart, (11) Ida Agnes   See 553

(10)(10)—**Margaret Stewart Thompson** (twin), born Aug 19, 1818, at Chillicothe, Ohio, died June 5, 1881, at Piper City, Ill   Unmarried

(10)(11)—**Gracy Thompson** (twin), born Aug 19, 1818, died Dec. 22, 1823

(10)(12)—**Thomas Boston Thompson,** born Jan 27, 1821; died Sept 22, 1821

18

BRANCH NO. 11.

(11)—**Peter Thomson** (called Uncle Peter), born —————, 1776, two miles from the present site of Thompsontown, at the home of John Thomson, the Pioneer; died Nov 3, 1831 According to his will in 1779, Pioneer John Thomson gave all of his lands to his sons James, Thomas and Peter. What became of the interests of James we do not know definitely, but Thomas, who evidently lived with his brother Peter, died a bachelor and willed his share of the home farm to Peter At that time the farm contained 433 acres In 1810 Peter Thomson erected on the old family farm, about 40 rods north of the site of the homestead of Pioneer John Thomson, the stone dwelling house in which most of his nine children were born This house is still in existence At the death of Peter Thomson, his son John Peter bought the interests of the other heirs and kept the homestead until 1865 when it was sold to Judge Samuel Hepburn, who sold it to Uriah Shuman, the present owner It is stated that the property passed from the control of John P Thompson as the result of an unsuccessful attempt to manufacture iron at the "Maria Furnace," the only furnace ever erected in Juniata County Peter Thomson married in 1804, in what is now Walker Township, Juniata County, Pa, Mary Patterson (born 1775 in Walker Township, died Dec 6, 1845, aged 70 years), daughter of Andrew and Jane (Purdy) Patterson, granddaughter of Alexander Patterson, and of James Purdy. Andrew Patterson, Scotchman, settled in York County, Pa., about 1745 His sons Andrew and James lived for a time in Bucks County, Pa, before moving to Juniata Valley about 1770 Mary (Patterson) Thompson was affectionately known by her friends as "Aunt Polly" She and Peter Patterson, called "Uncle Peter," were members of the "Seceder Congregation" which subsequently became the United Presbyterian Church at Mexico, Pa The portion of the congregation in their neighborhood met at the Peter Thompson homestead with "Aunt Polly" as leader and instructor in the Bible and the Catechism both before and after the death of Peter Thompson in 1837 Children of Peter and Mary (Patterson) Thompson, (1) John Peter, (2) Margaret, (3) Mary, (4) Samuel, (5) Susanna, (6) Silas, (7) Elenor, (8) Thomas Boal, (9) William Patterson

(11)1—**John Peter Thompson**, born Oct 6, 1806, at the homestead of John Thomson, Sr, died Apr 10, 1882 He purchased the interests of the other heirs and thereby acquired possession of the home farm of his father which was also that of his grandfather, Pioneer John Thomson On this he and George Moss erected in 1863 the "Maria Furnace" which they continued to operate until the sale of the homestead property including the stone house and the furnace, to

*" Lobenia " Home of Peter and Mary Patterson Thompson, Delaware
Township, Juniata Co., Pa.*

Built by them in 1810, on the homestead farm of Pioneer John Thomson.

(11) Mary (Patterson) Thomson.   (11)3 Mary (Thompson) Curran.

(11)3 James Curran.   (11)31 Ulysses Thompson Curran.

Judge Samuel Hepburn in 1865 He married on Jan 2, 1840, the
widow of his cousin (72) John Boal, Mrs Sarah Ann (Gilfillen)
Boal (born Aug 3, 1811; died Oct 16, 1883, buried two miles east
of Thompsontown, Pa), daughter of James and Sarah (Jones)
Gilfillen, granddaughter of James and Nancy (Watts) Gilfillen and
of Lewis and Patience (Londen) Jones, great-granddaughter of
Robert and Jean (McConnell) Gilfillen and of David and Sarah
(Bertram) Jones, and great-great-granddaughter of James and Mar-
garet (Briton) McConnell, and of Rev William Bertram   See 72
and (11)8 Children of John Peter and Sarah Ann (Gilfillen)
Thompson, (1) Theoris, (2) Irwin, (3) Henrietta, (4) William
Albanus Logan, (5) Emma, (6) Carrie

(11)11—Theoris Thompson, born Jan 1, 1840 at the Peter Thompson
    homestead, died Oct 10, 1888 Unmarried

(11)12—Irwin Thompson, born Aug 16, 1842, at the Peter Thompson
    homestead; died ——————. Lived at Topeka, Kan Unmarried

(11)13—Henrietta Thompson, born Aug —, 1844, at the Peter Thompson
    homestead in Juniata County, Pa Married in 1873 at Topeka,
    Kan, John Percy Watson Address, 3721 North 43rd St, Chicago,
    Ill Issue (1) Maude, (2) Percy, (3) Arthur, (4) Bessie

(11)131—Maude Watson, born —————— Married Edgar Burger, Chi-
    cago, Ill Issue (1) Edgar, (2) Evelyn No data

(11)132—Percy Watson, born ——————. Married Irene Leonard, Chi-
    cago, Ill Issue (1) Dorothea No data

(11)133—Arthur Watson, born ——————

(11)134—Bessie Watson, born —————— Married William Milliner,
    Chicago, Ill No data

(11)14—William Albanis Logan Thompson, born April 18, 1848, on the
    Peter Thompson farm in Juniata County, Pa ; died 1914 at Topeka,
    Kan He attended school at Thompsontown and Harrisburg He
    began his business career with Wm G Thompson, but later returned
    home to take charge of the store at the Iron Works In 1864 he
    went to Philadelphia where he became associated with the Stout
    Atkinson & Co Dry Goods Store, N E Corner 5th and Market He
    remained there until May, 1869, when he went to Kansas, first locat-
    ing at Park City , from there he went to Hutchinson where he car-
    ried on a merchantile business for 18 months He returned to To-
    peka and engaged in cattle raising and held in Jackson County for

three years   Later was associated in Topeka with Mr Funk in the gents furnishing goods   In August, 1878, he bought the Whitmer Hardware Co, and in 1884 he incorporated the W. A. L. Thompson Hardware Co., wholesale and retail, of which he became President   He was one of the organizers of the Merchants National Bank, vice-president, four years, president, ten years, and later chairman of the Board   President of the New England Building Co, the first six-story modern office building erected in Topeka   President of the Topeka Club of which he was a charter member, having organized in 1888   Member of the Country Club, also a Mason and member of the Elk's Club   He married on June 7, 1876, Ida Smith, daughter of Jacob and Jane (Von Cannon) Smith, and granddaughter of John and Elizabeth (Darshum) Smith   Jacob Smith was sergeant on Col Veale's staff, 2nd Regiment at the Battle of the Blue, Oct 24, 1864   Children (1) Helen, (2) Roy Smith.

(11)141—**Helen Thompson,** born Feb 16, 1878, at Topeka, Kan   Graduated College sisters of Bethany Topeka, 1898   Married on Oct. 26, 1907, at Topeka, Harry Wilson Donaldson (born Aug 26, 1876, in Indianapolis, Ind), son of Dr. Joseph Wilson and Jennie (Hanna) Donaldson   Address, 1212 Taylor St, Topeka, Kan

(11)142—**Roy Smith Thompson,** born Dec. 22, 1884, at Topeka, Kans   secretary-treasurer, W A L Thompson Hardware Co, Topeka, Kan   Graduated from Yale University, 1907   Married on Feb 9, 1912, at Topeka, Cornelia Gleed (born Oct. 8, 1892, at Topeka), daughter of Charles Samner and Mabel (Gore) Gleed.   Issue (1) Cornelia Gleed

(11)1421—**Cornelia Gleed Thompson,** born Nov. 20, 1912, at Topeka, Kans

(11)15—**Emma Thompson,** born July 30, 1849, in Juniata County, Pa.   Married on June 6, 1870, at Topeka, Kan , Lewis Butler McClintock (born July 14, 1848), son of Hamilton McClintock, Jr. (born Jan 19, 1820) and grandson of Hamilton McClintock, Sr (born May 31, 1775, died May 9, 1875) and his wife Mary (Culbertson) McClintock (born Sept 19, 1775, died June 27, 1863).   The wife of Hamilton McClintock, Jr, was Mary E (Jack) McClintock (born July 5, 1822; died July 17, 1899)   Address, 707 West 10th St , Topeka, Kan   Issue (1) Nellie, (2) Edna Irene, (3) Arthur Thompson

(11)151—**Nellie McClintock,** born Feb 27, 1874, in Topeka, Kans   Married on Apr. 5, 1899, Harry Augustus Weaver   He has been for a number of years engaged in the railroad business with the Kansas City Southern R. R   Present address, Kansas City, Mo

(11)152—**Edna Irene McClintock,** born Mar 3, 1878, at Topeka, Kans. Married on Apr 10, 1901, Johnathan Dorr Norton. He is engaged in the wholesale paint business in Kansas City, Mo   Issue (1) Johnathan Dorr, (2) William Sheffield

(11)1521—**Johnathan Dorr Norton,** died in infancy

(11)1522—**William Sheffield Norton,** born Mar. 2 ,1909, at Topeka, Kans

(11)153—**Arthur Thompson McClintock,** born Apr 5, 1882, at Topake, Kan   Married on Apr 20, 1904, Agnes Gunthor   He is manager of the Beatrice Creamery Co of Denver, Colo   Issue (1) Katherine

(11)1531—**Katherine McClintock,** born Oct 30, 1905.

(11)16—**Carrie Thompson,** born May 15, 1850, at the Peter Thompson homestead in Juniata County, Pa , died May 20, 1898   Married Bishop Crumrine.   No issue

(11)2—**Margaret Thompson** (twin of Mary), born Sept 7, 1809, at Thompsontown, Pa , died Mar 19, 1843, aged 34 years, 6 months and 12 days   Unmarried

(11)3—**Mary Thompson** (twin of Margaret), born Sept. 7, 1809, at Thompsontown, Pa , died June 30, 1887, at Sandusky, Ohio   Married on May 15, 1833, at the old Peter Thompson homestead, James Curran, Jr (born in Mifflintown, died June 26, 1882), son of James Curran, Sr , and Jane (Riddle) Curran of Ireland   In the early records of Juniata County the family name seems to have been spelled in several different ways   In the first of warrantees of land in the neighborhood of what is now Mifflintown appears the name of William Curran   On page 854 of the "History of Juniata and Susquehanna Valleys," under Walker Township, Juniata County, it is stated that the name of William Cochran appears among the list of warrantees and he took out a warrant for 103 acres of land, Mar 8, 1755   From all indications the name is the same as Corran and Curran and the one here given is the ancestor of the family who settled in this section of the country   His name as Curran appears in the assessment of Fermanagh in 1763, as owning 200 acres; in 1768 as William Corran owning 600 acres, and James Curran as in possession of 60 acres   William Corran remained here until 1771 when he appears to have removed to Donegal, Lancaster County, Pa   On Dec 17, 1772, William Cochran or Corran warranted a tract of land in Tuscarora Valley which he patented June 18, 1773, at "Williamsla _   In 1775 he is returned as having 10 acres cleared, and in Lee Township James Corran is assessed on

100 acres, and 20 acres cleared   William Curran, who died in
Rapahoe Township, Lancaster County, Pa, in 1787, designated his
sons Samuel and James as executors in his will   This James Curran
may or may not have been James Curran, Sr, who married Jane
Riddle, but it is probable that, in any event, James Curran, Jr, was
a descendant of William Curran   James and Mary (Thompson)
Curran lived in Brown County, Ohio, Monmouth, Ill, and Topeka,
Kan   Issue (1) Ulysses Thompson, (2) Theodore, (3) Silas Calvin,
(4) Margaret Eleanor, (5) James Caskey, (6) Mary Jane

(11)31—**Ulysses Thompson Curran,** born at Harrisburg, Pa., Mar 7, 1834;
died Feb 28, 1914 in New York City, buried at Sandusky, Ohio
He graduated from the Miami University, Ohio   Served as superintendent of schools at Sandusky, Ohio, judge of probate court,
Sandusky, Ohio, president of Ohio Teachers Association, life member of the National Teachers Association   Married Dec 29, 1859
at Chillicothe, Ohio, his cousin—(10)15—Elizabeth Thompson (born
May 24, 1833; died Jan 9, 1911 at Waco, Tex), daughter of Dr
John and Isabella (Johnson) Thompson   Issue (1) Charles Courtney, (2) Maribel, (3) Fannie May, (4) Stanley Arthur

(11)311—**Charles Courtney Curran,** born Feb. 13, 1861, at Hartford, Ky
Artist   Address, 39 W 67th St, New York   Married at Norwalk,
Ohio, Grace Wickham, daughter of Judge Charles P and Emily
(Wildman) Wickham   Issue (1) Louis Wickham, (2) Stanley
Thompson, (3) Emily

(11)3111—**Louis Wickham Curran,** born April 4. 1889, on the Isle de la
Cite, Paris, France   Graduated from the Baltimore College of
Forestry   Married, June 12, 1915, Erma Rebecca Whipple   Is-
sue (1) Laura Whipple

(11)31111—**Laura Whipple Curran,** born Oct. 16, 1916

(11)3112—**Stanley Thompson Curran,** born Apr. 21, 1894, at Norwalk,
Ohio   Attended the Wooster University, Ohio.   Address, 39 W.
67th St, New York

(11)3113—**Emily Curran,** born Aug 27 1903, at Norwalk, Ohio   Attended
the Felix Adler's School   Address, 39 W 67th St, New York

(11)312—**Maribel Curran,** born at Middletown, Ohio, Nov 17, 1862; died
in New York City on Oct 18, 1912   She graduated from the
Sandusky (Ohio) High School and the Wooster (Ohio) University, and served as professor of Latin in the Sandusky High
School   She married on July 24, 1895 in Detroit, Mich, her

cousin—(10)115—Edward Everett Thompson (born on May 5, 1865, at Metamora, Mexico), son of William Carson Stewart and Mary Virginia (Goode) Thompson, and grandson of Dr John and Isabella (Johnson) Thompson No issue

(11)313—Fannie May Curran, born May 21, 1864, at Middletown, Ohio, died Nov 16, 1914 Married at Sandusky, Ohio, Capt Frank I. Howells, son of Joseph Howells and grandson of Thomas Howells Address, Waco, Tex Issue (1) Bessie Curran, (2) Flossie Maribel, (3) Nanette

(11)3131—Bessie Curran Howells, born 1887, at Toledo, Ohio Married at Waco, Tex , John Ficklen Issue (1) John Howells.

(11)31311—John Howells Ficklen, born Apr. 18, 1912, at Waco, Tex Address, Waco, Tex

(11)3132—Flossie Maribel Howells, born Mar 14, 1887; died Feb. 7, 1892

(11)3133—Nanette Howells, born June 23, 1891, at Toledo, Ohio Married July —, 1915, at Waco, Tex , Joseph Francis McGrath Address, Waco, Tex. Issue (1) Frank Howell

(11)31331—Frank Howells McGrath, born Sept 6, 1914

(11)314—Stanley Arthur Curran, born May 28 1849 at Hartwell, Ohio, died Mar. 27, 1887.

(11)32—Theodore Curran, born Jan 17, 1836, at Harrisburg, Pa ; died Jan 10, 1910 Married at Middletown, Ohio, Sarah Brown, daughter of Rev S B Brown, Presbyterian minister Address, Mrs Sarah Brown Curran, 511 Grant Place, Chicago, Ill Issue (1) Ulysses, (2) Elizabeth, (3) Ward, (4) Edwin, (5) Clarence

(11)321—Ulysses Curran (twin of Elizabeth), born Sept 3, 1860, died Nov 17, 1860

(11)322—Elizabeth Curran (twin of Ulysses), born Sept 3, 1860, died Feb 22, 1861

(11)323—Ward Curran, born Jan 4 1865 died Mar 3, 1865

(11)324—Edwin Curran, born July 30, 1869, died Apr 4 1909.

(11)325—Clarence Curran, born June 23, 1862, died May 1, 1905. Married Nellie Sherman, daughter of N E Sherman—a brother of Gen W T S[...] , N [...] Address Mrs Nellie Sherman C[...] W [...]

(11)33—Silas Calvin Curran, born Apr. 17, 1838, at Centerville, Butler County, Pa ; died 1876 He was physician at Neosia Falls, Kan Married Sarah Hollingsworth Ferris Issue (1) William Ferris, (2) Ulysses, (3) daughter

(11)331—William Ferris Curran, born Feb. 20, 1873. For 14 years he was a cowboy in the "Panhandle" of Texas He studied medicine and surgery at the Maryland University, Baltimore, from which he graduated in 1904 From 1907 to 1911 during the construction of the Panama Canal, he was in the United States Government service at the Isthmus as physician in the sanitary department under Col W. C. Gorges. He is now engaged in private practice as a physician at Waco, Tex He married on April 20, 1909 at Waco, Tex, Lillian Margaret Eaton, daughter of John Curtis and Mary Pauline (Taylor) Eaton and granddaughter of John Dill and Margaret (Hart) Taylor Issue (1) Elizabeth, (2) Calvin

(11)3311—Elizabeth Curran, born Mar 9, 1911, at Waco, Tex.

(11)3312—Calvin Curran, born July 3, 1913, at Waco, Tex

(11)332—Ulysses Curran, born 1869, died in infancy.

(11)333—(daughter) Curran, born 1871, died in infancy

(11)34—Margaret Eleanor Curran, born Aug 8, 1841, at Russelville, Ohio; died Dec 19, 1906 Married March 18, 1868, at Carbondale, Ill, William Adam Romig (born May 14, 1844, Mifflin County, Pa), son of Adam Romig Address, Wellington, Kan Issue (1) Theodore William, (2) James Reuben, (3) Franklin Anthony, (4) George Morrison, (5) Ulysses General, (6) Frederick Calvin, (7) Willard Grant

(11)341—Theodore William Romig, born Aug 24, 1869. Address, Wellington, Kan. Married on Jan 21, 1897, at Wellington, Kan, Mary Eva Rynearson (born Feb. 12, 1869) No children

(11)342—James Reuben Romig, born Sept 2, 1871, at Carbondale, Ill. Address, Colorado Springs, Colo Unmarried

(11)343—Franklin Anthony Romig, born Jan 2, 1874, at Carbondale, Ill ; died in infancy.

(11)344—George Morrison Romig, born July 23, 1875. Address, Denver, Colo Married twice. No record

(11)345—Ulysses General Romig, born July 13, 1877, at Monmouth, Ill Address, Wellington, Kan   Married on Nov 6, 1907 at Wichita, Kan, Mary Elizabeth McIntyre (born June 9, 1878), daughter of Alex McIntyre of Wellington, Kan   Issue (1) Margaret Jean, (2) Calvin McIntyre, (3) Robert Ulysses, (4) Thomas Dean

(11)3451—Margaret Jean Romig, born Oct. 4, 1908. Address, Wellington, Kan

(11)3452—Calvin McIntyre Romig, born Aug. 10, 1910   Address, Wellington, Kan

(11)3453—Robert Ulysses Romig, born Nov. 5, 1914, at Wellington, Kan.

(11)3454—Thomas Dean Romig, born July 11, 1916, at Wellington, Kan

(11)346—Frederick Calvin Romig, born Jan 26, 1880, at Monmouth, Ill Graduated from the Manhattan (Kan) College   Assistant Postmaster, Manhattan, Kan   Married Aug 13, 1904 at Newman, Kan, Louise Belle Shirley (born Aug 25, 1880), daughter of John Lafayette and Plutina Shirley   Issue (1) Helen Belle, (2) James Edward.

(11)3461—Helen Belle Romig, born July 11, 1905. Address, Manhattan Kan

(11)3462—James Edward Romig, born Mar. 24, 1912. Address, Manhattan, Kan

(11)347—Willard Grant Romig, born at Monmouth, Ill, Apr 5, 1884 Address, Wellington, Kan   Married on Jan 1, 1905, Ida Josephine Stewart   Issue (1) James Stewart, (2) Earl Grant

(11)3471—James Stewart Romig, born Oct 7, 1905. Address, Wellington, Kan

(11)3472—Earl Grant Romig, born July 21, 1913

(11)35—James Caskey Curran, born at Russellville, Brown County, Ohio, died Dec, 1902 at Banco, Harper, Kan   Married Margaret Drake No children

(11)36—Mary Jane Curran, born Aug 4, 1850, at Russellville, Ohio; died ———— Married on ———— at ————, George Morrison ？ ⸳ Brooklyn N Y   ？   ？⸳ ？   — ⸳ No children

(11)4—Samuel Thompson, born July 9, 1810, died Nov 2, 1857, aged 47 years, buried at Spring Grove, Warren County, Ill Married his cousin—535—Jane Thompson (born May 31, 1813, died Aug 15, 1893, aged 80 years, 3 months, 15 days, buried at Galatia Barton County, Ohio), daughter of Robert and Elcy (Pauly) Thompson, granddaughter of Robert and Sarah (Mitchell) Thompson and great-granddaughter of Pioneer John Thompson and of James Mitchell. Issue (1) Pethenia, (2) George Addison, (3) Matilda, (4) Margaret

(11)41—Pethenia Thompson, born Oct 6, 1847, near the Peter Thompson farm between Millerstown and Thompsontown, Pa Married on Nov 26, 1896, at Tarkio, Mo, Jonathan Greek Gustin, son of Hugh and Jane (Greek) Gustin, and grandson of Dr. Amos and Mandy (Montgomery) Gustin and of Jonathan and Mandy (Stidwell) Greek No children.

(11)42—George Addison Thompson, born Oct 26, 1851, at Thompsontown, Pa Address, P O Box 505, Tarkio, Mo Married on Jan 12, 1875, at Monmouth, Ill, Jennie Brown, daughter of John and Margaret (Newbanks) Brown, and granddaughter of Samuel Brown and of William Newbanks. Issue (1) Howard Alton, (2) Effie Maude, (3) John Loran, (4) Nellie Lota, (5) Luella Belle, (6) Blanche Lillian

(11)421—Howard Alton Thompson, born Jan 2, 1876, at Gerlaw, Ill Address, Tarkio, Mo

(11)422—Effie Maude Thompson, born Feb 8, 1878, at Gerlaw, Ill. Address, Tarkio, Mo

(11)423—John Loran Thompson, born Jan 18, 1880, at Gerlaw, Ill, died May 11, 1901

(11)424—Nellie Lota Thompson, born Nov 3, 1884, at Gerlaw, Ill Married July 20, 1907, at Marysville, Mo, Walter Arnold Issue (1) Loran Pierce, (2) Ralph Harrison

(11)4241—Loran Pierce Arnold, born Jan 11, 1909, at Kansas City, Mo

(11)4242—Ralph Harrison Arnold, born Aug 20, 1912, at Kansas City, died Jan 13, 1914, at Kansas City, Mo

(11)425—Luella Belle Thompson, born Nov 17, 1890, at Russell, Kan Address, Tarkio, Mo

(11)426—Blanche Lillian Thompson, born July 1, 1893, at Russell, Kan School teacher, Tarkio, Mo

(11)43—**Matilda Thompson,** born ——————, died young

(11)44—**Margaret Thompson,** born ——————, died young

(11)5—**Susannah Thompson,** born Oct 3, 1812, in Juniata County, Pa, died Nov 25, 1852 Married May 25, 1837, Alexander Rodgers (born Nov 25, 1802, died in Kansas), son of Matthew and Mary (Kennedy) Rodgers and grandson of William and Margaret (Kelly) Rodgers William Rodgers who was born in England came to this country in 1760 settling in what was then Lancaster, and is now Dauphin County, Pa He held the rank of Colonel in the Revolutionary War Subsequently he moved to Perry County, Pa, where he farmed until his death in Sept, 1807 His wife Margaret (Kelly) Rodgers, who was of Scotch-Irish ancestry died in Aug, 1810 Their son Matthew Rodgers who was born in 1770 in Perry County, and died April 14, 1837, served in the War of 1812, first as captain of the state militia under Col Reese Hill and subsequently in 1814 as Colonel, being commissioned in each case by Governor Snyder In 1810 he married as his second wife Margaret or Mary Kennedy (born 1792 in Ireland, died May 28, 1854) Of their nine children two were married to Thompsons, namely, Alexander to Susannah Thompson—(11)5—and Sarah to "Bridge" John Thompson—527—while a daughter by his first wife Jane (Rodgers) Adams was the mother of Isabella Adams who married Thomas Boal Thompson—(11)8 Children of Alexander and Susannah (Thompson) Rodgers (1) Theophilus Patterson, (2) Margaret Eliza, (3) Alpheus Kennedy, (4) Alice, (5) Alphonzo Thompson, (6) Alfred Alexander

(11)51—**Theophilus Patterson Rodgers,** born July 4 1839 in Logansport, Ind, died Aug 11, 1913 Unmarried Served in the 46th Ind Infantry Volunteers as private and first lieutenant

(11)52—**Margaret Eliza Rodgers,** born Feb 26, 1842, at Logansport, Ind Married on March 12, 1863 at Idaville, Ind, Silas Benager Moon, son of Peleg Baxter and Mehitable (Taft) Moon The Moon family settled in North Carolina during the middle of the seventeenth century S B Moon was a corporal in the Civil War, his father was a soldier in the Mexican War and the War of 1812, and his grandfather was a soldier in the Revolutionary War S B Moon, died, Nov 13, 1914 Issue (1) Lula Belle, (2) Helen Ede, and eight others

(11)521—**Lula Belle Moon,** born June 16, 1871, died May 5, 1902 Married, June 9, 1891, at Logansport, Ind, William Otis Evans son of
W…………… ………… ………… ………… … … (1)
A…… ………… … ………… ………… a

(11)5211—**Maybelle Virginia Evans,** born July 15, 1892, died July 16, 1893

(11)5212—**Ethel Margaret Evans,** born Sept 21, 1894   Address, 1109 Broadway, Logansport, Ind

(11)5213—**Florence Rebecca Evans,** born May 1, 1896   Lived at Winona, Minn

(11)522—**Helen Ede Moon,** born Jan 19, 1878, at Logansport, Ind   Married twice. first on Jan 19, 1899, Ernest J Watson   Issue (1) Annie Laurie. Married secondly on Oct 27, 1902 at Logansport, Ind, Robert Gustave Callmyer, son of Gustave and Leonie (Forgnet) Callmer   Address, 6 Myrtle Ave, Newark, N. J

(11)5221—**Annie Laurie Watson,** born Oct 22, 1900.

(11)53—**Alpheus Kennedy Rodgers** (twin of Alice), born Dec. 6, 1844, at Logansport, Ind, died Mar 10, 1916, at Topeka, Kan   A K Rodgers served in the 142nd Ind. Volunteers as sergeant, and was mustered out at close of the Civil War   Served four years as county treasurer, Shawnee County, Kan, eight years as assistant postmaster, and eight years as postmaster, City of Topeka   Married on Nov 5, 1872, at Topeka, Kan, Anna May Dick, daughter of Dr. George and Deddy Ann Dick and granddaughter of George and Jane (Anderson) Dick   Address of Mrs A K Rodgers, 1334 Topeka Ave, Topeka, Kan   Issue (1) Willa Alice, (2) George Dick, (3) Ruth, (4) Esther, (5) Jean Dick

(11)531—**Willa Alice Rodgers,** born Sept. 6, 1873, at Topeka, Kan   Address, Topeka Ave, Topeka, Kan

(11)532—**George Dick Rodgers,** born Nov 14, 1876, at Topeka, Kan   Attorney, Muskogee, Okla. Married Dec 31, 1907, Georgiana Smith   No children

(11)533—**Ruth Rodgers,** born Mar. 8, 1881, died Nov. 23, 1884.

(11)534—**Esther Rodgers,** born Jan 21, 1889   Married Jan 1, 1912, Robert S Pierce (born Feb 14, 1886), son of Robert Pierce   Address, Topeka, Kan   Issue (1) William Rodgers

(11)5341—**William Rodgers Pierce,** born Aug 13, 1915

(11)535—**Jean Dick Rodgers,** born Oct. 8, 1891, at Topeka, Kan   Married May 14, 1913, Weldon A Morris (born ——— -; died Aug, 1913)   Address, Mrs W A Morris, 1334 Topeka Ave, Topeka, Kan.

(11)54—Alice Rodgers (twin of Alpheus Kennedy), born Dec. 6, 1844, at Logansport, Ind , died in infancy

(11)55—Alphonzo Thompson Rodgers, born Jan 22, 1846, at Logansport, Ind   Served in the Ind Volunteers in the Civil War as a private Died June 4, 1899, being killed in his own home by a burglar Married on Dec 9, 1881, at Topeka, Kan , Malvina Geiger, daughter of George and Rebecca Geiger. Issue (1) Rebecca, (2) Susana

(11)551—Rebecca Rodgers, born Aug 13, 1884, at Topeka, Kan. Married on Aug 22, 1900, at Topeka, Kan , Albert Garvin, son of Albert and Mary Garvin Automobile dealer. Address, Gallatin, Mo No issue

(11)552—Susanna Rodgers, born Mar 20, 1889, at Topeka, Kan. Married on Apr 20, 1911, at Topeka, Kan , George Rutter, son of C L and Elizabeth Rutter. In merchantile business Address, Gallatin, Mo No issue

(11)56—Alfred Alexander Rodgers, born Nov 15, 1852, at Logansport, Ind   During the winter of 1867-8 and 1868-9, he taught a district school in Indiana   From 1869 to 1884 he conducted a retail grocery store at Topeka, Kan   From 1884 to 1890 he retired from business, but in 1890 he entered the real estate, loan, bond and insurance business at Topeka He is a past-master of Orient Lodge, No 51, A F and A M ; a member of Topeka Royal Arch Chapter No 5, Zabud Council of Royal and Select Masters, Topeka Commandery No 5, Topeka Consistory No 1 Southern Jurisdiction, 33rd Degree Inspector General Hon Address, 110 W. 6th Ave, Topeka, Kan Married on Aug 21, 1890, at Washington, Kan , Ida Rowse, daughter of Wheeler and Sarah (Pancoast) Rowse, and granddaughter of Herman and Dovie (Stevenson) Rowse and of James and Mary (Yoder) Pancoast. Issue (1) Fred Alphonse, (2) Marjorie, (3) Mary Elizabeth.

(11)561—Fred Alphonse Rodgers, born May 27, 1891; died June 14, 1891.

(11)562—Marjorie Rodgers, born July 13, 1892 Unmarried

(11)563—Mary Elizabeth Rodgers, born Sept 2, 1901 Unmarried.

(11)6—Silas Thompson, born Nov. 14, 1814, died May 21, 1841 aged 26 years, 6 months and 7 days Unmarried.

(11)7—Elenor Thompson, born Mar 15, 1818, died Feb. 22, 1844, aged 25 years, 11 months and 7 days She was the first wife of her cousin —5-5 —James Thompson, rn 18-- died June 18, 1854, aged 35 years), son of John and J n (Gh'allen Thompson—see 5-5

(11)8—**Thomas Boal Thompson**, born Mar 25, 1825, at the Peter Thompson homestead in Juniata County, Pa He operated a store and a farm three miles north of Millerstown in Perry County, Pa In 1844 he engaged in the merchantile business in Logansport, Ind, and later in the banking business In August, 1854, he became cashier of the Planters and Mechanics Bank of Dalton, Ga In Feb 1859, he returned to his old home and lived on a farm in Perry County, Pa In 1870 he moved to Topeka, Kan, where he died May 29, 1891 He married twice first on April 27, 1848 at Mexico, Juniata County, Pa, Isabella Adams (born Dec 23, 1826; died March 23, 1853), daughter of John and Jane (Rodgers) Adams, and granddaughter of Jacob and Catherine (Lintner) Adams, and of Matthew and Margaret (Henderson) Rodgers, great-granddaughter of James and Isabella (Weldon) Adams, of Christian Lintner, and of William and Margaret (Kelly) Rodgers—see (11)5 James Adams (born Oct 30, 1734, died Oct, 1824) came from Chester, England and settled in Chester County, Pa He married Elizabeth Weldon (born Sept 24, 1736, died Sept, 1825) In 1795 their son, Jacob Adams (born Sept 23, 1758, died Aug 23, 1803) settled on a farm adjoining that of Robert Wilson (grandfather of Lucien Wilson—381) in what is now Fayette Township, Juniata County, Pa He married Mrs Catherine (Lintner) Wilson, widow of a younger brother of Robert Wilson. She was the daughter of Christian Lintner (born in Holland, died 1803 in Fermanagh Township, Mifflin County, Pa) whose daughter Elizabeth (Lintner) Banks was the mother of Judge David Banks —341 See "History of Juniata and Susquehanna Valleys," pp. 821 and 859 Of the four children of Jacob and Catherine (Lintner) Adams, two were ancestors of descendants of Pioneer John Thomson, namely, William Adams the father of Mrs. James Luther Thompson—5275; and John Adams the father of Mrs. Thomas Boal Thompson—(11)8 John Adams (born Feb, 1797 in Fermanagh Township, Juniata County, Pa ; died Nov, 1857) married Jane Rodgers (born July, 1802, in Walker Township, Juniata County, Pa , died Dec, 1879). Of the six children of John and Jane (Rodgers) Adams, two were married to Thompsons, namely, Catherine Adams to William Patterson Thompson—(11)9 and Isabella Adams to Thomas Boal Thompson Children of Thomas B and Isabella (Adams) Thompson (1) Alton Howard, (2) Arretta Bell, (3) Clara Jane Thomas B Thompson married secondly on Nov 29, 1859 in Perry County, Pa, his cousin—721—Jane Boal (born Dec 21, 1833, near Millerstown, Perry County, Pa , died Dec 5, 1910 at Topeka, Kan), daughter of John and Sarah Ann (Gifilllen) Boal; granddaughter of Capt. David and Susannah (Thompson) Boal and of James and Sarah (Jones) Gilfillen, a great-granddaughter of Pioneer John Thompson, of James and Nancy (Watts) Gilfillen and of Lewis and Patience (London) Jones, a great-great-granddaughter of Robert and Jean (McConnell) Gilfillen, of David and Sarah (Bertram) Jones, and a great-great-great-granddaughter of James and Margaret (Briton) McConnell and of Rev William Bertram—see 721 and (11)1 Children of Thomas B and Jane (Boal) Thompson, (4) Charles Stuart, (5) Minnie Alfareta, (6) Sarah Alberta, (7) Bessie Marguerite, (8) Frank Carroll, (9) Henrietta, (10) Mary Mabel, (11) Grace Eolene

(11)81—Alton Howard Thompson, born Apr. 8, 1849, in Logansport, Ind., died July 13, 1914 in Topeka, Kan He attended McAlisterville Academy and Airy View Academy in Juniata County, Pa, and graduated from the Dental College, Philadelphia, 1872 He assisted in establishing the Kansas City Dental College in 1884, and lectured there subsequently and until his death He lectured at the Philadelphia Dental College 1899-1900, and contributed frequently to dental journals and was the author of a text book on dental anatomy He was an elder in the Presbyterian Church He married twice, first on Dec 9, 1875 at Topeka, Kan, Fannie Geiger (born Jan 1, 1857, died Feb 17, 1903), daughter of George and Rebecca (Wallace) Geiger and granddaughter of John and Agnes (Culbertson) Wallace Issue (1) Isabella, (2) Wallace McGrath He married secondly on Oct 30, 1906 at Topeka, Kan, Helen Moon, daughter of John Ervin and Malvina (Price) Moon, a granddaughter of Jonathan and Rebecca Lemon (Ervin) Moon and of Hugh Roberts and Ann (Thomas) Price Jonathan Moon was born in Ireland, Hugh Roberts Price in Wales and Ann Thomas in England John Ervin Moon (born March 13, 1846 at Leesburg, Ind., died Aug 5, 1912) was first sergeant of Company C, 138th Indiana Regiment and first lieutenant of Company B, 151st Indiana Regiment during the Civil War. No issue

(11)811—Isabella Thompson, born Feb 2, 1880, at Topeka, Kans.; died June 17, 1897

(11)812—Wallace McGrath Thompson, born Aug 2 1883, at Topeka, Kans. He graduated from Washburn College, 1903, and was employed on newspapers and magazines in Topeka, New York City, Mexico City and Kansas City, until 1911 when he went to Paris Married on Sept 24, 1910 at Morrisville, Vt, Lillian Ellen Fisk, daughter of Henry Clay and Isabel Martha (Page) Fisk and granddaughter of Moses and Rebecca (Ferrin) Fisk, and of Russel Summer and Martha Malvina (Smalley) Page Lillian Fisk Thompson is an artist,—a portrait painter Address, Paramount Picture Co, 485 Fifth Ave, New York Issue (1) Jon Tomson

(11)8121— Jon Tomson Thompson

(11)82—**Annabella (Arnetta Bell) Thompson,** born Dec 23, 1850, died July 17, 1851

(11)83—**Clara Jane Thompson,** born Aug. 15, 1852, at Logansport, Ind After her mother' death in 1853, resulting from a cold contracted when her infant daughter Clara Jane was baptised at the Barnet Creek Church, she lived with her grandparents in Pennsylvania. Attended the Airy View Academy, Juniata County, Pa, and the Moravian Seminary, Bethlehem, Pa To her untiring efforts must be attributed the completeness and accuracy of the records of her branch of the Thompson family Address, Mifflintown, Pa

(11)84—**Charles Stuart Thompson,** born Jan 19, 1861, in Perry County, Pa, died Mar 27, 1870, in Perry County, Pa

(11)85—**Minnie Alfareta Thompson,** born Dec 23, 1863, in Perry County, Pa Married on Nov 19, 1884 at Topeka, Kan, Francis George Willard (born June 3, 1861 at Ironton, Ohio), son of George Willoughby and Emily Caroline (Burr) Willard and a descendant of Major Simon Willard who came from Kent County, England to Massachusetts Colony in 1634 settling in Cambridge in 1635 and leading the party which founded Concord Address, 1014, Topeka, Kan Issue (1) Alice Alberta, (2) George Thompson, (3) Thomas Burr, (4) Francis Alexander.

(11)851—**Alice Alberta Willard,** born Aug 28, 1885, at Topeka, Kan Married Dec 27, 1910 at Phoenix, Ariz, Samuel Grove Dolman, son of Charles Le Bar and Alice Annetta Kelley (Magil) Dolman S G Dolman graduated from the University of Kansas, 1909, and is a mining engineer with the Ray Consolidated Copper Company, Ray, Ariz Issue (1) Samuel Grove, (2) Willard Thompson

(11)8511—**Samuel Grove Dolman, Jr,** born Apr. 12, 1912, at Ray, Ariz

(11)8512—**Willard Thompson Dolman,** born Mar 19, 1916, at Ray, Ariz

(11)852—**George Thompson Willard,** born Mar. 13, 1889, at Topeka, Kan. Address, Rail Joint Company, Chicago, Ill

(11)853—**Thomas Burr Willard,** born April 29, 1891, at Topeka, Kan Address, General Manager's office, Chicago, Rock Island & Pacific R R, El Reno, Okla Married Sept 18, 1914, at Pueblo, Colo, Marcelle Renoux (born Jan 18, 1889, at Vallon-en-Sully, Allier, France), daughter of Gabriel and Catherine Virginie (Aurousseau) Renoux Issue (1) Alice Marcelle

(11)8531—**Alice Marcelle Willard,** born June 21, 1915

(11)854—Francis Alexander Willard, born Feb 2, 1894, at Topeka, Kan
Student Univ Mich, Class of 1918

(11)86—Sarah Alberta Thompson, born July 24, 1866, in Perry County, Pa
Married on June 6, 1888 at Topeka, Kan, Reid Alexander (born
Nov 1, 1860, died Oct 8, 1894, Topeka, Kan), son of Robert Tate
and Amanda Filzallan (Lydick) Alexander His father was born
in Rockbridge County, Va on March 2, 1825, married on March 17,
1856, at Grand View, Ill , died at Paris, Ill, Jan. 6, 1895 His mother
was born in Lynchburg, Va, Dec 3, 1831 and died Aug 25, 1895 at
Paris, Ill Reid Alexander graduated from the medical school of
the University of Pennsylvania in 1885. He was a partner of Dr.
David W Stormont, Topeka, Kan, up to the time of his death
1894 Issue (1) Henrietta, (2) Mary Alberta, (3) Jane Boal

(11)861—Henrietta Alexander, born Mar 11, 1889, at Topeka, Kans

(11)862—Mary Alberta Alexander, born Jan 2, 1892, at Topeka, Kans

(11)863—Jane Boal Alexander, born Apr. 30, 1894, at Topeka, Kans.

(11)87—Bessie Marguerite Thompson, born Sept 23, 1867, in Perry County,
Pa , died May 14, 1869, in Perry County, Pa

(11)88—Frank Carroll Thompson, born Oct 22, 1869, in Perry County, Pa ,
died Sept 4, 1880, in Topeka, Kans

(11)89—Henrietta Thompson, born Jan 17, 1875, at Topeka, Kans Married on April 29, 1896 at Topeka, Kans , Fred Buel Bonebrake, son
of Parkinson Isaiah and Martha (Lowe) Bonebrake, and grandson
of George Henry and Eliza (Adams) Bonebrake, and of Allen and
Mary (Cooley) Lowe Grain dealer Address, Osage City, Kans
Issue (1) Frederick Thompson, (2) Elizabeth

(11)891—Frederick Thompson Bonebrake, born Feb 7, 1897, at Osage
City, Kans Address, Topeka Kans

(11)892—Elizabeth Bonebrake, born Apr 7, 1901, at Osage City, Kan.
Address, Topeka, Kan

(11)8(10)—Mary Mabel Thompson, born July 30, 1875, at Topeka, Kan
Married Nov 4, 1914, at Topeka, Kan , Judge Leonard Summer
Ferry, son of John B and Elizabeth (Snowberger) Ferry, and
grandson of Leonard and Hannah (——————) Ferry, and of
i   ·   · n' · i·   s   ·ι ···' Address, 1419
·   · ·· W·, I·,ι·k   ·

19

(11)8(11)—Grace Eolene Thompson, born Feb 2, 1878, at Topeka, Kans ; died Sept 10, 1880

(11)9—William Patterson Thompson, born July 4, 1822, at the Peter Thompson homestead, Juniata County, Pa ; died March 29, 1871, at Logansport, Ind , aged 49 years He was engaged in the mercantile business at Logansport, Ind He married on Oct 8, 1851 in Juniata County, Pa , Catherine Adams (born April 22, 1831 in Walker Township, Juniata County, Pa , died Aug 9, 1900 at Logansport, Ind), daughter of John and Jane (Rodgers) Adams , a granddaughter of Jacob and Catherine (Lintner) Adams and of Matthew and Margaret (Henderson) Rodgers, great-granddaughter of James and Isabella (Weldon) Adams, of Christian Lintner and of William and Margaret (Kelly) Rodgers—see (11)5, and (11)8 Issue (1) Anna Blanche, (2) Boyd Adams, (3) Helen May, (4) Harry H

(11)91—Anna Blanche Thompson, born Sept 12 1852, at Logansport, Ind. Address, 403½ Broadway, Logansport, Ind. Unmarried

(11)92—Boyd Adams Thompson, born about 1856, died in infancy

(11)93—Helen May Thompson, born Feb. 15, 1860 at Logansport, Ind Married on May 19, 1890, at Logansport, John William Skaer Address, Wichita, Kan. Issue (1) Helen Margaret, (2) Eunice, (3) Cecil Gilbert, (4) Horace Allen.

(11)931—Helen Margaret Skaer, born Aug 16 1891 at Augusta, Kan. Married Oct 10, 1912, Quincy E Etnire Issue (1) Helen Margaret, (2) Bettie Louise

(11)9311—Helen Margaret Etnire, born Feb 25, 1914

(11)9312—Bettie Louise Etnire, born July 8, 1916

(11)932—Eunice Skaer, born Aug 5, 1893 Married June 17, 1912 John Milton Cooper, Severy, Kan

(11)933—Cecil Gilbert Skaer, born Oct 8, 1896. Address, 229 Chautauqua, St , Wichita, Kan

(11)934—Horace Allen Skaer, born Nov. 9 1898, died Aug 22, 1899

(11)94—Harry H Thompson, born Nov 8 1864 at Logansport Ind Address, 1826 North St , city civil engineer, Logansport, Ind Married on Aug 12 1891 at Dubuque, Iowa, Sarah Frances Upton, daughter ... granddaughter of ...

BRANCH NO. 12.

(12)—**Thomas Thomson,** born in Pennsylvania, died in Juniata County, Pa., two miles east of Thompsontown. He and his brothers James and Peter inherited the homestead property of Pioneer John Thomson. His brother James probably died before reaching the age of 18, under which condition his share in the estate passed automatically to Peter and Thomas by the provisions of their father's will, because the latter two early came into full possession of the homestead property. On Feb. 28, 1807 they purchased 84 acres of land from Frederick Keller, which had been patented in two tracts by Isaac Yost, which they sold on May 1, 1809 to their nephew—55—Andrew Thompson, the farmer. Thomas Thompson, who died a bachelor, doubtless at the home of his brother Peter Thompson, willed to Peter his share in the old farm which then embraced 433 acres.

BRANCH NO. 13.

(13)—**James Thomson,** born certainly after 1758 probably well after 1761, probably died young. He was joint heir with his brothers Thomas and James in the homestead property of Pioneer John Thomson, under the following provision in the will in 1779. "I do give all my land to my sons James, Thomas and Peter. If any of these heirs doth decease under the age of eighteen years, their part is to remain equally divided amongst the other heirs then living on the premises. I do allow my son James to have one horse and saddle when twenty-one years of age." The property transfer records are silent as to the interest of James, but show that the homestead estate was in the possession of Peter and Thomas at the time of the death of the latter who willed his share to Peter, and hence it is to be assumed that James Thomson died young, probably under eighteen years. See page 283

BRANCH NO. 14.

(14)———————— Thomson, possibly a child was born after Mar 2, 1779, when John Thomson wrote his will in which he said, "I do also allow to the child unborn whether son or daughter, when come to age of maturity to have equal with Thomas and Peter" There is nothing in available records to indicate that such a child ever reached maturity, and shared in the property of Thomas and Peter all of which finally became the property of the heirs of Peter Thompson However it might seem possible, though it is highly improbable, that this child was named Agnes and that she married a man named Black and lived in Blount County, Tenn, as implied on page 871 of the "History of Juniata and Susquehanna Valleys in Pennsylvania" The statement there found has been based on the fact that a certain Agnes Black wrote a letter, undated, to William Thomson, son of Pioneer John Thomson, whom she addressed as "Dear Brother," thanking him for some money he had sent her and requesting him to see that she obtained her share out of her father-in-law's estate. On Mar 2, 1812, a person evidently a son of Agnes Black wrote from Blount County, Tenn, to William Thomson, Thompsontown, Pa, stating that he is "six feet two inches" tall and has a brother of the same height, and that he is the "oldest of the family and looks after the family affairs" It might seem that this Agnes Black was indeed a sister to William Thomson and hence the posthumous child of Pioneer John Thomson However it would hardly be considered within the range of possibility for a person born after Mar 2, 1779, to become the mother of two sons over six feet tall less than 32 years later It is almost absolutely certain that Agnes Black was a sister-in-law and not a sister to William Thomson—see 3

APPENDIX

JOHN THOMSON'S BROTHER JAMES

In the "Thompson Family" pamphlet of 1887, it is stated that a brother of Pioneer John Thomson, who accompanied him to America, James Thomson, "settled along South Mountain, Cumberland Valley and County then (now Franklin County and Chambersburg), and his descendants reside there still" It has not proved possible to verify this statement. Dr. W H Egle, formerly State Librarian of Pennsylvania, who made a life study of Pennsylvania and its early inhabitants, expressed the opinion that James Thomson was Pioneer John Thomson's son and not his brother John Thomson did have a son James, to whom he left land at his death in 1779, and we have no other record of this son It is highly probable that this James Thomson died young, but he may indeed have "settled along South Mountain" It is said that Judge James Thomson, who lived in Chambersburg where he died before 1857, was of this branch A careful search of available records has failed to verify this statement

It is difficult to establish the identity of individuals whose names are found upon various lists, and it is unsafe to draw definite conclusions from such lists without independent sources of identification However, some interesting facts are disclosed by the assessment lists relating to Hanover Township, Dauphin County, Pa , at the time when our Pioneer John Thomson and his brother James are said to have lived there On the assessment list of 1750 for the east end of Hanover appear the names of John Thomson for 40 acres, William Thomson for 50 acres, and Alexander Thomson for 100 acres, and the name of Jas. Greenlee for 50 acres. On the 1756 list for the east end of Hanover appear the names of John Thomson and William Thomson, but not those of Alexander Thomson or Jas Greenlee There also appear the names of John Thompson and William Thompson on the 1756 list for the west end of Hanover In the 1769 list for the whole of Hanover Township, Dauphin County, appear the names of William Thompson (weaver) for 100 acres, James Greenlee for 100 acres; John Thompson for 200 acres; John Thompson for 100 acres, William Thomson for 80 acres, and

John Thomson for 100 acres   On the assessment list of the
Township for 1782 appear the names of John Thompson and
John Thompson, Sr   This was 14 years after our Pioneer John
Thomson purchased property in Juniata County, and presumably
sold his property in Dauphin County   It is noteworthy that the
name of James Thomson does not appear on any of the lists.

According to family tradition James Thomson, the brother of
Pioneer John Thomson, settled near Chambersburg. A search of
available records produces no evidence to substantiate this tradition, and it is possible that there may have been a confusion in
locations, given names or family connections   About five miles
northeast of Chambersburg on the Conococheague Creek there
was established by Scotch Covenanters named Thomson and
Torrence, a village called Scotland.   There came to this place in
1771-2 a certain Alexander Thompson with a large family and
purchased the land subsequently owned by S. Garve   Alexander
Thompson was said to have come to that locality directly from
Scotland, but it is possible that he removed from Chester or
Lancaster (Dauphin) County to Cumberland (Franklin) County
One of Alexander Thompson's thirteen children was James who
married Nancy Wright   It is possible that he was the James
Thompson who "settled in Cumberland Valley"   In families of
Scotch origin similarity in given names is of no importance, but
it is at least interesting that of the thirteen children of Pioneer
Alexander Thompson, six had given names identical with six of
the thirteen children of Pioneer John Thomson, namely· William, John, Andrew, James, Mary and Jean; his other children
were named Alexander, Archibald, Margaret, Barbara, Nancy,
Jennie, and Ann   All thirteen children reached maturity and
married

Among the early land warrants in Hanover Township, in
what was then Lancaster County, but is now Dauphin County,
Pa, were two to persons named Thompson, one for 100 acres,
to Alexander Thompson, dated Nov 26, 1748, and one for 150
acres to John Thompson, dated March 1, 1757   Alexander
Thompson may have been a son of James Thomson, whose
Chester County will of 1749 is referred to below, and John
Thompson may have been our Pioneer John Thompson who is
supposed to have located in Chester County before going to

Lancaster County with his brother James, and to have sold his land in Lancaster County, before removing in 1768 to what is now Juniata County, Pa.

In Chester County, Pa, Will Book C, page 163, is recorded the will of a certain James Thomson, of Londongrove Township, Chester County, Pa, dated Feb 3, 1748-9 and probated Oct 2, 1749 In this will James Thomson refers to his wife Ruth, and leaves his plantation to his sons Alexander. Samuel, James, Robert and William, "when the youngest is 21 years old" He appointed as his executors his wife Ruth and his brother John Thomson. The last-named may or may not have been our Pioneer John Thomson—but probably was not

In Jordan's "History of Juniata Valley and its People"—1913, Lewis Publishing Co, New York—it is stated that Rev James Thompson, who was the first minister of the Presbyterian Church, at Alexandria, Huntingdon County, Pa, where he died in 1830, was a descendant (grandson) of James Thomson, brother of our Pioneer John Thomson, as was also Capt James Thompson, the Indian fighter, whose family is referred to on page 1335 of "History of Susquehanna and Juniata Valleys." This statement may or may not be correct   Among the noteworthy descendants of Rev. James Thompson is his son William, born 1823 in Alexandria, and now living in Philadelphia at the age of 94 years. who was one of the donors of the Alexandria Memorial Library erected in memory of his mother, Mrs Elizabeth Gemmill (Stewart) Thompson. and Mrs Ann Maria Woolverton Kinsloe, granddaughters of Mrs Elizabeth (Porter) Gemmill, founder of that town

If the tradition concerning the existence of a brother of Pioneer John Thomson named James is correct—and its accuracy has certainly not been established—it is quite possible that the last-mentioned clue to descendants is the correct one. Of the known children in this line, the son James, called "Uncle Jimmie" was the well-known Indian fighter, Captain James Thompson, who lived in Spruce Creek, Union County, Pa., and in 1781 was captured by the Indians and carried to Canada with a Miss Young, who was sold in Montreal to a man named Young, who proved to be her cousin   es Thompson escaped, and returning to his family removed em to Chester County   He subsequently located in Buffalo Township, Union County, Pa, and died at the home of his son-in-law Gideon Smith, at the mouth of Little Buffalo near Jersey Shore, on Feb 9, 1837, aged 93 years, 9 months and 9 days. In addition to the daughter who married Gideon Smith, he had at least one child, William, who married in 1804 Susan Linn, daughter of John Linn, who was probably a son of William Linn, Jr., and grandson of William Linn, Sr, of Scotch-Irish stock, who emigrated to America about 1722, settling finally in Cumberland County, near Shippensburg. To this family belonged John Blair Linn, author of "Annals of Buffalo Valley" William and Susan (Linn) Thompson had four children. (1) James, who was killed by an explosion in 1833, (2) Ann, who married John B McCalmont, Esq., nephew of Judge McCalmont, and died in 1849; (3) John Linn, who died in Venango County, Pa., leaving a family; (4) William, who lived in New Brighton, Beaver County, Pa.

"Uncle Jimmie," Captain James Thompson, had a brother William, who married Jane Cochran, daughter of George and Ann (Henry) Cochran, and granddaughter of James and Isabella (Cochran) Cochran, and of Rev James Henry Of two of their children we have record, namely Ruth Thompson, born 1781, who died 1874 in Lewisburg, Pa, aged 93, and James Thompson (the Presbyterian minister already referred to), who was born 1791 in Buffalo Valley, Pa, and died Oct 8, 1830, aged 39 years, in Alexandria, Pa Rev. James Thompson married Elizabeth Gemmill Stewart, daughter of Thomas Harris and Annie (Gemmill) Stewart, and granddaughter of Zacharia and Elizabeth (Porter) Gemmill To the memory of Mrs. Elizabeth Gemmill (Stewart) Thompson, who died in 1877, after being a widow for 47 years, was dedicated the Alexandria Library by her son William, as already noted Rev. James and Elizabeth Gemmill (Stewart) Thompson had four children· (1) William, referred to above, unmarried, (2) Ann, who died unmarried; (3) Elizabeth, who died in infancy, (4) Jane, who died 1880, unmarried

INDEX TO DESCENDANTS OF PIONEER
JOHN THOMSON

Names of descendants are in bold-faced type The name of the father is also
in bold-faced type when he is a descendant of Pioneer John Thomson
In other cases the father's name is in light-faced type

INDEX TO ASSOCIATED FAMILY ANCESTORS

The "Descendant Number" referred to is the numeral by which has been designated (in accordance with the plan described on page 15) that individual descendant of Pioneer John Thomson of whose descendants these associated families are ancestors If each number be looked upon as a decimal fraction, as indicated below, one can readily locate the proper descendant, because the records of the individual descendants have been arranged throughout the book in exact agreement with a consecutive decimal notation.

See page 15

22

23

PLEASE READ CAREFULLY

The information we wish to obtain on the family tree, arranged in the order of importance, is as follows:—

FIRST:—The *Full Name* (not merely initials) of every descendant of the Pioneer, the *Full Name* of the person married in each case, and the *Full Name* of each child born to every couple.

SECOND·—The *Dates* of all births, marriages and deaths

THIRD.—The *Present Address* of every living descendant.

FOURTH:—The *Place* of birth, marriage and death of every descendant.

FIFTH:—A *Brief Life Sketch* of every descendant— giving only the important items, such as military service, training, education, profession and present occupation.

. SIXTH.—The *Ancestry*—with available dates—of each person who has married into any branch of our family. That is to say, we want the *Complete* available *Ancestral Record* of every descendant.

If in doubt as to exactly what is wanted, send all obtainable items of genealogical and biographical nature that would be of interest to any of the descendants of the Pioneer of our family.

It is appreciated that no one person can supply all of the information desired. It is hoped, however, that each person addressed will send all information obtainable and give *Clues* as to sources of additional information. Please send whatever you have, whether it is little or much

To the Thomson Cousins:

Now that the Christmas season is upon us, please turn your thoughts towards the best type of gift—one that is valued fully when first received and appreciated more and more as the years go by. To such a gift it is now within your power to contribute without cost to yourself and for the benefit of all your Thomson cousins of not only the present generation, but also the generations yet to come. We refer to the records of the decendants of "John Thomson, Pioneer and Patriot" partly in type and soon to be published in book form.

The value of these records will depend upon their accuracy and, completeness. In not one single line are the records as they now stand too elaborate—in some lines they are quite complete, while in others they are too brief to be dignified by the title "record."

No matter whether you have already sent in the records on your branch of the family or not, please devote a few moments of your time to sending, at once, complete records of your immediate family to the compiler,

ADDAMS S McALLISTER
261 West 23rd Street
New York

THE PRINTED RECORDS

We have no hesitancy in stating that every living descendant of John Thomson, if not now, will later want a copy of the book soon to be published—the grown ones for their own information and the children for use when they in turn grow up

For your convenience, in case you agree with this statement, an order blank is enclosed. The price has been placed at $5.00, every cent of which will represent money actually spent on the published book itself, the number of illustrations in each copy depending on the number of copies ordered in advance of publication. There will be no reprint, so if you want a copy for yourself or copies for the young ones of your family when they grow up, fill out at once the order blank and send it to

EDWARD 'S. THOMSON

Thomsontown,

Juniata Co., Pa.

PLEASE NOTE

Even though you do not order a copy of the book (which would be a valuable gift to yourself) please send in the records of your immediate family—which would be a highly prized gift to all of the other Thomson cousins.